THE DEMOCRACY READER

As the sun rose over Tiananmen Square in Beijing on May 30, 1989, university students worked to complete their "Goddess of Liberty," modelled after the American Statue of Liberty. For the few days of its existence, the Goddess of Liberty was a potent symbol of China's democratic aspirations. Then on June 4, 1989, troops and tanks took control of the Square, killing an unknown number of demonstrators and crushing the democracy movement. The symbol was destroyed, but the image and the idea lived on.

THE DEMOCRACY READER

CLASSIC AND MODERN SPEECHES, ESSAYS, POEMS, DECLARATIONS, AND DOCUMENTS ON FREEDOM AND HUMAN RIGHTS WORLDWIDE

Edited by

Diane Ravitch and Abigail Thernstrom

HarperCollins*Publishers*

Designed by Joan Greenfield
Photo research by Sabra Moore

Library of Congress Cataloging-in-Publication Data

The Democracy reader : classic and modern speeches,
     essays, poems, declarations, and documents on freedom
     and human rights worldwide / edited by Diane Ravitch
     and Abigail Thernstrom.
          p.   cm.
     Includes index.
     ISBN 0-06-270030-8
     1. Democracy—History.   I. Ravitch, Diane.
II. Thernstrom, Abigail M., 1936- .
JC421.D4635   1992
323.44′01—dc20   91-55393

---

92 93 94 95 96 PS / RRD 10 9 8 7 6 5 4 3 2 1

COVER PHOTO: *Liberty Enlightening the World*—better
known as the Statue of Liberty—was first assembled in
Paris. The statue was then disassembled, shipped to
Bedloe's Island in New York Harbor, and mounted on a
pedestal. The statue was formally dedicated amidst
great fanfare on October 28, 1886. Created by
Frederic-Auguste Bartholdi, the statue was a tribute to
Franco-American friendship and to the ideals of liberty.
It quickly became an international symbol of liberty, an
inspiration to all who treasured or longed for freedom
and democracy.

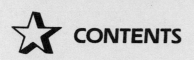# CONTENTS

CONTEMPORARY INTERNATIONAL DEMOCRATIC IDEAS

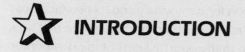

INTRODUCTION

We live in an age of democratic aspirations. The decade of the 1980s ended on a joyous note, as despotic regimes in many parts of the world loosened or abandoned their grip on power. Some were toppled by popular—and mostly peaceful—insurrections, others by free elections, or by the internal disintegration of totalitarianism. Poland, Nicaragua, Czechoslovakia, the Philippines, East Germany, South Korea, Chile, Romania, and even the Soviet Union, were merely a few of the countries that experienced the awakening of democratic movements. In China and Burma seismic democratic revolts were bloodily put down. The decade of the 1990s began on an amazing note, with the collapse of Communist totalitarian rule in the Soviet Union and a failed coup in August 1991 that led to a popular reaction against the Communist Party and strengthened the democratic movement in the Soviet republics and the Baltic states.

Where regimes fell, free elections usually followed. Revolution ceded to the frustrating task of creating democratic institutions, as well as the even more difficult goal of reconstructing the economy. One of the early leaders of the Solidarity movement in Poland, Adam Michnik, expressed the reality that followed the first flush of euphoria: "Dictatorship has been defeated and freedom has been won, yet the victory of freedom has not yet meant the triumph of democracy. Democracy is something more than freedom. Democracy is freedom institutionalized."

It quickly became apparent that revolution is the beginning of the process of political reconstruction, not its end. Democracy, the newly free discovered, is not an abstraction, but an absorbing activity. It requires revolutions to initiate it, but institutions to sustain it. Democratic culture, a free press, a stable social structure, representative government, institutional balance, an independent judiciary, experienced legislatures, a free and stable economy, educational institutions that honor academic freedom: these are among the essentials of a mature democracy, and the newly free countries look upon them with a certain bewilderment. Totalitarianism has attempted to control or eliminate these institutions. As became clear with the dawn of freedom, it is easier to destroy them than it is to create them.

The euphoria of revolution and the sobering task of democratization framed the compilation of *The Democracy Reader*. These pages hold words of inspiration, and also words of caution and doubt. The *Reader* offers reflections on what is necessary to turn freedom into democracy and, in the case of nations that already have strong democratic institutions, what is necessary to keep democracy democratic.

The *Reader* suggests, first, that the aspiration for democracy and its benefits today are universal. It offers evidence of democratic movements around the globe that seek the basic human and political rights guaranteed in the constitutions of the democratic nations. It then suggests that the achievement of democracy is a long, slow, and difficult process; that it takes decades, even generations, to build viable, effective democratic institutions; that the process of democratization is never finished but continues as societies mature and their problems change. It also suggests, perhaps to the disappointment of some, that the existence of democratic institutions does not in itself guarantee that political problems will always be solved correctly. Rather, democracy provides a process by which to solve problems fairly and with the highest degree of political consensus. It is a means as well as an end.

As the reader of these pages will observe, the commitment to political pluralism that makes a democratic society function must permeate the entire society, not just the formal structure of government. Democracy demands a broad dispersion of power and the engagement of the widest possible number of actors in civic and political life. In a democratic society, respect for pluralism and freedom pervades politics, culture, social life, and the economy. A democratic perspective is as important as democratic institutions and, in some ways, more difficult to sustain. What Americans think of as "checks and balances" is a set of institutional arrangements to prevent any branch of government from monopolizing political power. However, the belief that power must be dispersed and that citizens have a right to participate in their government goes deeper than institutional arrangements. Commitment to democracy is also a state of mind. It is the reaction of the ordinary citizen, who says, "Well, it's a free country," or "I know my rights . . ." The democratic society thrives to the extent that power—economic, political, cultural, and social—is broadly diffused. The totalitarian government seeks to gather all these powers and to regulate everyone's lives; the democratic society disperses these powers in order to protect individual freedom.

Important as universal suffrage is, it is no more important than those democratic institutions that temper its excesses: the rule of law, representative government, judicial review, the separation of powers. Democracy is not defined here merely by majority rule; it is also defined by its respect for the minority, for political liberty for the individual counts as much as political power for the masses. This balance is not an easy one, nor easily settled, and this constant tension between the rule of the majority and the rights of the individual—a democratic dilemma—is reflected in this volume.

The entries in this book demonstrate the powerful appeal of the democratic message. As the philosopher Sidney Hook pointed out in 1940, the greatest tribute nondemocratic governments pay to the idea of democracy is the adoption of democratic rhetoric in their constitutions: even though they shamefully abused the rights of their citizens, Hitler, Mussolini, and Stalin all insisted that their governments were "democratic." The lip service such leaders pay to democracy is a form of flattery, after all, but it also corrupts the vocabulary of democracy. Ironically, the dictators' constant invocation of democratic rhetoric probably serves to remind their subjects of the rights they do not have.

Where did we get this idea of democracy from in the first place? How was the idea of limited government established? Where did we get the idea that people have rights that the government cannot violate or take away? Who were the architects, polemicists, critics, philosophers, and poets of democratic thought? *The Democracy Reader* offers not singular answers to these questions, but rather a journey through the history of democratic ideas. Readers will not find here a blueprint for the ideal society; social blueprints are not democratic endeavors. They will find arguments, metaphors, questions, stories, poems, and manifestoes that tell of a search for legitimate and tolerant governance that is as open-ended now as it was when Pericles first defended it in ancient Athens.

For the most part, these passages defend democracy, but not uncritically, and not didactically. It is the hope of those who compiled this volume that the writing in it—by its very character—will provide a testimony to democratic culture and to the democratic sensibility. It was assembled in the spirit of open inquiry, and that is how we hope it will be read.

From Aristotle to Havel, from Jefferson to King, from Machiavelli to Paz; these authors have little in common but a passionate involvement with the democratic idea. The reader will find many American contributors and a concern with the evolution of American democracy. This is so not because we believe that the United States has more to offer than any other democratic nation, but because it is the nation we live in and know best. As today's global democratic revolution amply reveals, the passion for democracy—and for the freedoms and respect for human rights that democracy makes possible—is truly worldwide. Readers will find here voices from the Soviet Union, Eastern Europe, Africa, the Middle East, Asia, and Latin America.

Many of the contemporary writers have been instrumental in promoting democratic ideals in their societies. Some lived to see the overthrow of tyranny. Some experienced the beginnings of freedom, then saw their hopes destroyed by tanks and bullets. Some died in prison camps or in jail. Some are in exile. Some, even now as we write this, languish in prison.

What this whole volume reminds us, however, is that democracy has a long history and that its partisans have always been engaged in the political struggles of their time. Some were executed for their ideas, some suffered political oppression. Milton, Hobbes and Lincoln wrote in the midst of civil wars; the American Founders wrote in the midst of revolution. From the first authors in this collection to the last there is a great distance, but there are also enduring parallels.

The global democratic revolution of the late twentieth century has not been universally successful. Some popular insurrections were brutally crushed. Some despots continue to ignore demands for free elections, human rights, and the rule of law. Many governments that are members of the United Nations do not derive their authority from the consent of those they govern. Many do not hold free elections; do not permit a free press; do not observe other basic rights enumerated in the Universal Declaration of Human Rights.

For these reasons, we cannot say that the rise of democracy is preordained. The fate of those nations that have recently overthrown tyranny is likely to be precarious for many years to come. Given the difficulty of building democratic institutions, the impatience of long-suppressed peoples, the inexperience of new leaders, and the pain of shifting to political pluralism and free markets, we cannot be certain that democracy will survive. The course of human history contains too many setbacks and too many human-made disasters to support unbridled optimism.

We can say with assurance, however, that democracy is the best form of government yet devised. It is the form of government that provides the greatest freedom for human endeavor, the most enduring respect for human rights, and the best process for resolving conflicts peaceably. Our ability to sustain and extend democratic institutions throughout the world will largely determine the human prospect in the twenty-first century. In pursuing that goal, the words and ideas in these pages should be our constant companions.

The idea to create this volume was born during the glorious democratic moment in the autumn of 1989. The project was initiated by the Educational Excellence Network. We are grateful for the assistance provided by Chester Finn, Jr., and Ted Rebarber. It received encouragement from the American Federation of Teachers, which became convinced of the need for a comprehensive collection of documents about democracy on the part of free teachers' unions in nations struggling to achieve democracy. The Katherine Mabis McKenna Foundation provided needed support for the completion of the project. We are indebted to Andrew Sullivan for his contributions to the Classical and European Thought section. Samuel Thernstrom did much of the work of selecting and editing the American documents. We particularly thank Carol Cohen and Mary Kay Linge of HarperCollins Publishers for their commitment to the idea and the reality of this book.

Diane Ravitch
Abigail Thernstrom

THE DEMOCRACY READER

Plato and his pupil, Aristotle, were among the first in Western civilization to wrestle with the idea of democratic life and culture. This depiction of the two philosophers is a bas-relief from the facade of Giotto's campanile in Florence.

CLASSICAL AND EUROPEAN
THOUGHT

THE PELOPONNESIAN WAR

Thucydides (460–400 B.C.) was the son of a wealthy aristocrat in the fledgling democracy of Athens. In 424 B.C., he was appointed a general in the Athenian fleet, but was exiled from Athens after a military failure. He spent the next 20 years in Thrace and was recalled to Athens in 403 B.C., after the restoration of the Athenian democracy. *The Peloponnesian War* was written during his years in exile.

Thucydides' account of the statesman Pericles' oration at the ceremonial burial of the first Athenians killed in the war against Sparta is one of the first recorded defenses of democracy in western civilization. It is also, curiously, one of the most modern. Its context is international conflict, and the speech addresses the long-standing belief that democracies are inherently weak when faced with tyrannies in war.

In this passage, Pericles rebuts this idea, and justifies the conflict against martial Sparta in terms of the virtues that democratic Athens represents. Here, in a sense, is the first Cold War document; a ringing defense of both Athenian patriotism and the universal values of tolerance, diversity, free trade, and the rule of law. It is perhaps the most celebrated speech in defense of democracy ever given, and is rarely far from the thoughts of later democratic theorists and writers. See, for example, W. H. Auden's wartime musings some two millennia later (page 80).

Let me say that our system of government does not copy the institutions of our neighbours. It is more the case of our being a model to others, than of our imitating anyone else. Our constitution is called a democracy because power is in the hands not of a minority but of the whole people. When it is a question of settling private disputes, everyone is equal before the law: when it is a question of putting one person before another in positions of public responsibility, what counts is not membership of a particular class, but the actual ability which the man possesses. No one, so long as he has it in him to be of service to the state, is kept in political obscurity because of poverty. And, just as our political life is free and open, so is our day-to-day life in our relations with each other. We do not get into a state with our next-door neighbour if he enjoys himself in his own way, nor do we give him the kind of black looks which, though they do no real harm, still do hurt people's feelings. We are free and tolerant in our private lives; but in public affairs we keep to the law. This is because it commands our deep respect.

We give our obedience to those whom we put in positions of authority, and we obey the laws themselves, especially those which are for the protection of the oppressed, and those unwritten laws which it is an acknowledged shame to break.

And here is another point. When our work is over, we are in a position to enjoy all kinds of recreation for our spirits. There are various kinds of contests and sacrifices regularly throughout the year; in our own homes we find a beauty and a good taste which delight us every day and which drive away our cares. Then the greatness of our city brings it about that all the good things from all over the world flow in to us, so that to us it seems just as natural to enjoy foreign goods as our own local products.

Then there is a great difference between us and our opponents, in our attitude towards military security. Here are some examples: Our city is open to the world, and we have no periodical deportations in order to prevent people observing or finding out secrets which might be of military advantage to the enemy. This is because we rely, not on secret weapons, but on our own real courage and loyalty. There is a difference, too, in our educational systems. The Spartans, from their earliest boyhood, are submitted to the most laborious training in courage; we pass our lives without all these restrictions, and yet are just as ready to face the same dangers as they are. Here is a proof of this: When the Spartans invade our land, they do not come by themselves, but bring all their allies with them; whereas we, when we launch an attack abroad, do the job by ourselves, and, though fighting on foreign soil, do not often fail to defeat opponents who are fighting for their own hearths and homes. As a matter of fact none of our enemies has ever yet been confronted with our total strength, because we have to divide our attention between our navy and the many missions on which our troops are sent on land. Yet, if our enemies engage a detachment of our forces and defeat it, they give themselves credit for having thrown back our entire army; or, if they lose, they claim that they were beaten by us in full strength. There are certain advantages, I think, in our way of meeting danger voluntarily, with an easy mind, instead of with a laborious training, with natural rather than with state-induced courage. We do not have to spend our time practising to meet sufferings which are still in the future; and when they are actually upon us we show ourselves just as brave as these others who are always in strict training. This is one point in which, I think, our city deserves to be admired. There are also others:

Our love of what is beautiful does not lead to extravagance: our love of the things of the mind does not make us soft. We regard wealth as something to be properly used, rather than as something to boast about. As for poverty, no one need be ashamed to admit it: the real shame is in not taking practical measures to escape from it. Here each individual is interested not only in his own affairs but in the affairs of the state as well: even those who are mostly occupied with their own business are extremely well-informed on general politics—this is a peculiarity of ours: we do not say that a man who takes no interest in politics is a man who minds his own

business; we say that he has no business here at all. We Athenians, in our own persons, take our decisions on policy or submit them to proper discussions: for we do not think that there is an incompatibility between words and deeds; the worst thing is to rush into action before the consequences have been properly debated. And this is another point where we differ from other people. We are capable at the same time of taking risks and of estimating them beforehand. Others are brave out of ignorance; and, when they stop to think, they begin to fear. But the man who can most truly be accounted brave is he who best knows the meaning of what is sweet in life and of

Thucydides' *History of the Peloponnesian War* provides an early glimpse of a democracy's struggle against an authoritarian enemy.

what is terrible, and then goes out undeterred to meet what is to come.

Again, in questions of general good feeling there is a great contrast between us and most other people. We make friends by doing good to others, not by receiving good from them. This makes our friendship all the more reliable, since we want to keep alive the gratitude of those who are in our debt by showing continued goodwill to them: whereas the feelings of one who owes us something lack the same enthusiasm, since he knows that, when he repays our kindness, it will be more like paying back a debt than giving something spontaneously. We are unique in this. When we do kindnesses to others, we do not do them out of any calculations of profit or loss; we do them without afterthought, relying on our free liberality. Taking everything together then, I declare that our city is an education to Greece, and I declare that in my opinion each single one of our citizens, in all the manifold aspects of life, is able to show himself the rightful lord and owner of his own person, and do this, moreover, with exceptional grace and exceptional versatility. And to show that this is no empty boasting for the present occasion, but real tangible fact, you have only to consider the power which our city possesses and which has been won by those very qualities which I have mentioned. Athens, alone of the states we know, comes to her testing time in a greatness that surpasses what was imagined of her. In her case, and in her case alone, no invading enemy is ashamed at being defeated, and no subject can complain of being governed by people unfit for their responsibilities. Mighty indeed are the marks and monuments of our empire which we have left. Future ages will wonder at us, as the present age wonders at us now. We do not need the praises of a Homer, or of anyone else whose words may delight us for the moment, but whose estimation of facts will fall short of what is really true. For our adventurous spirit has forced an entry into every sea and into every land; and everywhere we have left behind us everlasting memorials of good done to our friends or suffering inflicted on our enemies.

This, then, is the kind of city for which these men, who could not bear the thought of losing her, nobly fought and nobly died. It is only natural that every one of us who survive them should be willing to undergo hardships in her service. And it was for this reason that I have spoken at such length about our city, because I wanted to make it clear that for us there is more at stake than there is for others who lack our advantages; also I wanted my words of praise for the dead to be set in the bright light of evidence. And now the most important of these words has been spoken. I have sung the praises of our city; but it was the courage and gallantry of these men, and of people like them, which made her splendid. Nor would you find it true in the case of many of the Greeks, as it is true of them, that no words can do more than justice to their deeds.

To me it seems that the consummation which has overtaken these men shows us the meaning of manliness in its first revelation and in its final proof. Some of them, no doubt, had their faults; but what we ought to remember first is their gallant conduct against the enemy in defence of their native land. They have blotted out evil with good, and done more service to the commonwealth than they ever did harm in their private lives. No one of these men weakened because he wanted to go on enjoying his wealth: no one put off the awful day in the hope that he might live to escape his poverty and grow rich. More to be desired than such things, they chose to check the enemy's pride. This, to them, was a risk most glorious, and they accepted it, willing to strike down the enemy and relinquish everything else. As for success or failure, they left that in the doubtful hands of Hope, and when the reality of battle was before their faces, they put their trust in their own selves. In the fighting, they thought it more honourable to stand their ground and suffer death than to give in and save their lives. So they fled from the reproaches of men, abiding with life and limb the brunt of battle; and, in a small moment of time, the climax of their lives, a culmination of glory, not of fear, were swept away from us.

So and such they were, these men—worthy

of their city. We who remain behind may hope to be spared their fate, but must resolve to keep the same daring spirit against the foe. It is not simply a question of estimating the advantages in theory. I could tell you a long story (and you know it as well as I do) about what is to be gained by beating the enemy back. What I would prefer is that you should fix your eyes every day on the greatness of Athens as she really is, and should fall in love with her. When you realize her greatness, then reflect that what made her great was men with a spirit of adventure, men who knew their duty, men who were ashamed to fall below a certain standard. If they ever failed in an enterprise, they made up their minds that at any rate the city should not find their courage lacking to her, and they gave to her the best contribution that they could. They gave her their lives, to her and to all of us, and for their own selves they won praises that never grow old, the most splendid of sepulchres—not the sepulchre in which their bodies are laid, but where their glory remains eternal in men's minds, always there on the right occasion to stir others to speech or to action. For famous men have the whole earth as their memorial: it is not only the inscriptions on their graves in their own country that mark them out; no, in foreign lands also, not in any visible form but in people's hearts, their memory abides and grows. It is for you to try to be like them. Make up your minds that happiness depends on being free, and freedom depends on being courageous.

★ PLATO
THE REPUBLIC

The Greek philosopher Socrates (469–399 B.C.) remains perhaps the archetypal democratic hero. His trial and execution in the late Athenian democracy on charges of heresy and corruption of the young make him an early martyr to the cause of free speech and inquiry. Yet, according to his student Plato (427–347 B.C.), his own views on democracy were more ambivalent than his death might suggest.

Plato, the son of an Athenian aristocrat, lived at a time when Athenian democracy was besieged by the Peloponnesian War. He left Athens in disgust after the execution of Socrates in 399 B.C., only to return later to found the Athenian Academy in 387 B.C., the prototype of the Western university. He taught there for 40 years.

In this passage from Plato's most celebrated writing on politics, *The Republic*, Socrates debates the tempestuous young Adeimantus on the nature of democratic regimes and the kind of citizens they produce. It is one of the earliest treatments of the subject, and one of the most finely balanced between admiration and scorn, concerned above all with the effect of politics on the individual soul.

" . . . And the absence of any compulsion to rule in this city," I said, "even if you are competent to rule, or again to be ruled if you don't want to be, or to make war when the others are making war, or to keep peace when the others are keeping it, if you don't desire peace; and, if some law prevents you from ruling or being a judge, the absence of any compulsion keeping you from ruling and being a judge anyhow, if you long to do so—isn't such a way of passing the time divinely sweet for the moment?"

"Perhaps," he said, "for the moment."

"And what about this? Isn't the gentleness toward some of the condemned exquisite? Or in such a regime haven't you yet seen men who have been sentenced to death or exile, nonethe-

The school of Athens was one of the first places where the merits and disadvantages of democratic life were discussed. This depiction is an engraving based on a painting by Raphael. Plato and Aristotle are debating in the center.

less staying and carrying on right in the middle of things; and, as though no one cared or saw, stalking the land like a hero?"

"Yes, many," he said.

"And this regime's sympathy and total lack of pettiness in despising what we were saying so solemnly when we were founding the city—that unless a man has a transcendent nature he would never become good if from earliest childhood his play isn't noble and all his practices aren't such—how magnificently it tramples all this underfoot and doesn't care at all from what kinds of practices a man goes to political action, but honors him if only he says he's well disposed toward the multitude?"

"It's a very noble regime," he said.

"Then, democracy," I said, "would have all this and other things akin to it and would be, as it seems, a sweet regime, without rulers and many-colored, dispensing a certain equality to equals and unequals alike."

"What you say," he said, "is quite well known."

"Reflect, then," I said, "who is the private man like this? Or, just as we did in the case of the regime, must we first consider how he comes to be?"

"Yes," he said.

"Isn't it this way? I suppose a son would be born to that stingy, oligarchic man, a son reared by his father in his dispositions."

"Of course."

"Now, this son too, forcibly ruling all the pleasures in himself that are spendthrifty and do not conduce to money-making, those ones that are called unnecessary—"

"Plainly," he said.

"So that we don't discuss in the dark," I said, "do you want us to define the necessary and the unnecessary desires?"

"Yes," he said, "that's what I want."

"Wouldn't those we aren't able to turn aside justly be called necessary, as well as all those whose satisfaction benefits us? We are by nature compelled to long for both of these, aren't we?"

"Quite so."

"Then we shall justly apply the term necessary to them."

"That is just."

"And what about this? If we were to affirm that all those are unnecessary of which a man could rid himself if he were to practice from youth on and whose presence, moreover, does no good—and sometimes even does the opposite of good—would what we say be fine?"

"Fine it would be."

"Then shall we choose an example of what each of them is so that we can grasp their general types?"

"Yes, we must."

"Wouldn't the desire of eating—as long as it is for health and good condition, the desire of mere bread and relish—be necessary?"

"I suppose so."

"The desire for bread, at least, is presumably necessary on both counts, in that it is beneficial and in that it is capable of putting an end to life."

"Yes."

"And so is the desire for relish, if in any way it is beneficial to good condition."

"Most certainly."

"But what about the desire that goes beyond toward sorts of food other than this, of which the many can be rid if it is checked in youth and educated, and is harmful to the body and to the soul with respect to prudence and moderation? Wouldn't it rightly be called unnecessary?"

"Most rightly indeed."

"Then wouldn't we also assert that the latter desires are spendthrifty, while the former are money-making because they are useful for our works?"

"Surely."

"Then won't we also assert the same about sex and the other desires?"

"Yes, we'll assert the same."

"And weren't we also saying that the man we just named a drone is full of such pleasures and desires and is ruled by the unnecessary ones, while the stingy oligarchic man is ruled by the necessary ones?"

"Of course we were."

"Well, then, going back again," I said, "let's say how the democratic man comes out of the oligarchic one. And it looks to me as though it happens in most cases like this."

"How?"

"When a young man, reared as we were just saying without education and stingily, tastes the drones' honey, and has intercourse with fiery, clever beasts who are able to purvey manifold and subtle pleasures with every sort of variety, you presumably suppose that at this point he begins his change from an oligarchic regime within himself to a democratic one."

"Most necessarily," he said.

"Then, just as the city was transformed when an alliance from outside brought aid to one party, like to like, is the young man also transformed in the same way when desires of a kindred and like form from without bring aid to one party of desires within him?"

"That's entirely certain."

"And, I suppose, if a counteralliance comes to the aid of the oligarchic party in him, either from the advice and scolding of his father or from other relatives, then faction and counterfaction arise in him and he does battle with himself."

"Surely."

"And I suppose that at times the democratic party gives way to the oligarchic; and, with some of the desires destroyed and others exiled, a certain shame arose in the young man's soul, and order was re-established."

"Sometimes that does happen," he said.

"But I suppose that once again other desires,

akin to the exiled ones, reared in secret due to the father's lack of knowledge about rearing, came to be, many and strong."

"At least," he said, "that's what usually happens."

"Then, drawn to the same associations, their secret intercourse bred a multitude."

"Of course."

"And, finally, I suppose they took the acropolis of the young man's soul, perceiving that it was empty of fair studies and practices and true speeches, and it's these that are the best watchmen and guardians in the thought of men whom the gods love."

"They are by far the best," he said.

"Then, in their absence, false and boasting speeches and opinions ran up and seized that place in such a young man."

"Indeed they did," he said.

"Doesn't he go back again to those Lotus-eaters and openly settle among them? And if some help should come to the stingy element in his soul from relatives, those boasting speeches close the gates of the kingly wall within him; they neither admit the auxiliary force itself nor do they receive an embassy of speeches of older private men, but doing battle they hold sway themselves; and naming shame simplicity, they push it out with dishonor, a fugitive; calling moderation cowardliness and spattering it with mud, they banish it; persuading that measure and orderly expenditure are rustic and illiberal, they join with many useless desires in driving them over the frontier."

"Indeed they do."

"Now, once they have emptied and purged these from the soul of the man whom they are seizing and initiating in great rites, they proceed to return insolence, anarchy, wastefulness, and shamelessness from exile, in a blaze of light, crowned and accompanied by a numerous chorus, extolling and flattering them by calling insolence good education; anarchy, freedom; wastefulness, magnificence; and shamelessness, courage. Isn't it in some such way," I said, "that a man, when he is young, changes from his rearing in necessary desires to the liberation and unleashing of unnecessary and useless pleasures?"

"Yes," he said, "it's quite manifestly that way."

"Then, I suppose that afterward such a man lives spending no more money, effort, and time on the necessary than on the unnecessary pleasures. However, if he has good luck and his frenzy does not go beyond bounds—and if, also, as a result of getting somewhat older and the great disturbances having passed by, he readmits a part of the exiles and doesn't give himself wholly over to the invaders—then he lives his life in accord with a certain equality of pleasures he has established. To whichever one happens along, as though it were chosen by the lot, he hands over the rule within himself until it is satisfied; and then again to another, dishonoring none but fostering them all on the basis of equality."

"Most certainly."

"And," I said, "he doesn't admit true speech or let it pass into the guardhouse, if someone says that there are some pleasures belonging to fine and good desires and some belonging to bad desires, and that the ones must be practiced and honored and the others checked and enslaved. Rather, he shakes his head at all this and says that all are alike and must be honored on an equal basis."

"That's exactly," he said, "what a man in this condition does."

"Then," I said, "he also lives along day by day, gratifying the desire that occurs to him, at one time drinking and listening to the flute, at another downing water and reducing; now practicing gymnastic, and again idling and neglecting everything; and sometimes spending his time as though he were occupied with philosophy. Often he engages in politics and, jumping up, says and does whatever chances to come to him; and if he ever admires any soldiers, he turns in that direction; and if it's money-makers, in that one. And there is neither order nor necessity in his life, but calling this life sweet, free, and blessed he follows it throughout." . . .

ARISTOTLE
THE POLITICS

Aristotle (384–322 B.C.) was for 20 years a student of Plato's at the Athenian Academy. On Plato's death, he left Athens and settled in Macedonia to take charge of the education of the young Alexander the Great. In 334, when Alexander began his Asiatic conquests, Aristotle returned to Athens to set up his own academy, the Lyceum. After Alexander's death, a charge of impiety was brought against Aristotle, and he fled Athens, to die a year later.

Aristotle's *Politics* remains the starting point for systematic Western discussion of political life. It was the first work to provide a comprehensive view of the different types of regimes, the virtues they support, the meaning of citizenship, and the role of education in political life. It was also, after Plato's *Republic*, one of the first texts to give an extended analysis of the nature of democracy.

For Aristotle, democracy was but one of a variety of regimes (monarchy, oligarchy, tyranny, and polity among them). His preference was for monarchy, but only if the monarch is an exemplary individual and rules in everybody's best interest. His view of the best practicable regime was polity, which is close to democracy, but with elements of oligarchy and moderation infused into it—a blueprint, in some respects, for modern constitutional democracy. In these passages, three notions that have lodged at the heart of democratic thinking are introduced: personal freedom, the rule of law, and the importance of a large middle class. That they are commonplace now says much about the perspicacity of their originator.

. . . The basis of a democratic state is liberty; which, according to the common opinion of men, can only be enjoyed in such a state;—this they affirm to be the great end of every democracy. One principle of liberty is for all to rule and be ruled in turn, and indeed democratic justice is the application of numerical not proportionate equality; whence it follows that the majority must be supreme, and that whatever the majority approve must be the end and the just. Every citizen, it is said, must have equality, and therefore in a democracy the poor have more power than the rich, because there are more of them, and the will of the majority is supreme. This, then, is one note of liberty which all democrats affirm to be the principle of their state. Another is that a man should live as he likes. This, they say, is the privilege of a freeman, since, on the other hand, not to live as a man likes is the mark of a slave. This is the second characteristic of democracy, whence has arisen the claim of men to be ruled by none, if possible, or, if this is impossible, to rule and be ruled in turns; and so it contributes to the freedom based upon equality.

Such being our foundation and such the principle from which we start, the characteristics of democracy are as follows:—the election of officers by all out of all; and that all should rule over each, and each in his turn over all; that the appointment to all offices, or to all but those which require experience and skill, should be made by lot; that no property qualification should be required for offices, or only a very low one; that a man should not hold the same office twice, or not often, or in the case of few except military offices: that the tenure of all offices, or of as many as possible, should be brief; that all men should sit in judgement, or that judges selected out of all should judge, in all matters, or in most and in the greatest and most important—such as the scrutiny of accounts, the constitution, and private contracts; that the assembly should be supreme over all causes, or at any rate over the most important, and the magistrates over none or only over a very few. Of all magistracies, a council is the most democratic when there is not the means of paying all the citizens, but when they are paid even this is robbed of its power; for the people then draw all cases to themselves, as I said in the previous discussion. The next characteristic of democracy is payment for services; assembly, law-courts, magistrates, everybody receives pay, when it is to be had; or when it is not to be had for all, then it is given to the law-courts and to the stated assemblies, to the council and to the magistrates, or at least to any of them who are compelled to have their meals together. And whereas oligarchy is characterized by birth, wealth, and education, the notes of democracy appear to be the opposite of these—low birth, poverty, mean employment. Another note is that no magistracy is perpetual, but if any such have survived some ancient change in the constitution it should be stripped of its power, and the holders should be elected by lot and no longer by vote. These are the points common to all democracies; but democracy and demos in their truest form are based upon the recognized principle of democratic justice, that all should count equally; for equality implies that the poor should have no more share in the government than the rich, and should not be the only rulers, but that all should rule equally according to their numbers. And in this way men think that they will secure equality and freedom in their state. . . .

Of forms of democracy first comes that which is said to be based strictly on equality. In such a democracy the law says that it is just for the poor to have no more advantage than the rich; and that neither should be masters, but both equal. For if liberty and equality, as is thought by some, are chiefly to be found in democracy, they will be best attained when all persons alike share in the government to the utmost. And since the people are the majority, and the opinion of the majority is decisive, such a government must necessarily be a democracy. Here then is one sort of democ-

racy. There is another, in which the magistrates are elected according to a certain property qualification, but a low one; he who has the required amount of property has a share in the government, but he who loses his property loses his rights. Another kind is that in which all the citizens who are under no disqualification share in the government, but still the law is supreme. In another, everybody, if he be only a citizen, is admitted to the government, but the law is supreme as before. A fifth form of democracy, in other respects, the same, is that in which, not the law, but the multitude, have the supreme power, and supersede the law by their decrees. This is a state of affairs brought about by the demagogues. For in democracies which are subject to the law the best citizens hold the first place, and there are no demagogues; but where the laws are not supreme, there demagogues spring up. For the people becomes a monarch, and is many in one; and the many have the power in their hands, not as individuals, but collectively. Homer says that "it is not good to have a rule of many," but whether he means this corporate rule, or the rule of many individuals, is uncertain. At all events this sort of democracy, which is now a monarch, and no longer under the control of law, seeks to exercise monarchical sway, and grows into a despot; the flatterer is held in honour; this sort of democracy being relatively to other democracies what tyranny is to other forms of monarchy. The spirit of both is the same, and they alike exercise a despotic rule over the better citizens. The decrees of the demos correspond to the edicts of the tyrant; and the demagogue is to the one what the flatterer is to the other. Both have great power;—the flatterer with the tyrant, the demagogue with democracies of the kind which we are describing. The demagogues make the decrees of the people override the laws, by referring all things to the popular assembly. And therefore they grow great, because the people have all things in their hands, and they hold in their hands the votes of the people, who are too ready to listen to them. Further, those who have any complaint to bring against the magistrates say, "let the people be judges"; the people are too happy to accept the invitation; and so the authority of every office is undermined. Such a democracy is fairly open to the objection that it is not a constitution at all; for where the laws have no authority, there is no constitution. The law ought to be supreme over all, and the magistracies should judge of particulars, and only this should be considered a constitution. So that if democracy be a real form of government, the sort of system in which all things are regulated by decrees is clearly not even a democracy in the true sense of the word, for decrees relate only to particulars.

These then are the different kinds of democracy. . . .

We have now to inquire what is the best constitution for most states, and the best life for most men, neither assuming a standard of virtue which is above ordinary persons, nor an education which is exceptionally favoured by nature and circumstances, nor yet an ideal state which is an aspiration only, but having regard to the life in which the majority are able to share, and to the form of government which states in general can attain. As to those aristocracies, as they are called, of which we were just now speaking, they either lie beyond the possibilities of the greater number of states, or they approximate to the so-called constitutional government, and therefore need no separate discussion. And in fact the conclusion at which we arrive respecting all these forms rests upon the same grounds. For if what was said in the *Ethics* is true, that the happy life is the life according to virtue lived without impediment, and that virtue is a mean, then the life which is in a mean, and in a mean attainable by every one, must be the best. And the same principles of virtue and vice are characteristic of cities and of constitutions; for the constitution is in a figure the life of the city.

Now in all states there are three elements: one class is very rich, another very poor, and a third is a mean. It is admitted that moderation and the mean are best, and therefore it will clearly be best to possess the gifts of fortune in moderation; for in that condition of life men are most ready to follow rational principle.

But he who greatly excels in beauty, strength, birth, or wealth, or on the other hand who is very poor, or very weak, or very much disgraced, finds it difficult to follow rational principle. Of these two the one sort grow into violent and great criminals, the others into rogues and petty rascals. And two sorts of offences correspond to them, the one committed from violence, the other from roguery. Again, the middle class is least likely to shrink from rule, or to be overambitious for it; both of which are injuries to the state. Again, those who have too much of the goods of fortune, strength, wealth, friends, and the like, are neither willing nor able to submit to authority. The evil begins at home; for when they are boys, by reason of the luxury in which they are brought up, they never learn, even at school, the habit of obedience. On the other hand, the very poor, who are in the opposite extreme, are too degraded. So that the one class cannot obey, and can only rule despotically; the other knows not how to command and must be ruled like slaves. Thus arises a city, not of freemen, but of masters and slaves, the one despising, the other envying; and nothing can be more fatal to friendship and good fellowship in states than this: for good fellowship springs from friendship; when men are at enmity with one another, they would rather not even share the same path. But a city ought to be composed, as far as possible, of equals and similars; and these are generally the middle classes. Wherefore the city which is composed of middle-class citizens is necessarily best constituted in respect of the elements of which we say the fabric of the state naturally consists. And this is the class of citizens which is most secure in a state, for they do not, like the poor, covet their neighbours' goods; nor do others covet theirs, as the poor covet the goods of the rich; and as they neither plot against others, nor are themselves plotted against, they pass through life safely. Wisely then did Phocylides pray—"Many things are best in the mean; I desire to be of a middle condition in my city."

Thus it is manifest that the best political community is formed by citizens of the middle class, and that those states are likely to be well-administered, in which the middle class is large, and stronger if possible than both the other classes, or at any rate than either singly; for the addition of the middle class turns the scale, and prevents either of the extremes from being dominant. Great then is the good fortune of a state in which the citizens have a moderate and sufficient property; for where some possess much, and the others nothing, there may arise an extreme democracy, or a pure oligarchy; or a tyranny may grow out of either extreme—either out of the most rampant democracy, or out of an oligarchy; but it is not so likely to arise out of the middle constitutions and those akin to them. I will explain the reason of this hereafter, when I speak of the revolutions of states. The mean condition of states is clearly best, for no other is free from faction; and where the middle class is large, there are least likely to be factions and dissensions. For a similar reason large states are less liable to faction than small ones, because in them the middle class is large; whereas in small states it is easy to divide all the citizens into two classes who are either rich or poor, and to leave nothing in the middle. And democracies are safer and more permanent than oligarchies, because they have a middle class which is more numerous and has a greater share in the government; for when there is no middle class, and the poor greatly exceed in number, troubles arise, and the state soon comes to an end. A proof of the superiority of the middle class is that the best legislators have been of a middle condition; for example, Solon, as his own verses testify; and Lycurgus, for he was not a king; and Charondas, and almost all legislators. . . .

THOMAS AQUINAS
SUMMA THEOLOGICA

In contemporary debates, it has become common to contrast modern political and cultural freedom with medieval Christian tyranny. Yet one of the striking things about the key texts urging religious and cultural tolerance in Western culture—Locke's *Letter Concerning Toleration* (page 31) and Milton's *Areopagitica* (page 16) for example—is that they are framed in essentially Christian contexts. The great medieval theologian and philosopher Thomas Aquinas (1225–1274) also provided important Christian arguments for tolerance and diversity of belief, a tolerance that was indeed reflected in early medieval society.

Aquinas was born in Italy, and served his novitiate as a Dominican monk in Paris. He was ordained as a priest in 1250, and was appointed Professor of Philosophy at the University of Paris in 1256. His philosophical system can be seen as an attempt to reconcile Christian theology with the natural philosophy of Aristotle.

This passage from the *Summa Theologica*, his masterwork, treats the subject of the imposition of moral virtue and argues for restraint on the part of government. It is but a small detail of a larger argument for a political authority based on the consent of the governed and the limits of human law.

. . . We *proceed thus to the Second Article:*
OBJECTION 1. It would seem that it belongs to human law to repress all vices. For Isidore says that "laws were made in order that, in fear thereof, man's audacity might be held in check." But it would not be held in check sufficiently unless all evils were repressed by law. Therefore human law should repress all evils.

OBJ. 2. Further, the intention of the lawgiver is to make the citizens virtuous. But a man cannot be virtuous unless he forbear from all kinds of vice. Therefore it belongs to human law to repress all vices.

OBJ. 3. Further, human law is derived from the natural law. . . . But all vices are contrary to the law of nature. Therefore human law should repress all vices.

ON THE CONTRARY. We read in *De libero arbitrio i. 5:* "It seems to me that the law which is written for the governing of the people rightly permits these things, and that divine providence punishes them." But divine providence punishes nothing but vices. Therefore human law rightly allows some vices, by not repressing them.

I ANSWER THAT, . . . law is framed as a rule or measure of human acts. Now a measure should be homogeneous with that which it measures, as stated in *Metaphysics x.* text. 3, 4, since different things are measured by different measures. Wherefore laws imposed on men should also be in keeping with their condition, for, as Isidore says, law should be "possible both according to nature, and according to the customs of the country." Now possibility or faculty of action is due to an interior habit or disposition, since the same thing is not possible to one who has not a virtuous habit as is possible to one who has. Thus the same is not possible to a child as to a full-grown man; for which reason the law for children is not the same as for adults, since many things are permitted to children which in an adult are punished by law or at any rate are open to blame. In like manner many things are permissible to men not perfect in virtue which would be intolerable in a virtuous man.

Now human law is framed for a number of human beings, the majority of whom are not perfect in virtue. Wherefore human laws do not forbid all vices from which the virtuous abstain, but only the more grievous vices from which it is possible for the majority to abstain; and chiefly those that are to the hurt of others, without the prohibition of which human society could not be maintained: thus human law prohibits murder, theft, and suchlike.

REPLY OBJ. 1. Audacity seems to refer to the assailing of others. Consequently it belongs to

Fra Angelico's haunting depiction of Thomas Aquinas shows the saint holding a book with blank pages. Aquinas's political philosophy allowed for a large degree of pluralism in the societies of a sinful humanity.

those sins chiefly whereby one's neighbor is injured; and these sins are forbidden by human law, as stated.

REPLY OBJ. 2. The purpose of human law is to lead men to virtue, not suddenly, but gradually. Wherefore it does not lay upon the multitude of imperfect men the burdens of those who are already virtuous, viz., that they should abstain from all evil. Otherwise these imperfect ones, being unable to bear such precepts, would break out into yet greater evils; thus it is written: "He that violently bloweth his nose, bringeth out blood"; and that if "new wine," i.e., precepts of a perfect life, is "put into old bottles," i.e., into imperfect men, "the bottles break, and the wine runneth out," i.e., the precepts are despised and those men, from contempt, break out into evils worse still.

REPLY OBJ. 3. The natural law is a participation in us of the eternal law, while human law falls short of the eternal law. Now Augustine says: "The law which is framed for the government of states allows and leaves unpunished many things that are punished by divine providence. Nor, if this law does not attempt to do everything, is this a reason why it should be blamed for what it does." Wherefore, too, human law does not prohibit everything that is forbidden by the natural law.

NICCOLÒ MACHIAVELLI
THE DISCOURSES

Although Niccolò Machiavelli (1469–1527) gave his name to a type of political ruthlessness, he was politically hapless. A Florentine, he worked for the Borgia family in a variety of functions, principally as a diplomatic envoy and a military specialist. In 1512, when the Medici familiy regained power in Florence, he was deprived of his office and banished. He never held any position of power again.

This political failure, however, gave rise to some of the finest works of political philosophy in the modern world. Machiavelli is rightly known as the original theorist of power-politics, the thinker who broke precedent by legitimizing an amoral politics distinct from classical notions of morality and propriety. It is less often acknowledged that this insight also led to some remarkable conclusions in Machiavelli's understanding of how modern states can be made to function effectively. In *The Discourses*, perhaps his most accomplished treatise, the origins of popular elections, media manipulation, constitutional checks and balances, and much paraphernalia now familiar to modern democrats were first mapped out in theory. A theory of democracy also emerges here, different from the classical notion, both more invigorating and more chilling. In this passage, the author who did so much to praise the power of the prince uses the same argument to assert the superiority of majority rule. He does so with his usual cynicism and wit.

. . . The nature of the masses, then, is no more reprehensible than is the nature of princes, for all do wrong and to the same extent when there is nothing to prevent them doing wrong. Of this there are plenty of examples besides those given, both among the Roman emperors and among other tyrants and princes; and in them we find a degree of inconstancy and changeability in behaviour such as is never found in the masses.

I arrive, then, at a conclusion contrary to the common opinion which asserts that populaces, when in power, are variable, fickle and ungrateful; and affirm that in them these faults are in no wise different from those to be found in certain princes. Were the accusation made against both the masses and princes, it would be true; but, if princes be excepted, it is false. For when the populace is in power and is well-ordered, it will be stable, prudent and grateful, in much the same way, or in a better way, than is a prince, however wise he be thought. And, on the other hand, a prince who condemns the laws, will be more ungrateful, fickle and imprudent than is the populace. Nor is inconstancy of behaviour due to a difference in nature, for they are pretty much the same, or, if one be better than the other, it is the populace: it is due to the greater or less respect which they have for the laws under which both alike are living.

If we consider the Roman populace it will be found that for four hundred years they were enemies to the very name of king and lovers of glory and of the common good of their country. Of both characteristics the Roman populace affords numerous and striking examples. And, should anyone bring up against me the ingratitude the populace displayed towards Scipio, my answer is that I have already discussed this question at length and have there shown the ingratitude of the populace to be less than that of princes. While in the matter of prudence and stability I claim that the populace is more prudent, more stable, and of sounder judgement than the prince. Not without good reason is the voice of the populace likened to that of God; for public opinion is remarkably accurate in its prognostications, so much so that it seems as if the populace by some hidden power discerned the evil and the good that was to befall it. With regard to its judgement, when two speakers of equal skill are heard advocating different alternatives, very rarely does one find the populace failing to adopt the better view or incapable of appreciating the truth of what it hears. While, if in bold actions and such as appear advantageous it errs, as I have said above, so does a prince often err where his passions are involved, and these are much stronger than those of the populace.

It is found, too, that in the election of magistrates the populace makes a far better choice than does the prince; nor can the populace ever be persuaded that it is good to appoint to such an office a man of infamous life or corrupt habits, whereas a prince may easily and in a vast variety of ways be persuaded to do this. Again, one finds that when the populace begins to have a horror of something it remains of the same mind for many centuries; a thing that is never observed in the case of a prince. For both these characteristics I shall content myself with the evidence afforded by the Roman populace, which in the course of so many hundreds of years and so many elections of consuls and tribunes did not make four elections of which it had to repent. So much,

This portrait of Niccolo Machiavelli hangs in the Palazzo Doria in Rome. A defender of republican rather than autocratic government, he was a political failure who tried to teach the secrets of political success.

too, as I have said, was the title of king hated that no service rendered by one of its citizens who ambitioned it, could render him immune from the penalties prescribed. Besides this, one finds that cities in which the populace is the prince, in a very short time extend vastly their dominions much more than do those which have always been under a prince; as Rome did after the expulsion of the kings, and Athens after it was free of Pisistratus.

This can only be due to one thing: government by the populace is better than government by princes. Nor do I care whether to this opinion of mine all that our historian has said in the aforesaid passage or what others have said, be objected; because if account be taken of all the disorders due to populaces and of all those due to princes, and of all the glories won by populaces and all those won by princes, it will be found that alike in goodness and in glory the populace is far superior. And if princes are superior to populaces in drawing up laws, codes of civic life, statutes and new institutions, the populace is so superior in sustaining what has been instituted, that it indubitably adds to the glory of those who have instituted them.

In short, to bring this topic to a conclusion, I say that, just as princely forms of government have endured for a very long time, so, too, have republican forms of government; and that in both cases it has been essential for them to be regulated by laws. For a prince who does what he likes is a lunatic, and a populace which does what it likes is unwise. If, therefore, it be a question of a prince subservient to the laws and of a populace chained up by laws, more virtue will be found in the populace than in the prince; and if it be a question of either of them loosed from control by the law, there will be found fewer errors in the populace than in the prince, and these of less moment and much easier to put right. For a licentious and turbulent populace, when a good man can obtain a hearing, can easily be brought to behave itself; but there is no one to talk to a bad prince, nor is there any remedy except the sword. From which an inference may be drawn

in regard to the importance of their respective maladies; for, if to cure the malady of the populace a word suffices and the sword is needed to cure that of a prince, no one will fail to see that the greater the cure, the greater the fault.

When the populace has thrown off all restraint, it is not the mad things it does that are terrifying, nor is it of present evils that one is afraid, but of what may come of them, for amidst such confusion there may come to be a tyrant. In the case of bad princes it is just the opposite: it is present evils that are terrifying, but for the future there is hope, since men are convinced that the evil ways of a bad prince may make for freedom in the end. Thus one sees the difference between the two cases amounts to the same thing as the difference between what is and what must come to be. The brutalities of the masses are directed against those whom they suspect of conspiring against the common good; the brutalities of a prince against those whom he suspects of conspiring against his own good. The reason why people are prejudiced against the populace is because of the populace anyone may speak ill without fear and openly, even when the populace is ruling. But of princes people speak with the utmost trepidation and the utmost reserve. . . .

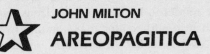

JOHN MILTON
AREOPAGITICA

Samuel Johnson said of John Milton: "He hated monarchs in the state and prelates in the church; for he hated all whom he was required to obey. It is to be suspected that his predominant desire was to destroy rather than establish, and that he felt not so much the love of liberty as repugnance to authority." This antiauthoritarianism makes Milton (1608–1674) one of the most eloquent democratic artists of the modern era—defender, among other things, of the right to divorce, and the autonomy of personal conscience in matters of religion.

Milton is perhaps best known today as the author of such epic poems as *Paradise Lost*, but he was involved in politics for much of his life, supporting the Parliamentary cause in the English Civil War. *Areopagitica* was written in 1644 in protest against Parliamentary attempts to regulate the printing press, using exactly the same mechanisms the King had previously used. In 1649 he was appointed foreign secretary by the government of the Commonwealth, a political posture that was to be rewarded with a short period of imprisonment under the royal restoration in 1660.

This work is perhaps the most exhilarating and far-ranging of any defenses of free speech: thorough, impassioned, and all the more powerful for being directed against people who were ostensibly his allies.

. . . Good and evil we know in the field of this world grow up together almost inseparably; and the knowledge of good is so involved and interwoven with the knowledge of evil, and in so many cunning resemblances hardly to be discerned, that those confused seeds which were imposed on Psyche as an incessant labor to cull out and sort asunder, were not more intermixed. It was from out the rind of one apple tasted, that the knowledge of good and evil, as two twins cleaving together, leaped forth into the world. And perhaps this is that doom which Adam fell into of knowing good and evil, that is to say, of knowing good by evil.

As therefore the state of man now is, what wisdom can there be to choose, what continence to forbear without the knowledge of evil? He that can apprehend and consider vice with all her baits and seeming pleasures, and yet abstain, and yet distinguish, and yet prefer that which is truly better, he is the true warfaring Christian. I cannot praise a fugitive and cloistered virtue, unexercised and unbreathed, that never sallies out and sees her adversary, but slinks out of the race where that immortal garland is to be run for, not without dust and heat. Assuredly we bring not innocence into the world, we bring impurity much rather: that which purifies us is trial, and trial is by what is contrary. That virtue therefore which is but a youngling in the contemplation of evil, and knows not the utmost that vice promises to her followers, and rejects it, is but a blank virtue, not a pure; her whiteness is but an excremental whiteness; which was the reason why our sage and serious poet Spenser, whom I dare be known to think a better teacher than Scotus or Aquinas, describing true temperance under the person of Guyon, brings him in with his palmer through the cave of Mammon and the bower of earthly bliss, that he might see and know, and yet abstain.

Since therefore, the knowledge and survey of vice is in this world so necessary to the constituting of human virtue, and the scanning of error to the confirmation of truth, how can we more safely and with less danger scout into the regions of sin and falsity than by reading all manner of tractates and hearing all manner of reason? And this is the benefit which may be had of books promiscuously read.

But of the harm that may result hence, three kinds are usually reckoned. First is feared the infection that may spread; but then all human learning and controversy in religious points must remove out of the world, yea the Bible itself; for that ofttimes relates blasphemy not nicely, it describes the carnal sense of wicked men not unelegantly, it brings in holiest men passionately murmuring against providence through all the arguments of Epicurus; in other great disputes it answers dubiously and darkly to the common reader; and ask a Talmudist what ails the modesty of his marginal Keri, that Moses and all the prophets cannot persuade him to pronounce the textual Chetiv. For these causes we all know the Bible itself put by the papist into the first rank of prohibited books. The ancientest fathers must be next removed, as Clement of Alexandria, and that Eusebian book of Evangelic preparation transmitting our ears through a hoard of heathenish obscenities to receive the Gospel. Who finds not that Irenæus, Epiphanius, Jerome, and others discover more heresies than they well confute, and that oft for heresy which is the truer opinion?

Nor boots it to say for these and all the heathen writers of greatest infection, if it must be thought so, with whom is bound up the life of human learning, that they writ in an unknown tongue, so long as we are sure those languages are known as well to the worst of men, who are both most able and most diligent to instil the poison they suck, first into the courts of princes, acquainting them with the choicest delights and criticisms of sin. As perhaps did that Petronius whom Nero called his Arbiter, the master of his revels; and that notorious ribald of Arezzo, dreaded, and yet dear to the Italian courtiers. I name not him for posterity's sake, whom Harry VIII named in merriment his Vicar of hell. By which compendious way all the contagion that foreign books can infuse, will find a passage to the people far easier and shorter than an Indian voyage, though it could be sailed either by the north of Cathay eastward, or of Canada westward, while our Spanish licensing gags the English press never so severely.

But, on the other side, that infection which is from books of controversy in religion, is more doubtful and dangerous to the learned than to the ignorant; and yet those books must be permitted untouched by the licenser. It will be hard to instance where any ignorant man hath been ever seduced by papistical book in English, unless it were commended and expounded to him by some of that clergy; and indeed all such tractates, whether false or true, are as the prophecy of Isaiah was to the eunuch, not to be "understood without a guide." But of our priests and doctors how many have been corrupted by studying the comments of Jesuits and Sorbonists, and how fast they could transfuse that corruption into the people, our experience is both late and sad. It is not forgot, since the acute and distinct Arminius was perverted merely by the perusing of a nameless discourse written at Delft, which at first he took in hand to confute.

Seeing, therefore, that those books, and those in great abundance which are likeliest to taint both life and doctrine, cannot be suppressed without the fall of learning, and of all ability in disputation; and that these books of either sort are most and soonest catching to the learned, from whom to the common people whatever is heretical or dissolute may quickly be conveyed; and that evil manners are as perfectly learned without books a thousand other ways which cannot be stopped; and evil doctrine not with books can propagate, except a teacher guide, which he might also do without writing, and so beyond prohibiting: I am not able to unfold how this cautelous enterprise of licensing can be exempted from the number of vain and impossible attempts. And he who were pleasantly disposed, could not well avoid to liken it to the exploit of that gallant man who thought to pound up the crows by shutting his park gate.

Besides another inconvenience, if learned men be the first receivers out of books and dispreaders both of vice and error, how shall the licensers themselves be confided in, unless we can confer upon them, or they assume to themselves above all others in the land, the grace of infallibility and uncorruptedness? And again, if it be true that a wise man, like a good refiner, can gather gold out of the drossiest volume, and that a fool will be a fool with the best book, yea or without book, there is no reason that we should deprive a wise man of any advantage to his wisdom, while we seek to restrain from a fool that which being restrained will be no hindrance to his folly. For if there should be so much exactness always used to keep that from him which is unfit for his reading, we should, in the judgment of Aristotle not only, but of Solomon and of our Savior, not vouchsafe him good precepts, and by consequence not willingly admit him to good books; as being certain that a wise man will make better use of an idle pamphlet than a fool will do of sacred scripture.

'Tis next alleged we must not expose ourselves to temptations without necessity, and, next to that, not employ our time in vain things. To both these objections one answer will serve, out of the grounds already laid; that to all men such books are not temptations nor vanities, but useful drugs and materials wherewith to temper and compose effective and strong medicines which man's life cannot want. The rest, as children and childish men, who have not the art to qualify and prepare these working minerals, well may be exhorted to forbear, but hindered forcibly they cannot be by all the licensing that sainted Inquisition could ever yet contrive. Which is what I promised to deliver next: that this order of licensing conduces nothing to the end for which it was framed; and hath almost prevented me by being clear already while thus much hath been explaining. See the ingenuity of Truth, who, when she gets a free and willing hand, opens herself faster than the pace of method and discourse can overtake her.

It was the task which I began with, to show that no nation, or well instituted state, if they valued books at all, did ever use this way of licensing; and it might be answered that this is a piece of prudence lately discovered. To which I return that as it was a thing slight and obvious to think on, so if it had been difficult to find out, there wanted not among them long since who suggested such a course; which they not following, leave us a pattern of their judgment that it was not the not knowing, but the not approving, which was the cause of their not using it.

Plato, a man of high authority indeed, but least of all for his commonwealth, in the book of his *Laws*, which no city ever yet received, fed his fancy with making many edicts to his airy burgomasters, which they who otherwise admire him, wish had been rather buried and excused in the genial cups of an Academic night-sitting. By which laws he seems to tolerate no kind of learning, but by unalterable decree, consisting most of practical traditions, to the attainment whereof a library of smaller bulk than his own dialogues would be abundant. And there also enacts that no poet should so much as read to any private man what he had written, until the judges and law-keepers had seen it and allowed it; but that Plato meant this law peculiarly to that commonwealth which he had imagined, and to no other, is evident. Why was he not else a law-giver to himself, but a transgressor, and to be expelled by his own magistrates; both for the wanton epigrams and dialogues which he made, and his perpetual reading of Sophron Mimus, and Aristophanes, books of grossest infamy; and also for commending the latter of them, though he were the malicious libeller of his chief friends, to be read by the

The visionary poet and philosopher John Milton, whose defense of free speech is perhaps the most eloquent in the English language, is shown here seated in his study.

tyrant Dionysius, who had little need of such trash to spend his time on? But that he knew this licensing of poems had reference and dependence to many other provisos there set down in his fancied republic, which in this world could have no place; and so neither he himself, nor any magistrate, or city ever imitated that course, which, taken apart from those other collateral injunctions, must needs be vain and fruitless.

For if they fell upon one kind of strictness, unless their care were equal to regulate all other things of like aptness to corrupt the mind, that single endeavor they knew would be but a fond labor; to shut and fortify one gate against corruption, and be necessitated to leave others round about wide open. If we think to regulate printing, thereby to rectify manners, we must regulate all recreations and pastimes, all that is delightful to man. No music must be heard, no song be set or sung, but what is grave and Doric. There must be licensing dancers, that no gesture, motion, or deportment be taught our youth, but what by their allowance shall be thought honest; for such Plato was provided of. It will ask more than the work of twenty licensers to examine all the lutes, the violins, and the guitars in every house; they must not be suffered to prattle as they do, but must be licensed what they may say. And who shall silence all the airs and madrigals that whisper softness in chambers? The windows also, and the balconies must be thought on; there are shrewd books, with dangerous frontispieces, set to sale; who shall prohibit them? Shall twenty licensers? The villages also must have their visitors to inquire what lectures the bagpipe and the rebeck reads even to the balladry and the gamut of every municipal fiddler, for these are the countryman's Arcadias, and his Monte Mayors.

Next, what more national corruption, for which England hears ill abroad, than household gluttony? Who shall be the rectors of our daily rioting? And what shall be done to inhibit the multitudes that frequent those houses where drunkenness is sold and harbored? Our garments also should be referred to the licensing of some more sober workmasters, to see them cut into a less wanton garb. Who shall regulate all the mixed conversation of our youth, male and female together, as is the fashion of this country? Who shall still appoint what shall be discoursed, what presumed, and no further? Lastly, who shall forbid and separate all idle resort, all evil company? These things will be and must be; but how they shall be least hurtful, how least enticing, herein consists the grave and governing wisdom of a state.

To sequester out of the world into Atlantic and Utopian polities, which never can be drawn into use, will not mend our condition; but to ordain wisely as in this world of evil, in the midst whereof God hath placed us unavoidably. Nor is it Plato's licensing of books will do this, which necessarily pulls along with it so many other kinds of licensing as will make us all both ridiculous and weary, and yet frustrate; but those unwritten, or at least unconstraining, laws of virtuous education, religious and civil nurture, which Plato there mentions as the bonds and ligaments of the commonwealth, the pillars and the sustainers of every written statute; these they be which will bear chief sway in such matters as these, when all licensing will be easily eluded. Impunity and remissness, for certain, are the bane of a commonwealth; but here the great art lies, to discern in what the law is to bid restraint and punishment, and in what things persuasion only is to work. If every action which is good or evil in man at ripe years, were to be under pittance and prescription and compulsion, what were virtue but a name, what praise could be then due to well-doing, what gramercy to be sober, just, or continent?

Many there be that complain of divine providence for suffering Adam to transgress. Foolish tongues! when God gave him reason, he gave him freedom to choose, for reason is but choosing; he had been else a mere artificial Adam, such an Adam as he is in the motions. We ourselves esteem not of that obedience, or love, or gift, which is of force. God therefore left him free, set before him a provoking object, ever almost in his eyes; herein consisted his merit, herein the right of his reward, the praise of his abstinence. Wherefore did he create passions within us, pleasures round about us, but that these rightly tempered are the very ingredients of virtue? They are not skillful considerers of human things who imagine to remove sin by removing the matter of sin. For, besides that it is a huge heap increasing under the very act of diminishing, though some part of it may for a time be withdrawn from some persons, it cannot from all, in such a universal thing as books are; and when this is done, yet the sin remains entire. Though ye take from a covetous man all his treasure, he has yet one jewel left—ye cannot bereave him of his covetousness. Banish all objects of lust, shut up all youth into the severest discipline that can be exercised in any hermitage, ye cannot make them chaste that came not thither so: such great care and wisdom is required to the right managing of this point.

Suppose we could expel sin by this means; look how much we thus expel of sin, so much we expel of virtue; for the matter of them both is the same; remove that, and ye remove them both alike. This justifies the high providence of God, who, though he command us temperance, justice, continence, yet pours out before us, even to a profuseness, all desirable things, and gives us minds that can wander beyond all limit and satiety. Why should we then affect a rigor contrary to the manner of God and of nature, by abridging or scanting those means which books freely permitted are, both to the trial of virtue and the exercise of truth?

It would be better done to learn that the law must needs be frivolous which goes to restrain things uncertainly and yet equally working to good and to evil. And were I the chooser, a dram of well-doing should be preferred before many times as much the forcible hindrance of evil-doing. For God sure esteems the growth and completing of one virtuous person more than the restraint of ten vicious. And albeit whatever thing we hear or see, sitting, walking, travelling, or conversing, may be fitly called our book, and is of the same effect that writings are; yet grant the thing to be prohibited were only books, it appears that this order hitherto is far insufficient to the end which it intends. Do we not see—not once or oftener, but weekly—that continued court-libel against the Parliament and City printed, as the wet sheets can witness, and dispersed among us, for all that licensing can do? Yet this is the prime service a man would think, wherein this Order should give proof of itself. If it were executed, you'll say. But certain, if execution be remiss or blindfold now, and in this particular, what will it be hereafter and in other books?

If then the Order shall not be vain and frustrate, behold a new labor, Lords and Commons. Ye must repeal and proscribe all scandalous and unlicensed books already printed and divulged (after ye have drawn them up into a list, that all may know which are condemned and which not) and ordain that no foreign books be delivered out of custody, till they have been read over. This office will require the whole time of not a few overseers, and those no vulgar men. There be also books which are partly useful and excellent, partly culpable and pernicious; this work will ask as many more officials, to make expurgations and expunctions, that the commonwealth of learning be not damnified. In fine, when the multitude of books increase upon their hands, ye must be fain to catalog all those printers who are found frequently offending, and forbid the importation of their whole suspected typography. In a word, that this your Order may be exact and not deficient, ye must reform it perfectly according to the model of Trent and Seville, which I know ye abhor to do.

Yet, though ye should condescend to this, which God forbid, the Order still would be but fruitless and defective to that end whereto ye meant it. If to prevent sects and schisms, who is so unread or so uncatechized in story that hath not heard of many sects refusing books as a hindrance, and preserving their doctrine unmixed for many ages, only by unwritten traditions? The Christian faith, for that was once a chism, is not unknown to have spread all over Asia, ere any Gospel or Epistle was seen in writing. If the amendment of manners be aimed at, look into Italy and Spain, whether those places be one scruple the better, the honester, the wiser, the chaster, since all the inquisitional rigor that hath been executed upon books.

Another reason whereby to make it plain that this Order will miss the end it seeks, consider by the quality which ought to be in every licenser. It cannot be denied but that he who is made judge to sit upon the birth or death of books, whether they may be wafted into this world or not, had need to be a man above the common measure, both studious, learned, and judicious. There may be else no mean mistakes in the censure of what is passable or not, which is also no mean injury. If he be of such worth as behoves him, there cannot be a more tedious and unpleasing journey-work, a greater loss of time levied upon his head, than to be made the perpetual reader of unchosen books and pamphlets, ofttimes huge volumes. There is no book that is acceptable unless at certain seasons; but to be enjoined the reading of that at all times, and in a hand scarce legible, whereof three pages would not down at any time in the fairest print, is an imposition which I cannot believe how he that values time and his own studies, or is but of a sensible nostril, should be able to endure.

In this one thing I crave leave of the present licensers to be pardoned for so thinking; who doubtless took this office up, looking on it through their obedience to the parliament, whose command perhaps made all things seem easy and unlaborious to them; but that this short trial hath wearied them out already, their own expressions and excuses to them who make so many journeys to solicit their license, are testimony enough. Seeing, therefore, those who now possess the employment, by all evident signs wish themselves well rid of it, and that no man of worth, none that is not a plain unthrift of his own hours, is ever likely to succeed them, except he mean to put himself to the salary of a press corrector, we may easily foresee what kind of licensers we are to expect hereafter, either ignorant, imperious, and remiss, or basely pecuniary. This is what I had to show, wherein this Order cannot conduce to that end whereof it bears the intention.

I lastly proceed from the no good it can do, to the manifest hurt it causes in being first the greatest discouragement and affront that can be offered to learning and to learned men.

It was the complaint and lamentation of prelates, upon every least breath of a motion to remove pluralities and distribute more equally church revenues, that then all learning would be for ever dashed and discouraged. But as for that opinion, I never found cause to think that the tenth part of learning stood or fell with the clergy; nor could I ever but hold it for a sordid and unworthy speech of any churchman who had a competency left him. If, therefore, ye be loth to dishearten utterly and discontent, not the

mercenary crew of false pretenders to learning, but the free and ingenuous sort of such as evidently were born to study and love learning for itself, not for lucre, or any other end but the service of God and of truth, and perhaps that lasting fame and perpetuity of praise which God and good men have consented shall be the reward of those whose published labors advance the good of mankind; then know, that so far to distrust the judgment and the honesty of one who hath but a common repute in learning, and never yet offended, as not to count him fit to print his mind without a tutor and examiner, lest he should drop a schism, or something of corruption, is the greatest displeasure and indignity to a free and knowing spirit that can be put upon him.

What advantage is it to be a man over it is to be a boy at school, if we have only scaped the ferula to come under the fescue of an Imprimatur; if serious and elaborate writings, as if they were no more than the theme of a grammar-lad under his pedagogue, must not be uttered without the cursory eyes of a temporizing and extemporizing licenser? He who is not trusted with his own actions, his drift not being known to be evil, and standing to the hazard of law and penalty, has no great argument to think himself reputed, in the commonwealth wherein he was born, for other than a fool or a foreigner.

When a man writes to the world, he summons up all his reason and deliberation to assist him; he searches, meditates, is industrious, and likely consults and confers with his judicious friends, after all which done he takes himself to be informed in what he writes, as well as any that writ before him. If in this the most consummate act of his fidelity and ripeness, no years, no industry, no former proof of his abilities can bring him to that state of maturity as not to be still mistrusted and suspected (unless he carry all his considerate diligence, all his midnight watchings, and expense of Palladian oil, to the hasty view of an unleisured licenser, perhaps much his younger, perhaps far his inferior in judgment, perhaps one who never knew the labor of book-writing), and if he be not repulsed, or slighted, must appear in print like a puny with his guardian, and his censor's hand on the back of his title to be his bail and surety that he is no idiot or seducer; it cannot be but a dishonor and derogation to the author, to the book, to the privilege and dignity of learning.

And what if the author shall be one so copious of fancy as to have many things well worth the adding, come into his mind after licensing, while the book is yet under the press, which not seldom happens to the best and diligentest writers; and that perhaps a dozen times in one book. The printer dares not go beyond his licensed copy. So often then must the author trudge to his leave-giver, that those his new insertions may be viewed, and many a jaunt will be made, ere that licenser, for it must be the same man, can either be found, or found at leisure. Meanwhile, either the press must stand still, which is no small damage, or the author lose his accuratest thoughts and send the book forth worse than he had made it, which to a diligent writer is the greatest melancholy and vexation that can befall.

And how can a man teach with authority, which is the life of teaching, how can he be a doctor in his book as he ought to be, or else had better be silent, whenas all he teaches, all he delivers, is but under the tuition, under the correction of his patriarchal licenser to blot or alter what precisely accords not with the hidebound humor which he calls his judgment? When every acute reader upon the first sight of a pedantic license, will be ready with these like words to ding the book a quoit's distance from him: "I hate a pupil teacher, I endure not an instructor that comes to me under the wardship of an overseeing fist. I know nothing of the licenser, but that I have his own hand here for his arrogance; who shall warrant me his judgment?"

"The state, sir," replies the stationer, but has a quick return: "The state shall be my governors, but not my critics; they may be mistaken in the choice of a licenser as easily as this licenser may be mistaken in an author; this is some common stuff"; and he might add from Sir Francis Bacon, "That such authorized books are but the language of the times." For though a licenser should

happen to be judicious more than ordinary, which will be a great jeopardy of the next succession, yet his very office and his commission enjoins him to let pass nothing but what is vulgarly received already.

Nay, which is more lamentable, if the work of any deceased author, though never so famous in his lifetime and even to this day, come to their hands for license to be printed, or reprinted; if there be found in his book one sentence of a venturous edge, uttered in the height of zeal, and who knows whether it might not be the dictate of a divine spirit, yet not suiting with every low, decrepit humor of their own, though it were Knox himself, the reformer of a kingdom, that spake it, they will not pardon him their dash; the sense of that great man shall to all posterity be lost, for the fearfulness, or the presumptuous rashness, of a perfunctory licenser. And to what an author this violence hath been lately done, and in what book of greatest consequence to be faithfully published, I could now instance, but shall forbear till a more convenient season.

Yet if these things be not resented seriously and timely by them who have the remedy in their power, but that such ironmolds as these shall have authority to gnaw out the choicest periods of exquisitest books, and to commit such a treacherous fraud against the orphan remainders of worthiest men after death, the more sorrow will belong to that hapless race of men whose misfortune it is to have understanding. Henceforth let no man care to learn, or care to be more than worldly wise; for certainly in higher matters to be ignorant and slothful, to be a common, steadfast dunce, will be the only pleasant life, and only in request.

And as it is a particular disesteem of every knowing person alive, and most injurious to the written labors and monuments of the dead, so to me it seems an undervaluing and vilifying of the whole nation. I cannot set so light by all the invention, the art, the wit, the grave and solid judgment which is in England, as that it can be comprehended in any twenty capacities how good soever; much less that it should not pass except their superintendence be over it, except it be sifted and strained with their strainers; that it should be uncurrent without their manual stamp. Truth and understanding are not such wares as to be monopolized and traded in by tickets and statutes and standards. We must not think to make a staple commodity of all the knowledge in the land, to mark and license it like our broadcloth and our woolpacks. What is it but a servitude like that imposed by the Philistines, not to be allowed the sharpening of our own axes and coulters, but we must repair from all quarters to twenty licensing forges.

Had anyone written and divulged erroneous things and scandalous to honest life, misusing and forfeiting the esteem had of his reason among men; if, after conviction, this only censure were adjudged him, that he should never henceforth write, but what were first examined by an appointed officer, whose hand should be annexed to pass his credit for him, that now he might be safely read; it could not be apprehended less than a disgraceful punishment.

Whence, to include the whole nation, and those that never yet thus offended, under such a diffident and suspectful prohibition, may plainly be understood what a disparagement it is. So much the more, whenas debtors and delinquents may walk abroad without a keeper, but unoffensive books must not stir forth without a visible jailor in their title. Nor is it to the common people less than a reproach; for if we be so jealous over them as that we dare not trust them with an English pamphlet, what do we but censure them for a giddy, vicious, and ungrounded people, in such a sick and weak estate of faith and discretion, as to be able to take nothing down but through the pipe of a licenser. That this is care or love of them, we cannot pretend, whenas in those popish places where the laity are most hated and despised, the same strictness is used over them. Wisdom we cannot call it, because it stops but one breach of license, nor that neither; whenas those corruptions which it seeks to prevent, break in faster at other doors which cannot be shut.

And in conclusion, it reflects to the disrepute of our ministers also, of whose labors we should hope better, and of the proficiency which their flock reaps by them, than that after all this light of the Gospel which is and is to be, and all this continual preaching, they should be still frequented with such an unprincipled, unedified, and laic rabble, as that the whiff of every new pamphlet should stagger them out of their catechism and Christian walking. This may have much reason to discourage the ministers, when such a low conceit is had of all their exhortations and the benefiting of their hearers, as that they are not thought fit to be turned loose to three sheets of paper without a licenser; that all the sermons, all the lectures preached, printed, vended in such numbers and such volumes as have now well nigh made all other books unsaleable, should not be armor enough against one single enchiridion, without the castle St. Angelo of an Imprimatur.

And lest some should persuade ye, Lords and Commons, that these arguments of learned men's discouragement at this your Order are mere flourishes, and not real, I could recount what I have seen and heard in other countries where this kind of inquisition tyrannizes; when I have sat among their learned men, for that honor I had, and been counted happy to be born in such a place of philosophic freedom as they supposed England was, while themselves did nothing but bemoan the servile condition into which learning amongst them was brought; that this was it which had damped the glory of Italian wits; that nothing had been there written now these many years but flattery and fustian. There it was that I found and visited the famous Galileo, grown old, a prisoner to the Inquisition for thinking in astronomy otherwise than the Franciscan and Dominican licensers thought. And though I knew that England then was groaning loudest under the prelatical yoke, nevertheless I took it as a pledge of future happiness that other nations were so persuaded of her liberty.

Yet was it beyond my hope that those worthies were then breathing in her air, who should be her leaders to such a deliverance as shall never be forgotten by any revolution of time that this world hath to finish. When that was once begun, it was as little in my fear, that what words of complaint I heard among learned men of other parts uttered against the Inquisition, the same I should hear by as learned men at home uttered in time of Parliament against an order of licensing; and that so generally, that when I had disclosed myself a companion of their discontent, I might say, if without envy, that he whom an honest quæstorship had endeared to the Sicilians, was not more by them importuned against Verres, than the favorable opinion which I had among many who honor ye, and are known and respected by ye, loaded me with entreaties and persuasions that I would not despair to lay together that which just reason should bring into my mind toward the removal of an undeserved thraldom upon learning.

That this is not, therefore, the disburdening of a particular fancy, but the common grievance of all those who had prepared their minds and studies above the vulgar pitch to advance truth in others, and from others to entertain it, thus much may satisfy. And in their name I shall for neither friend nor foe conceal what the general murmur is; that if it come to inquisitioning again and licensing, and that we are so timorous of ourselves and so suspicious of all men as to fear each book and the shaking of every leaf, before we know what the contents are; if some who but of late were little better than silenced from preaching, shall come now to silence us from reading, except what they please, it cannot be guessed what is intended by some but a second tyranny over learning; and will soon put it out of controversy that bishops and presbyters are the same to us both name and thing.

That those evils of prelaty which before from five or six and twenty sees were distributively charged upon the whole people, will now light wholly upon learning, is not obscure to us; whenas now the pastor of a small unlearned parish on the sudden shall be exalted archbishop over a large diocese of books, and yet not remove, but keep his other cure too, a mystical pluralist. He who but of late cried down the sole ordination of every novice bachelor of art, and denied sole jurisdiction over the simplest parish-

ioner, shall now at home in his private chair assume both these over worthiest and excellentest books and ablest authors that write them. This is not, ye covenants and protestations that we have made, this is not to put down prelaty; this is but to chop an episcopacy; this is but to translate the palace metropolitan from one kind of dominion into another; this is but an old canonical sleight of commuting our penance. To startle thus betimes at a mere unlicensed pamphlet will after a while be afraid of every conventicle, and a while after will make a conventicle of every Christian meeting.

But I am certain that a state governed by the rules of justice and fortitude, or a church built and founded upon the rock of faith and true knowledge, cannot be so pusillanimous. While things are yet not constituted in religion, that freedom of writing should be restrained by a discipline imitated from the prelates, and learnt by them from the Inquisition, to shut us up all again into the breast of a licenser, must needs give cause of doubt and discouragement to all learned and religious men. Who cannot but discern the fineness of this politic drift, and who are the contrivers: that while bishops were to be baited down, then all presses might be open; it was the people's birthright and privilege in time of parliament, it was the breaking forth of light?

But now, the bishops abrogated and voided out of the church, as if our reformation sought no more but to make room for others into their seats under another name, the episcopal arts begin to bud again; the cruse of truth must run no more oil; liberty of printing must be enthralled again under a prelatical commission of twenty, the privilege of the people nullified; and, which is worse, the freedom of learning must groan again, and to her old fetters: all this the parliament yet sitting. Although their own late arguments and defenses against the prelates might remember them that this obstructing violence meets for the most part with an event utterly opposite to the end which it drives at; instead of suppressing sects and schisms, it raises them and invests them with a reputation: "The punishing of wits enhances their authority," saith the Viscount St.

Albans, "and a forbidden writing is thought to be a certain spark of truth that flies up in the faces of them who seek to tread it out."

This Order, therefore, may prove a nursing mother to sects, but I shall easily show how it will be a stepdame to Truth; and first by disenabling us to the maintenance of what is known already.

Well knows he who uses to consider, that our faith and knowledge thrives by exercise, as well as our limbs and complexion. Truth is compared in scripture to a streaming fountain; if her waters flow not in a perpetual progression, they sicken into a muddy pool of conformity and tradition. A man may be a heretic in the truth; and if he believe things only because his pastor says so, or the Assembly so determines, without knowing other reason, though his belief be true, yet the very truth he holds becomes his heresy. There is not any burden that some would gladlier post off to another than the charge and care of their religion. There be, who knows not that there be, of protestants and professors who live and die in as arrant an implicit faith, as any lay papist of Loreto.

A wealthy man addicted to his pleasure and to his profits, finds religion to be a traffic so entangled, and of so many piddling accounts, that of all mysteries he cannot skill to keep a stock going upon that trade. What should he do? Fain he would have the name to be religious, fain he would bear up with his neighbors in that. What does he, therefore, but resolves to give over toiling, and to find himself out some factor to whose care and credit he may commit the whole managing of his religious affairs; some Divine of note and estimation that must be. To him he adheres, resigns the whole warehouse of his religion with all the locks and keys into his custody; and indeed makes the very person of that man his religion; esteems his associating with him a sufficient evidence and commendatory of his own piety. So that a man may say his religion is now no more within himself, but is become a dividual movable, and goes and comes near him, according as that good man frequents the house. He entertains him, gives him gifts, feasts him, lodges him. His religion comes home at night, prays, is liberally supped, and sumptuously laid to sleep, rises, is saluted, and after the malmsey, or some well spiced brewage, and better breakfasted than he whose morning appetite would have gladly fed on green figs between Bethany and Jerusalem, his religion walks abroad at eight, and leaves his kind entertainer in the shop trading all day without his religion.

Another sort there be, who, when they hear that all things shall be ordered, all things regulated and settled, nothing written but what passes through the custom-house of certain publicans that have the tonnaging and the poundaging of all free-spoken truth, will straight give themselves up into your hands, make 'em and cut 'em out what religion ye please. There be delights, there be recreations and jolly pastimes that will fetch the day about from sun to sun, and rock the tedious year as in a delightful dream. What need they torture their heads with that which others have taken so strictly and so unalterably into their own purveying? These are the fruits which a dull ease and cessation of our knowledge will bring forth among the people. How goodly, and how to be wished, were such an obedient unanimity as this, what a fine conformity would it starch us all into! Doubtless a staunch and solid piece of framework, as any January could freeze together.

Nor much better will be the consequence even among the clergy themselves. It is no new thing never heard of before, for a parochial minister, who has his reward, and is at his Hercules pillars in a warm benefice, to be easily inclinable, if he have nothing else that may rouse up his studies, to finish his circuit in an English concordance and a topic folio, the gatherings and savings of a sober graduateship, a harmony and a catena, treading the constant round of certain common doctrinal heads, attended with their uses, motives, marks, and means; out of which, as out of an alphabet or sol-fa, by forming and transforming, joining and disjoining variously a little bookcraft, and two hours' meditation, might furnish him unspeakably to the performance of more than a weekly charge of sermoning; not to reckon up the infinite helps of interlinearies, breviaries, synopses, and other loitering gear.

But as for the multitude of sermons ready printed and piled up on every text that is not difficult, our London trading St. Thomas in his vestry, and add to boot St. Martin and St. Hugh, have not within their hallowed limits more vendible ware of all sorts ready made; so that penury he never need fear of pulpit provision, having where so plenteously to refresh his magazine. But if his rear and flanks be not impaled, if his back door be not secured by the rigid licenser, but that a bold book may now and then issue forth and give the assault to some of his old collections in their trenches; it will concern him then to keep waking, to stand in watch, to set good guards and sentinels about his received opinions, to walk the round and counterround with his fellow inspectors, fearing lest any of his flock be seduced, who also then would be better instructed, better exercised and disciplined. And God send that the fear of this diligence, which must then be used, do not make us affect the laziness of a licensing church.

For if we be sure we are in the right, and do not hold the truth guiltily, which becomes not, if we ourselves condemn not our own weak and frivolous teaching, and the people for an untaught and irreligious, gadding rout, what can be more fair than when a man judicious, learned, and of a conscience, for aught we know, as good as theirs that taught us what we know, shall not privily from house to house, which is more dangerous, but openly by writing, publish to the world what his opinion is, what his reasons, and wherefore that which is now thought cannot be sound? Christ urged it as wherewith to justify himself that he preached in public; yet writing is more public than preaching; and more easy to refutation, if need be, there being so many whose business and profession merely it is, to be the champions of truth; which if they neglect, what can be imputed but their sloth or unability?

Thus much we are hindered and disinured by this course of licensing toward the true knowl-

edge of what we seem to know. For how much it hurts and hinders the licensers themselves in the calling of their ministry, more than any secular employment, if they will discharge that office as they ought, so that of necessity they must neglect either the one duty or the other, I insist not, because it is a particular, but leave it to their own conscience, how they will decide it there.

There is yet behind of what I purposed to lay open, the incredible loss and detriment that this plot of licensing puts us to. More than if some enemy at sea should stop up all our havens and ports and creeks, it hinders and retards the importation of our richest merchandise, truth. Nay, it was first established and put in practice by Antichristian malice and mystery, on set purpose to extinguish, if it were possible, the light of reformation, and to settle falsehood; little differing from that policy wherewith the Turk upholds his Alcoran, by the prohibition of printing. 'Tis not denied, but gladly confessed, we are to send our thanks and vows to Heaven, louder than most of nations, for that great measure of truth which we enjoy, especially in those main points between us and the Pope, with his appurtenances the prelates; but he who thinks we are to pitch our tent here, and have attained the utmost prospect of reformation that the mortal glass wherein we contemplate can show us, till we come to beatific vision, that man by this very opinion declares that he is yet far short of truth.

Truth indeed came once into the world with her divine Master, and was a perfect shape most glorious to look on. But when he ascended, and his apostles after him were laid asleep, then straight arose a wicked race of deceivers, who, as that story goes of the Egyptian Typhon with his conspirators, how they dealt with the good Osiris, took the virgin Truth, hewed her lovely form into a thousand pieces, and scattered them to the four winds. From that time ever since, the sad friends of Truth, such as durst appear, imitating the careful search that Isis made for the mangled body of Osiris, went up and down gathering up limb by limb still as they could find them. We have not yet found them all, Lords and Commons, nor ever shall do, till her Master's second coming. He shall bring together every joint and member, and shall mold them into an immortal feature of loveliness and perfection. Suffer not these licensing prohibitions to stand at every place of opportunity, forbidding and disturbing them that continue seeking, that continue to do our obsequies to the torn body of our martyred saint.

We boast our light; but if we look not wisely on the sun itself, it smites us into darkness. Who can discern those planets that are oft combust, and those stars of brightest magnitude that rise and set with the sun, until the opposite motion of their orbs bring them to such a place in the firmament, where they may be seen evening or morning. The light which we have gained, was given us, not to be ever staring on, but by it to discover onward things more remote from our knowledge. It is not the unfrocking of a priest, the unmitering of a bishop, and the removing him from off the Presbyterian shoulders that will make us a happy nation; no, if other things as great in the church, and in the rule of life both economical and political, be not looked into and reformed, we have looked so long upon the blaze that Zwinglius and Calvin hath beaconed up to us, that we are stark blind.

There be who perpetually complain of schisms and sects, and make it such a calamity that any man dissents from their maxims. It is their own pride and ignorance which causes the disturbing, who neither will hear with meekness, nor can convince, yet all must be suppressed which is not found in their syntagma. They are the troublers, they are the dividers of unity, who neglect and permit not others to unite those dissevered pieces which are yet wanting to the body of Truth. To be still searching what we know not by what we know, still closing up truth to truth as we find it (for all her body is homogeneal and proportional), this is the golden rule in theology as well as in arithmetic, and makes up the best harmony in a church; not the forced and outward union of cold and neutral and inwardly divided minds. . . .

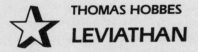

THOMAS HOBBES
LEVIATHAN

Thomas Hobbes (1588–1679) lived a long and fearful life as a political philosopher during the turbulent seventeenth century in England. He escaped into exile twice, first from England to France for 11 years, and then in the opposite direction. His complex treatises on the nature of politics, three of which he withheld from publication until after his death, were alternately praised and scorned by those on all points of the political spectrum.

To mention him in the context of democracy might be considered blasphemous. Hobbes is perhaps the supreme theorist of absolute sovereignty, a tutor to England's King Charles II, and a stern defender of the Royalists against the Parliamentarians in the English Civil War. Yet to view Hobbes as merely an apologist for power is to misunderstand his project entirely. For Hobbes, authority was necessary to protect people from one another. As he believed life without authority meant virtually no security, to him authority was the beginning of genuine liberty and not the end of it. By basing liberty on the low grounds of power-politics, Hobbes attempted to give it a firmer foothold than other thinkers. His argument lies behind the modern democratic concern with securing liberty under law. In this passage from *Leviathan*, written in 1651 at the height of the English Civil War, Hobbes outlines the rights of the individual in his commonwealth, and charts the impor-

. . . To come now to the particulars of the true Liberty of a Subject; that is to say, what are the things, which though commanded by the Soveraign, he may nevertheless, without Injustice, refuse to do; we are to consider, what Rights we passe away, when we make a Commonwealth; or (which is all one,) what Liberty we deny our selves, by owning all the Actions (without exception) of the Man, or Assembly we make our Soveraign. For in the act of our *Submission*, consisteth both our *Obligation*, and our *Liberty*; which must therefore be inferred by arguments taken from thence; there being no Obligation on any man, which ariseth not from some Act of his own; for all men equally, are by Nature Free. And because such arguments, must either be drawn from the expresse words, *I Authorise all his Actions*, or from the Intention of him that submitteth himselfe to his Power, (which Intention is to be understood by the End for which he so submitteth;) The Obligation, and Liberty of the Subject, is to be derived, either from those Words, (or others equivalent;) or else from the End of the Institution of Soveraignty; namely, the Peace of the Subjects within themselves, and their Defence against a common Enemy.

First therefore, seeing Soveraignty by Institution, is by Covenant of every one to every one; and Soveraignty by Acquisition, by Covenants of the Vanquished to the Victor, or Child to the Parent; It is manifest, that every Subject has Liberty in all those things, the right whereof cannot by Covenant be transferred. I have shewn before in the 14. Chapter, that Covenants, not to defend a mans own body, are voyd. Therefore,

If the Soveraign command a man (though justly condemned,) to kill, wound, or mayme himselfe; or not to resist those that assault him; or to abstain from the use of food, ayre, medicine, or any other thing, without which he cannot live; yet hath that man the Liberty to disobey.

If a man be interrogated by the Soveraign, or his Authority, concerning a crime done by himselfe, he is not bound (without assurance of Pardon) to confesse it; because no man (as I have shewn in the same Chapter) can be obliged by Covenant to accuse himselfe.

Again, the Consent of a Subject to Soveraign Power, is contained in these words, *I Authorise, or take upon me, all his actions*; in which there is no restriction at all, of his own former naturall Liberty: For by allowing him to *kill me*, I am not bound to kill my selfe when he commands me. 'Tis one thing to say, *Kill me, or my fellow, if you please*; another thing to say, *I will kill my selfe, or my fellow.* It followeth therefore, that

No man is bound by the words themselves, either to kill himselfe, or any other man; And consequently, that the Obligation a man may sometimes have, upon the Command of the Soveraign to execute any dangerous, or dishonourable Office, dependeth not on the Words of our Submission; but on the Intention; which is to be understood by the End thereof. When therefore our refusall to obey, frustrates the End for which the Soveraignty was ordained; then there is no Liberty to refuse: otherwise there is.

Upon this ground, a man that is commanded as a Souldier to fight against the enemy, though his Soveraign have Right enough to punish his refusall with death, may neverthelesse in many cases refuse, without Injustice; as when he substituteth a sufficient Souldier in his place: for in this case he deserteth not the service of the Common-wealth. And there is allowance to be made for naturall timorousnesse, not onely to women, (of whom no such dangerous duty is expected,) but also to men of feminine courage. When Armies fight, there is on one side, or both, a running away; yet when they do it not out of trechery, but fear, they are not esteemed to do it unjustly, but dishonourably. For the same reason, to avoyd battell, is not Injustice, but Cowardise. But he that inrowleth himselfe a Souldier, or

The frontispiece to Thomas Hobbes' *Leviathan* shows a giant—the state—made up entirely of its citizens. The Latin quotation is from the Book of Job, and describes the nature of the sovereign state: "There is no power upon the earth to compare with it."

taketh imprest mony, taketh away the excuse of a timorous nature; and is obliged, not onely to go to the battell, but also not to run from it, without his Captaines leave. And when the Defence of the Common-wealth, requireth at once the help of all that are able to bear Arms, every one is obliged; because otherwise the Institution of the Common-wealth, which they have not the purpose, or courage to preserve, was in vain.

To resist the Sword of the Common-wealth, in defence of another man, guilty, or innocent, no man hath Liberty; because such Liberty, takes away from the Soveraign, the means of Protecting us; and is therefore destructive of the very essence of Government. But in case a great many men together, have already resisted the Soveraign Power unjustly, or committed some Capitall crime, for which every one of them expecteth death, whether have they not the Liberty then to joyn together, and assist, and defend one another? Certainly they have: For they but defend their lives, which the Guilty man may as well do, as the Innocent. There was indeed injustice in the first breach of their duty; Their bearing of Arms subsequent to it, though it be to maintain what they have done, is no new unjust act. And if it be onely to defend their persons, it is not unjust at all. But the offer of Pardon taketh from them, to whom it is offered, the plea of self-defence, and maketh their perseverance in assisting, or defending the rest, unlawfull.

As for other Lyberties, they depend on the silence of the Law. In cases where the Soveraign has prescribed no rule, there the Subject hath the liberty to do, or forbeare, according to his own discretion. And therefore such Liberty is in some places more, and in some lesse; and in some times more, in other times lesse, according as they that have the Soveraignty shall think most convenient. As for Example, there was a time, when in *England* a man might enter in to his own Land, (and dispossesse such as wrongfully possessed it) by force. But in after-times, that Liberty of Forcible entry, was taken away by a Statute made (by the King) in Parliament. And in some places of the world, men have the Liberty of many wives: in other places, such Liberty is not allowed.

If a Subject have a controversie with his Soveraigne, of Debt, or of right of possession of lands or goods, or concerning any service required at his hands, or concerning any penalty corporall, or pecuniary, grounded on a precedent Law; He hath the same Liberty to sue for his right, as if it were against a Subject; and before such Judges, as are appointed by the Soveraign. For seeing the Soveraign demandeth by force of a former Law, and not by vertue of his Power; he declareth thereby, that he requireth no more, than shall appear to be due by that Law. The sute therefore is not contrary to the will of the Soveraign; and consequently the Subject hath the Liberty to demand the hearing of his Cause; and sentence, according to that Law. But if he demand, or take any thing by pretence of his Power; there lyeth, in that case, no action of Law: for all that is done by him in Vertue of his Power, is done by the Authority of every subject, and consequently, he that brings an action against the Soveraign, brings it against himselfe.

If a Monarch, or Soveraign Assembly, grant a Liberty to all, or any of his Subjects; which Grant standing, he is disabled to provide for their safety, the Grant is voyd; unlesse he directly renounce, or transferre the Soveraignty to another. For in that he might openly, (if it had been his will,) and in plain termes, have renounced, or transferred it, and did not; it is to be understood it was not his will; but that the Grant proceeded from ignorance of the repugnancy between such a Liberty and the Soveraign Power; and therefore the Soveraignty is still retayned; and consequently all those Powers, which are necessary to

the exercising thereof; such as are the Power of Warre, and Peace, of Judicature, of appointing Officers, and Councellours, of levying Mony, and the rest named in the 18th Chapter.

The Obligation of Subjects to the Soveraign, is understood to last as long, and no longer, than the power lasteth, by which he is able to protect them. For the right men have by Nature to protect themselves, when none else can protect them, can by no Covenant be relinquished. The Soveraignty is the Soule of the Common-wealth; which once departed from the Body, the members doe no more receive their motion from it. The end of Obedience is Protection; which, wheresoever a man seeth it, either in his own, or in anothers sword, Nature applyeth his obedience to it, and his endeavour to maintaine it. And though Soveraignty, in the intention of them that make it, be immortall; yet is it in its own nature, not only subject to violent death, by forreign war; but also through the ignorance, and passions of men, it hath in it, from the very institution, many seeds of a naturall mortality, by Intestine Discord. . . .

JOHN LOCKE
A LETTER CONCERNING TOLERATION

The influence of John Locke (1632–1704) on the thought of the founders of the United States is well documented, but Locke can also be seen as the philosophical father of more than just America. Virtually all the features of modern liberal democracy are mapped out in Locke's writings: a doctrine of religious toleration, a defense of individual self-determination, a theory of rebellion against unjust authority, and an absolute right to unlimited private property.

Locke's celebrated letter in defense of religious toleration has long been regarded as a classic of democratic literature. It was originally written in Latin when Locke was in exile in Holland in 1685, and only published in 1689 when the new regime of William of Orange, a Protestant, had been established by *coup d'état* in Britain. Under the new rule then established in Britain, the Toleration Act of 1689, religious freedom was only permitted to Protestants who affirmed the Holy Trinity and were prepared to sign an oath of allegiance to the Crown. All other dissenters—and of course Catholics—were denied religious freedom, a state of affairs that was to continue for another 150 years. Locke's letter was to achieve its most concrete affirmation on the American continent, where it

. . . The end of a religious society (as has already been said) is the publick worship of God, and by means thereof the acquisition of eternal life. All discipline ought therefore to tend to that end, and all ecclesiastical laws to be thereunto confined. Nothing ought, nor can be transacted in this society, relating to the possession of civil and worldly goods. No force is here to be made use of, upon any occasion whatsoever: for force belongs wholly to the civil magistrate, and the possession of all outward goods is subject to his jurisdiction.

But it may be asked, by what means then shall ecclesiastical laws be established, if they must be thus destitute of all compulsive power? I answer, they must be established by means suitable to the nature of such things, whereof the external profession and observation, if not proceeding from a thorow conviction and approbation of the mind, is altogether useless and unprofitable. The arms by which the members of this society are to be kept within their duty, are exhortations, admonitions, and advices. If by these means the offenders will not be reclaimed, and the erroneous convinced, there remains nothing farther to be done, but that such stubborn and obstinate persons, who give no ground to hope for their reformation, should be cast out and separated from the society. This is the last and utmost force of ecclesiastical authority: no other punishment can thereby be inflicted, than that, the relation ceasing between the body and the member which is cut off, the person so condemned ceases to be a part of that church.

These things being thus determined, let us inquire in the next place, how far the duty of toleration extends, and what is required from every one by it.

And first, I hold, that no church is bound by the duty of toleration to retain any such person in her bosom, as, after admonition, continues obstinately to offend against the laws of the society. For these being the condition of communion, and the bond of the society, if the breach of them were permitted without any animadversion, the society would immediately be thereby dissolved. But nevertheless, in all such cases care is to be taken that the sentence of excommunication, and the execution thereof, carry with it no rough usage, of word or action, whereby the ejected person may any wise be damnified in body or estate. For all force (as has often been said) belongs only to the magistrate, nor ought any private persons, at any time, to use force; unless it be in self-defence against unjust violence. Excommunication neither does, nor can, deprive the excommunicated person of any of those civil goods that he formerly possessed. All those things belong to the civil government, and are under the magistrate's protection. The whole force of excommunication consists only in this, that, the resolution of the society in that respect being declared, the union that was between the body and some member comes thereby to be dissolved, and that relation ceasing, the participation of some certain things, which the society communicated to its members, and unto which no man has any civil right, comes also to cease. For there is no civil injury done unto the excommunicated person, by the church-minister's refusing him that bread and wine, in the celebration of the Lord's Supper, which was not bought with his, but other mens money.

Secondly, No private person has any right, in any manner, to prejudice another person in his civil enjoyments, because he is of another church or religion. All the rights and franchises that belong to him as a man, or as a denison, are inviolably to be preserved to him. These are not the business of religion. No violence nor injury is to be offered him, whether he be Christian or pagan. Nay, we must not content our selves with the narrow measures of bare justice: charity, bounty, and liberality must be added to it. This the gospel enjoyns, this reason directs, and this that natural fellowship we are born into requires of us. If any man err from the right way, it is his own misfortune, no injury to thee: nor therefore art thou to punish him in the things of this life, because thou supposest he will be miserable in that which is to come.

What I say concerning the mutual toleration of private persons differing from one another in religion, I understand also of particular churches; which stand as it were in the same relation to each other as private persons among themselves, nor has any one of them any manner of jurisdiction over any other, no not even when the civil magistrate (as it sometimes happens) comes to be of this or the other communion. For the civil government can give no new right to the church, nor the church to the civil government. So that whether the magistrate joyn himself to any church, or separate from it, the church remains always as it was before, a free and voluntary society. It neither acquires the power of the sword by the magistrate's coming to it, nor does it lose the right of instruction and excommunication by his going from it. This is the fundamental and immutable right of a spontaneous society, that it has power to remove any of its members who transgress the rules of its institution: but it cannot, by the accession of any new members, acquire any right of jurisdiction over those that are not joined with it. And therefore peace, equity, and friendship, are always mutually to be observed by particular churches, in the same manner as by private persons, without any pretence of superiority or jurisdiction over one another.

That the thing may be made yet clearer by an example; let us suppose two churches, the one of *Arminians*, the other of *Calvinists*, residing in the city of *Constantinople.* Will any one say, that either of these churches has right to deprive the members of the other of their estates and liberty, (as we see practised elsewhere) because of their differing from it in some doctrines or ceremonies; whilst the *Turks* in the mean while silently stand by, and laugh to see with what inhumane cruelty Christians thus rage against Christians? But if one of these churches hath this power of

The seventeenth century philosopher John Locke's defense of private property and religious toleration was perhaps the single most powerful influence upon the Founders of the United States.

treating the other ill, I ask which of them it is to whom that power belongs, and by what right? It will be answered, undoubtedly, that it is the Orthodox Church which has the right of authority over the erroneous or heretical. This is, in great and specious words, to say just nothing at all. For every church is orthodox to it self; to others, erroneous or heretical. For whatsoever any church believes, it believes to be true; and the contrary unto those things, it pronounces to be error. So that the controversy between these churches about the truth of their doctrines, and the purity of their worship, is on both sides equal; nor is there any judge, either at *Constant-*

inople, or elsewhere upon earth, by whose sentence it can be determined. The decision of that question belongs only to the supream judge of all men, to whom also alone belongs the punishment of the erroneous. In the mean while, let those men consider how hainously they sin, who, adding injustice, if not to their error yet certainly to their pride, do rashly and arrogantly take upon them to misuse the servants of another master, who are not at all accountable to them.

Nay, further: if it could be manifest which of these two dissenting churches were in the right, there would not accrue thereby unto the orthodox any right of destroying the other. For churches have neither any jurisdiction in worldly matters, nor are fire and sword any proper instruments wherewith to convince mens minds of error, and inform them of the truth. Let us suppose, nevertheless, that the civil magistrate inclined to favour one of them, and to put his sword into their hands, that (by his consent) they might chastise the dissenters as they pleased. Will any man say, that any right can be derived unto a Christian church, over its brethren, from a Turkish emperor? An infidel, who has himself no authority to punish Christians for the articles of their faith, cannot confer such an authority upon any society of Christians, nor give unto them a right which he has not himself. This would be the case at *Constantinople*. And the reason of the thing is the same in any Christian kingdom. The civil power is the same in every place: nor can that power, in the hands of a Christian prince, confer any greater authority upon the church, than in the hands of a heathen: which is to say, just none at all.

Nevertheless, it is worthy to be observed, and lamented, that the most violent of these defenders of the truth, the opposers of errors, the exclaimers against schism, do hardly ever let loose this their zeal for God, with which they are so warmed and inflamed, unless where they have the civil magistrate on their side. But so soon as ever court-favour has given them the better end of the staff, and they begin to feel themselves the stronger, then presently peace and charity are to be laid aside: otherwise, they are religiously to be observed. Where they have not the power to carry on persecution, and to become masters, there they desire to live upon fair terms, and preach up toleration. When they are not strengthned with the civil power, then they can bear most patiently, and unmovedly, the contagion of idolatry, superstition, and heresie, in their neighbourhood; of which, in other occasions, the interest of religion makes them to be extreamly apprehensive. They do not forwardly attack those errors which are in fashion at court, or are countenanced by the government. Here they can be content to spare their arguments: which yet (with their leave) is the only right method of propagating truth, which has no such way of prevailing, as when strong arguments and good reason, are joined with the softness of civility and good usage.

No body therefore, in fine, neither single persons, nor churches, nay, nor even commonwealths, have any just title to invade the civil rights and worldly goods of each other, upon pretence of religion. Those that are of another opinion, would do well to consider with themselves how pernicious a seed of discord and war, how powerful a provocation to endless hatreds, rapines, and slaughters, they thereby furnish unto mankind. No peace and security, no not so much as common friendship, can ever be established or preserved amongst men, so long as this opinion prevails, That *Dominion is founded in Grace*, and that religion is to be propagated by force of arms.

In the third place: Let us see what the duty of toleration requires from those who are distinguished from the rest of mankind, (from the laity, as they please to call us) by some ecclesiastical character, and office; whether they be bishops, priests, presbyters, ministers, or however else dignified or distinguished. It is not my business to inquire here into the original of the power or dignity of the clergy. This only I say, that whence-soever their authority be sprung, since it is ecclesiastical, it ought to be confined within the bounds of the church, nor can it in any manner be extended to civil affairs; because the church it self is a thing absolutely separate and distinct from the commonwealth. The boundaries on both sides are fixed and immovable. He jumbles heaven and earth together, the things most remote and opposite, who mixes these two societies; which are in their original, end, business, and in every thing, perfectly distinct, and infinitely different from each other. No man therefore, with whatsoever ecclesiastical office he be dignified, can deprive another man that is not of his church and faith, either of liberty, or of any part of his worldly goods, upon the account of that difference between them in religion. For whatsoever is not lawful to the whole church, cannot, by any ecclesiastical right, become lawful to any of its members.

But this is not all. It is not enough that ecclesiastical men abstain from violence and rapine, and all manner of persecution. He that pretends to be a successor of the apostles, and takes upon him the office of teaching, is obliged also to admonish his hearers of the duties of peace, and good-will towards all men; as well towards the erroneous as the orthodox; towards those that differ from them in faith and worship, as well as towards those that agree with them therein: and he ought industriously to exhort all men, whether private persons or magistrates, (if any such there be in his church) to charity, meekness, and toleration; and diligently endeavour to allay and temper all that heat, and unreasonable averseness of mind, which either any mans fiery zeal for his own sect, or the craft of others, has kindled against dissenters. I will not undertake to represent how happy and how great would be the fruit, both in church and state, if the pulpits every where founded with this doctrine of peace and toleration; lest I should seem to reflect too severely upon those men whose dignity I desire not to detract from, nor would have it diminished either by others or themselves. But this I say, that thus it ought to be. And if any one that professes himself to be a minister of the word of God, a preacher of the gospel of peace, teach otherwise, he either understands not, or neglects the business of his calling, and shall one day give account thereof unto the prince of peace. If Christians are to be admonished that they abstain from all manner of revenge, even after repeated provocations and multiplied injuries, how much more ought they who suffer nothing, who have had no harm done them, forbear violence, and abstain from all manner of ill usage towards those from whom they have received none. This caution and temper they ought certainly to use towards those who mind only their own business, and are sollicitous for nothing but that (whatever men think of them) they may worship God in that manner which they are persuaded is acceptable to him, and in which they have the strongest hopes of eternal salvation. In private domestick affairs, in the management of estates, in the conservation of bodily health, every man may consider what suits his own conveniency, and follow what course he likes best. No man complains of the ill management of his neighbour's affairs. No man is angry with another for an error committed in sowing his land, or in marrying his daughter. No body corrects a spendthrift for consuming his substance in taverns. Let any man pull down, or build, or make whatsoever expences he pleases, no body murmurs, no body controuls him; he has his liberty. But if any man do not frequent the church, if he do not there conform his behaviour exactly to the accustomed ceremonies, or if he brings not his children to be initiated in the sacred mysteries of this or the other congregation; this immediately causes an uproar. The neighbourhood is filled with noise and clamour. Every one is ready to be the avenger of so great a crime. And the zealots hardly have the patience to refrain from violence and rapine, so long till the cause be heard, and the poor man be, according to form, condemned to the loss of liberty, goods, or life. Oh that our ecclesiastical orators, of every sect, would apply themselves with all the strength of arguments that they are able, to the confounding of mens errors! But let them spare their persons. Let them not supply their want of reasons with the instruments of force, which belong to another jurisdiction, and do ill become a churchman's hands. Let them not call in the magistrate's authority to the aid of their eloquence, or learning; lest, perhaps, whilst they pretend only love for the truth, this their intemperate zeal, breathing nothing but fire and sword, betray their ambition, and shew that what they desire is temporal dominion. For it will be very difficult to persuade men of sense, that he, who with dry eyes, and satisfaction of mind, can deliver his brother unto the executioner, to be burnt alive, does sincerely and heartily concern himself to save that brother from the flames of hell in the world to come.

In the last place. Let us now consider what is the magistrate's duty in the business of toleration: which certainly is very considerable.

We have already proved, that the care of souls does not belong to the magistrate: not a magisterial care, I mean, (if I may so call it) which consists in prescribing by laws, and compelling by punishments. But a charitable care, which consists in teaching, admonishing, and persuading, cannot be denied unto any man. The care therefore of every man's soul belongs unto himself, and is to be left unto himself. But what if he neglect the care of his soul? I answer, what if he neglect the care of his health, or of his estate, which things are nearlier related to the government of the magistrate than the other? Will the magistrate provide by an express law, that such an one shall not become poor or sick? Laws provide, as much as is possible, that the goods and health of subjects be not injured by the fraud or violence of others; they do not guard them from the negligence or ill-husbandry of the possessors themselves. No man can be forced to be rich or healthful, whether he will or no. Nay, God himself will not save men against their wills. Let us suppose, however, that some prince were desirous to force his subjects to accumulate riches, or to preserve the health and strength of their bodies. Shall it be provided by law, that they must consult none but *Roman* physicians, and shall every one be bound to live according to their prescriptions? What, shall no potion, no broth, be taken, but what is prepared either in the *Vatican*, suppose, or in a *Geneva* shop? Or, to make these subjects rich, shall they all be obliged by law to become merchants, or musicians? Or, shall every one turn victualler, or smith, because there are some that maintain their families plentifully, and grow rich in those professions? But it may be said, there are a thousand ways to wealth, but one only way to heaven. 'Tis well said indeed, especially by those that plead for compelling men into this or the other way. For if there were several ways that lead thither, there would not be so much as a pretence left for compulsion. But now if I be marching on with my utmost vigour, in that way which, according to the sacred geography, leads straight to *Jerusalem*; why am I beaten and ill used by others, because, perhaps, I wear not buskins; because my hair is not of the right cut; because perhaps I have not been dip't in the right fashion; because I eat flesh upon the road, or some other food which agrees with my stomach; because I avoid certain byways, which seem unto me to lead into briars or precipices; because amongst the several paths that are in the same road, I choose that to walk in which seems to be the straightest and cleanest; because I avoid to keep company with some travellers that are less grave, and others that are more sowre than they ought to be; or in fine, because I follow a guide that either is, or is not, clothed in white, and crowned with a miter? Certainly, if we consider right, we shall find that for the most part they are such frivolous things as these, that (without any prejudice to religion or the salvation of souls, if not accompanied with superstition or hypocrisie) might either be observed or omitted; I say they are such like things as these, which breed implacable enmities amongst Christian brethren, who are all agreed in the substantial and truly fundamental part of religion.

But let us grant unto these zealots, who condemn all things that are not of their mode, that from these circumstances arise different ends. What shall we conclude from thence? There is only one of these which is the true way to eternal happiness. But in this great variety of ways that men follow, it is still doubted which is this right one. Now neither the care of the commonwealth, nor the right of enacting laws, does discover this way that leads to heaven more certainly to the magistrate, than every private mans search and study discovers it unto himself. I have a weak body, sunk under a languishing disease, for which (I suppose) there is one only remedy, but that unknown. Does it therefore belong unto the magistrate to prescribe me a remedy, because there is but one, and because it is unknown? Because there is but one way for me to escape death, will it therefore be safe for me to do whatsoever the magistrate ordains? Those things that every man ought sincerely to enquire into himself, and by meditation, study, search, and his own endeavours, attain the knowledge of, cannot be looked upon as the peculiar possession of any one sort of men. Princes indeed are born superior unto other men in power, but in nature equal. Neither the right, nor the art of ruling, does necessarily carry along with it the certain knowledge of other things; and least of all of the true religion. For if it were so, how could it come to pass that the lords of the earth should differ so vastly as they do in religious matters? But let us grant that it is probable the way to eternal life may be better known by a prince than by his subjects; or at least, that in this incertitude of things, the safest and most commodious way for private persons is to follow his dictates. You will say, what then? If he should bid you follow merchandise for your livelihood, would you decline that course for fear it should not succeed? I answer: I would turn merchant upon the princes command, because in case I should have ill success in trade, he is abundantly able to make up my loss some other way. If it be true, as he pretends, that he desires I should thrive and grow rich, he can set me up again when unsuccessful voyages have broke me. But this is not the case, in the things that regard the life to come. If there I take a wrong course, if in that respect I am once undone, it is not in the magistrates power to repair my loss, to ease my suffering, nor to restore me in any measure, much less entirely, to a good estate. What security can be given for the kingdom of heaven?

Perhaps some will say that they do not suppose this infallible judgment, that all men are bound to follow in the affairs of religion, to be in the civil magistrate, but in the church. What the church has determined, that the civil magistrate orders to be observed; and he provides by his authority that no body shall either act or believe, in the business of religion, otherwise than the church teaches. So that the judgment of those things is in the church. The magistrate himself yields obedience thereunto, and requires the like obedience from others. I answer: who sees not how frequently the name of the church, which was so venerable in the time of the apostles, has been made use of to throw dust in peoples eyes, in following ages? But however, in the present case it helps us not. The one only narrow way which leads to heaven is not better known to the magistrate than to private persons, and therefore I cannot safely take him for my guide, who may probably be as ignorant of the way as my self, and who certainly is less concerned for my salvation than I my self am. Amongst so many kings of the *Jews*, how many of them were there whom any *Israelite*, thus blindly following, had not fall'n into idolatry, and thereby into destruction? Yet nevertheless, you bid me be of good courage, and tell me that all is now safe and secure, because the magistrate does not now enjoin the observance of his own decrees in matters of religion, but only the decrees of the church. Of what church I beseech you? Of that certainly which likes him best. As if he that compels me by laws and penalties to enter into this or the other church, did not interpose his own judgment in the matter. What difference is there whether he lead me himself, or deliver me over to be led by others? I depend both ways upon his will, and it is he that determines both ways of my eternal state. Would an *Israelite*, that had worshipped *Baal* upon the command of his king, have been in any better condition, because some body had told him that the king ordered nothing in religion upon his own head, nor commanded any thing to be done by his subjects in divine worship, but what was approved by the counsel of priests, and declared to be of divine right by the doctors of their church? If the religion of any church become therefore true and saving, because the head of that sect, the prelates and priests, and those of that tribe, do all of them, with all their might, extol and praise it; what religion can ever be accounted erroneous, false and destructive? I am doubtful concerning the doctrine of the *Socinians*, I am suspicious of the way of worship practised by the *Papists*, or *Lutherans*; will it be ever a jot the safer for me to join either unto the one or the other of those churches, upon the magistrates command, because he commands nothing in religion but by the authority and counsel of the doctors of that church? . . .

JOHN LOCKE
SECOND TREATISE OF CIVIL GOVERNMENT

John Locke was careful to distance himself from the bleak Hobbesian view that human nature was so depraved as to make absolute power for the sovereign authority a necessity. He argued instead for a view of humanity that would allow for a willingness to live in a tolerant and civil order without coercion.

In this passage from the influential *Second Treatise of Civil Government*, written in 1690, Locke outlines his essential case against absolute monarchy: that, with no basis in the consent of the governed, absolutism is not strictly speaking a political society at all; it is mere violence. The same argument was reiterated in the American Declaration of Independence nearly a century later.

. . . Man being born, as has been proved, with a title to perfect freedom, and an uncontrouled enjoyment of all the rights and privileges of the law of nature, equally with any other man, or number of men in the world, hath by nature a power, not only to preserve his property, that is, his life, liberty and estate, against the injuries and attempts of other men; but to judge of, and punish the breaches of that law in others, as he is persuaded the offence deserves, even with death itself, in crimes where the heinousness of the fact, in his opinion, requires it. But because no *political society* can be, nor subsist, without having in itself the power to preserve the property, and in order thereunto, punish the offences of all those of that society; there, and there only is *political society*, where every one of the members hath quitted this natural power, resigned it up into the hands of the community in all cases that exclude him not from appealing for protection to the law established by it. And thus all private judgment of every particular member being excluded, the community comes to be umpire, by settled standing rules, indifferent, and the same to all parties; and by men having author-ity from the community, for the execution of those rules, decides all the differences that may happen between any members of that society concerning any matter of right; and punishes those offences which any member hath committed against the society, with such penalties as the law has established: whereby it is easy to discern, who are, and who are not, in *political society* together. Those who are united into one body, and have a common established law and judicature to appeal to, with authority to decide controversies between them, and punish offenders, are in *civil society* one with another: but those who have no such common appeal, I mean on earth, are still in the state of nature, each being, where there is no other, judge for himself, and executioner; which is, as I have before shewed it, the perfect *state of nature.*

And thus the commonwealth comes by a power to set down what punishment shall belong to the several transgressions which they think worthy of it, committed amongst the members of that society, (which is the *power of making laws*) as well as it has the power to punish any injury done unto any of its members, by any one that is not of it, (which is the *power of war and peace*;) and all this for the preservation of the property of all the members of that society, as far as is possible. But though every man who has entered into civil society, and is become a member of any commonwealth, has thereby quitted his power to punish offences, against the law of *nature*, in prosecution of his own private judgment, yet with the judgment of offences, which he has given up to the legislative in all cases, where he can appeal to the magistrate, he has given a right to the commonwealth to employ his force, for the execution of the judgments of the commonwealth, whenever he shall be called to it; which indeed are his own judgments, they being made by himself, or his representative. And herein we have the original of the *legislative* and *executive power* of civil society, which is to judge by standing laws, how far offences are to be punished, when committed within the commonwealth; and also to determine, by occasional judgments founded on the present circumstances of the fact, how far injuries from without are to be vindicated; and in both these to employ all the force of all the members, when there shall be need.

Where-ever therefore any number of men are so united into one society, as to quit every one his executive power of the law of nature, and to resign it to the public, there and there only is a *political, or civil society.* And this is done, where-ever any number of men, in the state of nature, enter into society to make one people, one body politic, under one supreme government; or else when any one joins himself to, and incorporates with any government already made: for hereby he authorizes the society, or which is all one, the legislative thereof, to make laws for him, as the public good of the society shall require; to the execution whereof, his own assistance (as to his own decrees) is due. And this *puts men* out of a state of nature *into* that of a *common-wealth*, by setting up a judge on earth, with authority to determine all the controversies, and redress the injuries that may happen to any member of the common-wealth; which

judge is the legislative, or magistrates appointed by it. And where-ever there are any number of men, however associated, that have no such decisive power to appeal to, there they are still in *the state of nature.*

Hence it is evident, that *absolute monarchy*, which by some men is counted the only government in the world, is indeed *inconsistent with civil society*, and so can be no form of civil-government at all: for the *end of civil society*, being to avoid, and remedy those inconveniences of the state of nature, which necessarily follow from every man's being judge in his own case, by setting up a known authority, to which every one of that society may appeal upon any injury received, or controversy that may arise, and which every one of the society ought to obey; where-ever any persons are, who have not such an authority to appeal to, for the decision of any difference between them, there those persons are still *in the state of nature*; and so is every *absolute prince*, in respect of those who are under his *dominion.*

For he being supposed to have all, both legislative and executive power in himself alone, there is no judge to be found, no appeal lies open to any one, who may fairly, and indifferently, and with authority decide, and from whose decision relief and redress may be expected of any injury or inconviency, that may be suffered from the prince, or by his order: so that such a man, however intitled, *Czar*, or *Grand Seignior*, or how you please, is as much *in the state of nature*, with all under his dominion, as he is with the rest of mankind: for where-ever any two men are, who have no standing rule, and common judge to appeal to on earth, for the determination of controversies of right betwixt them, there they are still *in the state of nature*, and under all the inconveniencies of it, with only this woful difference to the subject, or rather slave of an absolute prince: that whereas, in the ordinary state of nature, he has a liberty to judge of his right, and according to the best of his power, to maintain it; now, whenever his property is invaded by the will and order of his monarch, he has not only no appeal, as those in society ought to have, but as if he were degraded from the common state of rational creatures, is denied a liberty to judge of, or to defend his right; and so is exposed to all the misery and inconveniencies, that a man can fear from one, who being in the unrestrained state of nature, is yet corrupted with flattery, and armed with power.

For he that thinks *absolute power purifies men's blood*, and corrects the baseness of human nature, need read but the history of this, or any other age, to be convinced of the contrary. He that would have been insolent and injurious in the woods of *America*, would not probably be much better in a throne; where perhaps learning and religion shall be found out to justify all that he shall do to his subjects, and the sword presently silence all those that dare question it. . . .

In *absolute monarchies* indeed, as well as other governments of the world, the subjects have an appeal to the law, and judges to decide any controversies, and restrain any violence that may happen betwixt the subjects themselves, one amongst another. This every one thinks necessary, and believes he deserves to be thought a declared enemy to society and mankind, who should go about to take it away. But whether this be from a true love of mankind and society, and such a charity as we owe all one to another, there is reason to doubt: for this is no more than what every man, who loves his own power, profit, or greatness, may and naturally must do, keep those animals from hurting, or destroying one another, who labour and drudge only for his pleasure and advantage; and so are taken care of, not out of any love the master has for them, but love of himself, and the profit they bring him: for if it be asked, what security, *what fence* is there, in such a state, *against the violence and oppression of this absolute ruler?* the very question can scarce be borne. They are ready to tell you, that it deserves death only to ask after safety. Betwixt subject and subject, they will grant, there must be measures, laws and judges, for their mutual peace and security: but as for the *ruler*, he ought to be *absolute*, and is above all such circumstances; because he has power to do more hurt and wrong, it is right when he does it. To ask how you may be guarded from harm, or injury, on that side where the strongest hand is to do it, is presently the voice of faction and rebellion: as if when men quitting the state of nature entered into society, they agreed that all of them but one, should be under the restraint of laws, but that he should still retain all the liberty of the state of nature, increased with power, and made licentious by impunity. This is to think, that men are so foolish, that they take care to avoid what mischiefs may be done them by *pole-cats*, or *foxes*; but are content, nay, think it safety, to be devoured by *lions*. . . .

☆ CHARLES DE MONTESQUIEU

THE SPIRIT OF LAWS

The Spirit of Laws was Montesquieu's masterwork, a sweeping analysis of the relationship between political systems and their cultural, geographical and historical contexts. Written in 1748, it stands as one of the subtlest and most influential works of the Enlightenment, and one of the most controversial—it was banned by the Catholic Church in 1751. It came to have a disproportionate influence on the founders of the United States of America.

Charles de Montesquieu (1689–1755) was born and brought up in Bordeaux and lived his life a subject of the Bourbon monarchy in France. His encounters with politics were largely regional and somewhat leisurely—he was president of the mainly powerless Bordeaux *parlement* from 1716 to 1728. He attended its meetings even less frequently than most of its indolent members. In 1728, he was elected to the Academie Francaise, and eventually sold his life interest in the presidency of the *parlement* in order to travel widely.

In this section, Montesquieu analyzes the various functions of government—legislative, executive and judicial—as they were reflected in the laws of eighteenth-century England. He sees in such a structure separate sources of authority for each, and in this separation, an aid to the maintenance of individual liberty. This insight led the American founders to formalize what was casually recognized in the English system and to construct a tri-partite government on lines recommended by this French aristocrat, a government divided into a president, a Congress, and a Supreme Court.

. . . In each state there are three sorts of powers: legislative power, executive power over the things depending on the right of nations, and executive power over the things depending on civil right.

By the first, the prince or the magistrate makes laws for a time or for always and corrects or abrogates those that have been made. By the second, he makes peace or war, sends or receives embassies, establishes security, and prevents invasions. By the third, he punishes crimes or judges disputes between individuals. The last will be called the power of judging, and the former simply the executive power of the state.

Political liberty in a citizen is that tranquillity of spirit which comes from the opinion each one has of his security, and in order for him to have this liberty the government must be such that one citizen cannot fear another citizen.

When legislative power is united with executive power in a single person or in a single body of the magistracy, there is no liberty, because one can fear that the same monarch or senate that makes tyrannical laws will execute them tyrannically.

Nor is there liberty if the power of judging is not separate from legislative power and from executive power. If it were joined to legislative power, the power over the life and liberty of the citizens would be arbitrary, for the judge would be the legislator. If it were joined to executive power, the judge could have the force of an oppressor.

All would be lost if the same man or the same body of principal men, either of nobles, or of the people, exercised these three powers: that of making the laws, that of executing public resolutions, and that of judging the crimes or the disputes of individuals.

In most kingdoms in Europe, the government is moderate because the prince, who has the first two powers, leaves the exercise of the third to his subjects. Among the Turks, where the three powers are united in the person of the sultan, an atrocious despotism reigns.

In the Italian republics, where the three powers are united, there is less liberty than in our monarchies. Thus, in order to maintain itself, the government needs means as violent as in the government of the Turks; witness the state inquisitors and the lion's maw into which an informer can, at any moment, throw his note of accusation.

Observe the possible situation of a citizen in these republics. The body of the magistracy, as executor of the laws, retains all the power it has given itself as legislator. It can plunder the state by using its general wills; and, as it also has the power of judging, it can destroy each citizen by using its particular wills.

There, all power is one; and, although there is none of the external pomp that reveals a despotic prince, it is felt at every moment.

Thus princes who have wanted to make themselves despotic have always begun by uniting in their person all the magistracies, and many kings of Europe have begun by uniting all the great posts of their state.

I do believe that the pure hereditary aristocracy of the Italian republics is not precisely like the despotism of Asia. The multitude of magistrates sometimes softens the magistracy; not all

Charles de Montesquieu, French aristocrat and philosopher, devised the theory of the separation of powers—the executive, legislative, and judicial—which formed a key part of the American democratic experiment, and is now copied around the world.

the nobles always concur in the same designs; there various tribunals are formed that temper one another. Thus, in Venice, the *Great Council* has legislation; the *Pregadi*, execution; *Quarantia*, the power of judging. But the ill is that these different tribunals are formed of magistrates taken from the same body; this makes them nearly a single power.

The power of judging should not be given to a permanent senate but should be exercised by persons drawn from the body of the people at certain times of the year in the manner prescribed by law to form a tribunal which lasts only as long as necessity requires.

In this fashion the power of judging, so terrible among men, being attached neither to a certain state nor to a certain profession, becomes, so to speak, invisible and null. Judges are not continually in view; one fears the magistracy, not the magistrates.

In important accusations, the criminal in cooperation with the law must choose the judges, or at least he must be able to challenge so many of them that those who remain are considered to be of his choice.

The two other powers may be given instead to magistrates or to permanent bodies because they are exercised upon no individual, the one being only the general will of the state, and the other, the execution of that general will.

But though tribunals should not be fixed, judgments should be fixed to such a degree that they are never anything but a precise text of the law. If judgments were the individual opinion of a judge, one would live in this society without knowing precisely what engagements one has contracted.

Further, the judges must be of the same condition as the accused, or his peers, so that he does not suppose that he has fallen into the hands of people inclined to do him violence.

If the legislative power leaves to the executive power the right to imprison citizens who can post bail for their conduct, there is no longer any liberty, unless the citizens are arrested in order to respond without delay to an accusation of a crime the law has rendered capital; in this case they are really free because they are subject only to the power of the law.

But if the legislative power believed itself endangered by some secret conspiracy against the state or by some correspondence with its enemies on the outside, it could, for a brief and limited time, permit the executive power to arrest suspected citizens who would lose their liberty for a time only so that it would be preserved forever.

And this is the only means consistent with reason of replacing the tyrannical magistracy of the *ephors* and the *state inquisitors* of Venice, who are also despotic.

As, in a free state, every man, considered to have a free soul, should be governed by himself, the people as a body should have legislative power; but, as this is impossible in large states and is subject to many drawbacks in small ones, the people must have their representatives do all that they themselves cannot do.

One knows the needs of one's own town better than those of other towns, and one judges the ability of one's neighbors better than that of one's other compatriots. Therefore, members of the legislative body must not be drawn from the body of the nation at large; it is proper for the inhabitants of each principal town to choose a representative from it.

The great advantage of representatives is that they are able to discuss public business. The people are not at all appropriate for such discussions; this forms one of the great drawbacks of democracy.

It is not necessary that the representatives, who have been generally instructed by those who have chosen them, be instructed about each matter of business in particular, as is the practice in the Diets of Germany. It is true that, in their way, the word of the deputies would better express the voice of the nation; but it would produce infinite delays and make each deputy the master of all the others, and on the most pressing occasions the whole force of the nation could be checked by a caprice. . . .

When the deputies represent a body of people, as in Holland, they should be accountable to those who have commissioned them; it is another thing when they are deputed by boroughs, as in England.

In choosing a representative, all citizens in the various districts should have the right to vote except those whose estate is so humble that they are deemed to have no will of their own.

A great vice in most ancient republics was that the people had the right to make resolutions for action, resolutions which required some exe-cution, which altogether exceeds the people's capacity. The people should not enter the government except to choose their representatives; this is quite within their reach. For if there are few people who know the precise degree of a man's ability, yet every one is able to know, in general, if the one he chooses sees more clearly than most of the others.

Nor should the representative body be chosen in order to make some resolution for action, a thing it would not do well, but in order to make laws or in order to see if those they have made have been well executed; these are things it can do very well and that only it can do well.

In a state there are always some people who are distinguished by birth, wealth, or honors; but if they were mixed among the people and if they had only one voice like the others, the common liberty would be their enslavement and they would have no interest in defending it, because most of the resolutions would be against them. Therefore, the part they have in legislation should be in proportion to the other advantages they have in the state, which will happen if they form a body that has the right to check the enterprises of the people, as the people have the right to check theirs.

Thus, legislative power will be entrusted both to the body of the nobles and to the body that will be chosen to represent the people, each of which will have assemblies and deliberations apart and have separate views and interests.

Among the three powers of which we have spoken, that of judging is in some fashion, null. There remain only two; and, as they need a power whose regulations temper them, that part of the legislative body composed of the nobles is quite appropriate for producing this effect.

The nobility should be hereditary. In the first place, it is so by its nature; and, besides, it must have a great interest in preserving its prerogatives, odious in themselves, and which, in a free state, must always be endangered.

But, as a hereditary power could be induced to follow its particular interests and forget those of the people, in the things about which one has a sovereign interest in corrupting, for instance, in the laws about levying silver coin, it must take part in legislation only through its faculty of vetoing and not through its faculty of enacting.

I call the right to order by oneself, or to correct what has been ordered by another, the *faculty of enacting.* I call the right to render null a resolution taken by another the *faculty of vetoing,* which was the power of the tribunes of Rome. And, although the one who has the faculty of vetoing can also have the right to approve, this approval is no more than a declaration that one does not make use of one's faculty of vetoing, and it derives from that faculty.

The executive power should be in the hands of a monarch, because the part of the government that almost always needs immediate action is better administered by one than by many, whereas what depends on legislative power is often better ordered by many than by one.

If there were no monarch and the executive power were entrusted to a certain number of persons drawn from the legislative body, there would no longer be liberty, because the two powers would be united, the same persons sometimes belonging and always able to belong to both.

If the legislative body were not convened for a considerable time, there would no longer be liberty. For one of two things would happen: either there would no longer be any legislative resolution and the state would fall into anarchy; or these resolutions would be made by the executive power, and it would become absolute.

It would be useless for the legislative body to be convened without interruption. That would inconvenience the representatives and besides would overburden the executive power, which would not think of executing, but of defending its prerogatives and its right to execute.

In addition, if the legislative body were continuously convened, it could happen that one would do nothing but replace the deputies who had died with new deputies; and in this case, if the legislative body were once corrupted, the ill would be without remedy. When various legisla-tive bodies follow each other, the people, holding a poor opinion of the current legislative body, put their hopes, reasonably enough, in the one that will follow; but if the legislative body were always the same, the people, seeing it corrupted, would expect nothing further from its laws; they would become furious or would sink into indolence.

The legislative body should not convene itself. For a body is considered to have a will only when it is convened; and if it were not convened unanimously, one could not identify which part was truly the legislative body, the part that was convened or the one that was not. For if it had the right to prorogue itself, it could happen that it would never prorogue itself; this would be dangerous in the event that it wanted to threaten executive power. Besides, there are some times more suitable than others for convening the legislative body; therefore, it must be the executive power that regulates, in relation to the circumstances it knows, the time of the holding and duration of these assemblies.

If the executive power does not have the right to check the enterprises of the legislative body, the latter will be despotic, for it will wipe out all the other powers, since it will be able to give to itself all the power it can imagine.

But the legislative power must not have the reciprocal faculty of checking the executive power. For, as execution has the limits of its own nature, it is useless to restrict it; besides, executive power is always exercised on immediate things. And the power of the tribunes in Rome was faulty in that it checked not only legislation but even execution; this caused great ills.

But if, in a free state, legislative power should not have the right to check executive power, it has the right and should have the faculty to examine the manner in which the laws it has made have been executed; and this is the advantage of this government over that of Crete and Lacedaemonia, where the *kosmoi* and the *ephors* were not held accountable for their administration.

But, whether or not this examination is made,

the legislative body should not have the power to judge the person, and consequently the conduct, of the one who executes. His person should be sacred because, as he is necessary to the state so that the legislative body does not become tyrannical, if he were accused or judged there would no longer be liberty.

In this case, the state would not be a monarchy but an unfree republic. But, as he who executes cannot execute badly without having as ministers wicked counsellors who hate the law although the laws favor them as men, these counsellors can be sought out and punished. . . .

Although in general the power of judging should not be joined to any part of the legislative power, this is subject to three exceptions founded on the particular interests of the one who is to be judged.

Important men are always exposed to envy; and if they were judged by the people, they could be endangered and would not enjoy the privilege of the last citizen of a free state, of being judged by his peers. Therefore, nobles must not be called before the ordinary tribunals of the nation but before that part of the legislative body composed of nobles.

It could happen that the law, which is simultaneously clairvoyant and blind, might be too rigorous in certain cases. But the judges of the nation are, as we have said, only the mouth that pronounces the words of the law, inanimate beings who can moderate neither its force nor its rigor. Therefore, the part of the legislative body, which we have just said is a necessary tribunal on another occasion, is also one on this occasion; it is for its supreme authority to moderate the law in favor of the law itself by pronouncing less rigorously than the law.

It could also happen that a citizen, in matters of public business, might violate the rights of the people and commit crimes that the established magistrates could not or would not want to punish. But, in general, the legislative power cannot judge, and even less so in this particular case, where it represents the interested party, the people. Therefore, it can be only the accuser. But,

before whom will it make its accusation? Will it bow before the tribunals of law, which are lower than it and are, moreover, composed of those who, being also of the people, would be swept along by the authority of such a great accuser? No: in order to preserve the dignity of the people and the security of the individual, that part of the legislature drawn from the people must make its accusation before the part of the legislature drawn from the nobles, which has neither the same interests nor the same passions.

This last is the advantage of this government over most of the ancient republics, where there was the abuse that the people were judge and accuser at the same time.

Executive power, as we have said, should take part in legislation by its faculty of vetoing; otherwise it will soon be stripped of its prerogatives. But if legislative power takes part in execution, executive power will equally be lost.

If the monarch took part in legislation by the faculty of enacting, there would no longer be liberty. But as in spite of this, he must take part in legislation in order to defend himself, he must take part in it by the faculty of vetoing.

The cause of the change in government in Rome was that the senate, which had one part of the executive power, and the magistrates, who had the other, did not have the faculty of vetoing, as the people had.

Here, therefore, is the fundamental constitution of the government of which we are speaking. As its legislative body is composed of two parts, the one will be chained to the other by their reciprocal faculty of vetoing. The two will be bound by the executive power, which will itself be bound by the legislative power.

The form of these three powers should be rest or inaction. But as they are constrained to move by the necessary motion of things, they will be forced to move in concert.

As executive power belongs to the legislative only through its faculty of vetoing, it cannot enter into the discussion of public business. It is not even necessary for it to propose, because, as it can always disapprove of resolutions, it can reject decisions on propositions it would have wanted left unmade.

In some ancient republics, where the people as a body discussed the public business, it was natural for the executive power to propose and discuss with them; otherwise, there would have been a strange confusion in the resolutions.

If the executive power enacts on the raising of public funds without the consent of the legislature, there will no longer be liberty, because the executive power will become the legislator on the most important point of legislation.

If the legislative power enacts, not from year to year, but forever, on the raising of public funds, it runs the risk of losing its liberty, because the executive power will no longer depend upon it; and when one holds such a right forever, it is unimportant whether that right comes from oneself or from another. The same is true if the legislative power enacts, not from year to year, but forever, about the land and sea forces, which it should entrust to the executive power.

So that the one who executes is not able to oppress, the armies entrusted to him must be of the people and have the same spirit as the people, as they were in Rome until the time of Marius. This can be so in only two ways: either those employed in the army must have enough goods to be answerable for their conduct to the other citizens and be enrolled for a year only, as was practiced in Rome; or, if the troops must be a permanent body, whose soldiers come from the meanest parts of the nation, legislative power must be able to disband them as soon as the legislature so desires; the soldiers must live with the citizens, and there must not be a separate camp, a barracks, or a fortified place.

Once the army is established, it should be directly dependent on the executive power, not on the legislative body; and this is in the nature of the thing, as its concern is more with action than with deliberation.

Men's manner of thinking is to make more of courage than of timidity; more of activity than of prudence; more of force than of counsel. The army will always scorn a senate and respect its officers. It will not make much of the orders sent from a body composed of people it believes timid and, therefore, unworthy to command it. Thus, whenever the army depends solely on the legislative body, the government will become military. And if the contrary has ever occurred, it is the effect of some extraordinary circumstances; it is because the army there is always separate, because it is composed of several bodies each of which depends upon its particular province, because the capitals are in excellent locations whose situation alone defends them and which have no troops.

Holland is even more secure than Venice; it could flood rebellious troops; it could leave them to die of hunger; since the troops are not in towns that could give them sustenance, their sustenance is precarious.

For if, in the case of an army governed by the legislative body, particular circumstances keep the government from becoming military, one will encounter other drawbacks; one of these two things must happen, either the army must destroy the government, or the government must weaken the army.

And this weakening will have a fatal cause: it will arise from the very weakness of the government.

If one wants to read the admirable work by Tacitus, *On the Mores of the Germans*, one will see that the English have taken their idea of political government from the Germans. This fine system was found in the forests.

Since all human things have an end, the state of which we are speaking will lose its liberty; it will perish. Rome, Lacedaemonia, and Carthage have surely perished. This state will perish when legislative power is more corrupt than executive power.

It is not for me to examine whether at present the English enjoy this liberty or not. It suffices for me to say that it is established by their laws, and I seek no further.

I do not claim hereby to disparage other governments, or to say that this extreme political liberty should humble those who have only a moderate one. How could I say that, I who believe that the excess even of reason is not always desirable and that men almost always accommodate themselves better to middles than to extremities?

Harrington, in his *Oceana*, has also examined the furthest point of liberty to which the constitution of a state can be carried. But of him it can be said that he sought this liberty only after misunderstanding it, and that he built Chalcedon with the coast of Byzantium before his eyes. . . .

JEAN-JACQUES ROUSSEAU

DISCOURSE ON THE ORIGIN AND FOUNDATIONS OF INEQUALITY

Apart from the American rebellion, the other great democratic experiment of the eighteenth century was the French Revolution. And if Locke could be said to be the intellectual father of the American Revolution, Jean-Jacques Rousseau (1712–1778) is clearly the philosophical patron of the French. His condemnation of absolute monarchy, his denunciation of European society as inherently oppressive and his demand for a root-and-branch attempt to reestablish human liberty are all classic statements of the European democratic tradition.

Rousseau was born in Switzerland, an orphan. After a tenuous adolescence, working as an apprentice engraver, he eventually ran away to Paris where he earned his living as a music teacher. In 1750 he won an essay competition, organized by the Academy of Dijon, for his essay, *The Discourse on the Sciences and the Arts*. His intellectual career began. The radical political, educational and social doctrines of his novel *La Nouvelle Heloise*, his teaching tract *Emile*, and his political masterpiece *The Social Contract*, earned the hostility of both French and Swiss governments, forcing him to seek exile in both Prussia and England, returning to France in 1768 under the assumed name Renou.

The arguments of his many works, taken out of context, have been criticized for containing within them the seeds of totalitarianism, and Rousseau's conception of a "general will," and of the need to establish freedom by a constant, communal democratic involvement can certainly be interpreted that way. But the more humanist and ironic passages of works such as *The Social Contract, Emile* and *La Nouvelle Heloise* suggest a more complicated thinker than his critics sometimes suggest.

In this passage from the *Discourse on the Origin and Foundations of Inequality*, his most significant work of political philosophy, Rousseau sketches his fundamental argument against arbitrary authority. For Rousseau, the fundamental freedom of human beings is destroyed as soon as they enter society. There, the strong manipulate the weak, and subsequently rationalize their might by specious arguments about justice. No one can seriously argue against humanity's inalienable right to freedom, Rousseau claims; nor can anyone defend the political subjugation Rousseau saw all around him.

. . . It would be no more reasonable to believe that at first peoples threw themselves into the arms of an absolute master without conditions and for all time, and that the first means of providing for the common security imagined by proud and unconquered men was to rush into slavery. In fact, why did they give themselves superiors if not to defend themselves against oppression, and to protect their goods, their freedoms, and their lives, which are, so to speak, the constituent elements of their being? Now in relations between one man and another, as the worst that can happen to one is to see himself at the discretion of the other, would it not have been contrary to good sense to begin by surrendering into the hands of a chief the only things they needed his help to preserve? What equivalent could he have offered them for the concession of so fine a right? And had he dared to require it under pretext of defending them, would he not promptly have received the answer of the allegory: What more will the enemy do to us? It is therefore incontestable, and it is the fundamental maxim of all political right, that peoples have given themselves chiefs to defend their freedom and not to enslave themselves. "If we have a prince," said Pliny to Trajan, "it is so that he may preserve us from having a master."

Our politicians make the same sophisms about love of freedom that our philosophers have made about the state of nature; by the things they see they make judgments about very different things which they have not seen. And they attribute to men a natural inclination to servitude due to the patience with which those who are before their eyes bear their servitude, without thinking that it is the same for freedom as for innocence and virtue—their value is felt only as long as one enjoys them oneself, and the taste for them is lost as soon as one has lost them. . . .

As an untamed steed bristles his mane, paws the earth with his hoof, and breaks away impetuously at the very approach of the bit, whereas a trained horse patiently endures whip and spur, barbarous man does not bend his head for the yoke that civilized man wears without a murmur, and he prefers the most turbulent freedom to tranquil subjection. Therefore it is not by the degradation of enslaved peoples that man's natural dispositions for or against servitude must be judged, but by the marvels done by all free peoples to guard themselves from oppression. I know that the former do nothing but boast incessantly of the peace and repose they enjoy in their

chains, and that *miserrimam servitutem pacem appellant*. But when I see the others sacrifice pleasures, repose, wealth, power, and life itself for the preservation of this sole good which is so disdained by those who have lost it; when I see animals born free and despising captivity break their heads against the bars of their prison; when I see multitudes of entirely naked savages scorn European voluptuousness and endure hunger, fire, the sword, and death to preserve only their independence, I feel that it does not behoove slaves to reason about freedom.

Regarding paternal authority, from which many have derived absolute government and all society, without having recourse to the contrary proofs of Locke and Sidney, it suffices to note that nothing in the world is farther from the ferocious spirit of despotism than the gentleness of that authority which looks more to the advantage of the one who obeys than to the utility of the one who commands; that by the law of nature, the father is master of the child only as long as his help is necessary for him; that beyond this stage they become equals, and the son, perfectly independent of the father, then owes him only respect and not obedience; for gratitude is certainly a duty which must be rendered, but not a right which one can require. Instead of saying that civil society is derived from paternal power, it should be said on the contrary that it is from civil society that this power draws its principle force. An individual was not recognized as the father of many until they remained assembled around him. The goods of the father, of which he is truly the master, are the bonds which keep his children dependent on him, and he can give them a share of his inheritance only in proportion as they shall have properly deserved it from him by continual deference to his wishes. Now subjects, far from having some similar favor to expect from their despot, since they and all they possess belong to him as personal belongings— or at least he claims this to be the case—are reduced to receiving as a favor what he leaves them of their own goods. He renders justice when he plunders them; he renders grace when he lets them live.

Continuing thus to test the facts by right, one would find no more solidity than truth in the voluntary establishment of tyranny; and it would be difficult to show the validity of a contract that would obligate only one of the parties, where all would be given to one side and nothing to the other, and that would only damage the one who binds himself. This odious system is very far from being, even today, that of wise and good monarchs, and especially of the Kings of France, as may be seen in various parts of their edicts and particularly in the following passage of a famous writing, published in 1667 in the name and by orders of Louis XIV:

> Let it not be said therefore that the sovereign is not subject to the laws of his State, since the contrary proposition is a truth of the law of nations, which flattery has sometimes attacked, but which good princes have always defended as a tutelary divinity of their States. How much more legitimate is it to say, with wise Plato, that the perfect felicity of a kingdom is that a prince be obeyed by his subjects, that the prince obey the law, and that the law be right and always directed to the public good.

I shall not stop to inquire whether, freedom being the most noble of man's faculties, it is not degrading one's nature, putting oneself on the level of beasts enslaved by instinct, even offending the author of one's being, to renounce without reservation the most precious of all his gifts and subject ourselves to committing all the crimes he forbids us in order to please a ferocious or insane master; nor whether this sublime workman must be more irritated to see his finest work destroyed than to see it dishonored. I shall neglect, if one wishes, the authority of Barbeyrac, who clearly declares, following Locke, that no one can sell his freedom to the point of subjecting himself to an arbitrary power which treats him according to its fancy: "Because," he adds, "that would be selling one's own life, of which one is not the master." I shall only ask by what right those who have not been afraid of so greatly debasing themselves have been able to subject their posterity to the same ignominy, and to re-

An uncharacteristically serene portrait of the passionate and brilliant French philosopher and essayist Jean-Jacques Rousseau, whose tirades against authoritarian government helped unleash the destructive power of the French Revolution.

nounce for it goods which do not depend on their liberality and without which life itself is burdensome to all who are worthy of it.

Pufendorf says that just as one transfers his goods to another by conventions and contracts, one can also divest himself of his freedom in favor of someone else. That, it seems to me, is very bad reasoning: for, first, the goods I alienate become something altogether foreign to me, the abuse of which is indifferent to me; but it matters to me that my freedom is not abused, and I cannot, without making myself guilty of the evil I shall be forced to do, risk becoming the instrument of crime. Moreover, as the right of property is only conventional and of human institution, every man can dispose at will of what he possesses. But it is not the same for the essential gifts of nature, such as life and freedom, which everyone is permitted to enjoy and of which it is at least doubtful that one has the right to divest himself: by giving up the one, one degrades his being, by giving up the other one destroys it insofar as he can; and as no temporal goods can compensate for the one or the other, it would offend both nature and reason to renounce them whatever the price. But if one could alienate his freedom like his goods, there would be a very great difference for children, who enjoy the father's goods only by transmission of his right; whereas since freedom is a gift they receive from nature by being men, their parents did not have

any right to divest them of it. So that just as to establish slavery violence had to be done to nature, nature had to be changed to perpetuate this right; and the jurists, who have gravely pronounced that the child of a slave would be born a slave, have decided in other terms that a man would not be born a man.

It therefore appears certain to me not only that governments did not begin by arbitrary power, which is only their corruption and extreme limit, and which finally brings them back to the sole law of the strongest for which they were originally the remedy; but also that even if they had begun thus, this power, being by its nature illegitimate, could not have served as a foundation for the rights of society, nor consequently for instituted inequality. . . .

EDMUND BURKE

ON ELECTION TO PARLIAMENT

Edmund Burke (1729–1797) was an Irish-born philosopher, polemicist, and politician who made his reputation in late eighteenth-century Britain. He entered Parliament in 1766, and there established a reputation as an orator and man of letters. He fought for the abolition of the slave trade, and argued passionately for the cause of the American colonists and the recently colonized people of India. Although a fervent Whig, he may be said to have founded the intellectual tradition of modern Toryism—to have begun a defense of democracy as liberal in its consequences as it is conservative in its premises.

Burke's speech given upon his selection as a member of Parliament for Bristol, a port on the west coast of England, is celebrated as a definitive account of an important democratic principle. In it, he defends what at first blush seems the opposite of democracy: the ability of the deputy to vote against the wishes of his constituents. Burke, however, argues that representative democracy means just that: that deputies are not delegates of their constituents' views, but rather representatives of their persons. He or she owes the voter nothing but judgment. If that judgment turns out to be faulty, the democratic process can, of course, unseat the representative by voting him or her out of office. Until then, the deputy is at liberty to say and do whatever he or she wants. As a principle it has become enshrined in the democratic tradition, although, of course, it has not always been followed in practice.

Certainly, gentlemen, it ought to be the happiness and glory of a representative to live in the strictest union, the closest correspondence, and

the most unreserved communication with his constituents. Their wishes ought to have great weight with him; their opinions high respect;

their business unremitted attention. It is his duty to sacrifice his repose, his pleasure, his satisfactions, to theirs—and above all, ever, and in all cases, to prefer their interest to his own.

But his unbiased opinion, his mature judgment, his enlightened conscience, he ought not to sacrifice to you, to any man, or to any set of men living. These he does not derive from your pleasure—no, nor from the law and the Constitution. They are a trust from Providence, for the abuse of which he is deeply answerable. Your representative owes you, not his industry only, but his judgment; and he betrays, instead of serving you, if he sacrifices it to your opinion.

My worthy colleague says, his will ought to be subservient to yours. If that be all, the thing is innocent. If government were a matter of will upon any side, yours, without question, ought to be superior. But government and legislation are matters of reason and judgment, and not of inclination; and what sort of reason is that in which the determination precedes the discussion, in which one set of men deliberate and another decide, and where those who form the conclusion are perhaps three hundred miles distant from those who hear the arguments?

To deliver an opinion is the right of all men; that of constituents is a weighty and respectable opinion, which a representative . . . ought always most seriously to consider. But *authoritative* instructions, *mandates* issued, which the member is bound blindly and implicitly to obey, to vote, and to argue for, though contrary to the clearest convictions of his judgment and conscience— these are things utterly unknown to the laws of this land, and which arise from a fundamental mistake of the whole order and tenor of our constitution.

Parliament is not a *congress* of ambassadors from different and hostile interests, which interests each must maintain, as an agent and advocate, against other agents and advocates; but Parliament is a *deliberative* assembly of *one* nation, with *one* interest, that of the whole—where not local purposes, not local prejudices, ought to guide, but the general good, resulting from the general reason of the whole. You choose a member, indeed; but when you have chosen him, he is not a member of Bristol, but he is a member of *Parliament*.

EDMUND BURKE

LETTER TO THE SHERIFFS OF BRISTOL

Edmund Burke's reputation as a conservative thinker has often obscured his Whig politics and his concern for civil liberties. In this document, Burke outlines the dangers for a democracy at war: how the exigencies of a national emergency can allow governments to encroach upon individual liberties of speech, action and thought—a dangerous precedent. (In this specific instance, he argues against any restriction of *habeas corpus* laws— essentially, legal guards against unlawful imprisonment.) Democracies, he also implies, are more naturally peaceful in their foreign affairs than other regimes.

. . . The main operative regulation of the act is to suspend the Common Law and the statute *Habeas Corpus* (the sole securities either for liberty or justice) with regard to all those who have been out of the realm, or on the high seas, within a given time. The rest of the people, as I understand, are to continue as they stood before.

I confess, Gentlemen, that this appears to me as bad in the principle, and far worse in its consequence, than an universal suspension of the *Habeas Corpus* Act; and the limiting qualification, instead of taking out the sting, does in my humble opinion sharpen and envenom it to a greater degree. Liberty, if I understand it at all, is a *general* principle, and the clear right of all the subjects within the realm, or of none. Partial freedom seems to me a most invidious mode of slavery. But, unfortunately, it is the kind of slavery the most easily admitted in times of civil discord: for parties are but too apt to forget their own future safety in their desire of sacrificing their enemies. People without much difficulty admit the entrance of that injustice of which they are not to be the immediate victims. In times of high proceeding it is never the faction of the predominant power that is in danger: for no tyranny chastises its own instruments. It is the obnoxious and the suspected who want the protection of law; and there is nothing to bridle the partial violence of state factions but this— "that, whenever an act is made for a cessation of law and justice, the whole people should be universally subjected to the same suspension of their franchises." The alarm of such a proceeding would then be universal. It would operate as a sort of *call of the nation.* It would become every man's immediate and instant concern to be made very sensible of *the absolute necessity* of this total eclipse of liberty. They would more carefully advert to every renewal, and more powerfully resist it. These great determined measures are not commonly so dangerous to freedom. They are marked with too strong lines to slide into use. No plea, nor pretence, of *inconvenience or evil example* (which must in their nature be daily and ordinary incidents) can be admitted as a reason for such mighty operations. But the true danger is when liberty is nibbled away, for expedients, and by parts. The *Habeas Corpus* Act supposes, contrary to the genius of most other laws, that the lawful magistrate may see particular men with a malignant eye, and it provides for that identical case. But when men, in particular descriptions, marked out by the magistrate himself, are delivered over by Parliament to this possible malignity, it is not the *Habeas Corpus* that is occasionally suspended, but its spirit that is mistaken, and its principle that is

subverted. Indeed, nothing is security to any individual but the common interest of all.

This act, therefore, has this distinguished evil in it, that it is the first *partial* suspension of the *Habeas Corpus* that has been made. The precedent, which is always of very great importance, is now established. For the first time a distinction is made among the people within this realm. Before this act, every man putting his foot on English ground, every stranger owing only a local and temporary allegiance, even negro slaves who had been sold in the colonies and under an act of Parliament, became as free as every other man who breathed the same air with them. Now a line is drawn, which may be advanced further and further at pleasure, on the same argument of mere expedience on which it was first described. There is no equality among us; we are not fellow-citizens, if the mariner who lands on the quay does not rest on as firm legal ground as the merchant who sits in his counting-house. Other laws may injure the community; this dissolves it. As things now stand, every man in the West Indies, every one inhabitant of three unoffending provinces on the continent, every person coming from the East Indies, every gentleman who has travelled for his health or education, every mariner who has navigated the seas, is, for no other offence, under a temporary proscription. Let any of these facts (now become presumptions of guilt) be proved against him, and the bare suspicion of the crown puts him out of the law. It is even by no means clear to me whether the negative proof does not lie upon the person apprehended on suspicion, to the subversion of all justice. . . .

The act of which I speak is among the fruits of the American war—a war in my humble opinion productive of many mischiefs, of a kind which distinguish it from all others. Not only our policy is deranged, and our empire distracted, but our laws and our legislative spirit appear to have been totally perverted by it. We have made war on our colonies, not by arms only, but by laws. As hostility and law are not very concordant ideas, every step we have taken in this business has

Edmund Burke, regarded as the founder of modern conservatism, was a staunch opponent of colonialism, a defender of individual liberties, especially in times of war, and an unapologetic believer in representative government.

been made by trampling on some maxim of justice or some capital principle of wise government. What precedents were established, and what principles overturned, (I will not say of English privilege, but of general justice,) in the Boston Port, the Massachusetts Charter, the Military Bill, and all that long array of hostile acts of Parliament by which the war with America has been begun and supported! Had the principles of any of these acts been first exerted on English ground, they would probably have expired as soon as they touched it. But by being removed from our persons, they have rooted in our laws, and the latest posterity will taste the fruits of them.

Nor is it the worst effect of this unnatural contention, that our *laws* are corrupted. Whilst *manners* remain entire, they will correct the vices of law, and soften it at length to their own temper. But we have to lament that in most of the late proceedings we see very few traces of that generosity, humanity, and dignity of mind, which formerly characterized this nation. War suspends the rules of moral obligation, and what is long suspended is in danger of being totally abrogated. Civil wars strike deepest of all into the manners of the people. They vitiate their politics; they corrupt their morals; they pervert even the natural taste and relish of equity and justice. By teaching us to consider our fellow-citizens in an hostile light, the whole body of our nation becomes gradually less dear to us. The very names of affection and kindred, which were the bond of charity whilst we agreed, become new incentives to hatred and rage when the communion of our country is dissolved. We may flatter ourselves that we shall not fall into this misfortune. But we have no charter of exemption, that I know of, from the ordinary frailties of our nature. . . .

⭐ THE DECLARATION OF THE RIGHTS OF MAN AND CITIZEN

This document is the preamble to the draft of a constitution for revolutionary France, put together in August 1789 as events in Paris were fast spinning out of control. In June of that year, an insurgent commoner caucus in the Estates General, in defiance of the nobility and the clergy, had declared itself the National Assembly, with the sole right to enact legislation. King Louis responded by depriving the National Assembly of its meeting hall. The subsequent meeting of the Assembly—on a Versailles tennis court—declared that it would not disband until it had drafted a new constitution for France. Pressured by growing civil unrest, the king ordered the nobility and clergy to rejoin the Assembly. As rioting spread throughout Paris, Louis also dismissed the popular Jacques Necker, director general of finance and minister of state, from the government and marshalled troops in his own defense. Further rioting ensued, culminating in the successful storm of the Bastille, a royal prison. It was in this atmosphere that the National Assembly lay down its gauntlet— the draft constitution that began with the following text.

In the new constitution, the monarchy was to be maintained, with carefully circumscribed powers. As it was, the document was to be rendered moot by the seismic violence then gripping French society, a violence that was to lead to the bloody overthrow of limited government and the authoritarian rule of Napoleon Bonaparte.

The language of the document reflects, to some extent, the rhetoric of the American Declaration of Independence. Noteworthy, in the context of what was to follow, is the Lockean emphasis on right to private property in sections 2 and 17, and the countervailing reference to the "general will" in section 6, which draws most obviously upon the ideas of Jean-Jacques Rousseau. Its language and moral certainty is exactly what Burke would later deplore and Wordsworth romanticize.

The representatives of the French people, organized in National Assembly, considering that ignorance, forgetfulness or contempt of the rights of man, are the sole causes of the public miseries and of the corruption of governments, have resolved to set forth in a solemn declaration the natural, inalienable, and sacred rights of man, in order that this declaration, being ever present to all the members of the social body, may unceasingly remind them of their rights and their duties; in order that the acts of the legislative power and those of the executive power may be each moment compared with the aim of every political institution and thereby may be more respected; and in order that the demands of citizens, grounded henceforth upon simple and incontestable principles, may always take the direction of maintaining the constitution and welfare of all.

In consequence, the National Assembly recognizes and declares, in the presence and under the auspices of the Supreme Being, the following rights of man and citizen.

1. Men are born and remain free and equal in rights. Social distinctions can be based only upon public utility.
2. The aim of every political association is the preservation of the natural and imprescriptible rights of man. These rights are liberty, property, security, and resistance to oppression.
3. The source of all sovereignty is essentially in

the nation; no body, no individual can exercise authority that does not proceed from it in plain terms.

4. Liberty consists in the power to do anything that does not injure others; accordingly, the exercise of the natural rights of each man has no limits except those that secure to the other members of society the enjoyment of these same rights. These limits can be determined only by law.

5. The law has the right to forbid only such actions as are injurious to society. Nothing can be forbidden that is not interdicted by the law, and no one can be constrained to do that which it does not order.

6. Law is the expression of the general will. All citizens have the right to take part personally, or by their representatives, in its formation. It must be the same for all, whether it protects or punishes. All citizens being equal in its eyes, are equally eligible to all public dignities, places, and employments, according to their capacities, and without other distinction than that of their virtues and their talents.

7. No man can be accused, arrested, or detained, except in the cases determined by the law and according to the forms that it has prescribed. Those who procure, expedite, execute, or cause to be executed arbitrary orders ought to be punished: but every citizen summoned or seized in virtue of the law ought to render instant obedience; he makes himself guilty by resistance.

8. The law ought to establish only penalties that are strictly and obviously necessary, and no one can be punished except in virtue of a law established and promulgated prior to the offence and legally applied.

9. Every man being presumed innocent until he has been pronounced guilty, if it is thought indispensable to arrest him, all severity that may not be necessary to secure his person ought to be strictly suppressed by law.

10. No one should be disturbed on account of his opinions, even religious, provided their manifestation does not derange the public order established by law.

11. The free communication of ideas and opinions is one of the most precious of the rights of man; every citizen then can freely speak, write, and print, subject to responsibility for the abuse of this freedom in the cases determined by law.

12. The guarantee of the rights of man and citizen requires a public force; this force then is instituted for the advantage of all and not for the personal benefit of those to whom it is entrusted.

13. For the maintenance of the public force and for the expenses of administration a general tax is indispensable; it ought to be equally apportioned among all the citizens according to their means.

14. All the citizens have the right to ascertain, by themselves or by their representatives, the necessity of the public tax, to consent to it freely, to follow the employment of it, and to determine the quota, the assessment, the collection, and the duration of it.

15. Society has the right to call for an account of his administration from every public agent.

16. Any society in which the guarantee of the rights is not secured, or the separation of powers not determined, has no constitution at all.

17. Property being a sacred and inviolable right, no one can be deprived of it, unless a legally established public necessity evidently demands it, under the condition of a just and prior indemnity.

BENJAMIN CONSTANT

THE LIBERTY OF THE ANCIENTS COMPARED WITH THAT OF THE MODERNS

Like Alexis de Tocqueville, Benjamin Constant (1767–1830) was a European who sought to spread the liberalism developing in Britain and America to the continent of Europe. He was born in Switzerland and educated at Oxford, Erlangen and Edinburgh. In 1795 he settled in revolutionary Paris, where he was appointed to the nation's ruling body, the Tribunate, in 1799. His opposition to Napoleon cost him his office, and in 1802 he went into exile. A novelist, politician, and associate of Madame de Stael, Goethe, and Schiller, he was later to edit two liberal periodicals, *Minerve Francaise* and *La Renomme.*

This extract is taken from his address to the *Athenèe Royale* in 1819. It is remarkable for its celebration of modern liberty against the ancients, its appreciation of the value of civil as well as political life, and its recognition of the importance of an autonomous civil society if democracy is to sustain itself. Democratic government, Constant argues, must not merely protect political liberty; it must defend civil liberty—the ability to trade, travel, associate, and express oneself freely, without undue social or political constraints.

. . . First ask yourselves, Gentlemen, what an Englishman, a Frenchman, and a citizen of the United States of America understand today by the word "liberty."

For each of them it is the right to be subjected only to the laws, and to be neither arrested, detained, put to death or maltreated in any way by the arbitrary will of one or more individuals. It is the right of everyone to express their opinion, choose a profession and practise it, to dispose of property, and even to abuse it; to come and go without permission, and without having to account for their motives or undertakings. It is everyone's right to associate with other individuals, either to discuss their interests, or to profess the religion which they and their associates prefer, or even simply to occupy their days or hours in a way which is most compatible with their inclinations or whims. Finally it is everyone's right to exercise some influence on the administration of the government, either by electing all or particular officials, or through representations, petitions, demands to which the authorities are more or less compelled to pay heed. Now compare this liberty with that of the ancients.

The latter consisted in exercising collectively, but directly, several parts of the complete sovereignty; in deliberating, in the public square, over war and peace; in forming alliances with foreign governments; in voting laws, in pronouncing judgements; in examining the accounts, the acts, the stewardship of the magistrates; in calling them to appear in front of the assembled people, in accusing, condemning or absolving them. But if this was what the ancients called liberty, they admitted as compatible with this collective freedom the complete subjection of the individual to the authority of the community. You find among them almost none of the enjoyments which we have just seen form part of the liberty of the moderns. All private actions were submitted to a severe surveillance. No importance was given to individual independence, neither in relation to opinions, nor to labour, nor, above all, to religion. The right to choose one's own religious affiliation, a right which we regard as one of the most precious, would have seemed to the ancients a crime and a sacrilege. In the domains which seem to us the most useful, the authority of the social body interposed itself and obstructed the will of individuals. Among the Spartans, Therpandrus could not add a string to his lyre without causing offence to the ephors. In the most domestic of relations the public authority again intervened. The young Lacedaemonian could not visit his new bride freely. In Rome, the censors cast a searching eye over family life. The laws regulated customs, and as customs touch on everything, there was hardly anything that the laws did not regulate.

Thus among the ancients the individual, almost always sovereign in public affairs, was a slave in all his private relations. As a citizen, he decided on peace and war; as a private individual, he was constrained, watched and repressed in all his movements; as a member of the collective body, he interrogated, dismissed, condemned, beggared, exiled, or sentenced to death his magistrates and superiors; as a subject of the collective body he could himself be deprived of his status, stripped of his privileges, banished, put to death, by the discretionary will of the whole to which he belonged. Among the moderns, on the contrary, the individual, independent in his private life, is, even in the freest of states, sovereign only in appearance. His sovereignty is restricted and almost always suspended. If, at fixed and rare intervals, in which he is again surrounded by precautions and obstacles, he exercises this sovereignty, it is always only to renounce it. . . .

Individual independence is the first need of the moderns: consequently one must never require from them any sacrifices to establish political liberty.

It follows that none of the numerous and too highly praised institutions which in the ancient republics hindered individual liberty is any longer admissible in the modern times.

You may, in the first place, think, Gentlemen, that it is superfluous to establish this truth. Several governments of our days do not seem in the least inclined to imitate the republics of antiquity. However, little as they may like republican institutions, there are certain republican usages for which they feel a certain affection. It is disturbing that they should be precisely those which allow them to banish, to exile, or to despoil. I remember that in 1802, they slipped into

the law on special tribunals an article which introduced into France Greek ostracism; and God knows how many eloquent speakers, in order to have this article approved, talked to us about the freedom of Athens and all the sacrifices that individuals must make to preserve this freedom! Similarly, in much more recent times, when fearful authorities attempted, with a timid hand, to rig the elections, a journal which can hardly be suspected of republicanism proposed to revive Roman censorship to eliminate all dangerous candidates.

I do not think therefore that I am engaging in a useless discussion if, to support my assertion, I say a few words about these two much vaunted institutions.

Ostracism in Athens rested upon the assumption that society had complete authority over its members. On this assumption it could be justified; and in a small state, where the influence of a single individual, strong in his credit, his clients, his glory, often balanced the power of the mass, ostracism may appear useful. But amongst us individuals have rights which society must respect, and individual interests are, as I have already observed, so lost in a multitude of equal or superior influences, that any oppression motivated by the need to diminish this influence is useless and consequently unjust. No-one has the right to exile a citizen, if he is not condemned by a regular tribunal, according to a formal law which attaches the penalty of exile to the action of which he is guilty. No-one has the right to tear the citizen from his country, the owner away from his possessions, the merchant away from his trade, the husband from his wife, the father from his children, the writer from his studious meditations, the old man from his accustomed way of life.

All political exile is a political abuse. All exile pronounced by an assembly for alleged reasons of public safety is a crime which the assembly itself commits against public safety, which resides only in respect for the laws, in the observance of forms, and in the maintenance of safeguards.

Roman censorship implied, like ostracism, a

Benjamin Constant, in democratic pose, haranguing the Tribune in Paris. A nineteenth century patrician, Constant attacked the fashionable belief that ancient Athens and Rome were morally superior to modern democracies.

discretionary power. In a republic where all the citizens, kept by poverty to an extremely simple moral code, lived in the same town, exercised no profession which might distract their attention from the affairs of the state, and thus constantly found themselves the spectators and judges of the usage of public power, censorship could on the one hand have greater influence: while on the other, the arbitrary power of the censors was restrained by a kind of moral surveillance exercised over them. But as soon as the size of the republic, the complexity of social relations and the refinements of civilization deprived this institution of what at the same time served as its basis and its limit, censorship degenerated even in Rome. It was not censorship which had created good morals; it was the simplicity of those morals which constituted the power and efficacy of censorship.

In France, an institution as arbitrary as censorship would be at once ineffective and intolerable. In the present conditions of society, morals are formed by subtle, fluctuating, elusive nuances, which would be distorted in a thousand ways if one attempted to define them more precisely. Public opinion alone can reach them; public opinion alone can judge them, because it is of the same nature. It would rebel against any positive authority which wanted to give it greater precision. If the government of a modern people wanted, like the censors in Rome, to censure a citizen arbitrarily, the entire nation would protest against this arrest by refusing to ratify the decisions of the authority.

What I have just said of the revival of censorship in modern times applies also to many other aspects of social organization, in relation to which antiquity is cited even more frequently and with greater emphasis. As for example, education; what do we not hear of the need to allow the government to take possession of new generations to shape them to its pleasure, and how many erudite quotations are employed to support this theory! The Persians, the Egyptians, Gaul, Greece and Italy are one after another set before us. Yet, Gentlemen, we are neither Persians subjected to a despot, nor Egyptians subjugated by priests, nor Gauls who can be sacrificed by their druids, nor, finally, Greeks or Romans, whose share in social authority consoled them for their private enslavement. We are modern men, who wish each to enjoy our own rights, each to develop our own faculties as we like best, without harming anyone; to watch over the development of these faculties in the children whom nature entrusts to our affection, the more enlightened as it is more vivid; and needing the authorities only to give us the general means of instruction which they can supply, as travellers accept from them the main roads without being told by them which route to take.

Religion is also exposed to these memories of bygone ages. Some brave defenders of the unity of doctrine cite the laws of the ancients against foreign gods, and sustain the rights of the Catholic church by the example of the Athenians, who killed Socrates for having undermined polytheism, and that of Augustus, who wanted the people to remain faithful to the cult of their fathers; with the result, shortly afterwards, that the first Christians were delivered to the lions.

Let us mistrust, Gentlemen, this admiration for certain ancient memories. Since we live in modern times, I want a liberty suited to modern times; and since we live under monarchies, I humbly beg these monarchies not to borrow from the ancient republics the means to oppress us.

Individual liberty, I repeat, is the true modern liberty. Political liberty is its guarantee, consequently political liberty is indispensable. But to ask the peoples of our day to sacrifice, like those of the past, the whole of their individual liberty to political liberty, is the surest means of detaching them from the former and, once this result has been achieved, it would be only too easy to deprive them of the latter. . . .

THOMAS BABINGTON MACAULAY
JEWISH DISABILITIES

Thomas Babington Macaulay (1800–1859) is best known as one of the magisterial British historians of the eighteenth and nineteenth centuries, along with Edward Gibbon, David Hume and Thomas Carlyle. Macaulay was a highly precocious child—before the age of ten, he had already written a world history. Educated at Cambridge University, his first foray into an intellectual career came in 1825 with the publication of an essay on John Milton in the *Edinburgh Review*. Macaulay complemented his literary career with politics, becoming a member of the House of Commons in 1830. Over the next decade, after playing an integral role in the passage of the 1832 Reform Bill, which drastically extended the electoral franchise in Britain, he was involved in Indian affairs. He spent four years in what was then a British colony, reforming the penal code and educational system. The latter part of his life he devoted to his literary pursuits, producing, among other works, his monumental *History of England*, which eventually covered the years 1685 through 1702.

What follows is an extract from a speech made early in his career in the House of Commons in 1833, arguing for an end to the ban on Jews holding public office in England. At that time all holders of civil office and all members of Parliament were required to take an oath as members of the Church of England. Catholics and dissenters had been granted waivers in 1828 and 1829, but at the time that Macaulay spoke, Jews remained barred. They were to stay so until 1858. Macaulay's call for equality of opportunity, like so many others, was ignored at the time, only to be honored later.

. . . My honorable friend, the Member for the University of Oxford, began his speech by declaring that he had no intention of calling in question the principles of religious liberty. He utterly disclaims persecution, that is to say, persecution as defined by himself. It would, in his opinion, be persecution to hang a Jew, or to flay him, or to draw his teeth, or to imprison him, or to fine him; for every man who conducts himself peaceably has a right to his life and his limbs, to his personal liberty and his property. But it is not persecution, says my honorable friend, to exclude any individual or any class from office; for nobody has a right to office: in every country official appointments must be subject to such regulations as the supreme authority may choose to make; nor can any such regulations be reasonably complained of by any member of the society as unjust. He who obtains an office obtains it, not as matter of right, but as matter of favour. He who does not obtain an office is not wronged; he is only in that situation in which the vast majority of every community must necessarily be. There are in the United Kingdom five and twenty million Christians without places; and, if they do not complain, why should five and twenty thousand Jews complain of being in the same case? In this way my honorable friend has convinced himself that, as it would be most absurd in him and me to say that we are wronged because we are not Secretaries of State, so it is most absurd in the Jews to say that they are wronged because they are, as a people, excluded from public employment.

Now, surely my honorable friend cannot have considered to what conclusions his reasoning leads. Those conclusions are so monstrous that he would, I am certain, shrink from them. Does he really mean that it would not be wrong in the legislature to enact that no man should be a judge unless he weighed twelve stone, or that no man should sit in parliament unless he were six feet high? We are about to bring in a bill for the government of India. Suppose that we were to insert in that bill a clause providing that no graduate of the University of Oxford should be Governor General or Governor of any Presidency, would not my honorable friend cry out against such a clause as most unjust to the learned body which he represents? And would he think himself sufficiently answered by being told, in his own words, that the appointment to office is a mere matter of favour, and that to exclude an individual or a class from office is no injury? Surely, on consideration, he must admit that official appointments ought not to be subject to regulations purely arbitrary, to regulations for which no reason can be given but mere caprice, and that those who would exclude any class from public employment are bound to show some special reason for the exclusion.

My honorable friend has appealed to us as Christians. Let me then ask him how he understands that great commandment which comprises the law and the prophets. Can we be said to do unto others as we would that they should do unto us if we wantonly inflict on them even the smallest pain? As Christians, surely we are bound to consider, first, whether, by excluding the Jews from all public trust, we give them pain; and, secondly, whether it be necessary to give them that pain in order to avert some greater evil. That by excluding them from public trust we inflict pain on them my honorable friend will not dispute. As a Christian, therefore, he is bound to relieve them from that pain, unless he can show, what I am sure he has not yet shown, that it is necessary to the general good that they should continue to suffer.

But where, he says, are you to stop, if once you admit into the House of Commons people who deny the authority of the Gospels? Will you let in a [Muslim]? Will you let in a Parsee? Will you let in a [Hindu], who worships a lump of stone with seven heads? I will answer my honorable friend's question by another. Where does he mean to stop? Is he ready to roast unbelievers at slow fires? If not, let him tell us why: and I will engage to prove that his reason is just as decisive against the intolerance which he thinks a duty as against the intolerance which he thinks a crime. Once admit that we are bound to inflict pain on a man because he is not of our religion; and where are you to stop? Why stop at the point fixed by my honorable friend rather than at the point fixed by the honorable Member for Oldham, who would make the Jews incapable of holding land? And why stop at the point fixed by the honorable Member for Oldham rather than at the point which would have been fixed by a Spanish Inquisitor of the sixteenth century? When once you enter on a course of persecution, I defy you to find any reason for making a halt till you have reached the extreme point. When my honorable friend tells us that he will allow the Jews to

The English historian Thomas Babington Macaulay combined his literary career with an attempt to reform the government of India and to extend the democratic franchise in Britain.

possess property to any amount, but that he will not allow them to possess the smallest political power, he holds contradictory language. Property is power. The honorable Member for Oldham reasons better than my honorable friend. The honorable Member for Oldham sees very clearly that it is impossible to deprive a man of political power if you suffer him to be the proprietor of half a county, and therefore very consistently proposes to confiscate the landed estates of the Jews. But even the honorable Member for Oldham does not go far enough. He has not proposed to confiscate the personal property of the Jews. Yet it is perfectly certain that any Jew who has a million may easily make himself very important in the state. By such steps we pass from official power to landed property, and from landed property to personal property, and from property to liberty, and from liberty to life. In truth, those persecutors who use the rack and the stake have much to say for themselves. They are convinced that their end is good; and it must be admitted that they employ means which are not unlikely to attain the end. Religious dissent has repeatedly been put down by sanguinary persecution. In that way the Albigenses were put down. In that way Protestantism was suppressed in Spain and Italy, so that it has never since reared its head. But I defy any body to produce an instance in which disabilities such as we are now considering have produced any other effect than that of making the sufferers angry and obstinate. My honorable friend should either persecute to some purpose, or not persecute at all. He dislikes the word persecution, I know. He will not admit that the Jews are persecuted. And yet I am confident that he would rather be sent to the King's Bench Prison for three months, or be fined a hundred pounds, than be subject to the disabilities under which the Jews lie. How can he then say that to impose such disabilities is not persecution, and that to fine and imprison is persecution? All his reasoning consists in drawing arbitrary lines. What he does not wish to inflict he calls persecution. What he does wish to inflict he will not call persecution. What he takes from the Jews he calls political power. What he is too good-natured to take from the Jews he will not call political power. The Jew must not sit in parliament: but he may be the proprietor of all the ten pound houses in a borough. He may have more fifty pound tenants than any peer in the kingdom. He may give the voters treats to please their palates, and hire bands of gipsies to break their heads, as if he were a Christian and a Marquess. All the rest of this system is of a piece. The Jew may be a jury-man, but not a judge. He may decide issues of fact, but not issues of law. He may give a hundred thousand pounds damages; but he may not in the most trivial case grant a new trial. He may rule the money market: he may influence the exchanges: he may be summoned to congresses of Emperors and Kings. Great potentates, instead of negotiating a loan with him by tying him in a chair and pulling out his grinders, may treat with him as with a great potentate, and may postpone the declaring of war or the signing of a treaty till they have conferred with him. All this is as it should be: but he must not be a Privy Councillor. He must not be called Right Honorable, for that is political power. And who is it that we are trying to cheat in this way? Even Omniscience. Yes, Sir; we have been gravely told that the Jews are under the divine displeasure, and that if we give them political power God will visit us in judgment. Do we then think that God cannot distinguish between substance and form? Does not He know that, while we withhold from the Jews the semblance and name of political power, we suffer them to possess the substance? The plain truth is that my honorable friend is drawn in one direction by his opinions, and in a directly opposite direction by his excellent heart. He halts between two opinions. He tries to make a compromise between principles which admit of no compromise. He goes a certain way in intolerance. Then he stops, without being able to give a reason for stopping. But I know the reason. It is his humanity. Those who formerly dragged the Jew at a horse's tail, and singed his beard with blazing furze-bushes, were much worse men than my honorable friend; but they were more consistent than he. . . .

WILLIAM WORDSWORTH
THE PRELUDE

William Wordsworth (1770–1850) grew up in England during the heady days of revolutionary democratic fervor in Europe. After graduating from Cambridge University in 1791, he spent a year in France and later wrote an account of his experiences in blank verse form, which was included in *The Prelude*. This long autobiographical poem is noteworthy not merely for themes it covers—most particularly the French Revolution—but also for the democratic vernacular in which it was written.

Wordsworth was at first intoxicated with the Revolution, engaging in a walking tour of France in the summer of 1790, then returning in the winter of 1791. The following year, he returned to Paris and witnessed the first public execution of what was to be a pathologically bloody period of mob rule. His disillusion with the effects of the revolution prompted him to return to his native England to concentrate on poetry. This passage from *The Prelude*, taken from the 1850 version of the poem, conveys the atmosphere of early reform and democratic inebriation that Wordsworth encountered in revolutionary France. It is one of the classics of revolutionary literature.

. . . An Englishman,
Born in a land whose very name appeared
To license some unruliness of mind;
A stranger, with youth's further privilege,
And the indulgence that a half-learnt speech
Wins from the courteous; I, who had been else
Shunned and not tolerated, freely lived
With these defenders of the Crown, and talked,
And heard their notions; nor did they disdain
The wish to bring me over to their cause.

But though untaught by thinking or by
    books
To reason well of polity or law,
And nice distinctions, then on every tongue,
Of natural rights and civil; and to acts
Of nations and their passing interests,
(If with unworldly ends and aims compared)
Almost indifferent, even the historian's tale
Prizing but little otherwise than I prized
Tales of the poets, as it made the heart
Beat high, and filled the fancy with fair forms,
Old heroes and their sufferings and their deeds;
Yet in the regal sceptre, and the pomp
Of orders and degrees, I nothing found
Then, or had ever, even in crudest youth,
That dazzled me, but rather what I mourned

And ill could brook, beholding that the best
Ruled not, and feeling that they ought to rule.

For, born in a poor district, and which yet
Retaineth more of ancient homeliness,
Than any other nook of English ground,
It was my fortune scarcely to have seen,
Through the whole tenor of my school-day
    time,
The face of one, who, whether boy or man,
Was vested with attention or respect
Through claims of wealth or blood; nor was it
    least
Of many benefits, in later years
Derived from academic institutes
And rules, that they held something up to view
Of a Republic, where all stood thus far
Upon equal ground; that we were brothers all
In honour, as in one community,
Scholars and gentlemen; where, furthermore,
Distinction lay open to all that came,
And wealth and titles were in less esteem
Than talents, worth, and prosperous industry.
Add unto this, subservience from the first
To presences of God's mysterious power
Made manifest in Nature's sovereignty,
And fellowship with venerable books,

To sanction the proud workings of the soul,
And mountain liberty. It could not be
But that one tutored thus should look with awe
Upon the faculties of man, receive
Gladly the highest promises, and hail,
As best, the government of equal rights
And individual worth. And hence, O Friend!
If at the first great outbreak I rejoiced
Less than might well befit my youth, the cause
In part lay here, that unto me the events
Seemed nothing out of nature's certain course,
A gift that was rather come late than soon.
No wonder, then, if advocates like these,

The poet William Wordsworth, pictured here in a
romantically anguished pose typical of the time, was
captivated in his youth by the radical idealism of the
French Revolution—only to become deeply
disillusioned later on.

Inflamed by passion, blind with prejudice,
And stung with injury, at this riper day,
Were impotent to make my hopes put on
The shape of theirs, my understanding bend
In honour to their honour: zeal, which yet
Had slumbered, now in opposition burst
Forth like a Polar summer: every word
They uttered was a dart, by counter-winds
Blown back upon themselves; their reason
    seemed
Confusion-stricken by a higher power
Than human understanding, their discourse
Maimed, spiritless; and, in their weakness
    strong,
I triumphed.
                Meantime, day by day, the
    roads
Were crowded with the bravest youth of
    France,
And all the promptest of her spirits, linked
In gallant soldiership, and posting on
To meet the war upon her frontier bounds.
Yet at this very moment do tears start
Into mine eyes: I do not say I weep—
I wept not then,—but tears have dimmed my
    sight,
In memory of the farewells of that time,
Domestic severings, female fortitude
At dearest separation, patriot love
And self-devotion, and terrestrial hope,
Encouraged with a martyr's confidence;
Even files of strangers merely, seen but once,
And for a moment, men from far with sound
Of music, martial tunes, and banners spread,
Entering the city, here and there a face,
Or person singled out among the rest,
Yet still a stranger and beloved as such;
Even by these passing spectacles my heart
Was oftentimes uplifted, and they seemed
Arguments sent from Heaven to prove the
    cause
Good, pure, which no one could stand up
    against,
Who was not lost, abandoned, selfish, proud,
Mean, miserable, wilfully depraved,
Hater perverse of equity and truth. . . .

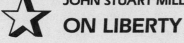

JOHN STUART MILL
ON LIBERTY

John Stuart Mill (1806–1873) is perhaps the most celebrated English theorist of democracy in modern times. The precocious son of a famous theorist of utilitarianism, James Mill, John Stuart Mill earned his living as an examiner for the East India Company, but his intellectual life dwarfed this career. Mill based his defense of democratic liberty on utilitarian grounds, arguing, among other things, that freedom of thought and action would lead to a steady improvement in the happiness of mankind. Good ideas would chase out bad; better ways of life, found by the experimentation only a free society allows, would crowd out inferior ways of living. Democracy was preferable not because of the *a priori* rights of individuals, but because it would raise the quality of life for all. In the increasingly materialist and secular culture of Victorian England, these arguments provided new foundations for democratic institutions.

His utilitarianism did not mean, however, that Mill was lax in asserting the absolute rights of the individual. Indeed, in *On Liberty*, his most famous work, his arguments extend beyond freedom from political oppression to a more general freedom from social oppression: the freedom from others' regulating private life, opinions, and predilections. Much of what we now understand as essential freedoms of privacy can be found in their earliest form in the writings of Mill.

. . . The distinction between the loss of consideration which a person may rightly incur by defect of prudence or of personal dignity, and the reprobation which is due to him for an offence against the rights of others, is not a merely nominal distinction. It makes a vast difference both in our feelings and in our conduct towards him whether he displeases us in things in which we think we have a right to control him or in things in which we know that we have not. If he displeases us, we may express our distaste, and we may stand aloof from a person as well as from a thing that displeases us; but we shall not therefore feel called on to make his life uncomfortable. We shall reflect that he already bears, or will bear, the whole penalty of his error; if he spoils his life by mismanagement, we shall not, for that reason, desire to spoil it still further; instead of wishing to punish him, we shall rather endeavour to alleviate his punishment by showing him how he may avoid or cure the evils his conduct tends to bring upon him. He may be to us an object of pity, perhaps of dislike, but not of anger or re-

sentment; we shall not treat him like an enemy of society; the worst we shall think ourselves justified in doing is leaving him to himself, if we do not interfere benevolently by showing interest or concern for him. It is far otherwise if he has infringed the rules necessary for the protection of his fellow creatures, individually or collectively. The evil consequences of his acts do not then fall on himself, but on others; and society, as the protector of all its members, must retaliate on him, must inflict pain on him for the express purpose of punishment, and must take care that it be sufficiently severe. In the one case, he is an offender at our bar, and we are called on not only to sit in judgment on him, but, in one shape or another, to execute our own sentence; in the other case, it is not our part to inflict any suffering on him, except what may incidentally follow from our using the same liberty in the regulation of our own affairs which we allow to him in his.

The distinction here pointed out between the part of a person's life which concerns only himself and that which concerns others, many persons will refuse to admit. How (it may be asked) can any part of the conduct of a member of society be a matter of indifference to the other members? No person is an entirely isolated being; it is impossible for a person to do anything seriously or permanently hurtful to himself without mischief reaching at least to his near connections, and often far beyond them. If he injures his property, he does harm to those who directly or indirectly derived support from it, and usually diminishes, by a greater or less amount, the general resources of the community. If he deteriorates his bodily or mental faculties, he not only brings evil upon all who depended on him for any portion of their happiness, but disqualifies himself for rendering the services which he owes to his fellow creatures generally, perhaps becomes a burden on their affection or benevolence; and if such conduct were very frequent hardly any offence that is committed would detract more from the general sum of good. Finally, if by his vices or follies a person does no direct harm to others, he is nevertheless (it may be said) injurious by his example, and ought to be compelled to control himself for the sake of those whom the sight or knowledge of his conduct might corrupt or mislead.

And even (it will be added) if the consequences of misconduct could be confined to the vicious or thoughtless individual, ought society to abandon to their own guidance those who are manifestly unfit for it? If protection against themselves is confessedly due to children and persons under age, is not society equally bound to afford it to persons of mature years who are equally incapable of self-government? If gambling, or drunkenness, or incontinence, or idleness, or uncleanliness are as injurious to happiness, and as great a hindrance to improvement, as many or most of the acts prohibited by law, why (it may be asked) should not law, so far as is consistent with practicability and social convenience, endeavour to repress these also? And as a supplement to the unavoidable imperfections of law, ought not opinion at least to organize a powerful police against these vices and visit rigidly with social penalties those who are known to practise

them? There is no question here (it may be said) about restricting individuality, or impeding the trial of new and original experiments in living. The only things it is sought to prevent are things which have been tried and condemned from the beginning of the world until now—things which experience has shown not to be useful or suitable to any person's individuality. There must be some length of time and amount of experience after which a moral or prudential truth may be regarded as established; and it is merely desired to prevent generation after generation from falling over the same precipice which has been fatal to their predecessors.

I fully admit that the mischief which a person does to himself may seriously affect, both through their sympathies and their interests, those nearly connected with him and, in a minor degree, society at large. When, by conduct of this sort, a person is led to violate a distinct and assignable obligation to any other person or persons, the case is taken out of the self-regarding class and becomes amenable to moral disapprobation in the proper sense of the term. If, for example, a man, through intemperance or extravagance, becomes unable to pay his debts, or, having undertaken the moral responsibility of a family, becomes from the same cause incapable of supporting or educating them, he is deservedly reprobated and might be justly punished; but it is for the breach of duty to his family or creditor, not for the extravagance. If the resources which ought to have been devoted to them had been diverted from them for the most prudent investment, the moral culpability would have been the same. George Barnwell murdered his uncle to get money for his mistress, but if he had done it to set himself up in business, he would equally have been hanged. Again, in the frequent case of a man who causes grief to his family by addiction to bad habits, he deserves reproach for his unkindness or ingratitude; but so he may for cultivating habits not in themselves vicious, if they are painful to those with whom he passes his life, or who from personal ties are dependent on him for their comfort. Whoever fails in the consideration generally due to the interests and feelings of others, not being compelled by some more imperative duty, or justified by allowable self-preference, is a subject of moral disapprobation for that failure, but not for the cause of it, nor for the errors, merely personal to himself, which may have remotely led to it. In like manner, when a person disables himself, by conduct purely self-regarding, from the performance of some definite duty incumbent on him to the public, he is guilty of a social offence. No person ought to be punished simply for being drunk; but a soldier or a policeman should be punished for being drunk on duty. Whenever, in short, there is a definite damage, or a definite risk of damage, either to an individual or to the public, the case is taken out of the province of liberty and placed in that of morality or law.

But with regard to the merely contingent or, as it may be called, constructive injury which a person causes to society by conduct which neither violates any specific duty to the public, nor occasions perceptible hurt to any assignable individual except himself, the inconvenience is one which society can afford to bear, for the sake of the greater good of human freedom. If grown persons are to be punished for not taking proper

The grandfather of modern liberalism, John Stuart Mill was a tireless defender of the rights of the individual against the state and the minority against the majority. He also campaigned for equal rights for women.

care of themselves, I would rather it were for their own sake than under pretence of preventing them from impairing their capacity or rendering to society benefits which society does not pretend it has a right to exact. But I cannot consent to argue the point as if society had no means of bringing its weaker members up to its ordinary standard of rational conduct, except waiting till they do something irrational, and then punishing them, legally or morally, for it. Society has had absolute power over them during all the early portion of their existence; it has had the whole period of childhood and nonage in which to try whether it could make them capable of rational conduct in life. The existing generation is master both of the training and the entire circumstances of the generation to come; it cannot indeed make them perfectly wise and good, because it is itself so lamentably deficient in goodness and wisdom; and its best efforts are not always, in individual cases, its most successful ones; but it is perfectly well able to make the rising generation, as a whole, as good as, and a little better than, itself. If society lets any considerable number of its members grow up mere children, incapable of being acted on by rational consideration of distant motives, society has itself to blame for the consequences. Armed not only with all the powers of education, but with the ascendancy which the authority of a received opinion always exercises over the minds who are least fitted to judge for themselves, and aided by the *natural* penalties which cannot be prevented from falling on those who incur the distaste or the contempt of those who know them—let not society pretend that it needs, besides all this, the power to issue commands and enforce obedience in the personal concerns of individuals in which, on all principles of justice and policy, the decision ought to rest with those who are to abide the consequences. Nor is there anything which tends more to discredit and frustrate the better means of influencing conduct than a resort to the worse. If there be among those whom it is attempted to coerce into prudence or temperance any of the material of which vigorous and independent characters are

made, they will infallibly rebel against the yoke. No such person will ever feel that others have a right to control him in his concerns, such as they have to prevent him from injuring them in theirs; and it easily comes to be considered a mark of spirit and courage to fly in the face of such usurped authority and do with ostentation the exact opposite of what it enjoins, as in the fashion of grossness which succeeded, in the time of Charles II, to the fanatical moral intolerance of the Puritans. With respect to what is said of the necessity of protecting society from the bad example set to others by the vicious or the self-indulgent, it is true that bad example may have a pernicious effect, especially the example of doing wrong to others with impunity to the wrongdoer. But we are now speaking of conduct which, while it does no wrong to others, is supposed to do great harm to the agent himself; and I do not see how those who believe this can think otherwise than that the example, on the whole, must be more salutary than hurtful, since, if it displays the misconduct, it displays also the painful or degrading consequences which, if the conduct is justly censured, must be supposed to be in all or most cases attendant on it.

But the strongest of all the arguments against the interference of the public with purely personal conduct is that, when it does interfere, the odds are that it interferes wrongly and in the wrong place. On questions of social morality, of duty to others, the opinion of the public, that is, of an overruling majority, though often wrong, is likely to be still oftener right, because on such questions they are only required to judge of their own interests, of the manner in which some mode of conduct, if allowed to be practised, would affect themselves. But the opinion of a similar majority, imposed as a law on the minority, on questions of self-regarding conduct is quite as likely to be wrong as right, for in these cases public opinion means, at the best, some people's opinion of what is good or bad for other people, while very often it does not even mean that—the public, with the most perfect indifference, passing over the pleasure or convenience of those whose conduct they censure and considering only their own preference. There are many who consider as an injury to themselves any conduct which they have a distaste for, and resent it as an outrage to their feelings; as a religious bigot, when charged with disregarding the religious feelings of others, has been known to retort that they disregard his feelings by persisting in their abominable worship or creed. But there is no parity between the feeling of a person for his own opinion and the feeling of another who is offended at his holding it, no more than between the desire of a thief to take a purse and the desire of the right owner to keep it. And a person's taste is as much his own peculiar concern as his opinion or his purse. It is easy for anyone to imagine an ideal public which leaves the freedom and choice of individuals in all uncertain matters undisturbed and only requires them to abstain from modes of conduct which universal experience has condemned. But where has there been seen a public which set any such limit to its censorship? Or when does the public trouble itself about universal experience? In its interferences with personal conduct it is seldom thinking of anything but the enormity of acting or feeling differently from itself; and this standard of judgement, thinly disguised, is held up to mankind as the dictate of religion and philosophy by nine-tenths of all moralists and speculative writers. These teach that things are right because they are right; because we feel them to be so. They tell us to search in our own minds and hearts for laws of conduct binding on ourselves and on all others. What can the poor public do but apply these instructions and make their own personal feelings of good and evil, if they are tolerably unanimous in them, obligatory on all the world?

The evil here pointed out is not one which exists only in theory; and it may perhaps be expected that I should specify the instances in which the public of this age and country improperly invests its own preferences with the character of moral laws. I am not writing an essay on the aberrations of existing moral feeling. That is too weighty a subject to be discussed parenthetically, and by way of illustration. Yet examples are necessary to show that the principle I maintain is of serious and practical moment, and that I am not endeavouring to erect a barrier against imaginary evils. And it is not difficult to show, by abundant instances, that to extend the bounds of what may be called moral police until it encroaches on the most unquestionably legitimate liberty of the individual is one of the most universal of all human propensities.

As a first instance, consider the antipathies which men cherish on no better grounds than that persons whose religious opinions are different from theirs do not practise their religious observances, especially their religious abstinences. To cite a rather trivial example, nothing in the creed or practice of Christians does more to envenom the hatred of Mohammedans against them than the fact of their eating pork. There are few acts which Christians and Europeans regard with more unaffected disgust than [Muslims] regard this particular mode of satisfying hunger. It is in the first place, an offence against their religion; but this circumstance by no means explains either the degree or the kind of their repugnance; for wine also is forbidden by their religion and to partake of it is by all [Muslims] accounted wrong, but not disgusting. Their aversion to the flesh of the "unclean beast" is, on the contrary, of that peculiar character, resembling an instinctive antipathy, which the idea of uncleanness, when once it thoroughly sinks into the feelings, seems always to excite even in those whose personal habits are anything but scrupulously cleanly, and of which the sentiment of religious impurity, so intense in the Hindus, is a remarkable example. Suppose now that in a people of whom the majority were [Muslims], that majority should insist upon not permitting pork to be eaten within the limits of the country. This would be nothing new in Mohammedan countries. Would it be a legitimate exercise of the moral authority of public opinion, and if not, why not? The practice is really revolting to such a public. They also sincerely think that it is forbidden and abhorred by the Deity. Neither could the prohibition be censured as religious persecution. It might be religious in its origin, but it would not be persecution for religion, since nobody's religion makes it a duty to eat pork. The only tenable ground of condemnation would be that with the personal tastes and self-regarding concerns of individuals the public has no business to interfere.

To come somewhat nearer home: the majority of Spaniards consider it a gross impiety, offensive in the highest degree to the Supreme Being, to worship him in any other manner than the Roman Catholic; and no other public worship is lawful on Spanish soil. The people of all southern Europe look upon a married clergy as not only irreligious, but unchaste, indecent, gross, disgusting. What do Protestants think of these perfectly sincere feelings, and of the attempt to enforce them against non-Catholics? Yet, if mankind are justified in interfering with each other's liberty in things which do not concern the interests of others, on what principle is it possible consistently to exclude these cases? Or who can blame people for desiring to suppress what they regard as a scandal in the sight of God and man? No stronger case can be shown for prohibiting anything which is regarded as a personal immorality than is made out for suppressing these practices in the eyes of those who regard them as impieties; and unless we are willing to adopt the logic of persecutors, and to say that we may persecute others because we are right, and that they must not persecute us because they are wrong, we must beware of admitting a principle of which we should resent as a gross injustice the application to ourselves.

The preceding instances may be objected to, although unreasonably, as drawn from contingencies impossible among us—opinion, in this country, not being likely to enforce abstinence from meats or to interfere with people for worshipping and for either marrying or not marrying, according to their creed or inclination. The next example, however, shall be taken from an interference with liberty which we have by no means passed all danger of. Wherever the Puritans have been sufficiently powerful, as in New England, and in Great Britain at the time of the Commonwealth, they have endeavoured, with considerable success, to put down all public, and nearly all private, amusements: especially music, dancing, public games, or other assemblages for purposes of diversion, and the theatre. There are still in this country large bodies of persons by whose notions of morality and religion these recreations are condemned; and those persons belonging chiefly to the middle class, who are the ascendant power in the present social and political condition of the kingdom, it is by no means impossible that persons of these sentiments may at some time or other command a majority in Parliament. How will the remaining portion of the community like to have the amusements that shall be permitted to them regulated by the religious and moral sentiments of the stricter Calvinists and Methodists? Would they not, with considerable peremptoriness, desire these intrusively pious members of society to mind their own business? This is precisely what should be said to every government and every public who have the pretension that no person shall enjoy any pleasure which they think wrong. But if the principle of the pretension be admitted, no one can reasonably object to its being acted on in the sense of the majority, or other preponderating power in the country; and all persons must be ready to conform to the idea of a Christian commonwealth as understood by the early settlers in New England, if a religious profession similar to theirs should ever succeed in regaining its lost ground, as religions supposed to be declining have so often been known to do. . . .

THE SUBJECTION OF WOMEN

This less well-known treatise of John Stuart Mill's, written in 1861 and published in 1869, also reflects very modern ideas. It emanates from his speeches as a member of Parliament on behalf of the Reform Bill of 1867, which extended the suffrage to all men in Britain, but not to women. The theme of the pamphlet is equality of opportunity, and it provides the archetypal liberal statement of the promise of democracy to extend its advantages to any individual, regardless of the characteristics with which he or she has been born. Many of the debates now raging in advanced Western democracies are in effect replays of this central question. Mill brings to this debate his usual ruthless logic and calm forensics; he is both impassioned and reasoned. What is interesting about this text is its apparent lack of interest in the rights of minorities as such, and its sole concentration on the rights of the individual. It is a plea for individual—not group—equality. It stands as a variation on one of Mill's richest themes: bettering the lot of those excluded from power and respect.

. . . For, what is the peculiar character of the modern world—the difference which chiefly distinguishes modern institutions, modern social ideas, modern life itself, from those of times long past? It is, that human beings are no longer born to their place in life, and chained down by an inexorable bond to the place they are born to, but are free to employ their faculties, and such favourable chances as offer, to achieve the lot which may appear to them most desirable. Human society of old was constituted on a very different principle. All were born to a fixed social position, and were mostly kept in it by law, or interdicted from any means by which they could emerge from it. As some men are born white and others black, so some were born slaves and others freemen and citizens; some were born patricians, others plebeians; some were born feudal nobles, others commoners and *roturiers*. A slave or serf could never make himself free, nor, except by the will of his master, become so. In most European countries it was not till towards the close of the middle ages, and as a consequence of the growth of regal power, that commoners could be ennobled. Even among nobles, the eldest son was born the exclusive heir to the paternal possessions, and a long time elapsed before it was fully established that the father could disinherit him. Among the industrious classes, only those who were born members of a guild, or were admitted into it by its members, could lawfully practise their calling within its local limits; and nobody could practise any calling deemed important, in any but the legal manner—by processes authoritatively prescribed. Manufacturers have stood in the pillory for presuming to carry on their business by new and improved methods. In modern Europe, and most in those parts of it which have participated most largely in all other modern improvements, diametrically opposite doctrines now prevail. Law and government do not undertake to prescribe by whom any social or industrial operation shall or shall not be conducted, or what modes of conducting them shall be lawful. These things are left to the unfettered choice of individuals. Even the laws which required that workmen should serve an apprenticeship, have in this country been repealed: there being ample assurance that in all cases in which an apprenticeship is necessary, its necessity will suffice to enforce it. The old theory was, that the least possible should be left to the choice of the individual agent; that all he had to do should, as far as practicable, be laid down for him by superior wisdom. Left to himself he was sure to go wrong. The modern conviction, the fruit of a thousand years of experience, is, that things in which the individual is the person directly interested, never go right but as they are left to his own discretion; and that any regulation of them by authority, except to protect the rights of others, is sure to be mischievous. This conclusion, slowly arrived at, and not adopted until almost every possible application of the contrary theory had been made with disastrous result, now (in the industrial department) prevails universally in the most advanced countries, almost universally in all that have pretensions to any sort of advancement. It is not that all processes are supposed to be equally good, or all persons to be equally qualified for everything; but that freedom of individual choice is now known to be the only thing which procures the adoption of the best processes, and throws each operation into the hands of those who are best qualified for it. Nobody thinks it necessary to make a law that only a strong-armed man shall be a blacksmith. Freedom and competition suffice to make blacksmiths strong-armed men, because the weak-armed can earn more by engaging in occupations for which they are more fit. In consonance with this doctrine, it is felt to be an overstepping of the proper bounds of authority to fix beforehand, on some general presumption, that certain persons are not fit to do certain things. It is now thoroughly known and admitted that if some such presumptions exist, no such presumption is infallible. Even if it be well grounded in a majority of cases, which it is very likely not to be, there will be a minority of exceptional cases in which it does not hold: and in those it is both an injustice to the individuals, and a detriment to society, to place barriers in the way of their using their faculties for their own benefit and for that of others. In the cases, on the other hand, in which the unfitness is real, the ordinary motives of human conduct will on the whole suffice to prevent the incompetent person from making, or from persisting in, the attempt.

If this general principle of social and economical science is not true; if individuals, with such help as they can derive from the opinion of those who know them, are not better judges than the law and the government, of their own capacities and vocation; the world cannot too soon abandon this principle, and return to the old system of regulations and disabilities. But if the principle is true, we ought to act as if we believed it, and not to ordain that to be born a girl instead of a boy, any more than to be born black instead of white, or a commoner instead of a nobleman, shall decide the person's position through all life—shall interdict people from all the more elevated social positions, and from all, except a few, respectable occupations. Even were we to admit the utmost that is ever pretended as to the superior fitness of men for all the functions now reserved to them, the same argument applies which forbids a legal qualification for Members of Parliament. If only once in a dozen years the conditions of eligibility exclude a fit person, there is a real loss, while the exclusion of thousands of unfit persons is no gain; for if the constitution of the electoral body disposes them to choose unfit persons, there are always plenty of such persons to choose from. In all things of any difficulty and importance, those who can do them well are fewer than the need, even with the most unrestricted latitude of choice: and any limitation of the field of selection deprives society of some chances of being served by the competent, without ever saving it from the incompetent.

At present, in the more improved countries, the disabilities of women are the only case, save one, in which laws and institutions take persons at their birth, and ordain that they shall never in all their lives be allowed to compete for certain things. The one exception is that of royalty. Persons still are born to the throne; no one, not of the reigning family, can ever occupy it, and no one even of that family can, by any means but the course of hereditary succession, attain it. All other dignities and social advantages are open to the whole male sex: many indeed are only attainable by wealth, but wealth may be striven for by anyone, and is actually obtained by many men of the very humblest origin. The difficulties, to the majority, are indeed insuperable without the aid of fortunate accidents; but no male human being is under any legal ban: neither law nor opinion superadd artificial obstacles to the natural ones. Royalty, as I have said, is excepted: but in this case everyone feels it to be an exception—an anomaly in the modern world, in marked opposition to its customs and principles, and to be justified only by extraordinary special expediences, which, though individuals and nations differ in estimating their weight, unquestionably do in fact exist. But in this exceptional case, in which a high social function is, for important reasons, bestowed on birth instead of being put up to competition, all free nations contrive to adhere in substance to the principle from which they nominally derogate; for they circumscribe this high function by conditions avowedly intended to prevent the person to whom it ostensibly belongs from really performing it; while the person by whom it is performed, the responsible minister, does obtain the post by a competition from which no full-grown citizen of the male sex is legally excluded. The disabilities, therefore, to which women are subject from the mere fact of their birth, are the solitary examples of the kind in modern legislation. In no instance except this, which comprehends half the human race, are the higher social functions closed against anyone by a fatality of birth which no exertions, and no change of circumstances, can overcome; for even religious disabilities (besides that in England and in Europe they have practically almost ceased to exist) do not close any career to the disqualified person in case of conversion.

The social subordination of women thus stands out an isolated fact in modern social institutions; a solitary breach of what has become their fundamental law; a single relic of an old world of thought and practice exploded in everything else, but retained in the one thing of most universal interest; as if a gigantic dolmen, or a vast temple of Jupiter Olympius, occupied the site of St. Paul's and received daily worship, while the surrounding Christian churches were only resorted to on fasts and festivals. This entire discrepancy between one social fact and all those which accompany it, and the radical opposition between its nature and the progressive movement which is the boast of the modern world, and which has successively swept away everything else of an analogous character, surely affords, to a conscientious observer of human tendencies, serious matter for reflection. . . .

WALTER BAGEHOT
THE ENGLISH CONSTITUTION

Walter Bagehot (1826–1877) was a financial and political journalist; indeed, one of the first writers who can be said to have sought the career of a political pundit. He became editor of *The Economist* in 1860 in part by marrying the daughter of its founder.

The first edition of *The English Constitution* appeared in 1867. It was essentially a defense of parliamentary, as opposed to presidential, democracy, and was written while the greatest test of the American system, the American Civil War, was in progress. Its most famous insight is a variation on Plato's notion of a "noble lie" at the heart of democratic government. All government, Bagehot implies, even democracy, rests to some extent on coercion and elitism. Making this palatable to democratic citizens is a difficult task—and the job is partly done by the ceremonial trappings of power. Government, he argues, must be mystified in order to work. There is something essentially mysterious about the nature of authority.

To Bagehot, the British system was preferable to the American, as it manages to separate ceremony and substance: the constitutional monarch provides the trappings of power—the *dignified* part—without its reality; the cabinet provides the essence of power—the *efficient* part—without the trappings. Neither is in danger of becoming too overbearing or of needing to be both dignified and efficient, as the American presidency is.

. . . No one can approach to an understanding of the English institutions, or of others which, being the growth of many centuries, exercise a wide sway over mixed populations, unless he divide them into two classes. In such constitutions there are two parts (not indeed separable with microscopic accuracy, for the genius of great affairs abhors nicety of division: first, those which excite and preserve the reverence of the population—the *dignified* parts, if I may so call them; and next, the *efficient* parts—those by which it, in fact, works and rules. There are two great objects which every constitution must attain to be successful, which every old and celebrated one must have wonderfully achieved: every constitution must first *gain* authority, and then *use* authority; it must first win the loyalty and confidence of mankind, and then employ that homage in the work of government.

There are indeed practical men who reject the dignified parts of government. They say, we want only to attain results, to do business: a constitution is a collection of political means for political ends, and if you admit that any part of a constitution does no business, or that a simpler machine would do equally well what it does, you admit that this part of the constitution, however dignified or awful it may be, is nevertheless in truth useless. And other reasoners, who distrust this bare philosophy, have propounded subtle arguments to prove that these dignified parts of old governments are cardinal components of the essential apparatus, great pivots of substantial utility; and so they manufactured fallacies which the plainer school have well exposed. But both schools are in error. The dignified parts of government are those which bring it force—which attract its motive power. The efficient parts only employ that power. The comely parts of a government *have* need, for they are those upon which its vital strength depends. They may not do anything definite that a simpler polity would

not do better; but they are the preliminaries, the needful prerequisites of *all* work. They raise the army, though they do not win the battle.

Doubtless, if all subjects of the same government only thought of what was useful to them, and if they all thought the same thing useful, and all thought that same thing could be attained in the same way, the efficient members of a constitution would suffice, and no impressive adjuncts would be needed. But the world in which we live is organized far otherwise.

The most strange fact, though the most certain in nature, is the unequal development of the human race. If we look back to the early ages of mankind, such as we seem in the faint distance to see them—if we call up the image of those dismal tribes in lake villages, or on wretched beaches—scarcely equal to the commonest material needs, cutting down trees slowly and painfully with stone tools, hardly resisting the attacks of huge, fierce animals—without culture, without leisure, without poetry, almost without thought—destitute of morality, with only a sort of magic for religion; and if we compare that imagined life with the actual life of Europe now, we are overwhelmed at the wide contrast—we can scarcely conceive ourselves to be of the same race as those in the far distance. There used to be a notion—not so much widely asserted as deeply implanted, rather pervadingly latent than commonly apparent in political philosophy— that in a little while, perhaps ten years or so, all human beings might, without extraordinary appliances, be brought to the same level. But now, when we see by the painful history of mankind at what point we began, by what slow toil, what favourable circumstances, what accumulated achievements, civilized man has become at all worthy in any degree so to call himself—when we realize the tedium of history and the painfulness of results—our perceptions are sharpened as to the relative steps of our long and gradual progress. We have in a great community like England crowds of people scarcely more civilized than the majority of two thousand years ago; we have others, even more numerous, such as the best people were a thousand years since. The lower orders, the middle orders, are still, when tried by what is the standard of the educated "ten thousand," narrow-minded, unintelligent, incurious. It is useless to pile up abstract words. Those who doubt should go out into their kitchens. Let an accomplished man try what seems to him most obvious, most certain, most palpable in intellectual matters, upon the housemaid and the footman, and he will find that what he says seems unintelligible, confused, and erroneous—that his audience think him mad and wild when he is speaking what is in his own sphere of thought the dullest platitude of cautious soberness. Great communities are like great mountains—they have in them the primary, secondary, and tertiary strata of human progress; the characteristics of the lower regions resemble the life of old times rather than the present life of the higher regions. And a philosophy which does not ceaselessly remember, which does not continually obtrude, the palpable differences of the various parts, will be a theory radically false, because it has omitted a capital reality—will be a theory essentially misleading, because it will lead men to expect what does not exist, and not to anticipate that which they will find.

Every one knows these plain facts, but by no means every one has traced their political importance. When a state is constituted thus, it is not true that the lower classes will be wholly absorbed in the useful; on the contrary, they do not like anything so poor. No orator ever made an impression by appealing to men as to their plainest physical wants, except when he could allege that those wants were caused by some one's tyranny. But thousands have made the greatest impression by appealing to some vague dream of glory, or empire, or nationality. The ruder sort of men—that is, men at *one* stage of rudeness—will sacrifice all they hope for, all they have, *themselves*, for what is called an idea—for some at-

Walter Bagehot, the well-known editor of *The Economist*, was one of the first political journalists to explain the importance of the theater and mystery in democratic politics—an early analyst of the politics of the television commercial and the sound bite.

traction which seems to transcend reality, which aspires to elevate men by an interest higher, deeper, wider than that of ordinary life. But this order of men are uninterested in the plain, palpable ends of government; they do not prize them; they do not in the least comprehend how they should be attained. It is very natural, therefore, that the most useful parts of the structure of government should by no means be those which excite the most reverence. The elements which excite the most easy reverence will be the *theatrical* elements—those which appeal to the senses, which claim to be embodiments of the greatest human ideas, which boast in some cases of far more than human origin. That which is mystic in its claims; that which is occult in its mode of action; that which is brilliant to the eye; that which is seen vividly for a moment, and then is seen no more; that which is hidden and unhidden; that which is specious, and yet interesting, palpable in its seeming, and yet professing to be more than palpable in its results; this, howsoever its form may change, or however we may define it or describe it, is the sort of thing—the only sort—which yet comes home to the mass of men. So far from the dignified parts of a constitution being necessarily the most useful, they are likely, according to outside presumption, to be the least so; for they are likely to be adjusted to the lowest orders—those likely to care least and judge worst about what *is* useful.

There is another reason which, in an old constitution like that of England, is hardly less important. The most intellectual of men are moved quite as much by the circumstances which they are used to as by their own will. The active voluntary part of a man is very small, and if it were not economized by a sleepy kind of habit, its results would be null. We could not do every day out of our own heads all we have to do. We should accomplish nothing, for all our energies would be frittered away in minor attempts at petty improvement. One man, too, would go off from the known track in one direction, and one in another; so that when a crisis came requiring massed combination, no two men would be near enough to act together. It is the dull traditional habit of mankind that guides most men's actions, and is the steady frame in which each new artist must set the picture that he paints. And all this traditional part of human nature is, *ex vi termini*, most easily impressed and acted on by that which is handed down. Other things being equal, yesterday's institutions are by far the best for today; they are the most ready, the most influential, the most easy to get obeyed, the most likely to retain the reverence which they alone inherit, and which every other must win. The most imposing institutions of mankind are the oldest; and yet so changing is the world, so fluctuating are its needs, so apt to lose inward force, though retaining outward strength, are its best instruments, that we must not expect the oldest institutions to be now the most efficient. We must expect what is venerable to acquire influence because of its inherent dignity; but we must not expect it to use that influence so well as new creations apt for the modern world, instinct with its spirit, and fitting closely to its life.

The brief description of the characteristic merit of the English Constitution is, that its dignified parts are very complicated and somewhat imposing, very old and rather venerable; while its efficient part, at least when in great and critical action, is decidedly simple and rather modern. We have made, or rather stumbled on, a constitution which—though full of every species of incidental defect, though of the worst *workmanship* in all out-of-the-way matters of any constitution in the world—yet has two capital merits: it contains a simple efficient part which, on occasion, and when wanted, *can* work more simply and easily, and better, than any instrument of government that has yet been tried; and it contains likewise historical, complex, august, theatrical parts, which it has inherited from a long past—which *take* the multitude—which guide by an insensible but an omnipotent influence the associations of its subjects. Its essence is strong with the strength of modern simplicity; its exterior is august with the Gothic grandeur of a more imposing age. Its simple essence may, *mutatis mutandis*, be transplanted to many very various countries, but its august outside—what most men think it is—is narrowly confined to nations with an analogous history and similar political materials.

The efficient secret of the English Constitution may be described as the close union, the nearly complete fusion, of the executive and legislative powers. No doubt by the traditional theory, as it exists in all the books, the goodness of our constitution consists in the entire separation of the legislative and executive authorities, but in truth its merit consists in their singular approximation. The connecting link is *the cabinet.* By that new word we mean a committee of the legislative body selected to be the executive body. The legislature has many committees, but this is the greatest. It chooses for this, its main committee, the men in whom it has most confidence. It does not, it is true, choose them directly; but it is nearly omnipotent in choosing them indirectly.... But as a rule, the nominal prime minister is chosen by the legislature, and the real prime minister for most purposes—the leader of the House of Commons—almost without exception is so. There is nearly always some one man plainly selected by the voice of the predominant party in the predominant house of the legislature to head that party, and consequently to rule the nation. We have in England an elective first magistrate as truly as the Americans have an elective first magistrate. The Queen is only at the head of the dignified part of the constitution. The prime minister is at the head of the efficient part. The Crown is, according to the saying, the "fountain of honour;" but the Treasury is the spring of business. Nevertheless our first magistrate differs from the American. He is not elected directly by the people; he is elected by the representatives of the people. He is an example of "double election." The legislature chosen, in name, to make laws, in fact finds its principal business in making and in keeping an executive....

FRIEDRICH NIETZSCHE
BEYOND GOOD AND EVIL

Friedrich Nietzsche (1844–1900) began his career as a classical philologist at the University of Bonn, and became a professor of philology at the University of Basel in 1869. His numerous works outlined a philosophy perhaps unique in modern times in its profundity and subtlety. He cannot be described as a conventional democrat. Indeed, his criticism of democracy is perhaps the most devastating since Plato's. In these passages from *Beyond Good and Evil*, his antidemocratic rhetoric is on full display. Particularly noteworthy is his gloomy view that democracy inherently debases what is noble in the human character.

Why, then, include him in a democracy reader? Because a close reading of Nietzsche reveals him as a man who accepted the inevitability of democratic development—indeed, he predicted the nature of modern democratic culture more accurately than any other thinker. He seemed to argue that democratic culture is essential for the emergence of the supremely creative individuality which alone warranted his admiration. Notice in this passage, for example, how Nietzsche viewed democracy as an inevitable force. Early scholars saw in Nietzsche a crass forerunner of Nazi totalitarianism. Contemporary critics are beginning to value the mastery and complexity of his social and philosophical critiques.

. . . Let us immediately say once more what we have already said a hundred times, for today's ears resist such truths—*our* truths. We know well enough how insulting it sounds when anybody counts man, unadorned and without metaphor, among the animals; but it will be charged against us as almost a *guilt* that precisely for the men of "modern ideas" we constantly employ such expressions as "herd," "herd instincts," and so forth. What can be done about it? We cannot do anything else; for here exactly lies our novel insight. We have found that in all major moral judgments Europe is now of one mind, including even the countries dominated by the influence of Europe: plainly, one now *knows* in Europe what Socrates thought he did not know and what that famous old serpent once promised to teach— today one "knows" what is good and evil.

Now it must sound harsh and cannot be heard easily when we keep insisting: that which here believes it knows, that which here glorifies itself with its praises and reproaches, calling itself good, that is the instinct of the herd animal, man, which has scored a breakthrough and attained prevalence and predominance over other instincts—and this development is continuing in accordance with the growing physiological approximation and assimilation of which it is the symptom. *Morality in Europe today is herd animal morality*—in other words, as we understand it, merely *one* type of human morality beside which, before which, and after which many other types, above all *higher* moralities, are, or ought to be, possible. But this morality resists such a "possibility," such an "ought" with all its power: it says stubbornly and inexorably, "I am morality itself, and nothing besides is morality." Indeed, with the help of a religion which indulged and flattered the most sublime herd-animal desires, we have reached the point where we find even in political and social institutions an ever more visible expression of this morality: the *democratic* movement is the heir of the Christian movement.

But there are indications that its tempo is still much too slow and sleepy for the more impatient, for the sick, the sufferers of the instinct mentioned: witness the ever madder howling of the anarchist dogs who are baring their fangs more and more obviously and roam through the alleys of European culture. They seem opposites of the peacefully industrious democrats and ideologists of revolution, and even more so of the doltish philosophasters and brotherhood enthusiasts who call themselves socialists and want a "free society"; but in fact they are at one with the lot in their thorough and instinctive hostility to every other form of society except that of the *autonomous* herd (even to the point of repudiating the very concepts of "master" and "servant"—*ni dieu ni maître* runs a socialist formula). They are at one in their tough resistance to every special claim, every special right and privilege (which means in the last analysis, *every* right: for once all are equal nobody needs "rights" any more). They are at one in their mistrust of punitive justice (as if it were a violation of those who are weaker, a wrong against the *necessary* consequence of all previous society). But they are also at one in the religion of pity, in feeling with all who feel, live, and suffer (down to the animal, up to "God"—the excess of a "pity with God" belongs in a democratic age). They are at one, the lot of them, in the cry and the impatience of pity, in their deadly hatred of suffering generally, in their almost feminine inability to remain spectators, to *let* someone suffer. They are at one in their involuntary plunge into gloom and unmanly tenderness under whose spell Europe seems threatened by a new Buddhism. They are at one in their faith in the morality of *shared* pity, as if that were morality in itself, being the height, the *attained* height of man, the sole hope of the future, the consolation of present man, the great absolution from all former guilt. They are at one, the lot of them, in their faith in the community as the *savior*, in short, in the herd, in "themselves"—

We have a different faith; to us the democratic movement is not only a form of the decay of political organization but a form of the decay, namely the diminution, of man, making him mediocre and lowering his value. Where, then, must *we* reach with our hopes?

Toward *new philosophers*; there is no choice; toward spirits strong and original enough to provide the stimuli for opposite valuations and to revalue and invert "eternal values"; toward forerunners, toward men of the future who in the present tie the knot and constraint that forces the will of millennia upon *new* tracks. To teach man the future of man as his *will*, as dependent on a human will, and to prepare great ventures and over-all attempts of discipline and cultivation by way of putting an end to that gruesome dominion of nonsense and accident that has so far been called "history"—the nonsense of the "greatest number" is merely its ultimate form: at some time new types of philosophers and commanders will be necessary for that, and whatever has existed on earth of concealed, terrible, and benevolent spirits, will look pale and dwarfed by comparison. It is the image of such leaders that we envisage: may I say this out loud, you free spirits? The conditions that one would have partly to create and partly to exploit for their genesis; the probable ways and tests that would enable a soul to grow to such a height and force that it would feel the *compulsion* for such tasks; a revaluation of values under whose new pressure and hammer a conscience would be steeled, a heart turned to bronze, in order to endure the weight of such responsibility; on the other hand, the necessity of such leaders, the frightening danger that they might fail to appear or that they might turn out badly or degenerate—these are *our* real worries and gloom— do you know that, you free spirits?—these are the heavy distant thoughts and storms that pass over the sky of *our* life.

There are few pains as sore as once having seen, guessed, felt how an extraordinary human being strayed from his path and degenerated. But anyone who has the rare eye for the over-all danger that "man" himself *degenerates*; anyone who, like us, has recognized the monstrous fortuity that has so far had its way and play regarding the future of man—a game in which no hand, and not even a finger, of God took part as a player; anyone who fathoms the calamity that lies concealed in the absurd guilelessness and blind confidence of "modern ideas" and even more in the whole Christian-European morality—suffers from an anxiety that is past all comparisons. With a single glance he sees what, given a favorable accumulation and increase of forces and tasks, might yet *be made of man*; he knows with all the knowledge of his conscience how man is still unexhausted for the greatest possibilities and how often the type "man" has already confronted enigmatic decisions and new paths—he knows still better from his most painful memories what wretched things have so far usually broken a being of the highest rank that was in the process of becoming, so that it broke, sank, and became contemptible.

The *over-all degeneration of man* down to what today appears to the socialist dolts and flat-

Friedrich Nietzsche, the disturbing, opaque German critic and philosopher, was contemptuous of modern democracies, and yet had a profound cultural effect upon them.

heads as their "man of the future"—as their ideal—this degeneration and diminution of man into the perfect herd animal (or, as they say, to the man of the "free society"), this animalization of man into the dwarf animal of equal rights and claims, is *possible*, there is no doubt of it. Anyone who has once thought through this possibility to the end knows one kind of nausea that other men don't know—but perhaps also a new *task!*—

W. H. AUDEN
SEPTEMBER 1, 1939

Arguably the greatest poet of his era, Wystan Hugh Auden (1907–1973) was not an ostensibly political figure, yet his very insistence on the importance of the aesthetic—and the autonomy of the aesthetic—is itself a political position, and a profoundly humane and democratic one.

At the beginning of the Second World War, Auden wrote the following poem while in exile in New York from his native England. It remains one of the finest statements of both the artist's independence from politics and his commitment to the world. The poem refers to Nijinsky's remark in his diary: "Some politicians are hypocrites like Diaghilev, who does not want universal love, but to be loved alone. I want universal love." Auden wrote in a letter at the time: "The day war was declared I opened Nijinsky's diary at random (the one he wrote as he was going mad) and read 'I want to cry but God orders me to go on writing. He does not want me to be idle.' And write I do, hoping that it is not only a deceptive form of idleness."

I sit in one of the dives
On Fifty-Second Street
Uncertain and afraid
As the clever hopes expire
Of a low dishonest decade:
Waves of anger and fear
Circulate over the bright
And darkened lands of the earth,
Obsessing our private lives;
The unmentionable odour of death
Offends the September night.

Accurate scholarship can
Unearth the whole offence
From Luther until now
That has driven a culture mad,
Find what occurred at Linz,
What huge imago made
A psychopathic god:
I and the public know
What all schoolchildren learn,
Those to whom evil is done
Do evil in return.

Exiled Thucydides knew
All that a speech can say
About Democracy,
And what dictators do,
The elderly rubbish they talk

To an apathetic grave;
Analysed all in his book,
The enlightenment driven away,
The habit-forming pain,
Mismanagement and grief:
We must suffer them all again.

Into this neutral air
Where blind skyscrapers use
Their full height to proclaim
The strength of Collective Man,
Each language pours its vain
Competitive excuse:
But who can live for long
In an euphoric dream;
Out of the mirror they stare,
Imperialism's face
And the international wrong.

Faces along the bar
Cling to their average day:
The lights must never go out,
The music must always play,
All the conventions conspire
To make this fort assume
The furniture of home;
Lest we should see where we are,
Lost in a haunted wood,
Children afraid of the night

Who have never been happy or good.

The windiest militant trash
Important Persons shout
Is not so crude as our wish:
What mad Nijinsky wrote
About Diaghilev
Is true of the normal heart;
For the error bred in the bone
Of each woman and each man
Craves what it cannot have,
Not universal love
But to be loved alone.

From the conservative dark
Into the ethical life
The dense commuters come,
Repeating their morning vow,
"I *will* be true to the wife,
I'll concentrate more on my work",
And helpless governors wake
To resume their compulsory game:
Who can release them now,
Who can reach the deaf,
Who can speak for the dumb?

All I have is a voice
To undo the folded lie,
The romantic lie in the brain
Of the sensual man-in-the-street
And the lie of Authority
Whose buildings grope the sky:
There is no such thing as the State
And no one exists alone;
Hunger allows no choice
To the citizen or the police;
We must love one another or die.

Defenceless under the night
Our world in stupor lies;
Yet, dotted everywhere,
Ironic points of light
Flash out wherever the Just
Exchange their messages:
May I, composed like them
Of Eros and of dust,
Beleaguered by the same
Negation and despair,
Show an affirming flame.

W. H. Auden, the English poet, dabbled in a range of
politics in his life, but always remained a passionate
defender of the autonomy of the artist in democratic
culture.

GEORGE ORWELL

ENGLAND, YOUR ENGLAND

As Franklin Delano Roosevelt confronted the strains to democracy caused by the Depression in America, the British novelist, essayist, and critic George Orwell (born Eric Arthur Blair, 1903–1950) looked to democratic culture as the only secure bulwark against a drift toward extremism. Orwell's most widely read works are his novels attacking totalitarianism—*Animal Farm* and *Nineteen Eighty-Four*—but his most perceptive democratic polemic often occurred in his journalism. In this essay, written at the height of the London blitz, Orwell muses on the culture that sustains democratic politics in modern England. His analysis is similar to Tocqueville's (page 147), although Orwell holds that English irreligion is a support for democracy. He is also more particularist than Tocqueville. This is no attempt at political science; rather, it is the celebration of a single flourish of democratic life in a small island off the European continent. What Orwell suggests is that each nation's democratic life is different, inseparable from its own culture, history and customs. He is content here to record his own.

. . . But here it is worth noticing a minor English trait which is extremely well marked though not often commented on, and that is a love of flowers. This is one of the first things that one notices when one reaches England from abroad, especially if one is coming from southern Europe. Does it not contradict the English indifference to the arts? Not really, because it is found in people who have no aesthetic feelings whatever. What it does link up with, however, is another English characteristic which is so much a part of us that we barely notice it, and that is the addiction to hobbies and spare-time occupations, the *privateness* of English life. We are a nation of flower-lovers, but also a nation of stamp-collectors, pigeon-fanciers, amateur carpenters, coupon-snippers, darts-players, crossword-puzzle fans. All the culture that is most truly native centres round things which even when they are communal are not official— the pub, the football match, the back garden, the fireside and the "nice cup of tea." The liberty of the individual is still believed in, almost as in the nineteenth century. But this has nothing to do with economic liberty, the right to exploit others for profit. It is the liberty to have a home of your own, to do what you like in your spare time, to choose your own amusements instead of having them chosen for you from above. The most hateful of all names in an English ear is Nosey Parker. It is obvious, of course, that even this purely private liberty is a lost cause. Like all other modern peoples, the English are in process of being numbered, labelled, conscripted, "coordinated." But the pull of their impulses is in the other direction, and the kind of regimentation that can be imposed on them will be modified in consequence. No party rallies, no Youth Movements, no coloured shirts, no Jew-baiting or "spontaneous" demonstrations. No Gestapo either, in all probability.

But in all societies the common people must live to some extent *against* the existing order. The genuinely popular culture of England is something that goes on beneath the surface, unofficially and more or less frowned on by the authorities. One thing one notices if one looks directly at the common people, especially in the big towns, is that they are not puritanical. They are inveterate gamblers, drink as much beer as their wages will permit, are devoted to bawdy jokes, and use probably the foulest language in the world. They have to satisfy these tastes in the face of astonishing, hypocritical laws (licensing laws, lottery acts, etc., etc.) which are designed to interfere with everybody but in practice allow everything to happen. Also, the common people are without definite religious belief, and have been so for centuries. The Anglican Church never had a real hold on them, it was simply a preserve of the landed gentry, and the Nonconformist sects only influenced minorities. And yet they have retained a deep tinge of Christian feeling, while almost forgetting the name of Christ. The power-worship which is the new religion of Europe, and which has infected the English intelligentsia, has never touched the common people. They have never caught up with power politics. The "realism" which is preached in Japanese and Italian newspapers would horrify them. One can learn a good deal about the spirit of England from the comic coloured postcards that you see in the windows of cheap stationers' shops. These things are a sort of diary upon which the English people have unconsciously recorded themselves. Their old-fashioned outlook, their graded snobberies, their mixture of bawdiness and hypocrisy, their extreme gentleness, their deeply moral attitude to life, are all mirrored there.

The gentleness of the English civilization is perhaps its most marked characteristic. You notice it the instant you set foot on English soil. It is a land where the bus conductors are good-tempered and the policemen carry no revolvers. In no country inhabited by white men is it easier to shove people off the pavement. And with this goes something that is always written off by European observers as "decadence" or hypocrisy, the English hatred of war and militarism. It is rooted deep in history, and it is strong in the lower-middle class as well as the working class. Successive wars have shaken it but not destroyed it. Well within living memory it was common for "the redcoats" to be booed at in the street and for the landlords of respectable public-houses to refuse to allow soldiers on the premises. In peacetime, even when there are two million unemployed, it is difficult to fill the ranks of the tiny standing Army, which is officered by the county gentry and a specialized stratum of the middle class, and manned by farm labourers and slum proletarians. The mass of the people are without military knowledge or tradition, and their atti-

tude toward war is invariably defensive. No politician could rise to power by promising them conquests or military "glory," no Hymn of Hate has ever made any appeal to them. In the last war the songs which the soldiers made up and sang of their own accord were not vengeful but humorous and mock-defeatist. The only enemy they ever named was the sergeant-major.

In England all the boasting and flag-wagging, the "Rule Britannia" stuff, is done by small minorities. The patriotism of the common people is not vocal or even conscious. They do not retain among their historical memories the name of a single military victory. English literature, like other literatures, is full of battle-poems, but it is worth noticing that the ones that have won for themselves a kind of popularity are always a tale of disasters and retreats. There is no popular poem about Trafalgar or Waterloo, for instance. Sir John Moore's army at Corunna, fighting a desperate rearguard action before escaping overseas (just like Dunkirk!) has more appeal than a brilliant victory. The most stirring battle-poem in English is about a brigade of cavalry which charged in the wrong direction. And of the last war, the four names which have really engraved themselves on the popular memory are Mons, Ypres, Gallipoli and Passchendaele, every time a disaster. The names of the great battles that finally broke the German armies are simply unknown to the general public.

The reason why the English anti-militarism disgusts foreign observers is that it ignores the existence of the British Empire. It looks like sheer hypocrisy. After all, the English have absorbed a quarter of the earth and held on to it by means of a huge navy. How dare they then turn round and say that war is wicked?

It is quite true that the English are hypocritical about their Empire. In the working class this hypocrisy takes the form of not knowing that the Empire exists. But their dislike of standing armies is a perfectly sound instinct. A navy employs comparatively few people, and it is an external weapon which cannot affect home politics directly. Military dictatorships exist everywhere, but there is no such thing as a naval dictatorship.

What English people of nearly all classes loathe from the bottom of their hearts is the swaggering officer type, the jingle of spurs and the crash of boots. Decades before Hitler was ever heard of, the word "Prussian" had much the same significance in England as "Nazi" has today. So deep does this feeling go that for a hundred years past the officers of the British Army, in peacetime, have always worn civilian clothes when off duty.

One rapid but fairly sure guide to the social atmosphere of a country is the parade-step of its army. A military parade is really a kind of ritual dance, something like a ballet, expressing a certain philosophy of life. The goose-step, for instance, is one of the most horrible sights in the world, far more terrifying than a dive-bomber. It is simply an affirmation of naked power; contained in it, quite consciously and intentionally, is the vision of a boot crashing down on a face. Its ugliness is part of its essence, for what it is saying is "Yes, I *am* ugly, and you daren't laugh at me," like the bully who makes faces at his victim. Why is the goose-step not used in England? There are, heaven knows, plenty of army officers who would be only too glad to introduce some such thing. It is not used because the people in the street would laugh. Beyond a certain point, military display is only possible in countries where the common people dare not laugh at the army. The Italians adopted the goose-step at about the time when Italy passed definitely under German control, and, as one would expect, they do it less well than the Germans. The Vichy government, if it survives, is bound to introduce a stiffer parade-ground discipline into what is left of the French army. In the British army the drill is rigid and complicated, full of memories of the eighteenth century, but without definite swagger; the march is merely a formalized walk. It belongs to a society which is ruled by the sword, no doubt, but a sword which must never be taken out of the scabbard.

And yet the gentleness of English civilization is mixed up with barbarities and anachronisms. Our criminal law is as out of date as the muskets in the Tower. Over against the Nazi Storm Trooper you have got to set that typically English figure, the hanging judge, some gouty old bully with his mind rooted in the nineteenth century, handing out savage sentences. In England people are still hanged by the neck and flogged with the cat-o'-nine-tails. Both of these punishments are obscene as well as cruel, but there has never been any genuinely popular outcry against them. People accept them (and Dartmoor, and Borstal) almost as they accept the weather. They are part of "the law," which is assumed to be unalterable.

Here one comes upon an all-important English trait: the respect for constitutionalism and legality, the belief in "the law" as something above the State and above the individual, something which is cruel and stupid, of course, but at any rate *incorruptible*.

It is not that anyone imagines the law to be just. Everyone knows that there is one law for the rich and another for the poor. But no one accepts the implications of this, everyone takes it for granted that the law, such as it is, will be respected, and feels a sense of outrage when it is not. Remarks like "They can't run me in; I haven't done anything wrong," or "They can't do that; it's against the law," are part of the atmosphere of England. The professed enemies of society have this feeling as strongly as anyone else. One sees it in prison-books like Wilfred Macartney's *Walls Have Mouths* or Jim Phelan's *Jail Journey*, in the solemn idiocies that take place at the trials of conscientious objectors, in letters to the papers from eminent Marxist professors, pointing out that this or that is a "miscarriage of British justice." Everyone believes in his heart that the law can be, ought to be, and on the whole, will be impartially administered. The totalitarian idea that there is no such thing as law, there is only power, has never taken root. Even the intelligentsia have only accepted it in theory.

An illusion can become a half-truth, a mask can alter the expression of a face. The familiar arguments to the effect that democracy is "just the same as" or "just as bad as" totalitarianism never take account of this fact. All such arguments boil down to saying that half a loaf is the same as no bread. In England such concepts as justice, liberty and objective truth are still believed in. They may be illusions, but they are very powerful illusions. The belief in them influences conduct, national life is different because of them. In proof of which, look about you. Where are the rubber truncheons, where is the castor oil? The sword is still in the scabbard, and while it stays there corruption cannot go beyond a certain point. The English electoral system, for instance, is an all-but open fraud. In a dozen obvious ways it is gerrymandered in the interest of the moneyed class. But until some deep change has occurred in the public mind, it cannot become *completely* corrupt. You do not arrive at the polling booth to find men with revolvers telling you which way to vote, nor are the votes miscounted, nor is there any direct bribery. Even hypocrisy is a powerful safeguard. The hanging judge, that evil old man in scarlet robe and horsehair wig, whom nothing short of dynamite will ever teach what century he is living in, but who will at any rate interpret the law according to the books and will in no circumstances take a money bribe, is one of the symbolic figures of England. He is a symbol of the strange mixture of reality and illusion, democracy and privilege, humbug and decency, the subtle network of compromises, by which the nation keeps itself in its familiar shape.

WINSTON CHURCHILL
THE IRON CURTAIN

Winston Churchill's epic life (1874–1965) spanned several generations in politics—from his emergence as a war hero in the Boer War in 1899 to his final stretch as prime minister of Britain from 1951 to 1955. In between, Churchill had been First Lord of the Admiralty in the First World War, Chancellor of the Exchequer in the 1920s, and legendary Prime Minister and war leader from 1940 until 1945. Churchill was a victim of democracy as much as a champion of it. For much of the 1930s he remained excluded from public office by his insistent and unpopular warnings about the menace of Nazi Germany. In 1945, after leading his besieged countrymen and women to victory in the war against Hitler, he was unceremoniously ejected from office in the postwar general election. Yet he was also a quintessential populist and democrat, never flinching from his famous formulation that democracy was the worst of all political systems—except for all the rest.

This speech was made during his second period in political exile. Given in Fulton, Missouri in 1946, Churchill argued in it that Soviet totalitarianism was of the same mold as Nazi totalitarianism. He said that the Western democracies faced a long, difficult struggle against its relentless propaganda and its armed might. Heard more sympathetically in the United States than in Great Britain, this speech may be said to have inaugurated the Cold War. Churchill echoes Pericles in his insistence on the inherent strength of democratic societies. In his unwavering faith in the eventual triumph of democratic ideas and societies over totalitarian ones, Churchill was, once again, prescient. The events of 1989 and 1990, as the Berlin Wall came down and democratic governments began to replace Communist ones in Central and Eastern Europe, seem to have proven him right.

I am glad to come to Westminster College this afternoon, and am complimented that you should give me a degree. The name "Westminster" is somehow familiar to me. I seem to have heard of it before. Indeed, it was at Westminster that I received a very large part of my education in politics, dialectic, rhetoric, and one or two other things. In fact we have both been educated at the same, or similar, or, at any rate, kindred establishments.

It is also an honour, perhaps almost unique, for a private visitor to be introduced to an academic audience by the President of the United States. Amid his heavy burdens, duties, and responsibilities—unsought but not recoiled from—the President has traveled a thousand miles to dignify and magnify our meeting here today and to give me an opportunity of addressing this kindred nation, as well as my own countrymen across the ocean, and perhaps some other countries too. The President has told you that it is his wish, as I am sure it is yours, that I should have full liberty to give my true and faithful counsel in these anxious and baffling times. I shall certainly avail myself of this freedom, and feel the more right to do so because any private ambitions I may have cherished in my younger days have been satisfied beyond my wildest dreams. Let me, however, make it clear that I have no official mission or status of any kind, and that I speak only for myself. There is nothing here but what you see.

I can therefore allow my mind, with the experience of a lifetime, to play over the problems which beset us on the morrow of our absolute victory in arms, and to try to make sure with what strength I have that what has been gained with so much sacrifice and suffering shall be preserved for the future glory and safety of mankind.

The United States stands at this time at the pinnacle of world power. It is a solemn moment for the American Democracy. For with primacy in power is also joined an awe-inspiring accountability to the future. If you look around you, you must feel not only the sense of duty done but also you must feel anxiety lest you fall below the level of achievement. Opportunity is here now, clear and shining for both our countries. To reject it or ignore it or fritter it away will bring upon us all the long reproaches of the after-time. It is necessary that constancy of mind, persistency of purpose and the grand simplicity of decision shall guide and rule the conduct of the English-

speaking peoples in peace as they did in war. We must, and I believe we shall, prove ourselves equal to this severe requirement.

When American military men approach some serious situation they are wont to write at the head of their directive the words "overall strategic concept." There is wisdom in this, as it leads to clarity of thought. What then is the overall strategic concept which we should inscribe today? It is nothing less than the safety and welfare, the freedom and progress, of all the homes and families of all the men and women in all the lands. And here I speak particularly of the myriad cottage or apartment homes where the wage-earner strives amid the accidents and difficulties of life to guard his wife and children from privation and bring the family up in the fear of the Lord, or upon ethical conceptions which often play their potent part.

To give security to these countless homes, they must be shielded from the two giant marauders, war and tyranny. We all know the frightful disturbances in which the ordinary family is plunged when the curse of war swoops down upon the bread-winner and those for whom he works and contrives. The awful ruin of Europe, with all its vanished glories, and of large parts of Asia glares us in the eyes. When the designs of wicked men or the aggressive urge of mighty States dissolve over large areas the frame of civilized society, humble folk are confronted with difficulties with which they cannot cope. For them all is distorted, all is broken, even ground to pulp.

When I stand here this quiet afternoon I shudder to visualize what is actually happening to millions now and what is going to happen in this period when famine stalks the earth. None can compute what has been called "the unestimated sum of human pain." Our supreme task and duty is to guard the homes of the common people from the horrors and miseries of another war. We are all agreed on that. . . .

Now I come to the second danger of these two marauders which threatens the cottage, the home, and the ordinary people—namely, tyranny. We cannot be blind to the fact that the liberties enjoyed by individual citizens throughout the British Empire are not valid in a considerable number of countries, some of which are very powerful. In these States control is enforced upon the common people by various kinds of all-embracing police governments. The power of the State is exercised without restraint, either by dictators or by compact oligarchies operating through a privileged party and a political police. It is not our duty at this time when difficulties are so numerous to interfere forcibly in the internal affairs of countries which we have not conquered in war. But we must never cease to proclaim in fearless tones the great principles of freedom and the rights of man which are the joint inheritance of the English-speaking world and which through Magna Carta, the Bill of Rights, the *Habeas Corpus*, trial by jury, and the English common law find their most famous expression in the American Declaration of Independence.

All this means that the people of any country have the right, and should have the power by constitutional action, by free unfettered elections, with secret ballot, to choose or change the character or form of government under which they dwell; that freedom of speech and thought should reign; that courts of justice, independent of the executive, unbiased by any party, should administer laws which have received the broad assent of large majorities or are consecrated by time and custom. Here are the title deeds of freedom which should lie in every cottage home. Here is the message of the British and American peoples to mankind. Let us preach what we practise—let us practise what we preach. . . .

A shadow has fallen upon the scenes so lately lighted by the Allied victory. Nobody knows what Soviet Russia and its Communist international organization intends to do in the immediate future, or what are the limits, if any, to their expansive and proselytizing tendencies. I have a strong admiration and regard for the valiant Russian people and for my wartime comrade, Marshal Stalin. There is deep sympathy and goodwill in Britain—and I doubt not here also—towards the peoples of all the Russias and a resolve to

Closely associated with the finest hour of the democracies in their twentieth-century battle with totalitarianism, Winston Churchill was himself an aristocrat, whose popularity at home was extremely volatile.

persevere through many differences and rebuffs in establishing lasting friendships. We understand the Russian need to be secure on her western frontiers by the removal of all possibility of German aggression. We welcome Russia to her rightful place among the leading nations of the world. We welcome her flag upon the seas. Above all, we welcome constant, frequent and growing contacts between the Russian people and our own people on both sides of the Atlantic. It is my duty, however, for I am sure you would wish me to state the facts as I see them to you, to place before you certain facts about the present position in Europe.

From Stettin in the Baltic to Trieste in the Adriatic, an iron curtain has descended across the Continent. Behind that line lie all the capitals of the ancient states of Central and Eastern Europe. Warsaw, Berlin, Prague, Vienna, Budapest, Belgrade, Bucharest and Sofia, all these famous cities and the populations around them lie in what I must call the Soviet sphere, and all are subject in one form or another, not only to Soviet influence but to a very high and, in many cases, increasing measure of control from Moscow. Athens alone—Greece with its immortal glories—is free to decide its future at an election under British, American and French observation. The Russian-dominated Polish Government has been encouraged to make enormous and wrongful inroads upon Germany, and mass expulsions of millions of Germans on a scale grievous and undreamed-of are now taking place. The Communist parties, which were very small in all these Eastern States of Europe, have been raised to preeminence and power far beyond their numbers and are seeking everywhere to obtain totalitarian control. Police governments are prevailing in nearly every case, and so far, except in Czechoslovakia, there is no true democracy.

Turkey and Persia [Iran] are both profoundly alarmed and disturbed at the claims which are being made upon them and at the pressure being exerted by the Moscow Government. An attempt is being made by the Russians in Berlin to build up a quasi-Communist party in their zone of Oc-cupied Germany by showing special favours to groups of left-wing German leaders. At the end of the fighting last June, the American and British Armies withdrew westwards, in accordance with an earlier agreement, to a depth at some points of 150 miles upon a front of nearly four hundred miles, in order to allow our Russian allies to occupy this vast expanse of territory which the Western Democracies had conquered.

If now the Soviet Government tries, by separate action, to build up a pro-Communist Germany in their areas, this will cause new serious difficulties in the British and American zones, and will give the defeated Germans the power of putting themselves up to auction between the Soviets and the Western Democracies. Whatever conclusions may be drawn from these facts—and facts they are—this is certainly not the Liberated Europe we fought to build up. Nor is it one which contains the essentials of permanent peace.

The safety of the world requires a new unity in Europe, from which no nation should be permanently outcast. It is from the quarrels of the strong parent races in Europe that the world wars we have witnessed, or which occurred in former times, have sprung. Twice in our own lifetime we have seen the United States, against their wishes and their traditions, against arguments, the force of which it is impossible not to comprehend, drawn by irresistible forces, into these wars in time to secure the victory of the good cause, but only after frightful slaughter and devastation had occurred. Twice the United States has had to send several millions of its young men across the Atlantic to find the war; but now war can find any nation, wherever it may dwell between dusk and dawn. Surely we should work with conscious purpose for a grand pacification of Europe, within the structure of the United Nations and in accordance with its Charter. That I feel is an open cause of policy of very great importance.

In front of the iron curtain which lies across Europe are other causes for anxiety. In Italy the Communist Party is seriously hampered by having to support the Communist-trained Marshal Tito's claims to former Italian territory at the head of the Adriatic. Nevertheless, the future of Italy hangs in the balance. Again one cannot imagine a regenerated Europe without a strong France. All my public life I have worked for a strong France and I never lost faith in her destiny, even in the darkest hours. I will not lose faith now. However, in a great number of countries, far from the Russian frontiers and throughout the world, Communist fifth columns are established and work in complete unity and absolute obedience to the directions they receive from the Communist centre. Except in the British Commonwealth and in the United States where Communism is in its infancy, the Communist parties or fifth columns constitute a growing challenge and peril to Christian civilization. These are sombre facts for anyone to have to recite on the morrow of a victory gained by so much splendid comradeship in arms and in the cause of freedom and democracy; but we should be most unwise not to face them squarely while time remains. . . .

I have felt bound to portray the shadow which, alike in the west and in the east, falls upon the world. I was a high minister at the time of the Versailles Treaty and a close friend of Mr. Lloyd George, who was the head of the British delegation at Versailles. I did not myself agree with many things that were done, but I have a very strong impression in my mind of that situation, and I find it painful to contrast it with that which prevails now. In those days there were high hopes and unbounded confidence that the wars were over, and that the League of Nations would become all-powerful. I do not see or feel that same confidence or even the same hopes in the haggard world at the present time.

On the other hand I repulse the idea that a new war is inevitable; still more that it is imminent. It is because I am sure that our fortunes are still in our own hands and that we hold the power to save the future, that I feel the duty to speak out now that I have the occasion and the opportunity to do so. I do not believe that Soviet Russia desires war. What they desire is the fruits of war and the indefinite expansion of their power and doctrines. But what we have to consider here today while time remains, is the permanent prevention of war and the establishment of conditions of freedom and democracy as rapidly as possible in all countries. Our difficulties and dangers will not be removed by closing our eyes to them. They will not be removed by mere waiting to see what happens; nor will they be removed by a policy of appeasement. What is needed is a settlement, and the longer this is delayed, the more difficult it will be and the greater our dangers will become.

From what I have seen of our Russian friends and Allies during the war, I am convinced that there is nothing they admire so much as strength, and there is nothing for which they have less respect than for weakness, especially military weakness. For that reason the old doctrine of a balance of power is unsound. We cannot afford, if we can help it, to work on narrow margins, offering temptations to a trial of strength. If the Western Democracies stand together in strict adherence to the principles of the United Nations Charter, their influence for furthering those principles will be immense and no one is likely to molest them. If, however, they become divided or falter in their duty and if these all-important years are allowed to slip away then indeed catastrophe may overwhelm us all.

Last time I saw it all coming and cried aloud to my own fellow-countrymen and to the world, but no one paid any attention. Up till the year 1933 or even 1935, Germany might have been saved from the awful fate which has overtaken her and we might all have been spared the miseries Hitler let loose upon mankind. There never was a war in all history easier to prevent by timely action than the one which has just desolated such great areas of the globe. It could have been prevented in my belief without the firing of a single shot, and Germany might be powerful, prosperous and honoured today; but no one would listen and one by one we were all sucked into the awful whirlpool. We surely must not let that happen again. . . .

ISAIAH BERLIN

TWO CONCEPTS OF LIBERTY

The contemporary political philosopher Isaiah Berlin's (1909–   ) 1958 lecture at Oxford University was modestly titled *Two Concepts of Liberty*. It recast the notion of liberty in the Western democratic tradition into two strands: "positive" and "negative" liberty. Positive liberty was described by Berlin as freedom *to* accomplish certain human goals; negative liberty, in contrast, was freedom *from* restraints of a political or social nature that infringe on an individual's autonomy. Both concepts of liberty are, according to Berlin, involved in the notion of democratic life, but the experience of the twentieth century suggests the dangers of positive liberty, of the state's forcing individuals to new levels of "freedom." The essential flaw in this, Berlin argues in this memorable passage, is that it depends upon a certainty of knowledge about the secret of human happiness, the very source of freedom, which is in fact inaccessible to us. Skepticism, he suggests, is at the root of all genuine liberty. Only recognizing the imperfection of personal knowledge allows the ability to grant others liberty to make mistakes. This lecture remains one of the quintessential restatements of the democratic idea in the face of competing totalitarianisms.

One belief, more than any other, is responsible for the slaughter of individuals on the altars of the great historical ideals—justice or progress or the happiness of future generations, or the sacred mission of emancipation of a nation or race or class, or even liberty itself, which demands the sacrifice of individuals for the freedom of society. This is the belief that somewhere, in the past or in the future, in divine revelation or in the mind of an individual thinker, in the pronouncements of history or science, or in the simple heart of an uncorrupted good man, there is a final solution. This ancient faith rests on the conviction that all the positive values in which men have believed must, in the end, be compatible, and perhaps even entail one another. "Nature binds truth, happiness, and virtue together as by an indissoluble chain," said one of the best men who ever lived, and spoke in similar terms of liberty, equality, and justice. But is this true? It is a commonplace that neither political equality nor efficient organization nor social justice is compatible with more than a modicum of individual liberty, and certainly not with unrestricted *laissez-faire*; that justice and generosity, public and private loyalties, the demands of genius and the claims of

society, can conflict violently with each other. And it is no great way from that to the generalization that not all good things are compatible, still less all the ideals of mankind. But somewhere, we shall be told, and in some way, it must be possible for all these values to live together, for unless this is so, the universe is not a cosmos, not a harmony; unless this is so, conflicts of values may be an intrinsic, irremovable element in human life. To admit that the fulfilment of some of our ideals may in principle make the fulfilment of others impossible is to say that the notion of total human fulfilment is a formal contradiction, a metaphysical chimaera. For every rationalist metaphysician, from Plato to the last disciples of Hegel or Marx, this abandonment of the notion of a final harmony in which all riddles are solved, all contradictions reconciled, is a piece of crude empiricism, abdication before brute facts, intolerable bankruptcy of reason before things as they are, failure to explain and to justify, to reduce everything to a system, which "reason" indignantly rejects. But if we are not armed with an *a priori* guarantee of the proposition that a total harmony of true values is somewhere to be found—perhaps in some ideal realm the characteristics of which we can, in our finite state, not so much as conceive—we must fall back on the ordinary resources of empirical observation and ordinary human knowledge. And these certainly give us no warrant for supposing (or even understanding what would be meant by saying) that all good things, or all bad things for that matter, are reconcilable with each other. The world that we encounter in ordinary experience is one in which we are faced with choices between ends equally ultimate, and claims equally absolute, the realization of some of which must inevitably involve the sacrifice of others. Indeed, it is because this is their situation that men place such immense value upon the freedom to choose; for if they had assurance that in some perfect state, realizable by men on earth, no ends pursued by them would ever be in conflict, the necessity and agony of choice would disappear, and with it the central importance of the freedom to choose. Any method of bringing this final state nearer would then seem fully justified, no matter how much freedom were sacrificed to forward its advance. It is, I have no doubt, some such dogmatic certainty that has been responsible for the deep, serene, unshakeable conviction in the minds of some of the most merciless tyrants and persecutors in history that what they did was fully justified by its purpose. I do not say that the ideal of self-perfection—whether for individuals or nations or churches or classes—is to be condemned in itself, or that the language which was used in its defence was in all cases the result of a confused or fraudulent use of words, or of moral or intellectual perversity. Indeed, I have tried to show that it is the notion of freedom in its "positive" sense that is at the heart of the demands for national or social self-direction which animate the most powerful and morally just public movements of our time, and that not to recognize this is to misunderstand the most vital facts and ideas of our age. But equally it seems to me that the belief that some single formula can in principle be found whereby all the diverse ends of men can be harmoniously realized is demonstrably false. If, as I believe, the ends of men are many, and not all of them are in principle compatible with each other, then the possibility of conflict—and of tragedy—can never wholly be eliminated from human life, either personal or social. The necessity of choosing between absolute claims is then an inescapable characteristic of the human condition. This gives its value to freedom as Acton had conceived of it—as an end in itself, and not as a temporary need, arising out of our confused notions and irrational and disordered lives, a predicament which a panacea could one day put right.

I do not wish to say that individual freedom is, even in the most liberal societies, the sole, or even the dominant, criterion of social action. We compel children to be educated, and we forbid public executions. These are certainly curbs to freedom. We justify them on the ground that ignorance, or a barbarian upbringing, or cruel pleasures and excitements are worse for us than the amount of restraint needed to repress them. This judgment in turn depends on how we determine good and evil, that is to say, on our moral, religious, intellectual, economic, and aesthetic values; which are, in their turn, bound up with our conception of man, and of the basic demands of his nature. In other words, our solution of such problems is based on our vision, by which we are consciously or unconsciously guided, of what constitutes a fulfilled human life, as contrasted with Mill's "cramped and warped," "pinched and hidebound" natures. To protest against the laws governing censorship or personal morals as intolerable infringements of personal liberty presupposes a belief that the activities which such laws forbid are fundamental needs of men as men, in a good (or, indeed, any) society. To defend such laws is to hold that these needs are not essential, or that they cannot be satisfied without sacrificing other values which come higher—satisfy deeper needs—than individual freedom, determined by some standard that is not merely subjective, a standard for which some objective status—empirical or *a priori*—is claimed.

The extent of a man's, or a people's, liberty to choose to live as they desire must be weighed against the claims of many other values, of which equality, or justice, or happiness, or security, or public order are perhaps the most obvious examples. For this reason, it cannot be unlimited. We are rightly reminded by R. H. Tawney that the liberty of the strong, whether their strength is physical or economic, must be restrained. This maxim claims respect, not as a consequence of some *a priori* rule, whereby the respect for the liberty of one man logically entails respect for the liberty of others like him; but simply because respect for the principles of justice, or shame at gross inequality of treatment, is as basic in men as the desire for liberty. That we cannot have everything is a necessary, not a contingent, truth. Burke's plea for the constant need to compensate, to reconcile, to balance; Mill's plea for novel "experiments in living" with their permanent possibility of error, the knowledge that it is not merely in practice but in principle impossible to reach clear-cut and certain answers, even in an ideal world of wholly good and rational men and wholly clear ideas—may madden those who seek for final solutions and single, all-embracing systems, guaranteed to be eternal. Nevertheless, it is a conclusion that cannot be escaped by those who, with Kant, have learnt the truth that out of the crooked timber of humanity no straight thing was ever made.

There is little need to stress the fact that monism, and faith in a single criterion, has always proved a deep source of satisfaction both to the intellect and to the emotions. Whether the standard of judgment derives from the vision of some future perfection, as in the minds of the *philosophes* in the eighteenth century and their technocratic successors in our own day, or is rooted in the past—*la terre et les morts*—as maintained by German historicists or French theocrats, or neo-Conservatives in English-speaking countries, it is bound, provided it is inflexible enough, to encounter some unforeseen and unforeseeable human development, which it will not fit; and will then be used to justify the *a priori* barbarities of Procrustes—the vivisection of actual human societies into some fixed pattern dictated by our fallible understanding of a largely imaginary past or a wholly imaginary future. To preserve our

absolute categories or ideals at the expense of human lives offends equally against the principles of science and of history; it is an attitude found in equal measure on the right and left wings in our days, and is not reconcilable with the principles accepted by those who respect the facts.

Pluralism, with the measure of "negative" liberty that it entails, seems to me a truer and more humane ideal than the goals of those who seek in the great, disciplined, authoritarian structures the ideal of "positive" self-mastery by classes, or peoples, or the whole of mankind. It is truer, because it does, at least, recognize the fact that human goals are many, not all of them commensurable, and in perpetual rivalry with one another. To assume that all values can be graded on one scale, so that it is a mere matter of inspection to determine the highest, seems to me to falsify our knowledge that men are free agents, to represent moral decision as an operation which a slide-rule could, in principle, perform. To say that in some ultimate, all-reconciling, yet realizable synthesis, duty *is* interest, or individual freedom *is* pure democracy or an authoritarian state, is to throw a metaphysical blanket over either self-deceit or deliberate hypocrisy. It is more humane because it does not (as the system builders do) deprive men, in the name of some remote, or incoherent, ideal, of much that they have found to be indispensable to their life as unpredictably self-transforming human beings. In the end, men choose between ultimate values; they choose as they do, because their life and thought are determined by fundamental moral categories and concepts that are, at any rate over large stretches of time and space, a part of their being and thought and sense of their own identity; part of what makes them human.

It may be that the ideal of freedom to choose ends without claiming eternal validity for them, and the pluralism of values connected with this, is only the late fruit of our declining capitalist civilization: an ideal which remote ages and primitive societies have not recognized, and one which posterity will regard with curiosity, even sympathy, but little comprehension. This may be so; but no sceptical conclusions seem to me to follow. Principles are not less sacred because their duration cannot be guaranteed. Indeed, the very desire for guarantees that our values are eternal and secure in some objective heaven is perhaps only a craving for the certainties of childhood or the absolute values of our primitive past. "To realise the relative validity of one's convictions," said an admirable writer of our time, "and yet stand for them unflinchingly, is what distinguishes a civilised man from a barbarian." To demand more than this is perhaps a deep and incurable metaphysical need; but to allow it to determine one's practice is a symptom of an equally deep, and more dangerous, moral and political immaturity.

MICHAEL OAKESHOTT
ON HUMAN CONDUCT

Michael Oakeshott (1901–1991) produced two major works in his lifetime, *Experience and its Modes* and *On Human Conduct*, although he is best known for his collection of essays, *Rationalism in Politics*. As a philosopher of politics, his writings on democracy have concentrated on the perils of the schemes constructed by modern democracies to transform society on rational grounds. His alternative to this "rationalism" has not, perhaps, been fully appreciated. It rests on a notion of "civil association," a loose grouping of self-sufficient individuals enjoying self-government under a minimalist interpretation of law. It is one of the most imaginative and elegant modern descriptions of free democratic societies. In this passage from the third essay of *On Human Conduct*, "On the Character of a Modern European State," Oakeshott traces the development of the personality necessary to engage in such a civil association, drawing an intellectual and cultural history of the character most at home in a modern democracy. There are few more graceful accounts of the tradition of European liberty now struggling to be reborn.

. . . A character in which this disposition is strong may exhibit it in a masterful egoism almost as careless of the concerns of some others as it is of their opinions, in a disdain for consequences or recognition, in a compelling versatility of response, or in a gracious or impatient intrusion into the affairs of the less well endowed. But, of course, since what we are considering is intelligent conduct, there is nothing whatever to identify this disposition with self-gratification. Such a character may display it habitually or only on important occasions, but he will always be a somewhat finicky chooser insisting upon doing things his own way. In his capacity for taking the initiative whilst others are laboriously marshalling their resources or seeking supporters, and in his ability to take responsibility upon himself and "to go about his business as if he had not a friend in the world" (as Halifax portrays him), he may be recognized as a useful character to have about the place. Possessing more than others he can afford to lose more without becoming destitute. He is more likely to perish in some quixotic adventure than to die in bed; but, either way, he will have a death of his own as he has a life of his own.

Or this disposition may express itself in a modest and an unaggressive self-reliance, in a man's acquiescence in his own capacity for self-enactment, whatever it may be; and even quite humbly in a man's knowing how to belong to himself and a preference for being related to others in these terms. And it may go along with an undismayed acknowledgement and admiration of the superiority of others, an aristocratic recognition of one's own unimportance, and a humility devoid of humiliation. On the other hand, one who understands himself to be the messenger of a god, to be "illuminated" from above, or to be the voice of destiny, who denies having any thoughts of his own to give meaning to what he does or says, and thus absolves himself from all responsibility for his actions and utterances, is a character of a different sort; he has resigned the character of a human being and has contracted out of the conversation of mankind. He is either an angel or a lunatic.

But further, this disposition or sentiment in favour of self-direction in conduct may be endowed with a more strictly moral character. Self-direction may be recognized not only to be useful, to be a source of considerable happiness, and to make life more interesting or more entertaining for everybody, but to be also an important virtue. And where personal autonomy is thus given a place in a moral practice, conduct will be recognized to have an excellence simply in respect of its authenticity and perhaps to be, in part, justifiable in these terms. In Luther's "*ich kann nicht anders*," the emphasis is upon the *ich* which is not feeling or mere "conscience" but judgement springing from self-understanding, and we have no difficulty in recognizing it as a sketch of a justification for his action. Of course this may be exaggerated into an exclusive moral ideal, excellence in conduct being identified with this authenticity; but this is a corruption which every disposition recognized as a virtue is apt to suffer at the hands of fanatics. And further, personal autonomy has been construed (by Rousseau and others) as a hypothetical organic feeling of self-identity, dissipated in reflective consciousness and unable to survive in conduct *inter homines*, or as the "idiocy" of idiots; and conduct springing from the self-understanding of an intelligent agent is, in consequence, declared to be necessarily unauthentic. But these and other such follies need not detain us.

What we have to do with, then, is a disposition to cultivate the "freedom" inherent in agency, to enjoy individuality, and added to this the disposition readily to concede virtue to this exercise of personal autonomy acquired in self-understanding. And we are concerned with them because this is a historic disposition notable not only in the *mœurs* of modern Europe but also reflected in the character attributed to states and the office attributed to governments.

But it would be a mistake to suppose that it first emerged in modern times. Like anything else in the modern European character this sentiment of individuality appeared there as a modification of the conditions of medieval life and thought. It was not generated in claims and assertions on behalf of individuality but in the gradual and intermittent dissolution, beginning perhaps in the twelfth century, of the self-contained seigneurial estate where choices, performances and responsibilities were circumscribed by an accepted prudential routine, of familiar relationships understood in terms of status and rarely extricated from the analogy of kinship, and of the powerful moral and religious orthodoxy which had been settling upon the Latin Christian world after the period of "conversion" was over. It displayed itself in the persons of younger sons making their own way in a world which had little place for them, of foot-loose adventurers who left the land to take to trade, of town-dwellers who had emancipated themselves from the communal ties of the countryside, of vagabond scholars, in the speculative audacities of Abelard, in venturesome heresy, in the lives of intrepid boys and men who left home to seek their fortunes each intent upon living a life for "a man like me," and in the relationships of men and women. It was reflected in the Latin and vernacular poetry of that memorable spring-time of the European spirit, in the singers and the songs of the Provençal idiom and in the admired characters of the men and women celebrated in the *Chansons de geste*: the proud and reckless *autonomia* of Roland which makes Roncevalles a memorable event in the history of European moral imagination, and the note of his horn an imperishable utterance, echoing down the centuries. And it was expressed in the morality of the Christian Knight (Parzival or Gawain) whose calling it was not to win victories, but to show *triuwe*, fidelity, in every human situation.

The vicissitudes of this disposition in the following centuries make a long and intricate story; not of steady diffusion but of climaxes and recessions, of confidence and apprehension, of extension to activities thitherto untouched by it, of modest and of magnificent endeavours, but of mounting self-consciousness. It emerged in the resuscitated heresy of the Albigenses, and in the Christianity of St. Francis; Burckhardt (who may still be recognized as its most perceptive historian) has described how Italy in the thirteenth century swarmed with serious and trivial expressions of this disposition; it was celebrated heroically in the sagas of the north, dourly in the sordid transactions of the Nibelungen, defiantly in Aucassin's *En paradis qu'ai je à faire?*, and lyrically in the loves of Tristan and Iseult; it was translated by Occam into a philosophical theorem; it was crowned in the crowning of Petrarch in 1341; it is alive in the characters of Boccaccio, and the Canterbury pilgrims of Chaucer are engaging illustrations of the poet's maxim, "let they ghost thee lead"; it is expressed elegiacally in the poems of Villon, with Teutonic seriousness in the Meistersinger of Nuremberg, flamboyantly by Cellini, and profoundly in the devotions of Thomas à Kempis and of St. John of the Cross. It was both evoked and endowed in the extended use of money during these centuries, it was promoted by the disruption occasioned by the bubonic plague, it was parodied in the vast emotional and intellectual chaos of the fifteenth century, it receded before the craft guilds when they imposed corporate organization upon towns which had thitherto been associations of individuals, and the universities were less friendly to it when they became corporations of licensed teachers, servants of a curriculum.

Nevertheless, the early years of modern European history were distinguished by the confidence with which this disposition was embraced, the energy with which its intimations were explored, and the scale of the engagement. Every practical undertaking and every intellectual pursuit revealed itself as an assemblage of opportunities for self-enactment; even religion became once more a matter of choice. With some, no doubt this disposition was all that was left to them after the collapse or the destruction of communal life to which the emergence of states made so considerable a contribution; to pick it up as best they could was to make a virtue of necessity. But they floated on a rising tide; it was a moment when this disposition burned with "a hard gem-like flame" and it received its classic expression in the *Essais* of Montaigne and (more formally) in Charron's *De la sagesse*: a reading of the human condition in which a man's life is understood as an adventure in personal self-enactment. Here there was no promise of salvation for the race or prevision that it would late or soon be gathered into one fold, no anticipation of a near or distant reassemblage of a "truth" fragmented at the creation of the world or expectation that if the human race were to go on researching long enough it will discover "the truth," and no prospect of a redemption in a technological break-through providing a more complete satisfaction of contingent wants; there was only a prompting not to be dismayed at our own imperfections and a recognition that "it is something almost divine for a man to know how to belong to himself" and to live by that understanding. Augustine come again to confound both Gnostics and Pelagians. And these were the lineaments of that *âge d'or* the birth of which Erasmus discerned in the confusions of his time and on which he congratulated the world, little knowing the revulsion it would evoke. . . .

This 1840 painting by Edward Hicks portrays the Continental Congress in the act of approving the Declaration of Independence.

THE AMERICAN EXPERIENCE

★ MASSACHUSETTS BODY OF LIBERTIES

Although the United States of America dates its existence to the beginning of its revolution against Britain more than two centuries ago, the American political and legal tradition has roots that extend far back into the English past. The representative political institutions the Americans created were modelled after the British Parliament. The concept of the rule of law and such protections as the right to trial by a jury of one's peers were likewise brought across the ocean with the first settlers. Britain was the freest country in Europe at the time the colonies were founded, and when the colonists deviated from English practice, it was invariably in the direction of even greater freedom of the individual.

The 1641 Massachusetts "Body of Liberties" was approved by the General Court of the colony a dozen years after the settlement's beginning in 1629, after prolonged and intense discussions in town meetings. It was an entire code of laws, with 98 sections, some with long and complex subpoints within them. Parts of it reflected the fact that the Puritans of Massachusetts believed fervently that theirs was the only true religion. Thus they imposed the death penalty for worship of any god but "the lord god"—as they conceived of him, of course. They prescribed death for witches as well. On the whole, though, their laws were more liberal versions of those already extant in the mother country.

The free fruition of such liberties Immunities and priveledges as humanitie, Civilitie, and Christianitie call for as due to every man in his place and proportion without impeachment and Infringement hath ever bene and ever will be the tranquillitie and Stabilitie of Churches and Commonwealths. And the deniall or deprivall thereof, the disturbance if not the ruine of both.

We hould it therefore our dutie and safetie whilst we are about the further establishing of this Government to collect and expresse all such freedomes as for present we foresee may concerne us, and our posteritie after us, And to ratify them with our sollemne consent. . . .

No mans life shall be taken away, no mans honour or good name shall be stayned, no mans person shall be arested, restrayned, banished, dismembred, nor any wayes punished, no man shall be deprived of his wife or children, no mans goods or estaite shall be taken away from him, nor any way indammaged under coulor of law or Countenance of Authoritie, unlesse it be by vertue or equitie of some expresse law of the Country waranting the same, established by a generall

Court and sufficiently published, or in case of the defect of a law in any parteculer case by the word of god. And in Capitall cases, or in cases concerning dismembring or banishment, according to that word to be judged by the Generall Court.

Every person within this Jurisdiction, whether Inhabitant or forreiner shall enjoy the same justice and law, that is generall for the plantation, which we constitute and execute one towards another without partialitie or delay. . . .

Every man whether Inhabitant or forreiner, free or not free shall have libertie to come to any publique Court, Councel, or Towne meeting, and either by speech or writeing to move any lawfull, seasonable, and materiall question, or to present any necessary motion, complaint, petition, Bill or information, whereof that meeting hath proper cognizance, so it be done in convenient time, due order, and respective manner. . . .

No Conveyance, Deede, or promise whatsoever shall be of validitie, If it be gotten by Illegal violence, imprisonment, threatenings, or any kinde of forcible compulsion called Dures. . . .

No man shall be twise sentenced by Civill Justice for one and the same Crime, offence, or Trespasse. . . .

All Jurors shall be chosen continuallie by the freemen of the Towne where they dwell. . . .

Any Shire or Towne shall have libertie to choose their Deputies whom and where they please for the Generall Court. So be it they be free men, and have taken there oath of fealtie, and Inhabiting in this Jurisdiction. . . .

The Freemen of every Towneship shall have power to make such by laws and constitutions as may concerne the wellfare of their Towne, provided they be not of a Criminall, but onely of a prudentiall nature, And that their penalties exceede not 20 sh. for one offence. And that they be not repugnant to the publique laws and orders of the Countrie. And if any Inhabitant shall neglect or refuse to observe them, they shall have power to levy the appointed penalties by distresse. . . .

If any man at his death shall not leave his wife a competent portion of his estaite, upon just complaint made to the Generall Court she shall be relieved.

Everie marryed woeman shall be free from bodilie correction or stripes by her husband, unlesse it be in his owne defence upon her assalt. If there be any just cause of correction complaint shall be made to Authoritie assembled in some Court, from which onely she shall receive it. . . .

If any servants shall flee from the Tiranny and crueltie of their masters to the howse of any freeman of the same Towne, they shall be there protected and susteyned till due order be taken for their relife. Provided due notice thereof be speedily given to their maisters from whom they fled. And the next Assistant or Constable where the partie flying is harboured. . . .

If any man after legall conviction shall have or worship any other god, but the lord god, he shall be put to death.

If any man or woeman be a witch, (that is hath or consulteth with a familiar spirit,) They shall be put to death. . . .

If any man rise up by false witnes, wittingly and of purpose to take away any mans life, he shall be put to death.

If any man shall conspire and attempt any invasion, insurrection, or publique rebellion against our commonwealth, or shall indeavour to surprize any Towne or Townes, fort or forts therein, or shall treacherously and perfediouslie attempt the alteration and subversion of our frame of politie or Government fundamentallie, he shall be put to death.

All the people of god within this Jurisdiction who are not in a church way, and be orthodox in Judgement, and not scandalous in life, shall have full libertie to gather themselves into a Church Estaite. Provided they doe it in a Christian way, with due observation of the rules of Christ revealed in his word.

Every Church hath full libertie to exercise all the ordinances of god, according to the rules of scripture.

Every Church hath free libertie of Election and ordination of all their officers from time to time, provided they be able, pious and orthodox. . . .

★
THOMAS JEFFERSON
THE DECLARATION OF INDEPENDENCE

When the Declaration of Independence from Britain was approved by the Continental Congress on July 4, 1776, the conflict that we know as the Revolutionary War had already been going on for more than a year. Fighting between the rebels and British authorities had first broken out at Lexington and Concord, Massachusetts, on April 19, 1775, but the

representatives of the thirteen colonies who had joined together in resistance to British rule through the Continental Congress maintained for many months to come that their quarrel was with Parliament rather than the king. They were loyal subjects of King George III, they insisted, who were merely resisting *Parliament's* allegedly unlawful decisions to tax them without representation and deny other of their rights as Englishmen. Shortly after the battles of Lexington and Concord, the Congress passed the Olive Branch Petition, which professed loyalty to the king and begged him to put an end to the oppressive actions of his "cruel" ministers. George III, not surprisingly, took no notice of the petition and proclaimed the colonies to be in a state of rebellion in need of suppression. By July of 1776 the rebels were ready to accept the logic of their earlier actions and to take the radical step of proclaiming the birth of new nation, fully independent from the mother country.

Thomas Jefferson (1743–1826) drafted the Declaration, with the aid of a distinguished committee that included another future President, John Adams, and Benjamin Franklin. Jefferson was a planter's son who had become a member of the Virginia bar in 1767 and was immediately caught up in the excitement of politics in the unfolding revolutionary crisis. He won election to the Virginia House of Burgesses in 1769 and then to the Continental Congress in 1775, where his literary skill won him appointment to the committee to draft the resolution setting forth America's reasons for severing its ties with Britain.

The document justified the actions of the colonists not in terms of the parochial rights of Englishmen but in terms of universal human rights sanctioned by "the laws of Nature and of Nature's God," a claim that would inspire other revolutions against tyrannical rule elsewhere around the globe. Its assertion of the "self-evident" truth that "all men are created equal" resonated through American history down to today.

When in the course of human events, it becomes necessary for one people to dissolve the political bands which have connected them with another, and to assume among the powers of the earth, the separate and equal station to which the laws of Nature and of Nature's God entitle them, a decent respect to the opinions of mankind requires that they should declare the causes which impel them to the separation.

We hold these truths to be self-evident, that all men are created equal, that they are endowed by their Creator with certain unalienable rights, that among these are life, liberty and the pursuit of happiness. That to secure these rights, governments are instituted among men, deriving their just powers from the consent of the governed. That whenever any form of government becomes destructive of these ends, it is the right of the people to alter or to abolish it, and to institute new government, laying its foundation on such principles and organizing its powers in such form, as to them shall seem most likely to effect their safety and happiness. Prudence, indeed, will dictate that governments long established should not be changed for light and transient causes; and accordingly all experience hath shown, that mankind are more disposed to suffer, while evils are sufferable, than to right themselves by abolishing the forms to which they are accustomed. But when a long train of abuses and usurpations, pursuing invariably the same object evinces a design to reduce them under absolute despotism, it is their right, it is their duty, to throw off such government, and to provide new guards for their future security—Such has been the patient sufferance of these colonies; and such is now the necessity which constrains them to alter their former systems of government. The history of the present King of Great Britain is a history of repeated injuries and usurpations, all having in direct object the establishment of an absolute tyranny over these states. To prove this, let facts be submitted to a candid world.

He has refused his assent to laws, the most wholesome and necessary for the public good.

He has forbidden his governors to pass laws of immediate and pressing importance, unless suspended in their operation till his assent should be obtained; and when so suspended, he has utterly neglected to attend to them.

He has refused to pass other laws for the accommodation of large districts of people, unless those people would relinquish the right of representation in the legislature, a right inestimable to them and formidable to tyrants only.

He has called together legislative bodies at places unusual, uncomfortable, and distant from the depository of their public records, for the sole purpose of fatiguing them into compliance with his measures.

He has dissolved representative houses repeatedly, for opposing with manly firmness his invasions on the rights of the people.

He has refused for a long time, after such dissolutions, to cause others to be elected; whereby the legislative powers, incapable of annihilation, have returned to the people at large for their exercise; the state remaining in the mean time exposed to all the dangers of invasion from without, and convulsions within.

He has endeavored to prevent the population of these states; for that purpose obstructing the laws for naturalization of foreigners; refusing to pass others to encourage their migration hither, and raising the conditions of new appropriations of lands.

He has obstructed the administration of justice, by refusing his assent to laws for establishing judiciary powers.

He has made judges dependent on his will alone, for the tenure of their offices, and the amount and payment of their salaries.

He has erected a multitude of new offices, and sent hither swarms of officers to harass our people, and eat out their substance.

He has kept among us, in times of peace, standing armies without the consent of our legislature.

He has affected to render the military independent of and superior to the civil power.

He has combined with others to subject us to a jurisdiction foreign to our constitution, and unacknowledged by our laws; giving his assent to their acts of pretended legislation:

For quartering large bodies of armed troops among us:

For protecting them, by a mock trial, from punishment for any murders which they should commit on the inhabitants of these states:

For cutting off our trade with all parts of the world:

For imposing taxes on us without our consent:

For depriving us in many cases, of the benefits of trial by jury:

For transporting us beyond seas to be tried for pretended offenses:

For abolishing the free system of English laws in a neighboring province, establishing therein an arbitrary government, and enlarging its boundaries so as to render it at once an example and fit instrument for introducing the same absolute rule into these colonies:

For taking away our charters, abolishing our most valuable laws; and altering fundamentally the forms of our governments:

For suspending our own legislatures, and declaring themselves invested with power to legislate for us in all cases whatsoever.

He has abdicated government here, by declaring us out of his protection and waging war against us.

He has plundered our seas, ravaged our coasts, burnt our towns, and destroyed the lives of our people.

He is at this time transporting large armies of foreign mercenaries to complete the works of death, desolation and tyranny, already begun with circumstances of cruelty and perfidy scarcely paralleled in the most barbarous ages, and totally unworthy the head of a civilized nation.

He has constrained our fellow citizens taken captive on the high seas to bear arms against their country, to become the executioners of their friends and brethren, or to fall themselves by their hands.

He has excited domestic insurrections amongst us, and has endeavored to bring on the inhabitants of our frontiers, the merciless Indian savages, whose known rule of warfare, is an undistinguished destruction of all ages, sexes and conditions.

In every stage of these oppressions we have petitioned for redress in the most humble terms. Our repeated petitions have been answered only by repeated injury. A prince, whose character is thus marked by every act which may define a tyrant, is unfit to be the ruler of a free people.

Nor have we been wanting in attention to our British brethren. We have warned them from time to time of attempts by their legislature to extend an unwarrantable jurisdiction over us. We have reminded them of the circumstances of our emigration and settlement here. We have appealed to their native justice and magnanimity, and we have conjured them by the ties of our common kindred to disavow these usurpations,

which would inevitably interrupt our connections and correspondence. They too have been deaf to the voice of justice and of consanguinity. We must, therefore, acquiesce in the necessity, which denounces our separation, and hold them, as we hold the rest of mankind, enemies in war, in peace friends.

We, therefore, the representatives of the united states of America, in General Congress, assembled, appealing to the Supreme Judge of the world for the rectitude of our intentions, do, in the name, and by authority of the good people of these colonies, solemnly publish and declare, that these united colonies are, and of right ought to be free and independent states; that they are absolved from all allegiance to the British Crown, and that all political connection between them and the state of Great Britain, is and ought to be totally dissolved; and that as free and independent states, they have full power to levy war, conclude peace, contract alliances, establish commerce, and to do all other acts and things which independent states may of right do. And for the support of this Declaration, with a firm reliance on the protection of Divine Providence, we mutually pledge to each other our lives, our fortunes and our sacred honor.

ABIGAIL AND JOHN ADAMS

CORRESPONDENCE ON WOMEN'S RIGHTS

Although "man" was used in the Declaration of Independence in a generic sense, meaning people of either sex, no society in the world in 1776 considered females to be autonomous beings with political rights. The family was the basic social unit, and the interests of dependent women and children were to be guarded by its male head. While waiting back home in Massachusetts to hear when the Continental Congress would declare "an independancy," the remarkable Abigail Adams (1744–1818) gently chided her husband John (1735–1826) to "Remember the Ladies" lest they "foment a Rebelion" of their own and refuse to hold themselves "bound by any laws in which we have no voice." Abigail, of course, was not a feminist in the modern sense; she accepted the traditional view of women as "Beings placed by providence" under male "protection." But her spirited independence pointed toward a time when what John called in his reply a "Tribe more numerous and powerfull than all the rest" would indeed grow "discontented" and successfully demand a greater voice.

ABIGAIL to JOHN   March 31, 1776

. . . I long to hear that you have declared an independancy—and by the way in the New Code of Laws which I suppose it will be necessary for you to make I desire you would Remember the Ladies, and be more generous and favourable to them than your ancestors. Do not put such unlimited power into the hands of the Husbands.

Remember all Men would be tyrants if they could. If perticuliar care and attention is not paid to the Laidies we are determined to foment a Rebelion, and will not hold ourselves bound by any laws in which we have no voice, or Representation.

That your Sex are Naturally Tyrannical is a Truth so thoroughly established as to admit of no dispute, but such of you as wish to be happy

These engravings of Abigail Adams, based on a portrait by C. Schessete, and John Adams, based on a painting by Gilbert Stuart, show the couple whose voluminous correspondence reflected all the burning issues of revolutionary America.

willingly give up the harsh title of Master for the more tender and endearing one of Friend. Why, then, not put it out of the power of the vicious and the Lawless to use us with cruelty and indignity with impunity. Men of Sense in all Ages abhor those customs which treat us only as the vassals of your Sex. Regard us then as Beings placed by providence under your protection and in immitation of the Supreme Being make use of that power only for our happiness.

Your ever faithful friend.

JOHN to ABIGAIL   April 14, 1776

. . . As to your extraordinary Code of Laws, I cannot but laugh. We have been told that our Struggle has loosened the bands of Government every where. That Children and Apprentices were disobedient—that schools and Colledges were grown turbulent—that Indians slighted their Guardians and Negroes grew insolent to their Masters. But your Letter was the first Intimation that another Tribe more numerous and powerfull than all the rest were grown discontented.—This is rather too coarse a Compliment but you are so saucy, I wont blot it out.

Depend upon it, We know better than to repeal our Masculine systems. Altho they are in full Force, you know they are little more than Theory. We dare not exert our Power in its full Latitude. We are obliged to go fair, and softly, and in Practice you know We are the subjects. We have only the Name of Masters, and rather than give up this, which would compleatly subject Us to the Despotism of the Peticoat, I hope General Washington, and all our brave Heroes would fight. I am sure every good Politician would plot, as long as he would against Despotism. Empire, Monarchy, Aristocracy, Oligarchy, or Ochlocracy.—A fine Story indeed. I begin to think the Ministry as deep as they are wicked. After stirring up Tories, Landjobbers, Trimmers, Bigots, Canadians, Indians, Negroes, Hanoverians, Hessians, Russians, Irish Roman Catholicks, Scotch Renegadoes, at last they have stimulated the ladies to demand new Priviledges and threaten to rebell.

GEORGE MASON

VIRGINIA BILL OF RIGHTS

When ratification of the proposed federal Constitution was being debated around the country following its drafting at Philadelphia in 1787, its lack of a Bill of Rights was the source of much controversy. In fact, to win the struggle Federalist proponents of ratification had to pledge that a Bill of Rights would be added immediately by the first Congress.

One reason for the initial omission was that most of the states had their own Bills of Rights, like the following one from Virginia. It was widely assumed—and was indeed true for many decades to come—that the effective governance of the country would be largely left to the states and local communities. Spelling out what the federal government could not do to intrude on the life of the individual seemed unnecessary to some, since its powers were limited and its business—carrying out foreign policy, dealing with the Indians, and delivering the mail, mainly—would be so remote from the concerns of the ordinary citizen.

Virginia's declaration was largely the work of George Mason (1725–1792), a close friend of and mentor to both Jefferson and James Madison. Like the Declaration, it sees government as the protector of the natural or inherent rights of people to enjoy "life and liberty," in need of reform, alteration, or abolition when it fails to protect them ade-

quately. Most of the guarantees of the federal Bill of Rights—of freedom of religion and the press, the right to a jury trial and reasonable bail, freedom from self-incrimination, and security against searches without a warrant—are to be found here.

SECTION 1. That all men are by nature equally free and independent, and have certain inherent rights, of which, when they enter into a state of society, they cannot, by any compact, deprive or divest their posterity; namely, the enjoyment of life and liberty, with the means of acquiring and possessing property, and pursuing and obtaining happiness and safety.

SECTION 2. That all power is vested in, and consequently derived from, the people; that magistrates are their trustees and servants, and at all times amenable to them.

SECTION 3. That government is, or ought to be, instituted for the common benefit, protection, and security of the people, nation, or community; of all the various modes and forms of government, that is best which is capable of producing the greatest degree of happiness and safety, and is most effectually secured against the danger of maladministration; and that, when any government shall be found inadequate or contrary to these purposes, a majority of the community hath an indubitable, inalienable, and indefeasible right to reform, alter, or abolish it, in such manner as shall be judged most conducive to the public weal.

SECTION 4. That no man, or set of men, are entitled to exclusive or separate emoluments or privileges from the community, but in consideration of public services; which, not being descendible, neither ought the offices of magistrate, legislator, or judge to be hereditary.

SECTION 5. That the legislative and executive powers of the State should be separate and distinct from the judiciary; and that the members of the two first may be restrained from oppression, by feeling and participating the burdens of the people, they should, at fixed periods, be reduced to a private station . . . and the vacancies be supplied by frequent, certain, and regular elections. . . .

SECTION 6. That elections of members to serve as representatives of the people, in assembly, ought to be free; and that all men, having sufficient evidence of permanent common interest with, and attachment to, the community; have the right of suffrage. . . .

SECTION 7. That all power of suspending laws, or the execution of laws, by any authority, without consent of the representatives of the people, is injurious to their rights, and ought not to be exercised.

SECTION 8. That in all capital or criminal prosecutions a man hath a right to demand the cause and nature of his accusation, to be confronted with the accusers and witnesses, to call for evidence in his favor, and to a speedy trial by an impartial jury . . . ; nor can he be compelled to give evidence against himself; that no man be deprived of his liberty, except by the law of the land or the judgment of his peers.

SECTION 9. That excessive bail ought not to be required, nor excessive fines imposed, nor cruel and unusual punishments inflicted.

SECTION 10. That general warrants, whereby an officer or messenger may be commanded to search suspected places without evidence of a fact committed, or to seize any person or persons not named, or whose offense is not particularly described and supported by evidence, are grievous and oppressive, and ought not to be granted.

SECTION 11. That in controversies respecting property, and in suits between man and man, the ancient trial by jury is preferable to any other. . . .

SECTION 12. That the freedom of the press is one of the great bulwarks of liberty, and can never be restrained but by despotic governments.

SECTION 13. That a well-regulated militia . . . is the proper . . . defense of a free state; that standing armies, in time of peace, should be avoided, as dangerous to liberty; and that in all cases the military should be under strict subordination to, and governed by, the civil power. . . .

SECTION 16. That religion, or the duty which we owe to our Creator, and the manner of discharging it, can be directed only by reason and conviction, not by force or violence; and therefore all men are equally entitled to the free exercise of religion, according to the dictates of conscience; and that it is the mutual duty of all to practice Christian forbearance, love, and charity towards each other.

MASSACHUSETTS SLAVE PETITION

In the years of turmoil leading up to the Revolution, patriots charged again and again that the British were making them "slaves." The Declaration that justified their rebellion to the world out of "a decent respect to the opinions of mankind" stated the self-evident truth that all men are created equal. How, then, could Americans possibly justify continuing to hold almost a fifth of their own people, black Africans, in bondage?

The question was raised by slaves themselves in petitions for freedom that they lodged with the authorities. This one, sent to the Massachusetts legislature in 1777, called their treatment a violation of "Laws of Nature and of Nations" that was particularly unjustifiable because it was inflicted upon them by people who had shown the "spirit to Resent the unjust efforts of others to Reduce them to a state of Bondage and Subjugation." It was hard to deny the truth of the contention that "Every Principle from which America has Acted in the Cours of their unhappy Dificultes with Great Briton Pleads Stronger than A thousand arguments in favours of your petitioners."

The egalitarian impulses generated by the Revolution did bring a quick end to slavery in northern states like Massachusetts, where the practice was not widespread and it did not play an essential role in the economy. In 1783 the Massachusetts Supreme Court struck down slavery as a violation of the state's constitution, and other northern states did likewise through judicial or legislative action.

The same egalitarian impulses that made slavery seem so anomalous in a free society were felt in the South as well, and they led a substantial number of individual planters to set free—to "manumit"—their slaves. George Washington did so in his will, for example. But the institution was the basis of the plantation economy there, and it was never possible to generate white majority support for its elimination. The Revolution thus did not result in the mass abolition of slavery. It did, however, bring about its denationalization. Confining the institution to one particular section of the American polity was a major step down the road toward its elimination, but it would take several decades before that destination was reached.

To the Honorable Counsel & House of [Representa]tives for the State of Massachusetts Bay in General Court assembled, January 13, 1777

The petition of A Great Number of Blackes detained in a State of slavery in the Bowels of a free & Christian Country Humbly sheweth that your Petitioners apprehend that they have in Common with all other men a Natural and Unalienable Right to that freedom which the Grat Parent of the Unavers hath Bestowed equalley on all menkind and which they have Never forfeited by any Compact or agreement whatever—but that wher Unjustly Dragged by the hand of cruel Power from their Derest friends and sum of them Even torn from the Embraces of their tender Parents—from A populous Pleasant and plentiful country and in violation of Laws of Nature and off Nations and in defiance of all the tender feelings of humanity Brough hear Either to Be sold Like Beast of Burthen & Like them Condemnd to Slavery for Life—Among A People Profesing the mild Religion of Jesus A people Not Insensible of the Secrets of Rational Being Nor without spirit to Resent the unjust endeavours of others to Reduce them to a state of Bondage and Subjection your honouer Need not to be informed that A Live of Slavery Like that of your petioners Deprived of Every social privilege of Every thing Requisit to Render Life Tolable is far worse then Nonexistence.

[In imitat]ion of the Lawdable Example of the Good People of these States your petitiononers have Long and Patiently waited the Evnt of petition after petition By them presented to the Legislative Body of this state and cannot but with Grief Reflect that their Sucess hath ben but too similar they Cannot but express their Astonishment that It have Never Bin Consirdered that Every Principle from which Amarica has Acted in the Cours of their unhappy Dificultes with Great Briton Pleads Stronger than A thousand arguments in favours of your petioners they therfor humble Beseech your honours to give this petion its due weight & consideration & cause an act of the Legislatur to be past Wherby they may be Restored to the Enjoyments of that which is the Naturel Right of all men—and their Children who wher Born in this Land of Liberty may not be heald as Slaves after they arive at the age of twenty one years so may the Inhabitance of this Stats No longer chargeable with the inconsistancey of acting themselves the part which they condem and oppose in others Be prospered in their present Glorious struggle for Liberty and have those Blessing to them, &c.

THOMAS JEFFERSON

NOTES ON THE STATE OF VIRGINIA—RELIGION

Although by the time of the Revolution there was a wider degree of toleration for dissenting religious sects in the American colonies than anywhere else in the world, that toleration had developed not so much out of popular support for the principle of religious freedom as out of practical necessity. Immigrants from many different religious backgrounds came to British North America, and colonial governments were generally too weak to force them to adhere to the tenets of the majority religion (although the Puritan colonies of New England did so with some success for most of the seventeenth century). Enforcing a particular religious orthodoxy might repel settlers who would contribute to the growth and prosperity of a settlement. The directors of the Dutch West India Company, who ruled New Netherlands (later known as New York), confronted the issue in 1663 when they ordered that Jews and Quakers be admitted to the colony. "Although we heartily desire that these and other sectarians remained away from there," they said grudgingly, "we very much doubt whether we can proceed rigorously against them without diminishing the population and stopping immigration."

For Thomas Jefferson, a child of the Enlightenment, freedom of religion and of inquiry of all kinds was a positive good, not an unwelcome necessity. Note, though, that he appears to be willing to have the testimony of his neighbor who believes in "twenty gods, or no God" disallowed in Court. The practice of barring testimony from witnesses whose oath on the Bible to tell the truth was suspect on religious grounds continued long after in some states.

The error seems not sufficiently eradicated, that the operations of the mind, as well as the acts of the body, are subject to the coercion of the laws. But our rulers can have authority over such natural rights only as we have submitted to them. The rights of conscience we never submitted, we could not submit. We are answerable for them to our God. The legitimate powers of government extend to such acts only as are injurious to others. But it does me no injury for my neighbour to say there are twenty gods, or no god. It neither picks my pocket nor breaks my leg. If it be said, his testimony in a court of justice cannot be relied on, reject it then, and be the stigma on him. Constraint may make him worse by making him a hypocrite, but it will never make him a truer man. It may fix obstinately in his errors, but will not cure them. Reason and free enquiry are the only effectual agents against error. Give a loose to them, they will support the true religion, by bringing every false one to their tribunal, to the test of their investigation. . . . It is error alone which needs the support of government. Truth can stand by itself. Subject opinion to coercion: whom will you make your inquisitors? Fallible men; men governed by bad passions, by private as well as public reasons. And why subject it to coercion? To produce uniformity. But is uniformity of opinion desireable? No more than of face and stature. Introduce the bed of Procrustes then, and as there is danger that the large men may beat the small, make us all of a size, by lopping the former and stretching the latter. Difference of opinion is advantageous in religion. The several sects perform the office of a *Censor morum* over each other. Is uniformity attainable? Millions of innocent men, women, and children, since the introduction of Christianity, have been burnt, tortured, fined, imprisoned; yet we have not advanced one inch towards uniformity. What has been the effect of coercion? To make one half the world fools, and the other half hypocrites. To support roguery and error all over the earth. Let us reflect that it is inhabited by a thousand millions of people. That these profess probably a thousand different systems of religion. That ours is but one of that thousand. That if there be but one right, and ours that one, we should wish to see the 999 wandering sects gathered into the fold of truth. But against such a majority we cannot effect this by force. Reason and persuasion are the only practicable instruments. To make way for these, free enquiry must be indulged; and how can we wish others to indulge it while we refuse it ourselves.

BENJAMIN FRANKLIN

SPEECH AT THE CONSTITUTIONAL CONVENTION

At the ripe age of 81, Benjamin Franklin (1706–1790) was the oldest man at the Philadelphia Convention, and arguably the wisest one as well. He spoke rarely and briefly, but to great effect. His remarks here, the closing speech at the convention, are in the spirit that would become a defining trait of the American democratic tradition—the spirit of pragmatic compromise rather than ideological utopianism. Few delegates, he conceded, found the proposed Constitution perfect in every detail. For him it was sufficient that the plan for a new frame of government for the nation approached "so near to perfection as it does." Franklin's motion for unanimous approval of the convention's work passed without a dissenting voice.

I confess, that I do not entirely approve of this Constitution at present; but, Sir, I am not sure I shall never approve it; for, having lived long, I have experienced many instances of being obliged, by better information or fuller consideration, to change my opinions even on important subjects, which I once thought right, but found to be otherwise. It is therefore that, the older I grow, the more apt I am to doubt my own judgment of others. Most men, indeed, as well as most sects in religion, think themselves in possession of all truth, and that wherever others differ from them, it is so far error. Steele, a Protestant, in a dedication, tells the Pope, that the only difference between our two churches in their opinions of the certainty of their doctrine, is, the Romish Church is *infallible*, and the Church of England is *never in the wrong*. But, though many private Persons think almost as highly of their own infallibility as of that of their Sect, few express it so naturally as a certain French Lady, who, in a little dispute with her sister, said, "But I meet with nobody but myself that is *always* in the right." *"Je ne trouve que moi qui aie toujours raison."*

In these sentiments, Sir, I agree to this Consti-

In this 1778 lithograph by the French artist Jean Claude Richard de St.-Non, Benjamin Franklin is being crowned by the Goddess Liberty. French enthusiasm for the cause of American independence led to the forging of a French-American alliance that same year, an alliance that provided military support necessary for the victory of the rebellious colonists.

tution, with all its faults,—if they are such; because I think a general Government necessary for us, and there is no *form* of government but what may be a blessing to the people, if well administered; and I believe, farther, that this is likely to be well administered for a course of years, and can only end in despotism, as other forms have done before it, when the people shall become so corrupted as to need despotic government, being incapable of any other. I doubt, too, whether any other Convention we can obtain, may be able to make a better constitution; for, when you assemble a number of men, to have the advantage of their joint wisdom, you inevitably assemble with those men all their prejudices, their passions, their errors of opinion, their local interests, and their selfish views. From such an assembly can a *perfect* production be expected? It therefore astonishes me, Sir, to find this system approaching so near to perfection as it does; and I think it will astonish our enemies, who are waiting with confidence to hear, that our councils are confounded like those of the builders of Babel, and that our States are on the point of separation, only to meet hereafter for the purpose of cutting one another's throats. Thus I consent, Sir, to this Constitution, because I expect no better, and because I am not sure that it is not the best. The opinions I have had of its *errors* I

sacrifice to the public good. I have never whispered a syllable of them abroad. Within these walls they were born, and here they shall die. If every one of us, in returning to our Constituents, were to report the objections he has had to it, and endeavour to gain Partisans in support of them, we might prevent its being generally received, and thereby lose all the salutary effects and great advantages resulting naturally in our favour among foreign nations, as well as among ourselves, from our real or apparent unanimity. Much of the strength and efficiency of any government, in procuring and securing happiness to the people, depends on *opinion*, on the general opinion of the goodness of that government, as well as of the wisdom and integrity of its governors. I hope, therefore, for our own sakes, as a part of the people, and for the sake of our posterity, that we shall act heartily and unanimously in recommending this Constitution, wherever our Influence may extend, and turn our future thoughts and endeavours to the means of having it *well administered.*

On the whole, Sir, I cannot help expressing a wish, that every member of the Convention who may still have objections to it, would with me on this occasion doubt a little of his own infallibility, and to make *manifest* our *unanimity*, put his name to this Instrument.

⭐ THE CONSTITUTION OF THE UNITED STATES OF AMERICA

The Constitution of the United States (without, of course, the 26 amendments that have since been added) was the work of 55 delegates who spent the long hot summer of 1787 in Philadelphia composing it. The meeting at Philadelphia was the result of growing dissatisfaction over the feeble central government provided under the Articles of Confederation, which had been ratified in 1781 to create a loose confederation of the states. It was a government more notable for the powers that it lacked than the powers that it had. It could not tax the states or their citizens; it could only beg state legislatures for appropriations. It could not raise an army, nor regulate commerce, either international or among the states. It had no chief executive, only a committee with little power, and no judicial branch at all. Legislation passed by its Congress required the approval of nine of the thirteen states, and any amendment to alter the Articles needed unanimous backing, making serious modifications almost impossible.

The Philadelphia meeting was called by the Congress to write amendments to the Articles of Confederation, even though it seemed a futile exercise in light of the veto power held by each individual state. Any significant alteration proposed was surely destined to be shot down by at least one dissenter. However, George Washington, James Madison, Benjamin Franklin, Alexander Hamilton, and the other luminaries who gathered there audaciously exceeded their mandate. Instead of tinkering with the Articles, they junked them and wrote a new Constitution from scratch. They failed to meekly submit the new frame of government to the Congress for ratification, as the law seemed to require. Knowing that such a submission was doomed to defeat because of the unanimous approval required for amendments, they instead provided that it should be debated and voted upon in popular conventions in the states, and would go into effect when at least nine of the thirteen former colonies had approved it. Once nine positive votes had been won and the new union was a reality, the other four states would not have a choice of sticking with the existing arrangement any longer. There would be a new central government whether they liked it or not, and their only choices would be to go in or to stay out. Madison offered a powerful justification for this evasion of established procedures. To have a Constitution that was more than the result of haggling back and forth between thirteen often selfish and jealous states, it was necessary to root it in the will of the American people as expressed in popular conventions. The opening words of the Constitution, "We the people of the United States," would thus be truly grounded in a way otherwise impossible.

We the People of the United States, in Order to form a more perfect Union, establish Justice, insure domestic Tranquility, provide for the common defence, promote the general Welfare, and secure the Blessings of Liberty to ourselves and our Posterity, do ordain and establish this Constitution for the United States of America.

Article I.

SECTION 1. All legislative Powers herein granted shall be vested in a Congress of the United States, which shall consist of a Senate and House of Representatives.

SECTION 2. The House of Representatives shall be composed of Members chosen every second Year by the People of the several States, and the Electors in each State shall have the Qualifications requisite for Electors of the most numerous Branch of the State Legislature.

No Person shall be a Representative who shall not have attained to the Age of twenty five Years, and been seven Years a Citizen of the United States, and who shall not, when elected, be an Inhabitant of that State in which he shall be chosen.

Representatives and direct Taxes shall be apportioned among the several States which may be included within this Union, according to their respective Numbers, which shall be determined by adding to the whole Number of free Persons, including those bound to Service for a Term of Years, and excluding Indians not taxed, three fifths of all other Persons. The actual Enumeration shall be made within three Years after the first Meeting of the Congress of the United States, and within every subsequent Term of ten Years, in such Manner as they shall by Law direct. The Number of Representatives shall not exceed one for every thirty Thousand, but each State shall have at Least one Representative; and until such enumeration shall be made, the State of New Hampshire shall be entitled to chuse three, Massachusetts eight, Rhode Island and Providence Plantations one, Connecticut five, New-York six,

New Jersey four, Pennsylvania eight, Delaware one, Maryland six, Virginia ten, North Carolina five, South Carolina five, and Georgia three.

When vacancies happen in the Representation from any State, the Executive Authority thereof shall issue Writs of Election to fill such Vacancies.

The House of Representatives shall chuse their Speaker and other Officers; and shall have the sole Power of Impeachment.

SECTION 3. The Senate of the United States shall be composed of two Senators from each State, chosen by the Legislature thereof, for six Years; and each Senator shall have one Vote.

Immediately after they shall be assembled in Consequence of the first Election, they shall be divided as equally as may be into three Classes. The Seats of the Senators of the first Class shall be vacated at the Expiration of the second Year, of the second Class at the Expiration of the fourth Year, and of the third Class at the Expiration of the sixth Year, so that one third may be chosen every second Year; and if Vacancies happen by Resignation, or otherwise, during the Recess of the Legislature of any State, the Executive thereof may make temporary Appointments until the next Meeting of the Legislature, which shall then fill such Vacancies.

No Person shall be a Senator who shall not have attained to the Age of thirty Years, and been nine Years a Citizen of the United States, and who shall not, when elected, be an Inhabitant of that State for which he shall be chosen.

The Vice President of the United States shall be President of the Senate, but shall have no Vote, unless they be equally divided.

The Senate shall chuse their other Officers, and also a President pro tempore, in the Absence of the Vice President, or when he shall exercise the Office of President of the United States.

The Senate shall have the sole Power to try all Impeachments. When sitting for that Purpose, they shall be on Oath or Affirmation. When the President of the United States is tried the Chief Justice shall preside: And no Person shall be convicted without the Concurrence of two thirds of the Members present.

Judgment in Cases of Impeachment shall not extend further than to removal from Office, and disqualification to hold and enjoy any Office of honor, Trust or Profit under the United States: but the Party convicted shall nevertheless be liable and subject to Indictment, Trial, Judgment and Punishment, according to Law.

SECTION 4. The Times, Places and Manner of holding Elections for Senators and Representatives, shall be prescribed in each State by the Legislature thereof; but the Congress may at any time by Law make or alter such Regulations, except as to the Places of chusing Senators.

The Congress shall assemble at least once in every Year, and such Meeting shall be on the first Monday in December, unless they shall by Law appoint a different Day.

SECTION 5. Each House shall be the Judge of the Elections, Returns and Qualifications of its own Members, and a Majority of each shall constitute a Quorum to do Business; but a smaller Number may adjourn from day to day, and may be authorized to compel the Attendance of absent Members, in such Manner, and under such Penalties as each House may provide.

Each House may determine the Rules of its Proceedings, punish its Members for disorderly Behaviour, and, with the Concurrence of two thirds, expel a Member.

Each House shall keep a Journal of its Proceedings, and from time to time publish the same, excepting such Parts as may in their Judgment require Secrecy; and the Yeas and Nays of the Members of either House on any question shall, at the Desire of one fifth of those Present, be entered on the Journal.

Neither House, during the Session of Congress, shall, without the Consent of the other, adjourn for more than three days, nor to any other Place than that in which the two Houses shall be sitting.

SECTION 6. The Senators and Representatives shall receive a Compensation for their Services, to be ascertained by Law, and paid out of the Treasury of the United States. They shall in all Cases, except Treason, Felony and Breach of the Peace, be privileged from Arrest during their Attendance at the Session of their respective Houses, and in going to and returning from the same; and for any Speech or Debate in either House, they shall not be questioned in any other Place.

No Senator or Representative shall, during the Time for which he was elected, be appointed to any civil Office under the Authority of the United States, which shall have been created, or the Emoluments whereof shall have been encreased during such time; and no Person holding any Office under the United States, shall be a Member of either House during his Continuance in Office.

SECTION 7. All Bills for raising Revenue shall originate in the House of Representatives; but the Senate may propose or concur with amendments as on other Bills.

Every Bill which shall have passed the House of Representatives and the Senate, shall, before it become a Law, be presented to the President of the United States; If he approve he shall sign it, but if not he shall return it, with his Objections to that House in which it shall have originated, who shall enter the Objections at large on their Journal, and proceed to reconsider it. If after such Reconsideration two thirds of that House shall agree to pass the Bill, it shall be sent, together with the Objections, to the other House, by which it shall likewise be reconsidered, and if approved by two thirds of that House, it shall become a Law. But in all such Cases the Votes of both Houses shall be determined by Yeas and Nays, and the Names of the Persons voting for and against the Bill shall be entered on the Journal of each House respectively. If any Bill shall not be returned by the President within ten Days (Sunday excepted) after it shall have been presented to him, the Same shall be a Law, in like Manner as if he had signed it, unless the Congress by their Adjournment prevent its Return, in which Case it shall not be a Law.

Every Order, Resolution, or Vote to which the Concurrence of the Senate and House of Representatives may be necessary (except on a question of Adjournment) shall be presented to the President of the United States; and before the Same shall take Effect, shall be approved by him, or being disapproved by him, shall be repassed by two thirds of the Senate and House of Representatives, according to the Rules and Limitations prescribed in the Case of a Bill.

SECTION 8. The Congress shall have Power To lay and collect Taxes, Duties, Imposts and Excises, to pay the Debts and provide for the common Defence and general Welfare of the United States; but all Duties, Imposts and Excises shall be uniform throughout the United States;

To borrow Money on the credit of the United States;

To regulate Commerce with foreign Nations, and among the several States, and with the Indian Tribes;

To establish an uniform Rule of Naturalization, and uniform Laws on the subject of Bankruptcies throughout the United States;

To coin Money, regulate the Value thereof, and of foreign Coin, and fix the Standard of Weights and Measures;

To provide for the Punishment of counterfeiting the Securities and current Coin of the United States;

To establish Post Offices and post Roads;

To promote the Progress of Science and useful Arts, by securing for limited Times to Authors and Inventors the exclusive Right to their respective Writings and Discoveries;

To constitute Tribunals inferior to the supreme Court;

To define and punish Piracies and Felonies committed on the high Seas, and Offences against the Law of Nations;

To declare War, grant Letters of Marque and Reprisal, and make Rules concerning Captures on Land and Water;

To raise and support Armies, but no Appropriation of Money to that Use shall be for a longer Term than two Years;

To provide and maintain a Navy;

To make Rules for the Government and Regulation of the land and naval Forces;

To provide for calling forth the Militia to execute the Laws of the Union, suppress Insurrections and repel Invasions;

To provide for organizing, arming, and disciplining, the Militia, and for governing such Part of them as may be employed in the Service of the United States, reserving to the States respectively, the Appointment of the Officers, and the Authority of training the Militia according to the discipline prescribed by Congress;

To exercise exclusive Legislation in all Cases whatsoever, over such District (not exceeding ten Miles square) as may, by Cession of particular States, and the Acceptance of Congress, become the Seat of the Government of the United States, and to exercise like Authority over all Places purchased by the Consent of the Legislature of the State in which the Same shall be, for the Erection of Forts, Magazines, Arsenals, dock-Yards, and other needful Buildings;—And

To make all Laws which shall be necessary and proper for carrying into Execution the foregoing Powers, and all other Powers vested by this Constitution in the Government of the United States, or in any Department or Officer thereof.

SECTION 9. The Migration or Importation of such Persons as any of the States now existing shall think proper to admit, shall not be prohibited by the Congress prior to the Year one thousand eight hundred and eight, but a Tax or duty may be imposed on such Importation, not exceeding ten dollars for each Person.

The Privilege of the Writ of Habeas Corpus shall not be suspended, unless when in Cases of Rebellion or Invasion the public Safety may require it.

No Bill of Attainder or ex post facto Law shall be passed.

No Capitation, or other direct, Tax shall be laid, unless in Proportion to the Census or Enumeration herein before directed to be taken.

No Tax or Duty shall be laid on Articles exported from any State.

No Preference shall be given by any Regulation of Commerce or Revenue to the Ports of one State over those of another; nor shall Vessels bound to, or from, one State, be obliged to enter, clear or pay Duties in another.

No Money shall be drawn from the Treasury, but in Consequence of Appropriations made by Law; and a regular Statement and Account of the Receipts and Expenditures of all public Money shall be published from time to time.

No Title of Nobility shall be granted by the United States: And no Person holding any Office of Profit or Trust under them, shall, without the Consent of the Congress, accept of any present, Emolument, Office, or Title, of any kind whatever, from any King, Prince or foreign State.

SECTION 10. No State shall enter into any Treaty, Alliance, or Confederation; grant Letters of Marque and Reprisal; coin Money; emit Bills of Credit; make any Thing but gold and silver Coin a Tender in Payment of Debts; pass any Bill of Attainder, ex post facto Law, or Law impairing the Obligation of Contracts, or grant any Title of Nobility.

No State shall, without the Consent of the Congress, lay any Imposts or Duties on Imports or Exports, except what may be absolutely necessary for executing its inspection Laws: and the net Produce of all Duties and Imposts, laid by any State on Imports or Exports, shall be for the Use of the Treasury of the United States; and all such Laws shall be subject to the Revision and Controul of the Congress.

No State shall, without the Consent of Congress, lay any Duty of Tonnage, keep Troops, or Ships of War in time of Peace, enter into any Agreement or Compact with another State, or with a foreign Power, or engage in War, unless actually invaded, or in such imminent Danger as will not admit of delay.

Article II.

SECTION 1. The executive Power shall be vested in a President of the United States of America. He shall hold his Office during the Term of four Years, and, together with the Vice President, chosen for the same Term, be elected, as follows

Each State shall appoint, in such Manner as the Legislature thereof may direct, a Number of Electors, equal to the whole Number of Senators and Representatives to which the State may be entitled in the Congress: but no Senator or Representative, or Person holding an Office of Trust or Profit under the United States, shall be appointed an Elector.

The Electors shall meet in their respective States, and vote by Ballot for two Persons, of whom one at least shall not be an Inhabitant of the same State with themselves. And they shall make a List of all the Persons voted for, and of the Number of Votes for each; which List they shall sign and certify, and transmit sealed to the Seat of the Government of the United States, directed to the President of the Senate. The President of the Senate shall, in the Presence of the Senate and House of Representatives, open all the Certificates, and the Votes shall then be counted. The Person having the greatest Number of Votes shall be the President, if such Number be a Majority of the whole Number of Electors appointed; and if there be more than one who have such Majority, and have an equal Number of Votes, then the House of Representatives shall immediately chuse by Ballot one of them for President; and if no Person have a Majority, then from the five highest on the List the said House shall in like Manner chuse the President. But in chusing the President, the Votes shall be taken by States, the Representation from each State having one Vote; a quorum for this Purpose shall consist of a Member or Members from two thirds of the States, and a Majority of all the States shall be necessary to a Choice. In every Case, after the Choice of the President, the Person having the greatest Number of Votes of the Electors shall be the Vice President. But if there should remain two or more who have equal Votes, the Senate shall chuse from them by Ballot the Vice President.

The Congress may determine the Time of chusing the Electors, and the Day on which they shall give their Votes; which Day shall be the same throughout the United States.

No Person except a natural born Citizen, or a Citizen of the United States, at the time of the Adoption of this Constitution, shall be eligible to the Office of President; neither shall any Person be eligible to that Office who shall not have attained to the Age of thirty five Years, and been fourteen Years a Resident within the United States.

In Case of the Removal of the President from Office, or of his Death, Resignation, or Inability to discharge the Powers and Duties of the said Office, the Same shall devolve on the Vice President, and the Congress may by Law provide for the Case of Removal, Death, Resignation or Inability, both of the President and Vice President, declaring what Officer shall then act as President, and such Officer shall act accordingly, until the Disability be removed, or a President shall be elected.

The President shall, at stated Times, receive for his Services, a Compensation, which shall neither be encreased nor diminished during the Period for which he shall have been elected, and he shall not receive within that Period any other Emolument from the United States, or any of them.

Before he enter on the Execution of his Office, he shall take the following Oath or Affirmation:—"I do solemnly swear (or affirm) that I will faithfully execute the Office of President of the United States, and will to the best of my Ability, preserve, protect and defend the Constitution of the United States."

SECTION 2. The President shall be Commander in Chief of the Army and Navy of the United States, and of the Militia of the several States, when called into the actual Service of the United States; he may require the Opinion, in writing, of the principal Officer in each of the executive Departments, upon any Subject relating to the Duties of their respective Offices, and he shall have Power to grant Reprieves and Pardons for Offences against the United States, except in Cases of Impeachment.

He shall have Power, by and with the Advice and Consent of the Senate, to make Treaties, provided two thirds of the Senators present concur; and he shall nominate, and by and with the Advice and Consent of the Senate, shall appoint Ambassadors, other public Ministers and Consuls, Judges of the supreme Court, and all other Officers of the United States, whose Appointments are not herein otherwise provided for, and which shall be established by Law: but the Congress may by Law vest the Appointment of such inferior Officers, as they think proper, in the President alone, in the Courts of Law, or in the Heads of Departments.

The President shall have Power to fill up all Vacancies that may happen during the Recess of the Senate, by granting Commissions which shall expire at the End of their next Session.

SECTION 3. He shall from time to time give to the Congress Information of the State of the Union, and recommend to their Consideration such Measures as he shall judge necessary and expedient; he may, on extraordinary Occasions, convene both Houses, or either of them, and in Case of Disagreement between them, with Respect to the Time of Adjournment, he may adjourn them to such Time as he shall think proper; he shall receive Ambassadors and other public Ministers; he shall take Care that the Laws be faithfully executed, and shall Commission all the Officers of the United States.

SECTION 4. The President, Vice President and all Civil Officers of the United States, shall be removed from Office on Impeachment for, and Conviction of, Treason, Bribery, or other high Crimes and Misdemeanors.

Article III.

SECTION 1. The judicial Power of the United States, shall be vested in one supreme Court, and in such inferior Courts as the Congress may from time to time ordain and establish. The Judges, both of the supreme and inferior Courts, shall hold their Offices during good Behaviour, and shall, at stated Times, receive for their Services, a Compensation, which shall not be diminished during their Continuance in Office.

SECTION 2. The judicial Power shall extend to all Cases, in Law and Equity, arising under this Constitution, the Laws of the United States, and Treaties made, or which shall be made, under their Authority;—to all Cases affecting Ambassadors, other public Ministers and Consuls;—to all Cases of admiralty and maritime Jurisdiction;—to Controversies to which the United States shall be a Party;—to Controversies between two or more States;—between a State and Citizens of another State;—between Citizens of different States;—between Citizens of the same State claiming Lands under Grants of different States, and between a State, or the Citizens thereof, and foreign States, Citizens or Subjects.

In all Cases affecting Ambassadors, other public Ministers and Consuls, and those in which a State shall be Party, the Supreme Court shall have original Jurisdiction. In all the other Cases before mentioned, the supreme Court shall have appellate Jurisdiction, both as to Law and Fact, with such Exceptions, and under such Regulations as the Congress shall make.

The Trial of all Crimes, except in Cases of Impeachment, shall be by Jury; and such Trial shall be held in the State where the said Crimes shall have been committed; but when not committed within any State, the Trial shall be at such Place or Places as the Congress may by Law have directed.

SECTION 3. Treason against the United States, shall consist only in levying War against them, or in adhering to their Enemies, giving them Aid and Comfort. No Person shall be convicted of Treason unless on the Testimony of two Witnesses to the same overt Act, or on Confession in open Court.

The Congress shall have Power to declare the Punishment of Treason, but no Attainder of Treason shall work Corruption of Blood, or Forfeiture except during the Life of the Person attainted.

Article IV.

SECTION 1. Full Faith and Credit shall be given in each State to the public Acts, Records, and judicial Proceedings of every other State. And the Congress may by general Laws prescribe the Manner in which such Acts, Records and Proceedings shall be proved, and the Effect thereof.

SECTION 2. The Citizens of each State shall be entitled to all Privileges and Immunities of Citizens in the several States.

A Person charged in any State with Treason,

Felony, or other Crime, who shall flee from Justice, and be found in another State, shall on Demand of the executive Authority of the State from which he fled, be delivered up, to be removed to the State having Jurisdiction of the Crime.

No Person held to Service or Labour in one State, under the Laws thereof, escaping into another, shall, in Consequence of any Law or Regulation therein, be discharged from such Service or Labour, but shall be delivered up on Claim of the Party to whom such Service or Labour may be due.

SECTION 3. New States may be admitted by the Congress into this Union; but no new State shall be formed or erected within the Jurisdiction of any other State; nor any State be formed by the Junction of two or more States, or Parts of States, without the Consent of the Legislatures of the States concerned as well as of the Congress.

The Congress shall have Power to dispose of and make all needful Rules and Regulations respecting the Territory or other Property belonging to the United States; and nothing in this Constitution shall be so construed as to Prejudice any Claims of the United States, or of any particular State.

SECTION 4. The United States shall guarantee to every State in this Union a Republican Form of Government, and shall protect each of them against Invasion; and on Application of the Legislature, or of the Executive (when the Legislature cannot be convened) against domestic Violence.

Article V.

The Congress, whenever two thirds of both Houses shall deem it necessary, shall propose Amendments to this Constitution, or, on the Application of the Legislatures of two thirds of the several States, shall call a Convention for proposing Amendments, which, in either Case, shall be valid to all Intents and Purposes, as Part of this Constitution, when ratified by the Legislatures of three fourths of the several States, or by Conventions in three fourths thereof, as the one or the other Mode of Ratification may be proposed by the Congress; Provided that no Amendment which may be made prior to the Year One thousand eight hundred and eight shall in any Manner affect the first and fourth Clauses in the Ninth Section of the first Article; and that no State, without its Consent, shall be deprived of its equal Suffrage in the Senate.

Article VI.

All Debts contracted and Engagements entered into, before the Adoption of this Constitution, shall be as valid against the United States under this Constitution, as under the Confederation.

This Constitution, and the Laws of the United States which shall be made in Pursuance thereof; and all Treaties made, or which shall be made, under the Authority of the United States, shall be the supreme Law of the Land; and the Judges in every State shall be bound thereby, any Thing in the Constitution or Laws of any State to the Contrary notwithstanding.

The Senators and Representatives before mentioned, and the Members of the several State Legislatures, and all executive and judicial Officers, both of the United States and of the several States, shall be bound by Oath or Affirmation, to support this Constitution; but no religious Test shall ever be required as a Qualification to any Office or public Trust under the United States.

Article VII.

The Ratification of the Conventions of nine States, shall be sufficient for the Establishment of this Constitution between the States so ratifying the Same.

Articles in addition to, and amendment of, the Constitution of the United States of America, proposed by Congress, and ratified by the several states, pursuant to the Fifth Article of the original Constitution.

Amendment I [1791].

Congress shall make no law respecting an establishment of religion, or prohibiting the free exercise thereof; or abridging the freedom of speech, or of the press; or the right of the people peaceably to assemble, and to petition the Government for a redress of grievances.

Amendment II [1791].

A well regulated Militia, being necessary to the security of a free State, the right of the people to keep and bear Arms, shall not be infringed.

Amendment III [1791].

No Soldier shall, in time of peace be quartered in any house, without the consent of the Owner, nor in time of war, but in a manner to be prescribed by law.

Amendment IV [1791].

The right of the people to be secure in their persons, houses, papers, and effects, against unreasonable searches and seizures, shall not be violated, and no Warrants shall issue, but upon probable cause, supported by Oath or affirmation, and particularly describing the place to be searched, and the persons or things to be seized.

Amendment V [1791].

No person shall be held to answer for a capital, or otherwise infamous crime, unless on a presentment or indictment of a Grand Jury, except in cases arising in the land or naval forces, or in the Militia, when in actual service in time of War or public danger; nor shall any person be subject for the same offence to be twice put in jeopardy of life or limb; nor shall be compelled in any criminal case to be a witness against himself, nor be deprived of life, liberty, or property, without due process of law; nor shall private property be taken for public use, without just compensation.

Amendment VI [1791].

In all criminal prosecutions, the accused shall enjoy the right to a speedy and public trial, by an impartial jury of the State and district wherein the crime shall have been committed, which district shall have been previously ascertained by law, and to be informed of the nature and cause of the accusation; to be confronted with the witnesses against him; to have compulsory process for obtaining Witnesses in his favor, and to have the Assistance of Counsel for his defence.

Amendment VII [1791].

In Suits at common law, where the value in controversy shall exceed twenty dollars, the right of trial by jury shall be preserved, and no fact tried by a jury, shall be otherwise re-examined in any Court of the United States, than according to the rules of the common law.

Amendment VIII [1791].

Excessive bail shall not be required, nor excessive fines imposed, nor cruel and unusual punishments inflicted.

Amendment IX [1791].

The enumeration in the Constitution, of certain rights, shall not be construed to deny or disparage others retained by the people.

Amendment X [1791].

The powers not delegated to the United States by the Constitution, nor prohibited by it to the States, are reserved to the States respectively, or to the people.

Amendment XI [1798].

The Judicial power of the United States shall not be construed to extend to any suit in law or equity, commenced or prosecuted against one of the United States by Citizens of another State, or by Citizens or Subjects of any Foreign State.

Amendment XII [1804].

The Electors shall meet in their respective states and vote by ballot for President and Vice-President, one of whom, at least, shall not be an inhabitant of the same state with themselves; they shall name in their ballots the person voted for as President, and in distinct ballots the person voted for as Vice-President, and they shall make distinct lists of all persons voted for as President, and of all persons voted for as Vice-President, and of the number of votes for each, which lists they shall sign and certify, and transmit sealed to the seat of the government of the United States, directed to the President of the Senate;—The President of the Senate shall, in the presence of the Senate and House of Representatives, open all the certificates and the votes shall then be counted;—The person having the greatest number of votes for President, shall be the President, if such number be a majority of the whole number of Electors appointed; and if no person have such majority, then from the persons having the highest numbers not exceeding three on the list of those voted for as President, the House of Representatives shall choose immediately, by ballot, the President. But in choosing the President, the votes shall be taken by states, the representation from each state having one vote; a quorum for this purpose shall consist of a member or members from two-thirds of the states, and a majority of all the states shall be necessary to a choice. And if the House of Representatives shall not choose a President whenever the right of choice shall devolve upon them, before the fourth day of March next following, then the Vice-President shall act as President, as in the case of the death or other constitutional disability of the President—The person having the greatest number of votes as Vice-President, shall be the Vice-President, if such number be a majority of the whole number of Electors appointed, and if no person have a majority, then from the two highest numbers on the list, the Senate shall choose the Vice-President; a quorum for the purpose shall consist of two-thirds of the whole number of Senators, and a majority of the whole number shall be necessary to a choice. But no person constitutionally ineligible to the office of President shall be eligible to that of Vice-President of the United States.

Amendment XIII [1865].

SECTION 1. Neither slavery nor involuntary servitude, except as a punishment for crime whereof the party shall have been duly convicted, shall exist within the United States, or any place subject to their jurisdiction.

SECTION 2. Congress shall have power to enforce this article by appropriate legislation.

Amendment XIV [1868].

SECTION 1. All persons born or naturalized in the United States and subject to the jurisdiction thereof, are citizens of the United States and of the State wherein they reside. No State shall make or enforce any law which shall abridge the privileges or immunities of citizens of the United States; nor shall any State deprive any person of life, liberty, or property, without due process of law; nor deny to any person within its jurisdiction the equal protection of the laws.

SECTION 2. Representatives shall be apportioned among the several States according to their respective numbers, counting the whole number of persons in each State, excluding Indians not taxed. But when the right to vote at any election for the choice of electors for President and Vice President of the United States, Representatives in Congress, the Executive and Judicial officers of a State, or the members of the Legislature thereof, is denied to any of the male inhabitants of such State, being twenty-one years of age, and citizens of the United States, or in any way abridged, except for participation in rebellion, or other crime, the basis of representation therein shall be reduced in the proportion which the number of such male citizens shall bear to the whole number of male citizens twenty-one years of age in such State.

SECTION 3. No person shall be a Senator or Representative in Congress, or elector of President and Vice President, or hold any office, civil or military, under the United States, or under any State, who, having previously taken an oath, as a member of Congress, or as an officer of the United States, or as a member of any State legislature, or as an executive or judicial officer of any State, to support the Constitution of the United States, shall have engaged in insurrection or rebellion against the same, or given aid or comfort to the enemies thereof. But Congress may by a vote of two-thirds of each House, remove such disability.

SECTION 4. The validity of the public debt of the United States, authorized by law, including debts incurred for payment of pensions and bounties for services in suppressing insurrection or rebellion, shall not be questioned. But neither the United States nor any State shall assume or pay any debt or obligation incurred in aid of insurrection or rebellion against the United States, or any claim for the loss of emancipation of any slave; but all such debts, obligations and claims shall be held illegal and void.

SECTION 5. The Congress shall have power to enforce, by appropriate legislation, the provisions of this article.

Amendment XV [1870].

SECTION 1. The right of citizens of the United States to vote shall not be denied or abridged by the United States or by any State on account of race, color, or previous condition of servitude.

SECTION 2. The Congress shall have power to enforce this article by appropriate legislation.

Amendment XVI [1913].

The Congress shall have power to lay and collect taxes on incomes, from whatever source derived, without apportionment among the several States, and without regard to any census or enumeration.

Amendment XVII [1913].

The Senate of the United States shall be composed of two Senators from each State, elected by the people thereof, for six years; and each Senator shall have one vote. The electors in each State shall have the qualifications requisite for electors of the most numerous branch of the State legislatures.

When vacancies happen in the representation of any State in the Senate, the executive authority of such State shall issue writs of election to fill such vacancies: *Provided*, That the legislature of any State may empower the executive thereof to make temporary appointments until the people fill the vacancies by election as the legislature may direct.

This amendment shall not be so construed as to affect the election or term of any Senator chosen before it becomes valid as part of the Constitution.

Amendment XVIII [1919].

SECTION 1. After one year from the ratification of this article the manufacture, sale, or transportation of intoxicating liquors within, the importation thereof into, or the exportation thereof from the United States and all territory subject to the jurisdiction thereof for beverage purposes is hereby prohibited.

SECTION 2. The Congress and the several States shall have concurrent power to enforce this article by appropriate legislation.

SECTION 3. This article shall be inoperative unless it shall have been ratified as an amendment to the Constitution by the legislatures of the several States, as provided in the Constitution, within seven years from the date of the submission hereof to the States by the Congress.

Amendment XIX [1920].

The right of citizens of the United States to vote shall not be denied or abridged by the United States or by any State on account of sex.

Congress shall have power to enforce this article by appropriate legislation.

Amendment XX [1933].

SECTION 1. The terms of the President and Vice President shall end at noon on the 20th day of January, and the terms of Senators and Representatives at noon on the 3d day of January, of the years in which such terms would have ended if this article had not been ratified; and the terms of their successors shall then begin.

SECTION 2. The Congress shall assemble at least once in every year, and such meeting shall begin at noon on the 3d day of January, unless they shall by law appoint a different day.

SECTION 3. If, at the time fixed for the beginning of the term of the President, the President elect shall have died, the Vice President elect shall become President. If a President shall not have been chosen before the time fixed for the beginning of his term, or if the President elect shall have failed to qualify, then the Vice President elect shall act as President until a President shall have qualified; and the Congress may by law provide for the case wherein neither a President elect nor a Vice President elect shall have qualified, declaring who shall then act as President, or the manner in which one who is to act shall be selected, and such person shall act accordingly until a President or Vice President shall have qualified.

SECTION 4. The Congress may by law provide for the case of the death of any of the persons from whom the House of Representatives may choose a President whenever the right of choice shall have devolved upon them, and for the case of the death of any of the persons from whom the Senate may choose a Vice President whenever the right of choice shall have devolved upon them.

SECTION 5. Sections 1 and 2 shall take effect on the 15th day of October following the ratification of this article.

SECTION 6. This article shall be inoperative unless it shall have been ratified as an amendment to the Constitution by the legislatures of three-fourths of the several States within seven years from the date of its submission.

Amendment XXI [1933].

SECTION 1. The eighteenth article of amendment to the Constitution of the United States is hereby repealed.

SECTION 2. The transportation or importation into any State, Territory, or possession of the United States for delivery or use therein of intoxicating liquors, in violation of the laws thereof, is hereby prohibited.

SECTION 3. This article shall be inoperative unless it shall have been ratified as an amendment to the Constitution by conventions in the several States, as provided in the Constitution, within seven years from the date of the submission hereof to the States by the Congress.

Amendment XXII [1951].

SECTION 1. No person shall be elected to the office of the President more than twice, and no person who has held the office of President, or acted as President, for more than two years of a term to which some other person was elected

President shall be elected to the office of the President more than once. But this Article shall not apply to any person holding the office of President when this Article was proposed by the Congress, and shall not prevent any person who may be holding the office of President, or acting as President, during the term within which this Article becomes operative from holding the office of President or acting as President during the remainder of such term.

SECTION 2. This article shall be inoperative unless it shall have been ratified as an amendment to the Constitution by the legislatures of three-fourths of the several States within seven years from the date of its submission to the States by the Congress.

Amendment XXIII [1961].

SECTION 1. The District constituting the seat of Government of the United States shall appoint in such manner as the Congress may direct:

A number of electors of President and Vice President equal to the whole number of Senators and Representatives in Congress to which the District would be entitled if it were a State, but in no event more than the least populous State; they shall be in addition to those appointed by the States, but they shall be considered, for the purposes of the election of President and Vice President, to be electors appointed by a State; and they shall meet in the District and perform such duties as provided by the twelfth article of amendment.

SECTION 2. The Congress shall have power to enforce this article by appropriate legislation.

Amendment XXIV [1964].

SECTION 1. The right of citizens of the United States to vote in any primary or other election for President or Vice President, for electors for President or Vice President, or for Senator or Representative in Congress, shall not be denied or abridged by the United States or any State by reason of failure to pay any poll tax or other tax.

SECTION 2. The Congress shall have power to enforce this article by appropriate legislation.

Amendment XXV [1967].

SECTION 1. In case of the removal of the President from office or of his death or resignation, the Vice President shall become President.

SECTION 2. Whenever there is a vacancy in the office of the Vice President, the President shall nominate a Vice President who shall take office upon confirmation by a majority vote of both Houses of Congress.

SECTION 3. Whenever the President transmits to the President pro tempore of the Senate and the Speaker of the House of Representatives his written declaration that he is unable to discharge the powers and duties of his office, and until he transmits to them a written declaration to the contrary, such powers and duties shall be discharged by the Vice President as Acting President.

SECTION 4. Whenever the Vice President and a majority of either the principal officers of the executive departments or of such other body as Congress may by law provide, transmit to the President pro tempore of the Senate and the Speaker of the House of Representatives their written declaration that the President is unable to discharge the powers and duties of his office, the Vice President shall immediately assume the powers and duties of the office as Acting President.

Thereafter, when the President transmits to the President pro tempore of the Senate and the Speaker of the House of Representatives his written declaration that no inability exists, he shall resume the powers and duties of his office unless the Vice President and a majority of either the principal officers of the executive department or of such other body as Congress may by law provide, transmit within four days to the President pro tempore of the Senate and the Speaker of the House of Representatives their written declaration that the President is unable to discharge the powers and duties of his office. Thereupon Congress shall decide the issue, assembling within forty-eight hours for that purpose if not in session. If the Congress, within twenty-one days after receipt of the latter written declaration, or, if Congress is not in session, within twenty-one days after Congress is required to assemble, determines by two-thirds vote of both Houses that the President is unable to discharge the powers and duties of his office, the Vice President shall continue to discharge the same as Acting President; otherwise, the President shall resume the powers and duties of his office.

Amendment XXVI [1971].

SECTION 1. The right of citizens of the United States, who are eighteen years of age or older, to vote shall not be denied or abridged by the United States or by any State on account of age.

SECTION 2. The Congress shall have power to enforce this article by appropriate legislation.

ALEXANDER HAMILTON, JAMES MADISON AND JOHN JAY
THE FEDERALIST

The Federalist was a series of 85 essays written in defense of the proposed Constitution for a New York newspaper in the winter of 1787–88, and then published in book form. Signed "Publius," the articles were chiefly written by James Madison and Alexander Hamilton, with John Jay responsible for 5. In 1788 Thomas Jefferson called them "the best commentaries on the principles of government . . . ever written," and two centuries later they still rank as the most impressive statements of American political philosophy.

The Federalist No. 9 expresses confidence in a "science of politics" that would guard the new union from the disorders that had plagued republican regimes in the past. It is a useful reminder of what is so easy to forget today—the fact that the framers of the

Constitution were engaged in a risky experiment. It was not yet clear that the pessimists were wrong to maintain that free government was "inconsistent with the order of society."

A firm union will be of the utmost moment to the peace and liberty of the States, as a barrier against domestic faction and insurrection. It is impossible to read the history of the petty republics of Greece and Italy without feeling sensations of horror and disgust at the distractions with which they were continually agitated, and at the rapid succession of revolutions by which they were kept in a state of perpetual vibration between the extremes of tyranny and anarchy. If they exhibit occasional calms, these only serve as short-lived contrasts to the furious storms that are to succeed. . . .

From the disorders that disfigure the annals of those republics the advocates of despotism have drawn arguments, not only against the forms of republican government, but against the very principles of civil liberty. They have decried all free government as inconsistent with the order of society, and have indulged themselves in malicious exultation over its friends and partisans. . . .

But it is not to be denied that the portraits they have sketched of republican government were too just copies of the originals from which they were taken. . . .

The science of politics, however, like most other sciences, has received great improvement. The efficacy of various principles is now well understood, which were either not known at all, or imperfectly known to the ancients. The regular distribution of power into distinct departments; the introduction of legislative balances and checks; the institution of courts composed of judges holding their offices during good behavior; the representation of the people in the legislature by deputies of their own election: these are wholly new discoveries, or have made their principal progress towards perfection in modern times. They are means, and powerful means, by which the excellences of republican government may be retained and its imperfections lessened or avoided. . . .

Perhaps the most famous of these essays, *No. 10*, takes up the argument that free governments will inevitably be torn apart by "faction." How is it possible to prevent some group whose "passions" or "interests" are antithetical to the general welfare from exerting disastrous influence on the whole society? Madison here rejects strategies aimed at wiping out factions altogether, either by destroying the liberty in which they can flourish or by somehow forcing every citizen into the same mold, so that all will have "the same opinions, the same passions, and the same interests." The first of these cures, he states, is worse than the disease; the second is impossible and contrary to "the nature of man."

Factions cannot be eliminated, but Madison argues that under the Constitution they can be controlled. Not so in a pure or direct democracy, however. In a pure democracy the majority itself can be a dangerous faction. What's needed is a republic—a *representative* democracy. In a republic the elected legislators may be expected to have the wisdom to "best discern the true interest of their country," even when the majority temporarily loses sight of them.

In a second argument, Madison attacks the assumption that republics can only work in countries with very small populations. To the contrary, he says. An "extended republic" will have such a wide array of competing factions that it becomes highly unlikely that any one of them can mobilize majority support. "Factious leaders" might be able to "kindle a flame within their particular States," but could never triumph in the Union at large. The broad "extent and proper structure of the Union" thus offered "a republican remedy for the diseases most incident to republican government."

Surprisingly, nowhere does the Constitution mention the institutions that have since become a fundamental part of our democratic order—political parties and the two-party system. "Party," after all, is simply a euphemism for "faction." Paradoxically, it was Madison, along with his friend Jefferson, who took the lead in forming a new political party because of their dissatisfaction with the course of policy in George Washington's administration. (The Democratic–Republican party challenged Washington's chosen successor, John Adams, in the election of 1796, and was successful when Jefferson won the Presidency in 1800.) The idea that competing political parties clarify the alternatives before the electorate and promote national cohesion developed only very slowly, and was not securely established until "the second party system" developed in the 1830s.

Among the numerous advantages promised by a well-constructed Union, none deserves to be more accurately developed than its tendency to break and control the violence of faction. . . .

By a faction, I understand a number of citizens, whether amounting to a majority or minority of the whole, who are united and actuated by some common impulse of passion, or of interest, adverse to the rights of other citizens, or to the permanent and aggregate interests of the community.

There are two methods of curing the mischiefs of faction: the one, by removing its cause; the other, by controlling its effects.

There are again two methods of removing the causes of faction: the one, by destroying the liberty which is essential to its existence; the other, by giving to every citizen the same opinions, the same passions, and the same interests.

It could never be more truly said than of the first remedy, that it was worse than the disease. Liberty is to faction what air is to fire, an aliment without which it instantly expires. But it could not be less folly to abolish liberty, which is essential to political life, because it nourishes faction, than it would be to wish the annihilation of air, which is essential to animal life, because it imparts to fire its destructive agency.

The second expedient is as impracticable as the first would be unwise. As long as the reason of man continues fallible, and he is at liberty to exercise it, different opinions will be formed. As long as the connection subsists between his reason and his self-love, his opinions and his passions will have a reciprocal influence on each other; and the former will be objects to which the latter will attach themselves. The diversity in the faculties of men, from which the rights of property originate, is not less an insuperable obstacle to a uniformity of interests. The protection of these faculties is the first object of government. From the protection of different and unequal faculties of acquiring property, the possession of different degrees and kinds of property immediately results; and from the influence of these on the sentiments and views of the respective proprietors, ensues a division of the society into different interests and parties.

The latent causes of faction are thus sown in the nature of man and we see them everywhere brought into different degrees of activity, according to the different circumstances of civil society. . . .

The inference to which we are brought is, that the *causes* of faction cannot be removed, and that relief is only to be sought in the means of controlling its *effects*.

If a faction consists of less than a majority, relief is supplied by the republican principle, which enables the majority to defeat its sinister views by regular vote. It may clog the administration, it may convulse the society; but it will be unable to execute and mask its violence under the forms of the Constitution. When a majority is included in a faction, the form of popular government, on the other hand, enables it to sacrifice to

A nineteenth-century engraving of James Madison, who is known today as "the father of the U.S. Constitution."

its ruling passion or interest both the public good and the rights of other citizens. To secure the public good and private rights against the danger of such a faction, and at the same time to preserve the spirit and the form of popular government, is then the great object to which our inquiries are directed. . . .

By what means is this object obtainable? . . . A pure democracy, by which I mean a society consisting of a small number of citizens, who assemble and administer the government in person, can admit of no cure for the mischiefs of faction. A common passion or interest will, in almost every case, be felt by a majority of the whole; a communication and concert result from the form of government itself; and there is nothing to check the inducements to sacrifice the weaker party or an obnoxious individual. . . .

A republic, by which I mean a government in which the scheme of representation takes place, opens a different prospect, and promises the cure for which we are seeking. Let us examine the points in which it varies from pure democracy, and we shall comprehend both the nature of the cure and the efficacy which it must derive from the Union.

The two great points of difference between a democracy and a republic are: first, the delegation of the government, in the latter, to a small number of citizens elected by the rest; secondly, the greater number of citizens, and greater sphere of country, over which the latter may be extended.

The effect of the first difference is, on the one hand, to refine and enlarge the public views, by passing them through the medium of a chosen body of citizens, whose wisdom may best discern the true interest of their country, and whose patriotism and love of justice will be least likely to sacrifice it to temporary or partial considerations. . . .

The other point of difference is, the greater number of citizens and extent of territory which may be brought within the compass of republican than of democratic government; and it is this circumstance principally which renders factious combinations less to be dreaded in the former than in the latter. The smaller the society, the fewer probably will be the distinct parties and interests composing it; the fewer the distinct parties and interests, the more frequently will a majority be found of the same party; and the smaller the number of individuals composing a majority, and the smaller the compass within which they are placed, the more easily will they concert and execute their plans of oppression. Extend the sphere and you take in a greater variety of parties and interests; you make it less probable that a majority of the whole will have a common motive to invade the rights of other citizens; or if such a common motive exists, it will be more difficult for all who feel it to discover their own strength, and to act in unison with each other. . . .

Hence, it clearly appears, that the same advantage which a republic has over a democracy, in controlling the effects of faction, is enjoyed by a large over a small republic—is enjoyed by the Union over the States composing it. . . .

The influence of factious leaders may kindle a flame within their particular States, but will be unable to spread a general conflagration through the other States. A religious sect may degenerate into a political faction in a part of the Confederacy; but the variety of sects dispersed over the entire face of it must secure the national councils against any danger from that source. A rage for paper money, for an abolition of debts, for an equal division of property, or for any other improper or wicked project, will be less apt to pervade the whole body of the Union than a particular member of it; in the same proportion as such a malady is more likely to taint a particular county or district, than an entire State.

In the extent and proper structure of the Union, therefore, we behold a republican remedy for the diseases most incident to republican government. And according to the degree of pleasure and pride we feel in being republicans, ought to be our zeal in cherishing the spirit and supporting the character of Federalists.

No. 39 sought to establish that the form of government introduced by the Constitution was "strictly republican," in the sense that it "derives all its powers directly or indirectly from the great body of the people." Madison easily demonstrates that it satisfies that criterion, though when he reaches the fact that federal judges are appointed by the president for life he has to concede that they are the choice of the people only in a "remote" sense of the term.

He then wrestles with a different and very delicate issue raised by the opponents of ratification—the charge that the Constitution created a new national government and destroyed the existing federal system under the Articles government, in which the Union was "a confederacy of sovereign states." It was a shrewd tactic of the supporters of the new Constitution to call themselves "Federalists," and to dub their opponents "Antifederalists." The latter were truly federalists, as the term was then understood. Madison, on the other hand, was an ardent nationalist at this point in his career—although he would change course drastically a few years later—and would have liked an even more centralized and "consolidated" national government than the Constitution provided. However, it would not have been prudent for him to admit that before a New York audience, where the contest over ratification was a close one and Antifederalist fears on the point were strong.

His desire here to stake out what would look like a sensible middle ground leads him into complex and rather slippery arguments. Consent to the Constitution, he notes, is to be given not by the people "as individuals composing one entire nation" but rather "as composing the distinct and independent States to which they respectively belong." In that somewhat strained sense, ratification would be "not a *national* but a *federal* act." (Earlier Madison had argued, in contradiction to this, that the Constitution was to be ratified by the people, rather than by the Articles Congress, so that it would be the expression of "we the people.") The form of representation in the House of Representatives, based upon population, was "national" in character, he had to concede. But the Senate, with an equal voice for each state whatever its size, was apportioned in accord with "federal" principles. The complex system for electing the president (a choice that Madison, like others at the time, assumed would usually be made by the House of Representatives in the absence of a majority decision by the Electoral College) had both national and federal features. The new government would operate more in a national than in a federal fashion. On the other hand, the power of the central government was limited to "certain enumerated objects only," leaving to the states sovereignty over "all other objects." In sum, Madison believes, the Constitution was not quite fish and not quite fowl, neither national nor federal, but "a composition of both." That was, in his mind, a happy medium.

These fine distinctions may seem to us to border on the metaphysical. However, the question of the character of the Union and of the relative power of the federal and state governments was the central issue of constitutional debate in the United States from the ratification of the Constitution to the Civil War, and these issues would crop up again and again in the decades to come.

The last paper having concluded the observations which were meant to introduce a candid survey of the plan of government reported by the convention, we now proceed to the execution of that part of our undertaking.

The first question that offers itself is, whether the general form and aspect of the government be strictly republican. It is evident that no other form would be reconcilable with the genius of the people of America; with the fundamental principles of the Revolution; or with that honorable determination which animates every votary of freedom, to rest all our political experiments on the capacity of mankind for self-government. If the plan of the convention, therefore, be found to depart from the republican character, its advocates must abandon it as no longer defensible.

What, then, are the distinctive characters of the republican form? . . .

If we resort for a criterion to the different principles on which different forms of government are established, we may define a republic to be, or at least may bestow that name on, a government which derives all its powers directly or indirectly from the great body of the people, and is administered by persons holding their offices during pleasure, for a limited period, or during good behavior. It is *essential* to such a government that it be derived from the great body of the society, not from an inconsiderable proportion, or a favored class of it; otherwise a handful of tyrannical nobles, exercising their oppressions by a delegation of their powers, might aspire to the rank of republicans, and claim for their government the honorable title of republic. It is *sufficient* for such a government that the persons administering it be appointed, either directly or indirectly, by the people; and that they hold their appointments by either of the tenures just specified; otherwise every government in the United States, as well as every other popular government that has been or can be well organized or well executed, would be degraded from the republican character. . . .

On comparing the Constitution planned by the convention with the standard here fixed, we perceive at once that it is, in the most rigid sense, conformable to it. The House of Representatives, like that of one branch at least of all the State legislatures, is elected immediately by the great body of the people. The Senate, like the present Congress, and the Senate of Maryland, derives its appointment indirectly from the people. The President is indirectly derived from the choice of the people, according to the example in most of the States. Even the judges with all other officers of the Union, will, as in the several States, be the choice, though a remote choice, of the people themselves. The duration of the appointments is equally conformable to the republican standard, and to the model of State constitutions. . . .

"But it was not sufficient," say the adversaries of the proposed Constitution, "for the convention to adhere to the republican form. They ought, with equal care, to have preserved the *federal* form, which regards the Union as a *Confederacy* of sovereign states; instead of which, they have framed a *national* government, which regards the Union as a *consolidation* of the States." And it is asked by what authority this bold and radical innovation was undertaken? . . .

First. —In order to ascertain the real character of the government, it may be considered in relation to the foundation on which it is to be established; to the sources from which its ordinary powers are to be drawn; to the operation of those powers; to the extent of them; and to the authority by which future changes in the government are to be introduced.

On examining the first relation, it appears, on one hand, that the Constitution is to be founded on "the assent and ratification of the people of America, given by deputies elected for the special purpose; but, on the other, that this assent and ratification is to be given by the people, not as individuals composing one entire nation, but as composing the distinct and independent States to which they respectively belong. It is to be the assent and ratification of the several States, derived from the supreme authority in each State,—the authority of the people themselves. The act, therefore, establishing the Constitution, will not be a *national*, but a *federal* act.

That it will be a federal and not a national act, as these terms are understood by the objectors; the act of the people, as forming so many independent States, not as forming one aggregate nation, is obvious from this single consideration, that it is to result neither from the decision of a *majority* of the people of the Union, nor from that of a *majority* of the States. It must result from the *unanimous* assent of the several States that are parties to it, ...

Each State, in ratifying the Constitution, is considered as a sovereign body, independent of all others, and only to be bound by its own voluntary act. In this relation, then, the new Constitution will, if established, be a *federal*, and not a *national* constitution.

The next relation is, to the sources from which the ordinary powers of government are to be derived. The House of Representatives will derive its powers from the people of America; and the people will be represented in the same proportion, and on the same principle, as they are in the legislature of a particular State. So far the government is *national*, not *federal*. The Senate, on the other hand, will derive its powers from the States, as political and coequal societies;

and these will be represented on the principle of equality in the Senate, as they now are in the existing Congress. So far the government is *federal*, not *national.* The executive power will be derived from a very compound source. The immediate election of the President is to be made by the States in their political characters. The votes allotted to them are in a compound ratio, which considers them partly as distinct and coequal societies, partly as unequal members of the same society. The eventual election, again, is to be made by that branch of the legislature which consists of the national representatives; but in this particular act they are to be thrown into the form of individual delegations, from so many distinct and coequal bodies politic. From this aspect of the government, it appears to be of a mixed character, presenting at least as many *federal* as *national* features.

The difference between a federal and national government, as it relates to the *operation of the government*, is supposed to consist in this, that in the former the powers operate on the political bodies composing the Confederacy, in their political capacities; in the latter, on the individual citizens composing the nation, in their individual capacities. On trying the Constitution by this criterion, it falls under the *national*, not the *federal* character; though perhaps not so completely as has been understood. In several cases, and particularly in the trial of controversies to which States may be parties, they must be viewed and proceeded against in their collective and political capacities only. So far the national countenance of the government on this side seems to be disfigured by a few federal features. But this blemish is perhaps unavoidable in any plan; and the operation of the government on the people, in their individual capacities; in its ordinary and most essential proceedings, may, on the whole, designate it, in this relation, a *national* government.

But if the government be national with regard to the *operation* of its powers, it changes its aspect again when we contemplate it in relation to the extent of its powers. The idea of a national government involves in it, not only an authority over the individual citizens, but an indefinite supremacy over all persons and things, so far as they are objects of lawful government. Among a people consolidated into one nation, this supremacy is completely vested in the national legislature. Among communities united for particular purposes, it is vested partly in the general and partly in the municipal legislatures. In the former case, all local authorities are subordinate to the supreme; and may be controlled, directed, or abolished by it at pleasure. In the latter, the local or municipal authorities form distinct and independent portions of the supremacy, no more subject, within their respective spheres, to the general authority, than the general authority is subject to them, within its own sphere. In this relation, then, the proposed government cannot be deemed a *national* one; since its jurisdiction extends to certain enumerated objects only, and leaves to the several States a residuary and inviolable sovereignty over all other objects. . . .

The proposed Constitution, therefore, is, in strictness, neither a national nor a federal Constitution, but a composition of both. In its foundation it is federal, not national; in the sources from which the ordinary powers of the government are drawn, it is partly federal and partly national; in the operation of these powers, it is national, not federal; in the extent of them, again, it is federal, not national; and, finally, in the authoritative mode of introducing amendments, it is neither wholly federal nor wholly national.

No. 51 sets forth the logic behind the "checks and balances" contained in the Constitution, the features that give each branch of government some power to influence or offset actions taken by those in the other branches. Madison's view of human nature is a skeptical one. He concedes that the need to make ambition "counteract ambition" is an unfortunate reflection on human nature, but so too is the need for government itself. Angels do not need government, but we do, and cannot rely upon one run by angels. In a government "administered by men over men," it is necessary both to "enable the government to control the governed" and then to "oblige it to control itself."

To what expedient, then, shall we finally resort, for maintaining in practice the necessary partition of power among the several departments, as laid down in the Constitution? The only answer that can be given is, that as all these exterior provisions are found to be inadequate, the defect must be supplied, by so contriving the interior structure of the government as that its several constituent parts may, by their mutual relations, be the means of keeping each other in their proper places. . . .

The great security against a gradual concentration of the several powers in the same department, consists in giving to those who administer each department the necessary constitutional means and personal motives to resist encroachments of the others. The provision for defence must in this, as in all other cases, be made commensurate to the danger of attack. Ambition must be made to counteract ambition. The interest of the man must be connected with the constitutional rights of the place. It may be a reflection on human nature, that such devices should be necessary to control the abuses of government. But what is government itself, but the greatest of all reflections on human nature? If men were angels, no government would be necessary. If angels were to govern men, neither external nor internal controls on government would be necessary. In framing a government which is to be administered by men over men, the great difficulty lies in this: you must first enable the government to control the governed; and in the next place oblige it to control itself. A dependence on the people is, no doubt, the primary control on the government; but experience has taught mankind the necessity of auxiliary precautions.

This policy of supplying, by opposite and

rival interests, the defect of better motives, might be traced through the whole system of human affairs, private as well as public. We see it particularly displayed in all the subordinate distributions of power, where the constant aim is to divide and arrange the several offices in such a manner as that each may be a check on the other—that the private interest of every individual may be a sentinel over the public rights. These inventions of prudence cannot be less requisite in the distribution of the supreme powers of the State.

No. 70, written by Alexander Hamilton, deals with one of the hottest issues raised by the new Constitution—its provision for a strong, independent chief executive, the president. The hatred of the royal governors and of King George III that had developed during the revolutionary crisis had resulted in a general distrust of executive leadership in the former colonies. A number of the new state constitutions written in those years made the executive officer so dependent upon the legislature that he played no independent role; Pennsylvania's, in fact, provided for no governor at all. The Articles of Confederation were shaped by the same fears, creating only an executive committee with little power to act.

Hamilton had been one of the most forceful advocates of a strong presidency at the Philadelphia Convention. It was fortunate for his political future that its sessions were closed to the public (all that we know about what transpired comes from the detailed notes Madison kept, which were not made public until 1840). Hamilton was a great admirer of the British system of government, and argued behind closed doors at Philadelphia for a president who would be an "elected monarch" serving a life term, like a Supreme Court Justice. Political realities, of course, required that Hamilton disguise his monarchical sympathies here. He argues that "energy in the executive" is essential to good government, and that the necessary energy cannot be had except by lodging the responsibility in a single person. Legislatures are by definition made up of many voices, and that is appropriate for the functions they serve. The "vigor and expedition" required in the executive branch, especially in the realm of foreign affairs, mandates that it have a single head. The extent of the power over foreign policy given the president by Article II of the Constitution—his command of the armed forces and control over the making of treaties—would inspire much later debate, most recently in the clash between Congress and the Reagan administration over aid to the Nicaraguan *contras* and the War Powers Act, and in Congressional debate on the eve of the Persian Gulf War.

There is an idea, which is not without its advocates, that a vigorous executive is inconsistent with the genius of republican government. The enlightened well-wishers to this species of government must at least hope that the supposition is destitute of foundation; since they can never admit its truth, without, at the same time, admitting the condemnation of their own principles. Energy in the executive is a leading character in the definition of good government. It is essential to the protection of the community against foreign attacks; it is not less essential to the steady administration of the laws, to the protection of property against those irregular and high-handed combinations, which sometimes interrupt the ordinary course of justice, to the security of liberty against the enterprises and assaults of ambition, of faction, and of anarchy. . . .

A feeble executive implies a feeble execution of the government. A feeble execution is but another phrase for a bad execution; and a government ill executed, whatever it may be in theory, must be, in practice, a bad government.

Taking it for granted, therefore, that all men of sense will agree in the necessity of an energetic executive, it will only remain to inquire, what are the ingredients which constitute this energy? How far can they be combined with those other ingredients, which constitute safety in the republican sense? And how far does this combination characterize the plan which has been reported by the convention?

The ingredients which constitute energy in the executive are, unity; duration; an adequate provision for its support; competent powers.

The ingredients which constitute safety in the republican sense are, a due dependence on the people; a due responsibility. . . .

In the legislature, promptitude of decision is oftener an evil than a benefit. The differences of opinion, and the jarrings of parties in that department of the government, though they may sometimes obstruct salutary plans, yet often promote deliberation and circumspection; and serve to check excesses in the majority. When a resolution, too, is once taken, the opposition must be at an end. That resolution is a law, and resistance to it punishable. But no favorable circumstances palliate, or atone for the disadvantages of dissention in the executive department. . . .

They constantly counteract those qualities in the executive, which are the most necessary ingredients in its composition—vigor and expedition; and this without any counterbalancing good. In the conduct of war, in which the energy of the executive is the bulwark of the national security, everything would be to be apprehended from its plurality.

Alexander Hamilton was Madison's great collaborator at the Philadelphia Convention and in writing *The Federalist*, later his bitter enemy as the most ardent and partisan leader of the Federalist party.

THOMAS JEFFERSON

WHAT I LIKE AND DON'T

Thomas Jefferson was conspicuously absent from the Philadelphia Convention because he was serving as American Ambassador to France. He depended upon his close friend Madison to keep him informed of developments. In this letter to Madison he offers his verdict on the final product that emerged from the deliberations. It is interesting, in light of Jefferson's later reputation as a great believer in the wisdom of the people, that he suggests that the popularly elected House of Representatives will be "very illy qualified" to legislate wisely, though he supports the plan on the grounds that taxation should only be imposed by representatives directly chosen by the people, in his mind a "fundamental principle" that outweighs all other considerations.

Jefferson expresses two reservations about the Constitution as written. He argues strongly for the addition of a Bill of Rights, rejecting Pennsylvania delegate James Wilson's argument that it was unnecessary because the new central government would only have powers expressly delegated to it. Such guarantees of rights, Wilson contended, were needed only in the states—the "particular" governments Jefferson refers to— because the states alone could be presumed to have the power to do anything they wanted that was not expressly forbidden them in their constitutions. Jefferson believed that the people were entitled to a bill of rights to protect them against "every government on earth, general or particular." This objection, of course, was rendered moot by the passage of the first ten amendments to the Constitution, approved in the first session of Congress and promptly ratified by the states.

Jefferson's other reservation was that the new government had no requirement for "rotation in office." This had been a feature of the Articles government, which sought to guard against the emergence of a national political elite by making members of Congress subject to annual election and forbidding them from holding office more than three years out of six. Most of the delegates at Philadelphia regarded such compulsory turnover of elected officials to be a source of weakness in need of repair. Jefferson was particularly worried about the prospect that the first president, who was sure to be George Washington, "will always be reelected" and would be "an officer for life." Without a constitutional check of the kind Jefferson would have favored, Washington set a precedent for a two-term presidency by refusing to run again in 1796, one unbroken until Franklin D. Roosevelt was elected to a third term in 1940. The Twenty-Second Amendment, adopted in 1951, made it impossible for the election of another president "for life." Whether there should be limits on terms served in Congress has become a widely debated issue in recent years.

I like much the general idea of framing a government which should go on of itself peaceably, without needing continual recurrence to the state legislatures. I like the organization of the government into Legislative, Judiciary and Executive. I like the power given the Legislature to levy taxes; and for that reason solely approve of the greater house being chosen by the people directly. For tho' I think a house chosen by them will be very illy qualified to legislate for the Union, for foreign nations &c. yet this evil does not weigh against the good of preserving inviolate the fundamental principle that the people are not to be taxed but by representatives cho-sen immediately by themselves. I am captivated by the compromise of the opposite claims of the great and little states, of the latter to equal, and the former to proportional influence. I am much pleased too with the substitution of the method of voting by persons, instead of that of voting by states: and I like the negative given to the Executive with a third of either house, though I should have liked it better had the Judiciary been associated for that purpose, or invested with a similar and separate power. There are other good things of less moment. I will now add what I do not like. First the omission of a bill of rights providing clearly and without the aid of sophisms for freedom of religion, freedom of the press, protection against standing armies, restriction against monopolies, the eternal and unremitting force of the *habeas corpus* laws, and trials by jury in all matters of fact triable by the laws of the land and not by the law of Nations. To say, as Mr. Wilson does that a bill of rights was not necessary because all is reserved in the case of the general government which is not given, while in the particular ones all is given which is not reserved might do for the Audience to whom it was addressed, but is surely *gratis dictum*, opposed by strong inferences from the body of the instrument, as well as from the omission of the clause of our present confederation which had declared that in express terms. It was a hard conclusion to say because there has been no uniformity among the states as to the cases triable by jury, because some have been so incau-tious as to abandon this mode of trial, therefore the more prudent states shall be reduced to the same level of calamity. It would have been much more just and wise to have concluded the other way that as most of the states had judiciously preserved this palladium, those who had wandered should be brought back to it, and to have established general right instead of general wrong. Let me add that a bill of rights is what the people are entitled to against every government on earth, general or particular, and what no just government should refuse, or rest on inference. The second feature I dislike, and greatly dislike, is the abandonment in every instance of the necessity of rotation in office, and most particularly in the case of the President. Experience concurs with reason in concluding that the first magistrate will always be re-elected if the constitution permits it. He is then an officer for life. . . .

THOMAS JEFFERSON
ON THE BILL OF RIGHTS

Jefferson finally succeeded in persuading Madison that a Bill of Rights should be added to the Constitution. Here he expresses satisfaction at Madison's conversion to his point of view, and goes on to review and reject the various arguments that had been made against such a declaration. He concedes that spelling out guarantees of the rights of citizens "may cramp government in its useful exertions." It might be annoying, to take a contemporary example, to have a First Amendment that prevented Congress from enforcing a law banning flag-burning, but that seemed to him a small price to pay. The great danger to liberty, in his view, was "the tyranny of the legislatures." That was a fear shared by Madison, Hamilton, and other Federalists. Hence their willing submission to the demand for the prompt addition to the Constitution of a Bill of Rights.

. . . Your thoughts on the subject of the Declaration of rights in the letter of Oct. 17. I have weighed with great satisfaction. Some of them had not occurred to me before, but were acknoleged just in the moment they were presented to my mind. In the arguments in favor of a declaration of rights, you omit one which has great weight with me, the legal check which it puts into the hands of the judiciary. This is a body, which if rendered independent, and kept strictly to their own department merits great confidence for their learning and integrity. . . . I am happy to find that on the whole you are a friend to this amendment. The Declaration of rights is like all other human blessings alloyed with some inconveniences, and not accomplishing fully it's object. But the good in this instance vastly overweighs the evil. I cannot refrain from making short answers to the objections which your letter states to have been raised. 1. That the rights in question are reserved by the manner in which the federal powers are granted. Answer. A constitutive act may certainly be so formed as to need no declaration of rights. . . .

But in a constitutive act which leaves some precious articles unnoticed, and raises implications against others, a declaration of rights becomes necessary by way of supplement. This is the case of our new federal constitution. This instrument forms us into one state as to certain

A lithograph of Thomas Jefferson shows him pointing to the Declaration of Independence, which he had drafted. A bust of Franklin sits next to it on the table, while to his side and rear are various of Jefferson's inventions.

objects, and gives us a legislative and executive body for these objects. It should therefore guard us against their abuses of power within the field submitted to them. 2. A positive declaration of some essential rights could not be obtained in the requisite latitude. Answer. Half a loaf is better than no bread. If we cannot secure all our rights, let us secure what we can. 3. The limited powers of the federal government and jealousy of the subordinate governments afford a security which exists in no other instance. Answer. The first member of this seems resolvable into the 1st. objection before stated. The jealousy of the subordinate governments is a precious reliance. But observe that those governments are only agents. They must have principles furnished them whereon to found their opposition. The declaration of rights will be the text whereby they will try all the acts of the federal government. In this view it is necessary to the federal government also: as by the same text they may try the opposition of the subordinate governments. 4. Experience proves the inefficacy of a bill of rights. True. But tho it is not absolutely efficacious under all circumstances, it is of great potency always, and rarely inefficacious. A brace the more will often keep up the building which would have fallen with that brace the less. There is a remarkable difference between the characters of the Inconveniencies which attend a Declaration of rights, and those which attend the want of it. The inconveniences of the Declaration are that it may cramp government in it's useful exertions. But the evil of this is shortlived, moderate, and reparable. The inconveniences of the want of a Declaration are permanent, afflicting and irreparable: they are in constant progression from bad to worse. The executive in our governments is not the sole, it is scarcely the principal object of my jealousy. The tyranny of the legislatures is the most formidable dread at present, and will be for long years. . . .

GEORGE WASHINGTON
FAREWELL ADDRESS

George Washington (1732–1799) was a wealthy Virginia planter who acquired extensive military experience fighting for the British during the French and Indian War of 1754–1763. A key member of the Virginia House of Burgesses, he was elected to the First Continental Congress in 1774, and was the obvious choice to be the commander of American forces when the Revolutionary War broke out. He resigned from the army when peace came in 1783, but was so distressed at the weakness of the central government under the Articles of Confederation that he lent his enormous prestige to the drive for reform that led to the drafting of a new national constitution at Philadelphia in 1787. He was the consensus choice to preside over the Philadelphia convention and, in the elections that followed popular ratification of the Constitution, was elected without opposition as the first President of the United States.

In his last major address, President Washington offered an emphatic warning against tinkering with the Constitution in a way that might "impair the energy of the system." "Experience" was the true test of whether the new system would work, and it should be left to "time and habit" to determine whether or not fundamental alterations in the future would be wise.

Washington's greatest fear was the emerging "Spirit of Party." Although Washington felt himself to be above party, he could hardly fail to notice that Hamilton and John Adams, on the one side, and Madison and Jefferson on the other, clearly considered themselves members of opposing camps. One key point of disagreement concerned the major war Britain and France had been engaged in since 1793. There was bitter internal division over whether the U.S. should stay out of the conflict and quietly side with the British, as Hamilton and Adams preferred, or tilt in favor of France—then a revolutionary republic, soon to be transformed into a dictatorship under Napoleon. Jefferson and Madison were much more sympathetic to France, and sharply opposed the pro-British Jay Treaty of 1795 that the Washington administration had negotiated. Although the Federalists were every bit as partisan as the Jeffersonians, it is always easier for the party in power to proclaim that it represents not the views of a particular faction or party but merely the national interest. Here, Washington does concede that parties can serve some positive functions in free countries, but he is far more impressed with their dangers. He particularly worries that party ties could undermine the separation of powers and checks and balances built into the Constitution. For instance, Republican legislators and Republican judges might show undue deference to a Republican president, acting more in accord with their partisan allegiances than their duty to act independently in the sphere that belonged to them.

Finally, Washington makes an argument that runs against the grain of *The Federalist No. 9*'s optimistic boast about understanding "the new science of politics," though he does not make the point explicitly. The best possible formal political arrangements, he suggests, would not be enough to preserve free government without certain preconditions. "Religion and morality," he asserts, are inseparably intertwined, and are "the firmest props" of good government. Virtue and morality, in turn, depend upon "the general diffusion of knowledge" so that "public opinion will be enlightened." If true, this argument has sobering implications in a secular age.

. . . Resist with care the spirit of innovation upon its principles however specious the pretexts, one method of assault may be to effect, in the forms of the Constitution, alterations which will impair the energy of the system, and thus to undermine what cannot be directly overthrown. In all the changes to which you may be invited, remember that time and habit are at least as necessary to fix the true character of Governments, as of other human institutions; that experience is the surest standard, by which to test the real tendency of the existing Constitution of a country; that facility in changes upon the credit of mere hypotheses and opinion exposes to perpetual change, from the endless variety of hypotheses and opinion: and remember, especially, that for the efficient management of your common interests, in a country so extensive as ours, a Government of as much vigour as is consistent with the perfect security of Liberty is indispensable. Liberty itself will find in such a Government, with powers properly distributed and adjusted, its surest Guardian. It is indeed little else than a name, where the Government is too feeble to withstand the enterprises of faction, to confine each member of the Society within the limits prescribed by the laws and to maintain all in the secure and tranquil enjoyment of the rights of person and property.

I have already intimated to you the danger of Parties in the State, with particular reference to the founding of them on Geographical discriminations. Let me now take a more comprehensive view, and warn you in the most solemn manner against the baneful effects of the Spirit of Party, generally.

This spirit, unfortunately, is inseperable from our nature, having its root in the strongest passions of the human Mind. It exists under different shapes in all Governments, more or less stifled, controuled, or repressed; but, in those of the popular form it is seen in its greatest rankness and is truly their worst enemy.

The alternate domination of one faction over

This printed kerchief showing George Washington and his horse was produced for the celebration of the Centennial of the Declaration of Independence in 1876.

entirely out of sight) the common and continual mischiefs of the spirit of Party are sufficient to make it the interest and the duty of a wise People to discourage and restrain it.

It serves always to distract the Public Councils and enfeeble the Public administration. It agitates the Community with ill founded jealousies and false alarms, kindles the animosity of one part against another, foments occasionally riot and insurrection. It opens the door to foreign influence and corruption, which find a facilitated access to the government itself through the channels of party passions. Thus the policy and the will of one country, are subjected to the policy and will of another.

There is an opinion that parties in free countries are useful checks upon the Administration of the Government and serve to keep alive the spirit of Liberty. This within certain limits is probably true, and in Governments of a Monarchical cast Patriotism may look with endulgence, if not with favour, upon the spirit of party. But in those of the popular character, in Governments purely elective, it is a spirit not to be encouraged. From their natural tendency, it is certain there will always be enough of that spirit for every salutary purpose. And there being constant danger of excess, the effort ought to be, by force of public opinion, to mitigate and assuage it. A fire not to be quenched; it demands a uniform vigilance to prevent its bursting into a flame, lest instead of warming it should consume.

It is important, likewise, that the habits of thinking in a free Country should inspire caution in those entrusted with its administration, to confine themselves within their respective Constitutional spheres; avoiding in the exercise of the Powers of one department to encroach upon another. The spirit of encroachment tends to consolidate the powers of all the departments in one, and thus to create whatever the form of government, a real despotism. A just estimate of that love of power, and proneness to abuse it, which predominates in the human heart is sufficient to satisfy us of the truth of this position. The necessity of reciprocal checks in the exercise of political power; by dividing and distributing it

another, sharpened by the spirit of revenge natural to party dissention, which in different ages and countries has perpetrated the most horrid enormities, is itself a frightful despotism. But this leads at length to a more formal and permanent despotism. The disorders and miseries, which result, gradually incline the minds of men to seek security and repose in the absolute power of an Individual: and sooner or later the chief of some prevailing faction more able or more fortunate than his competitors, turns this disposition to the purposes of his own elevation, on the ruins of Public Liberty.

Without looking forward to an extremity of this kind (which nevertheless ought not to be into different depositories, and constituting each the Guardian of the Public Weal against invasions by the others, has been evinced by experiments ancient and modern; some of them in our country and under our own eyes. To preserve them must be as necessary as to institute them. If in the opinion of the People, the distribution or modification of the Constitutional powers be in any particular wrong, let it be corrected by an amendment in the way which the Constitution designates. But let there be no change by usurpation; for though this, in one instance, may be the instrument of good, it is the customary weapon by which free governments are destroyed. The precedent must always greatly overbalance in permanent evil any partial or transient benefit which the use can at any time yield.

Of all the dispositions and habits which lead to political prosperity, Religion and morality are indispensable supports. In vain would that man claim the tribute of Patriotism, who should labour to subvert these great Pillars of human happiness, these firmest props of the duties of Men and citizens. The mere Politician, equally with the pious man ought to respect and to cherish them. A volume could not trace all their connections with private and public felicity. Let it simply be asked where is the security for property, for reputation, for life, if the sense of religious obligation desert the oaths, which are the instruments of investigation in Courts of Justice? And let us with caution indulge the supposition, that morality can be maintained without religion. Whatever may be conceded to the influence of refined education on minds of peculiar structure, reason and experience both forbid us to expect that National morality can prevail in exclusion of religious principle.

'Tis substantially true, that virtue or morality is a necessary spring of popular government. The rule indeed extends with more or less force to every species of free Government. Who that is a sincere friend to it, can look with indifference upon attempts to shake the foundation of the fabric.

Promote then as an object of primary importance, Institutions for the general diffusion of knowledge. In proportion as the structure of a government gives force to public opinion, it is essential that public opinion should be enlightened. . . .

THOMAS JEFFERSON
FIRST INAUGURAL ADDRESS

Jefferson's election as president has been called "the revolution of 1800," the first instance of the peaceful transfer of power from one party to another as a result of a mass election. The idea of Jefferson in the White House appalled most Federalists, who regarded him as a wild man who might well usher in something like the Reign of Terror that had scarred the French Revolution a few years before. Thus he took pains in his First Inaugural Address to insist at the outset that, while "the will of the majority is in all cases to prevail," the "minority possess their equal rights, which equal laws must protect." He distinguishes here between differences of political opinion and differences of principle, and argues that Federalists and Republicans are equally dedicated to republican principles, differing only in their opinions as to how best to preserve them. To those who doubted the capacity of humans to govern themselves Jefferson asks: if they cannot, how then can kings, who are not after all angels, do it for them? He then provides a classic analysis of the essential principles upon which the government he considered "the world's best hope" rested, "the creed of our political faith."

. . . During the contest of opinion through which we have passed, the animation of discussion and of exertions has sometimes worn an aspect which might impose on strangers unused to think freely and to speak and to write what they think; but this being now decided by the voice of the nation, announced according to the rules of the constitution, all will, of course, arrange themselves under the will of the law, and unite in common efforts for the common good. All, too, will bear in mind this sacred principle, that though the will of the majority is in all cases to prevail, that will, to be rightful, must be reasonable; that the minority possess their equal rights, which equal laws must protect, and to violate which would be oppression. Let us, then, fellow citizens, unite with one heart and one mind. Let us restore to social intercourse that harmony and affection without which liberty and even life itself are but dreary things. And let us reflect that having banished from our land that religious intolerance under which mankind so long bled and suffered, we have yet gained little if we countenance a political intolerance as despotic, as wicked, and capable of as bitter and bloody persecutions. . . .

[E]very difference of opinion is not a difference of principle. We have called by different names brethren of the same principle. We are all republicans—we are all federalists. If there be any among us who would wish to dissolve this Union or to change its republican form, let them stand undisturbed as monuments of the safety with which error of opinion may be tolerated where reason is left free to combat it. I know, indeed, that some honest men fear that a republican government cannot be strong; that this government is not strong enough. But would the honest patriot, in the full tide of successful experiment, abandon a government which has so far kept us free and firm, on the theoretic and visionary fear that this government, the world's best hope, may by possibility want energy to preserve itself? I trust not. I believe this, on the contrary, the strongest government on earth. I believe it is the only one where every man, at the call of the laws, would fly to the standard of the law, and would meet invasions of the public order as his own personal concern. Sometimes it is said that man cannot be trusted with the government of himself. Can he, then, be trusted with the government of others? Or have we found angels in the forms of kings to govern him? Let history answer this question. . . .

[I]t is proper that you should understand what I deem the essential principles of our government, and consequently those which ought to shape its administration. I will compress them within the narrowest compass they will bear, stating the general principle, but not all its limitations. Equal and exact justice to all men, of whatever state or persuasion, religious or political; peace, commerce, and honest friendship, with all nations—entangling alliances with none; the support of the state governments in all their rights, as the most competent administrations for our domestic concerns and the surest bulwarks against anti-republican tendencies; the preservation of the general government in its whole constitutional vigor, as the sheet anchor of our peace at home and safety abroad; a jealous care of the right of election by the people—a mild and safe corrective of abuses which are lopped by the sword of the revolution where peaceable remedies are unprovided; absolute acquiescence in the decisions of the majority—the vital principle of republics, from which there is no appeal but to force, the vital principle and immediate parent of despotism; a well-disciplined militia—our best reliance in peace and for the first moments of war, till regulars may relieve them; the supremacy of the civil over the military authority; economy in the public expense, that labor may be lightly burdened; the honest payment of our debts and sacred preservation of the public faith; encouragement of agriculture, and of commerce as its handmaid; the diffusion of information and the arraignment of all abuses at the bar of public reason; freedom of religion; freedom of the press; freedom of person under the protection of the *habeas corpus*; and trial by juries impartially selected—these principles form the bright constellation which has gone before us, and guided our steps through an age of revolution and reformation. The wisdom of our sages and the blood of our heroes have been devoted to their attainment. They should be the creed of our political faith—the text of civil instruction—the touchstone by which to try the services of those we trust; and should we wander from them in moments of error or alarm, let us hasten to retrace our steps and to regain the road which alone leads to peace, liberty, and safety.

JOHN MARSHALL
MARBURY V. MADISON

The Supreme Court, at the apex of the federal judicial system, has the last word on the meaning of the Constitution of the United States. That is, it has the power to say with finality what is constitutional and what is not—whether, for instance, legislation prohibiting organized public resistance to the military draft in wartime violates the First Amendment's promise that "Congress shall make no law . . . abridging the freedom of speech." Or whether a university's admissions policy violates the "equal protection" clause if black applicants are preferred over those who are white.

In exercising its power of judicial review, the court often has a great deal of interpretive leeway. Some clauses in the Constitution are specific and straightforward, but many are not. It is thus up to the court to define such words as "liberty" and "property," such phrases as "due process of law" and "equal protection of the laws," and such doctrines (implicit in the document) as that of the separation of powers. In defining such words, phrases and ideas, the court shapes the life of the nation in fundamental ways.

The enormous power of the Supreme Court is neither explicitly conferred nor clearly implied in the Constitution. It was created by the court itself. The process began, however, very early—in 1803, to be exact, when *Marbury v. Madison* was decided.

The decision was the work of the first great Chief Justice, John Marshall (1755–1835). The case laid the foundation for the wide-ranging exercise of judicial power that has now become central to the American political system. The immediate issue was the validity of the appointment of William Marbury to a minor judicial post. In the last days of the presidency of John Adams, Marbury and 41 colleagues had been given positions, but their commissions had never been properly delivered, an administrative oversight on the part of the Federalists that was welcomed by the new Jefferson administration, which denied them their jobs. Marbury and his friends appealed to the Supreme Court, seeking a writ of mandamus, an order compelling the new secretary of state, James Madison, to deliver their commissions.

Marshall condemned the action of the president, but denied the court's power to rule in Marbury's favor. The Supreme Court could not issue the writ of mandamus, Marshall reasoned, because the power to do so rested in an unconstitutional provision in the 1789 Judiciary Act. Fourteen years earlier, in other words, Congress had passed an unconstitutional act; since the Constitution is superior to any ordinary act of the legislature, the legislation itself was invalid.

The reasoning was pure Alexander Hamilton. While the argument was stirring, it was also dubious and inadequate. It skirted, in fact, the real issue that is at the heart of the question of judicial review: When a constitutional question is not clear, which branch of government should have the authority to decide that a legislative act violates the nation's fundamental law? Arguably, the states or Congress or the executive branch or even the people themselves (by means of a vote) are equally entitled to decide what is constitutional and what is not. Although Marshall took the initiative to give the Supreme Court this power, the question is one that, in different forms, is still debated today.

. . . The authority . . . given to the supreme court by the act establishing the judicial courts of the United States, to issue writs of *mandamus* to public officers, appears not to be warranted by the constitution; and it becomes necessary to inquire, whether a jurisdiction so conferred can be exercised.

The question, whether an act, repugnant to the constitution, can become the law of the land, is a question deeply interesting to the United States; but, happily, not of an intricacy proportioned to its interest. It seems only necessary to recognise certain principles, supposed to have been long and well established, to decide it. That the people have an original right to establish, for their future government, such principles as, in their opinion, shall most conduce to their own happiness, is the basis on which the whole American fabric has been erected. The exercise of this original right is a very great exertion; nor can it, nor ought it, to be frequently repeated. The principles, therefore, so established, are deemed fundamental: and as the authority from which they proceed is supreme, and can seldom act, they are designed to be permanent.

This original and supreme will organizes the government, and assigns to different departments their respective powers. It may either stop here, or establish certain limits not to be transcended by those departments. The government of the United States is of the latter description. The powers of the legislature are defined and limited; and that those limits may not be mistaken or forgotten, the constitution is written. To what purpose are powers limited, and to what purpose is that limitation committed to writing, if these limits may, at any time, be passed by those intended to be restrained? The distinction

between a government with limited and unlimited powers is abolished, if those limits do not confine the persons on whom they are imposed, and if acts prohibited and acts allowed, are of equal obligation. It is a proposition too plain to be contested, that the constitution controls any legislative act repugnant to it; or that the legislature may alter the constitution by an ordinary act.

Between these alternatives, there is no middle ground. The constitution is either a superior paramount law, unchangeable by ordinary means, or it is on a level with ordinary legislative acts, and, like other acts, is alterable when the legislature shall please to alter it. If the former part of the alternative be true, then a legislative act, contrary to the constitution, is not law: if the latter part be true, then written constitutions are absurd attempts, on the part of the people, to limit a power, in its own nature, illimitable.

Certainly, all those who have framed written constitutions contemplate them as forming the fundamental and paramount law of the nation, and consequently, the theory of every such government must be, that an act of the legislature, repugnant to the constitution, is void. This theory is essentially attached to a written constitution, and is, consequently, to be considered, by this court, as one of the fundamental principles of our society. It is not, therefore, to be lost sight of, in the further consideration of this subject.

If an act of the legislature, repugnant to the constitution, is void, does it, notwithstanding its invalidity, bind the courts, and oblige them to give it effect? Or, in other words, though it be not law, does it constitute a rule as operative as if it was a law? This would be to overthrow, in fact, what was established in theory; and would seem, at first view, an absurdity too gross to be insisted on. It shall, however, receive a more attentive consideration.

It is, emphatically, the province and duty of the judicial department, to say what the law is. Those who apply the rule to particular cases, must of necessity expound and interpret that rule. If two laws conflict with each other, the courts must decide on the operation of each. So, if a law be in opposition to the constitution; if both the law and the constitution apply to a particular case, so that the court must either decide that case, conformable to the law, disregarding the constitution; or conformable to the constitution, disregarding the law; the court must determine which of these conflicting rules governs the case: this is of the very essence of judicial duty. If then, the courts are to regard the constitution, and the constitution is superior to any ordinary act of the legislature, the constitution, and not such ordinary act, must govern the case to which they both apply.

An engraving of Chief Justice John Marshall, showing in the background the home of the U.S. Supreme Court over which he presided.

Those, then, who controvert the principle, that the constitution is to be considered, in court, as a paramount law, are reduced to the necessity of maintaining that courts must close their eyes on the constitution, and see only the law. This doctrine would subvert the very foundation of all written constitutions. It would declare that an act which, according to the principles and theory of our government, is entirely void, is yet, in practice, completely obligatory. It would declare, that if the legislature shall do what is expressly forbidden, such act, notwithstanding the express prohibition, is in reality effectual. It would be giving to the legislature a practical and real omnipotence, with the same breath which professes to restrict their powers within narrow limits. It is prescribing limits, and declaring that those limits may be passed at pleasure. That it thus reduces to nothing, what we have deemed the greatest improvement on political institutions, a written constitution, would, of itself, be sufficient, in America, where written constitutions have been viewed with so much reverence, for rejecting the construction. But the peculiar expressions of the constitution of the United States furnish additional arguments in favor of its rejection. The judicial power of the United States is extended to all cases arising under the constitution. Could it be the intention of those who gave this power, to say, that in using it, the constitution should not be looked into? That a case arising under the constitution should be decided, without examining the instrument under which it arises? This is too extravagant to be maintained. In some cases, then, the constitution must be looked into by the judges. And if they can open it at all, what part of it are they forbidden to read or to obey?

There are many other parts of the constitution which serve to illustrate this subject. It is declared, that "no tax or duty shall be laid on articles exported from any state." Suppose, a duty on the export of cotton, of tobacco or of flour; and a suit instituted to recover it. Ought judgment to be rendered in such a case? ought the judges to close their eyes on the constitution, and only see the law?

The constitution declares "that no bill of attainder or *ex post facto* law shall be passed." If, however, such a bill should be passed, and a person should be prosecuted under it; must the court condemn to death those victims whom the constitution endeavors to preserve?

"No person," says the constitution, "shall be convicted of treason, unless on the testimony of two witnesses to the same *overt* act, or on confession in open court." Here, the language of the constitution is addressed especially to the courts. It prescribes, directly for them, a rule of evidence not to be departed from. If the legislature should change that rule, and declare one witness, or a confession out of court, sufficient for conviction, must the constitutional principle yield to the legislative act?

From these, and many other selections which might be made, it is apparent, that the framers of the constitution contemplated that instrument as a rule for the government of courts, as well as of the legislature. Why otherwise does it direct the judges to take an oath to support it? This oath certainly applies in an especial manner, to their conduct in their official character. How immoral to impose it on them, if they were to be used as the instruments, and the knowing instruments, for violating what they swear to support!

The oath of office, too, imposed by the legislature, is completely demonstrative of the legislative opinion on this subject. It is in these words: "I do solemnly swear, that I will administer justice, without respect to persons, and do equal right to the poor and to the rich; and that I will faithfully and impartially discharge all the duties incumbent on me as ———, according to the best of my abilities and understanding, agreeably to the constitution and laws of the United States." Why does a judge swear to discharge his duties agreeably to the constitution of the United States, if that constitution forms no rule for his government? if it is closed upon him, and cannot be inspected by him? If such be the real state of things, this is worse than solemn mockery. To prescribe, or to take this oath, becomes equally a crime.

It is also not entirely unworthy of observation, that in declaring what shall be the supreme law of the land, the constitution itself is first mentioned; and not the laws of the United States, generally, but those only which shall be made in pursuance of the constitution, have that rank.

Thus, the particular phraseology of the constitution of the United States confirms and strengthens the principle, supposed to be essential to all written constitutions, that a law repugnant to the constitution is void; and that courts, as well as other departments, are bound by that instrument.

The rule must be discharged.

ANDREW JACKSON
PROCLAMATION ON NULLIFICATION

President Andrew Jackson (1767–1845) was both a Southern slaveholder and an ardent believer in a strong national government for the United States. During his years in the White House (1829–1837), the dominant planter class of the South was becoming increasingly fearful of the concentration of power in Washington and increasingly insistent that "states' rights" were more important than national power. Jackson's 1832 Nullification Proclamation was his response to the South Carolina *Exposition*, in which the legislature of that state refused to allow federal officials to collect tariffs within its boundaries, on the grounds that a majority of South Carolinians believed that a tariff bill recently approved by Congress was unconstitutional.

The immediate economic issues at stake were fairly trivial, but a vital general principle was involved. Could a majority of voters in one state decide on the constitutionality of federal laws, and refuse to abide by those they objected to? Vice President John C. Calhoun, a brilliant political theorist and South Carolina's most prominent leader, insisted that it could. The United States was not a nation, he argued, but only "a confederacy of separate and sovereign states," and any of its members were free to "nullify"—to render null and void—any federal law that it disliked.

President Jackson agreed that the tariff in question was too high, but believed that South Carolina's position would lead to anarchy. Having first won national fame as a general during the War of 1812, "Old Hickory" was furious about this attempt to undermine the authority of the national government he presided over. He promptly dispatched reinforcements to federal forts in South Carolina and naval vessels to patrol its coastline, promised the state's Congressional delegation that if blood were shed in defiance of the law he would hang the guilty parties on the first tree he could find, and issued this forceful proclamation. The Constitution, he declared, had brought into being a new national government that derived directly from the American people. The union it created was not a mere "league" of states whose members were free to leave whenever they wished. Secession would be a revolutionary act, and Jackson would use all of his powers to prevent it. With the threat of rebel hangings by federal troops as the stick and a modest tariff reduction voted by Congress in the interim as the carrot, South Carolina eventually backed down.

South Carolina, though, would not have become so conciliatory had it been able to

win the backing of the other Southern states in the crisis. Several others did lodge emphatic protests against the tariff, but no others were prepared to stick their necks out far enough to risk a war with the government of the United States.

Whereas a convention assembled in the State of South Carolina have passed an ordinance by which they declare "that the several acts and parts of acts of the Congress of the United States purporting to be laws for the imposing of duties and imposts on the importation of foreign commodities . . . are null and void and no law"; . . .

[And] whereas the said ordinance prescribes to the people of South Carolina a course of conduct in direct violation of their duty as citizens . . . and having for its object the destruction of the Union. . . . To preserve this bond of our political existence from destruction, . . . I, Andrew Jackson, President of the United States, have thought proper to issue this my proclamation, . . .

E. W. Earle's portrait of Andrew Jackson suggests the president's firmness and self-confidence, if not his fiery temperament.

declaring the course which duty will require me to pursue, and, appealing to the understanding and patriotism of the people, warn them of the consequences that must inevitably result from an observance of the dictates of the convention. . . .

The ordinance is founded . . . on the strange position that any one state may not only declare an act of Congress void, but prohibit its execution. . . . There is no appeal from the state decision. . . . But reasoning on this subject is superfluous, when our social compact, in express terms, declares that the laws of the United States, its Constitution, and treaties made under it are the supreme law of the land; and, for greater caution, adds "that the judges in every state shall be bound thereby, anything in the constitution or laws of any state to the contrary notwithstanding." . . . No federative government could exist without a similar provision. . . .

I consider, then, the power to annul a law of the United States, assumed by one state, incompatible with the existence of the Union, contradicted expressly by the letter of the Constitution, unauthorized by its spirit, inconsistent with every principle on which it was founded, and destructive of the great object for which it was formed. . . .

The Constitution of the United States . . . forms a government, not a league; and whether it be formed by compact between the states or in any other manner, its character is the same. It is a government in which all the people are represented, which operates directly on the people individually, not upon the states. . . . Each state . . . cannot . . . possess any right to secede, because such secession does not break a league, but destroys the unity of a nation; and any injury to that unity is . . . an offense against the whole Union. . . . Secession, like any other revolutionary act, may be morally justified by the extremity of oppression; but to call it a constitutional right is confounding the meaning of terms. . . .

Because the Union was formed by a compact, it is said the parties to that compact may, when they feel themselves aggrieved, depart from it; but it is precisely because it is a compact that they cannot. A compact is an agreement or binding obligation. It may by its terms have a sanction or penalty for its breach, or it may not. . . . A government . . . always has a sanction, express or implied; and in our case it is both necessarily implied and expressly given. An attempt, by force of arms, to destroy a government is an offense . . . and such government has the right by the law of self-defense to pass acts for punishing the offender. . . .

This, then, is the position in which we stand.

A small majority of the citizens of one state in the Union have elected delegates to a state convention; that convention has ordained that all the revenue laws of the United States must be repealed, or that they are no longer a member of the Union. . . . It is the intent of this instrument to *proclaim*, not only that the duty imposed on me by the Constitution "to take care that the laws be faithfully executed" shall be performed to the extent of the powers already vested in me by law, . . . but to warn the citizens of South Carolina . . . of the danger they will incur by obedience to the illegal and disorganizing ordinance of the convention.

ALEXIS DE TOCQUEVILLE

DEMOCRACY IN AMERICA

No book has ever offered as many penetrating insights into the character of American democracy and the nature of American life as Alexis de Tocqueville's two-volume classic *Democracy in America*. Tocqueville (1805–1859) was a French aristocrat who toured the United States between 1831 and 1832 seeking to discern what lessons the workings of American democracy might have for Europeans, who were at an earlier stage in the democratic revolution sweeping the Western world in the nineteenth century.

The first of these selections discusses one of the perennial problems of democratic society, that of "the tyranny of the majority." Although the American Constitution gives very broad protection to freedom of speech, the press, and religion, Tocqueville found "less independence of mind and true freedom of discussion" in America in the age of Jackson than he did in European countries still ruled by despots. Even the most absolute of monarchs, he says, cannot "hold all the forces of society in his hand," but a majority of the people, who *are* the society, can make it tempting for everyone to jump on its bandwagon or suffer ostracism.

It can be argued that much of the pressure for popular conformity that Tocqueville observed reflected the fairly primitive level of social development in the United States of the 1830s. Still, there are later examples of mass hysteria—the Red Scare that followed World War I and the McCarthyism of the 1950s, for instance—that seem to reinforce Tocqueville's conclusion.

It is in the examination of the exercise of thought in the United States, that we clearly perceive how far the power of the majority surpasses all the powers with which we are acquainted in Europe. Thought is an invisible and subtle power, that mocks all the efforts of tyranny. At the present time, the most absolute monarchs in Europe cannot prevent certain opinions hostile to their authority from circulating in secret through their dominions, and even in their courts. It is not so in America; as long as the majority is still undecided, discussion is carried on; but as soon as its decision is irrevocably pronounced, every one is silent, and the friends as well as the opponents of the measure unite in assenting to its propriety. The reason of this is perfectly clear: no monarch is so absolute as to combine all the powers of society in his own hands, and to conquer all opposition, as a majority is able to do, which has the right both of making and of executing the laws.

The authority of a king is physical, and controls the actions of men without subduing their will. But the majority possesses a power which is physical and moral at the same time, which acts upon the will as much as upon the actions, and represses not only all contest, but all controversy.

I know of no country in which there is so little independence of mind and real freedom of discussion as in America. In any constitutional state in Europe, every sort of religious and political theory may be freely preached and disseminated; for there is no country in Europe so subdued by any single authority, as not to protect the man who raises his voice in the cause of truth from the consequences of his hardihood. If he is unfortunate enough to live under an absolute government, the people are often upon his side; if he inhabits a free country, he can, if necessary, find a shelter behind the throne. The aristocratic part of society supports him in some countries, and the democracy in others. But in a nation where democratic institutions exist, organized like those of the United States, there is but one authority, one element of strength and success, with nothing beyond it.

In America, the majority raises formidable barriers around the liberty of opinion: within these barriers, an author may write what he pleases; but woe to him if he goes beyond them. Not that he is in danger of an *auto-da-fé*, but he is exposed to continued obloquy and persecution. His political career is closed forever, since he has offended the only authority which is able to open it. Every sort of compensation, even that of celebrity, is refused to him. Before publishing his opinions, he imagined that he held them in common with others; but no sooner has he declared them, than he is loudly censured by his opponents, whilst those who think like him, without having the courage to speak out, abandon him in silence. He yields at length, overcome by the daily effort which he has to make, and subsides into silence, as if he felt remorse for having spoken the truth.

Fetters and headsmen were the coarse instruments which tyranny formerly employed; but the civilization of our age has perfected despotism itself, though it seemed to have nothing to learn. Monarchs had, so to speak, materialized oppression: the democratic republics of the present day have rendered it as entirely an affair of the mind, as the will which it is intended to coerce. Under the absolute sway of one man, the body was attacked in order to subdue the soul; but the soul escaped the blows which were directed against it, and rose proudly superior. Such is not the course adopted by tyranny in democratic republics; there the body is left free, and the soul is enslaved. The master no longer says, "You shall think as I do, or you shall die"; but he says, "You are free to think differently from me, and to retain your life, your property, and all that you possess; but you are henceforth a stranger among your people."

In this second selection Tocqueville stresses the extent to which American democracy was rooted in heritage of political freedom the early settlers brought with them from Britain, a country with a much stronger tradition of liberty than his native France. It is not quite true that all of the early immigrants "spoke the same tongue." A good number spoke German, Dutch, Welsh, or Gaelic. However, they quickly adopted English, and he is correct that the possession of a *lingua franca* is a vital source of national cohesion (a point too often forgotten today by those who deny that the "melting pot" ever worked and even reject it as an ideal).

Tocqueville has been criticized by later scholars for having exaggerated the extent to which "rags to riches" stories were a reality in nineteenth century America. However, social mobility was indeed widespread, and the relative equality of economic and social conditions it brought about was a force making for political democracy as well.

The emigrants who came at different periods to occupy the territory now covered by the American Union differed from each other in many respects; their aim was not the same, and they governed themselves on different principles. These men had, however, certain features in common, and they were all placed in an analogous situation. The tie of language is, perhaps, the strongest and the most durable that can unite mankind. All the emigrants spoke the same tongue; they were all offsets from the same people. Born in a country which had been agitated for centuries by the struggles of faction, and in which all parties had been obliged in their turn to place themselves under the protection of the laws, their political education had been perfected in this rude school; and they were more conversant with the notions of right, and the principles of true freedom, than the greater part of their European contemporaries. At the period of the first emigrations, the township system, that fruitful germ of free institutions, was deeply rooted in the habits of the English; and with it the doctrine of the sovereignty of the people. . . .

Another remark, to which we shall hereafter have occasion to recur, is applicable not only to the English, but to . . . all the Europeans who successively established themselves in the New World. All these European colonies contained the elements, if not the development, of a complete democracy. Two causes led to this result. It may be said generally, that on leaving the mother country the emigrants had, in general, no notion of superiority one over another. The happy and the powerful do not go into exile, and there are no surer guaranties of equality among men than poverty and misfortune. It happened, however, on several occasions, that persons of rank were driven to America by political and religious quarrels. Laws were made to establish a gradation of ranks; but it was soon found that the soil of America was opposed to a territorial aristocracy. To bring that refractory land into cultivation, the constant and interested exertions of the owner himself were necessary; and when the ground was prepared, its produce was found to be insufficient to enrich a proprietor and a farmer at the same time. The land was then naturally broken up into small portions, which the proprietor cultivated for himself. Land is the basis of an aristocracy, which clings to the soil that supports it; for it is not by privileges alone, nor by birth, but by landed property handed down from generation to generation, that an aristocracy is constituted. A nation may present immense fortunes and extreme wretchedness; but unless those fortunes are territorial, there is no true aristocracy, but simply the class of the rich and that of the poor. . . .

I do not mean that there is any lack of wealthy individuals in the United States; I know of no country, indeed, where the love of money has taken stronger hold on the affections of men, and where a profounder contempt is expressed for the theory of the permanent equality of property. But wealth circulates with inconceivable rapidity, and experience shows that it is rare to find two succeeding generations in the full enjoyment of it. . . .

. . . The social condition of the Americans is eminently democratic; this was its character at the foundation of the colonies, and it is still more strongly marked at the present day. . . . America, then, exhibits in her social state an extraordinary phenomenon. Men are there seen on a greater equality in point of fortune and intellect, or, in other words, more equal in their strength, than in any other country of the world, or in any age of which history has preserved the remembrance.

The political consequences of such a social condition as this are easily deducible. It is impossible to believe that equality will not eventually find its way into the political world, as it does everywhere else. To conceive of men remaining forever unequal upon a single point, yet equal on all others, is impossible; they must come in the end to be equal upon all. . . .

In this selection Tocqueville calls attention to one of the most striking traits of the American people—their remarkable capacity to form voluntary associations to realize their collective aims, instead of leaving everything up to "the authorities." Jefferson's belief that "that government is best which governs least," and President Ronald Reagan's later pledges to "get the government off our backs," would seem very strange in most societies, where formal political institutions dominate the channels of social action. It does not appear to be odd in the United States. This American view does not represent a radical and ruthless individualism that boasts "every man for himself and let the devil take the hindmost." It stems rather from a tradition in which government is not the only, or even the most important, instrument of social action.

In no country in the world has the principle of association been more successfully used, or applied to a greater multitude of objects, than in America. Besides the permanent associations, which are established by law, under the names of townships, cities, and counties, a vast number of others are formed and maintained by the agency of private individuals.

The citizen of the United States is taught from infancy to rely upon his own exertions, in order to resist the evils and the difficulties of life; he looks upon the social authority with an eye of mistrust and anxiety, and he claims its assistance only when he is unable to do without it. This habit may be traced even in the schools, where the children in their games are wont to submit to rules which they have themselves established, and to punish misdemeanors which they have themselves defined. The same spirit pervades every act of social life. If a stoppage occurs in a thoroughfare, and the circulation of vehicles is hindered, the neighbors immediately form themselves into a deliberative body; and this extemporaneous assembly gives rise to an executive power, which remedies the inconvenience before anybody has thought of recurring to a preexisting authority superior to that of the persons immediately concerned. If some public pleasure is concerned, an association is formed to give more splendor and regularity to the entertainment. Societies are formed to resist evils which are exclusively of a moral nature, as to diminish the vice of intemperance. In the United States, associations are established to promote the public safety, commerce, industry, morality, and religion. There is no end which the human will despairs of attaining through the combined power of individuals united into a society. . . .

It cannot be denied that the unrestrained liberty of association for political purposes is the privilege which a people is longest in learning how to exercise. If it does not throw the nation into anarchy, it perpetually augments the chances of that calamity. On one point, however, this perilous liberty offers a security against dangers of another kind; in countries where associations are free, secret societies are unknown. In America, there are factions, but no conspiracies.

The most natural privilege of man, next to the right of acting for himself, is that of combining his exertions with those of his fellow-creatures, and of acting in common with them. The right of association therefore appears to me almost as inalienable in its nature as the right of personal liberty.

As this fourth selection suggests, although Tocqueville was struck by the importance of voluntary associations in giving order to American society, he nonetheless found no lack of political activity. Indeed, he found politics in America to be pervasive, to the point at which it was virtually the only topic of conversation. Without it, he says, Americans "would find an immense void" in their lives. This does not always produce good government, to be sure. "Democratic liberty rarely completes its projects with the skills of an adroit despotism," Tocqueville writes. It does, though, create "an all-pervading and restless activity, a superabundant force, an energy which will produce wonders however unfavorable circumstances may be."

. . . It is not impossible to conceive the surprising liberty which the Americans enjoy; some idea may likewise be formed of their extreme equality; but the political activity which pervades the United States must be seen in order to be understood. No sooner do you set foot upon American ground, than you are stunned by a kind of tumult; a confused clamor is heard on every side; and a thousand simultaneous voices demand the satisfaction of their social wants. Everything is in motion around you; here, the people of one quarter of a town are met to decide upon the building of a church; there, the election of a representative is going on; a little further, the delegates of a district are posting to the town in order to consult some local improvements; in another place, the laborers of a village quit their ploughs to deliberate upon the project of a road or a public school. Meetings are called for the sole purpose of declaring their disapprobation of the conduct of the government; whilst in other assemblies, citizens salute the authorities of the day as the fathers of their country. Societies are formed which regard drunkenness as the principal cause of the evils of the state, and solemnly bind themselves to give an example of temperance. The great political agitation of American legislative bodies, which is the only one that attracts the attention of foreigners, is a mere episode, or a sort of continuation, of that universal movement which originates in the lowest classes of the people, and extends successively to all the ranks of society. It is impossible to spend more effort in the pursuit of happiness.

The cares of politics engross a prominent place in the occupations of a citizen in the United States; and almost the only pleasure which an American knows is to take a part in the government, and to discuss its measures. This feeling pervades the most trifling habits of life; even the women frequently attend public meetings, and listen to political harangues as a recreation from

A caricature of Alexis de Tocqueville by the great French painter and satirist, Honore Daumier.

their household labors. Debating clubs are, to a certain extent, a substitute for theatrical entertainments: an American cannot converse, but he can discuss; and his talk falls into a dissertation. He speaks to you as if he was addressing a meeting; and if he should chance to become warm in the discussion, he will say "Gentlemen" to the person with whom he is conversing.

In some countries, the inhabitants seem unwilling to avail themselves of the political privileges which the law gives them; it would seem that they set too high a value upon their time to spend it on the interests of the community; and they shut themselves up in a narrow selfishness, marked out by four sunk fences and a quickset hedge. But if an American were condemned to confine his activity to his own affairs, he would be robbed of one half of his existence; he would feel an immense void in the life which he is accustomed to lead, and his wretchedness would be unbearable. I am persuaded, that, if ever a despotism should be established in America, it will be more difficult to overcome the habits which freedom has formed, than to conquer the love of freedom itself.

This ceaseless agitation which democratic government has introduced into the political world, influences all social intercourse. I am not sure that, upon the whole, this is not the greatest advantage of democracy; and I am less inclined to applaud it for what it does, than for what it causes to be done. It is incontestable that the people frequently conduct public business very ill; but it is impossible that the lower orders should take a part in public business without extending the circle of their ideas, and quitting the ordinary routine of their thoughts. The humblest individual who co-operates in the government of society acquires a certain degree of self-respect; and as he possesses authority, he can command the services of minds more enlightened than his own. He is canvassed by a multitude of applicants, and, in seeking to deceive him in a thousand ways, they really enlighten him. He takes a part in political undertakings which he did not originate, but which give him a taste for undertakings of the kind. New improvements are daily pointed out to him in the common property, and this gives him the desire of improving that property which is his own. He is perhaps neither happier nor better than those who came before him, but he is better informed and more active. I have no doubt that the democratic institutions of the United States, joined to the physical constitution of the country, are the cause (not the direct, as is so often asserted, but the indirect cause) of the prodigious commercial activity of the inhabitants. It is not created by the laws, but the people learn how to promote it by the experience derived from legislation.

When the opponents of democracy assert that a single man performs what he undertakes better than the government of all, it appears to me that they are right. The government of an individual, supposing an equality of knowledge on either side, is more consistent, more persevering, more uniform, and more accurate in details, than that of a multitude, and it selects with more discrimination the men whom it employs. If any deny this, they have never seen a democratic government, or have judged upon partial evidence. It is true that, even when local circumstances and the dispositions of the people allow democratic institutions to exist, they do not display a regular and methodical system of government. Democratic liberty is far from accomplishing all its projects with the skill of an adroit despotism. It frequently abandons them before they have borne their fruits, or risks them when the consequences may be dangerous; but in the end, it produces more than any absolute government; if it does fewer things well, it does a greater number of things. Under its sway, the grandeur is not in what the public administration does, but in what is done without it or outside of it. Democracy does not give the people the most skilful government, but it produces what the ablest governments are frequently unable to create; namely, an all-pervading and restless activity, a superabundant force, and an energy which is inseparable from it, and which may, however unfavorable circumstances may be, produce wonders. These are the true advantages of democracy.

INTRODUCTION TO *DEMOCRATIC REVIEW*

The United States Magazine and Democratic Review, usually known as the *Democratic Review*, was a literary and political journal founded in 1837. It was financially supported by many Democratic politicians, including Andrew Jackson, who had just retired from the presidency. The introduction printed in the first issue sets forth some basic tenets of the American democratic faith as understood by Democrats. "The best government is that which governs least" was a Jeffersonian principle rejected by the opposing party, the Whigs, just as Democrats in the 1980s dismissed Ronald Reagan's efforts to "get the government off our backs." The Whigs of the day favored Henry Clay's "American system" of high protective tariffs and federal aid for transportation improvements to stimulate economic growth, just as Democrats in recent years supported federal social programs the Reagan administration sought to kill. (In this sense, the modern Republican Party is closer to the Democratic tradition of Thomas Jefferson and Andrew Jackson than the modern Democrats are.)

The *Democratic Review*, which charged the Whigs with elitism and aristocratic sympathies, argued for the superior wisdom of the common people. Their instincts could be trusted so long as government did not overstep the bounds of its authority.

The best government is that which governs least. No human depositories can, with safety, be trusted with the power of legislation upon the general interests of society so as to operate directly or indirectly on the industry and property of the community. Such power must be perpetually liable to the most pernicious abuse, from the natural imperfection, both in wisdom of judgment and purity of purpose, of all human legislation, exposed constantly to the pressure of partial interests; interests which, at the same time that they are essentially selfish and tyrannical, are ever vigilant, persevering, and subtle in all the arts of deception and corruption. In fact, the whole history of human society and government may be safely appealed to, in evidence that the abuse of such power a thousand fold more than overbalances its beneficial use. . . .

It is a common error to overrate our own capacities, and underrate those of others. There is a vulgar pride gratified in depreciating the integrity and information of the great mass. The arrogant vanity of the rich, the haughty pretension of the privileged, the insolence of the unprincipled, the pomposity of the learned, and the inflated conceit of the selfish and superficial "business man" delight to disparage the intellectual or moral claims of "the multitude." They are stigmatized as the lower orders, but a little, if any, removed from the brute; they are spoken of as the wild, ferocious herd; passed by with the rude jest or the scornful look, or at times crushed in the dust like crawling, loathsome earthworms. But there is a native instinct in the general mind more unerring in its decisions than prejudiced instruction—a practical sagacity, which sets the most subtle or far-reaching intellect at naught—the conviction of great truths, which sink deep, deep into the heart, and guide its sympathies and movements aright. So long as the many shall know their rights—while they can distinguish moral rectitude from guilt—while they are judges of the means most conducive to their happiness and growth—and while they may be addressed by every variety of persuasion and appeal, it is no frightful absurdity to rely confidently on their will.

Most especially may they be trusted when government is confined by its legitimate bounds. The details of a consolidated government based on unwritten laws, perpetually changing—comprehending an infinity of functions—

fettered by a vast variety of checks, balances and restrictions—connected directly with every interest of society—mingling in all the gambling and speculation of trade—entrenching itself behind immense civil, ecclesiastical and military establishments, and operating through a machinery as intricate as the differential calculus, it is true, would puzzle their heads, as they do the most experienced statesmen themselves. But the Democratic creed contemplates no such complicated arrangement. That creed is consistent with itself throughout. It does not construct an engine of adjustments and relations so multiplied and abstruse, that the most practised wisdom is alone adequate to their comprehension. It does not abuse the people for not controlling what is beyond their capacity to understand. It does not hang laws far above their heads, and then Draco-like, execute a terrible penalty upon every infringement. While it asserts the competency of the whole to govern themselves, it restricts government to its natural uses; it curtails the number of its functions, separates its action from partial interests; simplifies the mode of its operation, and reduces the principles of legislation to the simplest expression compatible with some form of national organization. It insists strenuously on popular rights, because it believes the popular body sufficient to the discharge of its public duties. There is intelligence enough abroad to answer the purposes required of it.

SENECA FALLS DECLARATION OF SENTIMENTS AND RESOLUTIONS

On the eve of the Declaration of Independence, the American challenge to the legitimacy of Britain's traditional authority over the colonies had led Abigail Adams to question the legitimacy of a far more ancient and deeply rooted tradition—that of the subjugation of women to male authority. Women played a significant role in the great burst of American reform activity of the 1830s and 1840s, working for such causes as temperance, abolition, and educational progress. A small number, led by Elizabeth Cady Stanton and Lucretia Mott, took up the cause of what today would be called "women's liberation." The 1848 Seneca Falls convention on "the social, civil, and religious rights of women" was attended by about 300 people, 40 of them men. It attracted very little attention at the time, but expressed the fundamental concerns that would be the focus of women's organized political activities for many decades to come.

The first four complaints registered in the declaration are variants of the same grievance—that women were not allowed the right to vote. Winning the suffrage was the central aim of the women's movement from Seneca Falls until the Nineteenth Amendment became law in 1920. The predominantly non-immigrant white middle class character of the suffrage cause then and later is indicated by the blunt references to the voting of "the most ignorant and degraded men—both natives and foreign." Votes for women were frequently urged to offset the allegedly evil influence of immigrants, workers, and (after slavery was ended) black men. Several other of the complaints listed in the Declaration, concerning property rights, divorce law, and education, were largely remedied well before 1920. The demands concerning access to certain occupations, an end to the double standard of morality, and independence and self-respect for women are obviously of some continuing relevance.

When, in the course of human events, it becomes necessary for one portion of the family of man to assume among the people of the earth a position different from that which they have hitherto occupied, but one to which the laws of nature and of nature's God entitle them, a decent respect to the opinions of mankind requires that they should declare the causes that impel them to such a course. . . .

The history of mankind is a history of repeated injuries and usurpations on the part of man toward woman, having in direct object the establishment of an absolute tyranny over her. To prove this, let facts be submitted to a candid world.

He has never permitted her to exercise her inalienable right to the elective franchise.

He has compelled her to submit to laws, in the formation of which she had no voice.

He has withheld from her rights which are given to the most ignorant and degraded men—both natives and foreigners.

Having deprived her of this first right of a citizen, the elective franchise, thereby leaving her without representation in the halls of legislation, he has oppressed her on all sides.

He has made her, if married, in the eye of the law, civilly dead.

He has taken from her all right in property, even to the wages she earns.

He has made her, morally, an irresponsible being, as she can commit many crimes with impunity, provided they be done in the presence of her husband. In the covenant of marriage, she is compelled to promise obedience to her husband, he becoming, to all intents and purposes, her master—the law giving him power to deprive her of her liberty, and to administer chastisement.

He has so framed the laws of divorce, as to what shall be the proper causes, and in case of separation, to whom the guardianship of the children shall be given, as to be wholly regardless of the happiness of women—the law, in all cases, going upon a false supposition of the supremacy of man, and giving all power into his hands.

After depriving her of all rights as a married woman, if single, and the owner of property, he has taxed her to support a government which recognizes her only when her property can be made profitable to it.

He has monopolized nearly all the profitable employments, and from those she is permitted to follow, she receives but a scanty remuneration. He closes against her all the avenues to wealth and distinction which he considers most honorable to himself. As a teacher of theology, medicine or law, she is not known.

He has denied her the facilities for obtaining a thorough education, all colleges being closed against her.

He allows her in church, as well as state, but a subordinate position, claiming apostolic authority for her exclusion from the ministry, and, with some exceptions, from any public participation in the affairs of the church.

He has created a false public sentiment by giving to the world a different code of morals for men and women, by which moral delinquencies which exclude women from society, are not only tolerated, but deemed of little account in man. . . .

He has endeavored, in every way that he could, to destroy her confidence in her own powers, to lessen her self-respect, and to make her willing to lead a dependent and abject life.

Now, in view of this entire disfranchisement of one-half the people of this country, their social and religious degradation—in view of the unjust laws above mentioned, and because women do feel themselves aggrieved, oppressed and fraudulently deprived of their most sacred rights, we insist that they have immediate admission to all the rights and privileges which belong to them as citizens of the United States.

In entering upon the great work before us, we anticipate no small amount of misconception, misrepresentation and ridicule; but we shall use every instrumentality within our power to effect our object. We shall employ agents, circulate tracts, petition the state and national legislatures, and endeavor to enlist the pulpit and the press in our behalf.

HENRY DAVID THOREAU

CIVIL DISOBEDIENCE

Henry David Thoreau (1817–1862) grew up in Concord, Massachusetts, and graduated from Harvard in 1837, the year in which his mentor Ralph Waldo Emerson delivered his famous address "The American Scholar" there. Like Emerson, Thoreau was a "transcendalist," who saw nature as man's greatest teacher. His classic *Walden* offers his meditations on two years spent living alone in a cabin on the banks of Walden Pond. Despite his preference for the solitude of the Concord woods, he was a sharp social critic and political activist and a strong supporter of the abolition of slavery. "Civil Disobedience," an essay that influenced Mahatma Gandhi and Reverend Martin Luther King, Jr., was inspired by his opposition to the Mexican War. In 1845 the James K. Polk administration bullied Mexico into a war, and forced it to sell the U.S. about a third of its territory in exchange for peace. Like many Northerners, Thoreau was appalled both at the slenderness of the pretext upon which Polk declared war and at the fact that the conflict would clearly result in a great expansion of territory into which slavery would spread. When the fighting broke out he personally seceded from the union, as it were, refusing to pay his taxes to carry on what he regarded as an unjust war. Thoreau spent a night in the Concord jail before an unidentified person—possibly his aunt—bailed him out, and four years later he published this striking statement of his beliefs.

Thoreau carried the doctrine that "that government is best which governs least" to its extreme, and perhaps logical, conclusion: if less is better, the government that is truly best is one "which governs not at all." Respect for the law for him was less important than "respect for the right." The essay is a stirring call to the individual to stand up against Tocqueville's "tyranny of the majority."

It is also, though, an arrogant assertion that the author belongs to the "wise minority," walking in the footsteps of Christ, Copernicus, and Luther. But once one not only opposes but refuses to abide by majority political decisions one thinks misguided, the only way to settle disputes is by force—a stance hardly compatible with the spirit of compromise that is so necessary to the smooth running of a democratic government.

I heartily accept the motto,—"That government is best which governs least;" and I should like to see it acted up to more rapidly and systematically. Carried out, it finally amounts to this, which also I believe,—"That government is best which governs not at all;" and when men are prepared for it, that will be the kind of government which they will have. Government is at best but an expedient; but most governments are usually, and all governments are sometimes, inexpedient. The objections which have been brought against a standing army, and they are many and weighty, and deserve to prevail, may also at last be brought against a standing govern-

ment. The standing army is only an arm of the standing government. The government itself, which is only the mode which the people have chosen to execute their will, is equally liable to be abused and perverted before the people can act through it. . . .

Must the citizen ever for a moment, or in the least degree, resign his conscience to the legislator? Why has every man a conscience, then? I think that we should be men first, and subjects afterward. It is not desirable to cultivate a respect for the law, so much as for the right. The only obligation which I have a right to assume is to do at any time what I think right. It is truly enough said, that a corporation has no conscience; but a corporation of conscientious men is a corporation *with* a conscience. Law never made men a whit more just; and, by means of their respect for it, even the well-disposed are daily made the agents of injustice. A common and natural result of an undue respect for law is, that you may see a file of soldiers, colonel, captain, corporal, privates, powder-monkeys, and all, marching in admirable order over hill and dale to the wars, against their wills, ay, against their common sense and consciences, which makes it very steep marching indeed, and produces a palpitation of the heart. They have no doubt that it is a damnable business in which they are concerned; they are all peaceably inclined. . . .

The mass of men serve the state thus, not as men mainly, but as machines, with their bodies. They are the standing army, and the militia, jailors, constables, posse comitatus, etc. In most cases there is no free exercise whatever of the judgment or of the moral sense; but they put themselves on a level with wood and earth and stones; and wooden men can perhaps be manufactured that will serve the purpose as well. Such command no more respect than men of straw or a lump of dirt. They have the same sort of worth only as horses and dogs. Yet such as these even are commonly esteemed good citizens. Others— as most legislators, politicians, lawyers, ministers, and office-holders—serve the state chiefly with their heads; and, as they rarely make any moral distinctions, they are as likely to serve the Devil, without *intending* it, as God. A very few, as heroes, patriots, martyrs, reformers in the great sense, and *men*, serve the state with their consciences also, and so necessarily resist it for the most part; and they are commonly treated as enemies by it. . . .

How does it become a man to behave toward this American government to-day? I answer, that he cannot without disgrace be associated with it. I cannot for an instant recognize that political organization as *my* government which is the *slave's* government also. . . .

Unjust laws exist: shall we be content to

Henry David Thoreau in 1856, two years after the publication of his most famous work, *Walden.*

obey them, or shall we endeavor to amend them, and obey them until we have succeeded, or shall we transgress them at once? Men generally, under such a government as this, think that they ought to wait until they have persuaded the majority to alter them. They think that, if they should resist, the remedy would be worse than the evil. But it is the fault of the government itself that the remedy *is* worse than the evil. *It* makes it worse. Why is it not more apt to anticipate and provide for reform? Why does it not cherish its wise minority? Why does it cry and resist before it is hurt? Why does it not encourage its citizens to be on the alert to point out its faults, and *do* better than it would have them? Why does it always crucify Christ, and excommunicate Copernicus and Luther, and pronounce Washington and Franklin rebels? . . .

I do not hesitate to say, that those who call themselves Abolitionists should at once effectually withdraw their support, both in person and property, from the government of Massachusetts and not wait till they constitute a majority of one, before they suffer the right to prevail through them. I think that it is enough if they have God on their side, without waiting for that other one. Moreover, any man more right than his neighbors constitutes a majority of one already. . . .

Under a government which imprisons any unjustly, the true place for a just man is also a prison. . . .

Is a democracy, such as we know it, the last improvement possible in government? Is it not possible to take a step further towards recognizing and organizing the rights of man? There will never be a really free and enlightened State until the State comes to recognize the individual as a higher and independent power, from which all its own power and authority are derived, and treats him accordingly. I please myself with imagining a State at last which can afford to be just to all men, and to treat the individual with respect as a neighbor; which even would not think it inconsistent with its own repose if a few were to live aloof from it, not meddling with it, nor embraced by it, who fulfilled all the duties of neighbors and fellow-men. A State which bore this kind of fruit, and suffered it to drop off as fast as it ripened, would prepare the way for a still more perfect and glorious State, which also I have imagined, but not yet anywhere seen.

ABRAHAM LINCOLN
SPEECH AT PEORIA

One of the greatest debates in American history, the Lincoln–Douglas debate, took place in Illinois in 1858 between Democratic Congressman Stephen Douglas (1813–1861) and his challenger Abraham Lincoln (1809–1865). Lincoln was a lawyer who had served a term in the U.S. House of Representatives, and had become a leader of the Republican Party shortly after its founding in 1854. Republicans like Lincoln opposed slavery, but were not outright abolitionists like Henry David Thoreau, who wanted slavery banished immediately. No serious politician in the 1850s was an abolitionist; to state such a radical view would have been outright political suicide. Lincoln was an intensely practical and pragmatic politician who believed that an institution that embraced so many people and was the source of much of the wealth of a large portion of the United States could only be phased out gradually, with financial compensation to those who had invested their savings in slave property. However, he felt very deeply that slavery was morally wrong and incompatible with the fundamental premises of a free society, and hence that it had to be set upon "a course towards ultimate extinction." The first vital step was "free soil," the Republican demand that slavery not be allowed to spread into American territories that had not yet become populated enough to be states.

In his debate with Douglas at Peoria, Lincoln hammered away at the inconsistency of professing to hold traditional American beliefs about liberty and equality while supporting the enslavement of a race. He worried that the Americans of his day were abandoning their principles, "giving up the old for the new faith." The old faith was that all men were created equal, the new that the right to enslave others was, as Southern leaders like John C. Calhoun insisted, a "sacred right of self-government." Once the moral wrong of slavery was admitted, Lincoln would grant that it had "existing legal rights" and that arguments of "necessity" had some force. The slave system, he knew, could not be safely overturned overnight with the wave of a wand, but he felt the moral indifference toward slavery that Douglas expressed was not acceptable.

Douglas beat Lincoln in the Senate race. However, Lincoln's strong performance gave him new national prominence and a crack at the Republican presidential nomination two years later.

Equal justice to the South, it is said, requires us to consent to the extension of slavery to new countries. That is to say, inasmuch as you do not object to my taking my hog to Nebraska, therefore I must not object to you taking your slave. Now, I admit that this is perfectly logical, if there is no difference between hogs and negroes. But while you thus require me to deny the humanity of the negro, I wish to ask whether you of the South, yourselves, have ever been willing to do as much? It is kindly provided that of all those who come into the world only a small percentage are natural tyrants. That percentage is no larger in the slave states than in the free. The great majority South, as well as North, have human sympathies, of which they can no more divest themselves than they can of their sensibility to physical pain. These sympathies in the bosoms of the Southern people manifest, in many ways, their sense of the wrong of slavery, and their consciousness that, after all, there is humanity in the negro. If they deny this, let me address them a few plain questions. In 1820 you joined the North, almost unanimously, in declaring the African slave-trade piracy, and in annexing to it the punishment of death. Why did you do this? If you did not feel that it was wrong, why did you join in providing that men should be hung for it? The practice was no more than bringing wild negroes from Africa to such as would buy them. But you never thought of hanging men for catching and selling wild horses, wild buffaloes, or wild bears. . . .

The doctrine of self-government is right,—absolutely and eternally right,—but it has no just application as here attempted. Or perhaps I should rather say that whether it has such application depends upon whether a negro is not or is a man. If he is not a man, in that case he who is a man may as a matter of self-government do just what he pleases with him.

But if the negro is a man, is it not to that extent a total destruction of self-government to say that he too shall not govern himself? When the white man governs himself, that is self-government; but when he governs himself and also governs another man, that is more than self-government—that is despotism. If the negro is a man, why then my ancient faith teaches me that "all men are created equal," and that there can be no moral right in connection with one man's making a slave of another. . . .

. . . [N]o man is good enough to govern another man without that other's consent. I say this is the leading principle, the sheet-anchor of American republicanism. Our Declaration of Independence says:

> We hold these truths to be self-evident: That all men are created equal; that they are endowed by their Creator with certain inalienable rights; that among these are life, liberty and the pursuit of happiness. That to secure these rights, governments are instituted among men, DERIVING THEIR JUST POWERS FROM THE CONSENT OF THE GOVERNED.

I have quoted so much at this time merely to show that, according to our ancient faith, the just powers of governments are derived from the consent of the governed. Now the relation of master and slave is *pro tanto* a total violation of this principle. The master not only governs the slave without his consent, but he governs him by a set of rules altogether different from those which he prescribes for himself. Allow all the governed an equal voice in the government, and that, and that only, is self-government.

Let it not be said I am contending for the

A lithograph entitled "President Lincoln, Writing the Proclamation of Freedom."
The anguished Lincoln is surrounded by symbols of the great struggle—anti-
slavery petitions, a draft poster, the secessionist writings of Calhoun and John
Randolph, a poster of the opposition Peace Democrats, Daniel Webster's
nationalistic interpretation of the Constitution, the Bible, and many more.

establishment of political and social equality between the whites and blacks. I have already said
the contrary. I am not combating the argument
of necessity, arising from the fact that the blacks
are already among us; but I am combating what is
set up as moral argument for allowing them to be
taken where they have never yet been—arguing
against the extension of a bad thing, which,
where it already exists, we must of necessity
manage as we best can. . . .

Repeal the Missouri Compromise, repeal all
compromises, repeal the Declaration of Independence, repeal all past history, you still cannot
repeal human nature. . . .

Little by little, but steadily as man's march to
the grave, we have been giving up the old for the
new faith. Near eighty years ago we began by
declaring that all men are created equal; but now
from that beginning we have run down to the
other declaration, that for some men to enslave
others is a "sacred right of self-government."
These principles cannot stand together. They are
as opposite as God and Mammon; and whoever
holds to the one must despise the other. . . .

The spirit of seventy-six and the spirit of Nebraska are utter antagonisms; and the former is being rapidly displaced by the latter. . . .

Our republican robe is soiled and trailed in the dust. Let us repurify it. Let us turn and wash it white in the spirit, if not the blood, of the Revolution. Let us turn slavery from its claims of "moral right" back upon its existing legal rights and its arguments of "necessity." Let us return it to the position our fathers gave it, and there let it rest in peace. Let us readopt the Declaration of Independence, and with it the practices and policy which harmonize with it. Let North and South—let all Americans—let all lovers of liberty everywhere join in the great and good work. If we do this, we shall not only have saved the Union, but we shall have so saved it as to make and to keep it forever worthy of the saving. We shall have so saved it that the succeeding millions of free, happy people, the world over, shall rise up and call us blessed to the latest generations.

SOUTH CAROLINA SECESSION STATEMENT

Abraham Lincoln won the Republican nomination in 1860 and was able to win the presidency over the divided Democrats with about 40 percent of the popular vote. He was the first purely sectional candidate in American history to win the White House, carrying only 2 of the more than 1100 southern counties and not even appearing on the ballot in ten states.

Upon Lincoln's election, the South Carolina legislature said farewell to the Union in a statement that rehashed the history of the American Revolution and declared that the state was only claiming the same right of resistance that the patriots of 1776 had exercised. It insisted that the bonds between the state and the federal government were a "compact," that the failure of one party to live up to the contract allows the other to break it, and that in cases "where no arbiter is provided" each party must make its own judgment on the matter. This historical argument is open to a good deal of question. A stronger case can be made for the view that the Constitution was not a mere compact or "league" between the states but instead a government rooted in the assent of "we the people," and could not be dissolved at the will of one discontented party. The federal government was the proper arbiter in disputes among the states and between it and one or more states, but the South Carolina legislators were not historians searching for the truth; they were debaters who succeeded in making a case.

It is tempting to see an analogy between South Carolina's challenge to the authority of the central government and that of Lithuania, Armenia, and other Soviet republics in our era. One obvious difference is that South Carolina's secession was motivated by a desire to deprive a large fraction of its own population—its black slaves—of any human rights. A second is that South Carolina voluntarily ratified the Constitution and surrendered part of its sovereignty to Washington, while the Soviet empire was created by force. The moral case for the right of secession is far stronger when the union under challenge was not the result of initial voluntary consent.

. . . And now the State of South Carolina having resumed her separate and equal place among nations, deems it due to herself, to the remaining United States of America, and to the nations of the world, that she should declare the immediate causes which have led to this act.

In the year 1765, that portion of the British Empire embracing Great Britain undertook to make laws for the Government of that portion composed of the thirteen American Colonies. A struggle for the right of self-government ensued, which resulted, on the 4th of July, 1776, in a Declaration, by the Colonies, "that they are, and of right ought to be, *free and independent states*; and that, as free and independent States, they have full power to levy war, conclude peace, contract alliances, establish commerce, and to do all other acts and things which independent States may of right do."

They further solemnly declared that whenever any "form of government becomes destructive of the ends for which it was established, it is the right of the people to alter or abolish it, and to institute a new government." Deeming the Government of Great Britain to have become destructive of these ends, they declared that the Colonies "are absolved from all allegiance to the British Crown, and that all political connection between them and the State of Great Britain is, and ought to be, totally dissolved." . . .

Thus were established the two great principles asserted by the Colonies, namely, the right of a State to govern itself; and the right of a people to abolish a Government when it becomes destructive of the ends for which it was instituted. And concurrent with the establishment of these principles, was the fact, that each Colony became and was recognized by the mother country as *a free, sovereign and independent state.* . . .

We hold that the Government thus established is subject to the two great principles asserted in the Declaration of Independence; and we hold further, that the mode of its formation subjects it to a third fundamental principle, namely, the law of compact. We maintain that in every compact between two or more parties, the obligation is mutual; that the failure of one of the contracting parties to perform a material part of the agreement, entirely releases the obligation of the other; and that, where no arbiter is provided, each party is remitted to his own judgment to determine the fact of failure, with all its consequences. . . .

The ends for which this Constitution was framed are declared by itself to be "to form a more perfect union, establish justice, insure domestic tranquillity, provide for the common defence, promote the general welfare, and secure the blessings of liberty to ourselves and our posterity."

These ends it endeavored to accomplish by a Federal Government, in which each State was recognized as an equal, and had separate control over its own institutions. The right of property in slaves was recognized by giving to free persons distinct political rights; by giving them the right to represent, and burdening them with direct

This illustration decorated the sheet music for "Secession Quick Step," a Confederate song by Herman Schreiner, published in Macon, Georgia. The rattlesnake with the legend *"noli me tangere"* (don't touch me) derives from a flag of the Revolutionary era.

taxes for, three-fifths of their slaves; by authorizing the importation of slaves for twenty years; and by stipulating for the rendition of fugitives from labor.

We affirm that these ends for which this Government was instituted have been defeated, and the Government itself has been destructive of them by the action of the non-slaveholding States. Those States have assumed the right of deciding upon the propriety of our domestic institutions; and have denied the rights of property established in fifteen of the States and recognized by the Constitution; they have denounced as sinful the institution of Slavery; they have permitted the open establishment among them of societies, whose avowed object is to disturb the peace of and eloin the property of the citizens of other States. They have encouraged and assisted thousands of our slaves to leave their homes; and those who remain, have been incited by emissaries, books, and pictures, to servile insurrection.

ABRAHAM LINCOLN

FIRST INAUGURAL ADDRESS

Lincoln took office on March 4, 1861 in unprecedented circumstances. Seven out of the 34 existing states, all of them in the Deep South, had voted to leave the Union and join the would-be rival nation South Carolina had taken the lead in organizing, the Confederate States of America. A number of others in the Upper South were considering doing the same. Lincoln began his address in these tense circumstances with assurances, not reproduced here, that he would abide strictly by the law and the Constitution, and do nothing to endanger "the property, peace, and security" of any section of the country. As slavery was lawful in many states, the laws enforcing it would thus be upheld like any others.

Lincoln then set forth his grounds for insisting that the Constitution had created a perpetual Union. His argument about the consequences of a minority decision to "secede rather than acquiesce" is of enormous relevance to the problems of Yugoslavia, the U.S.S.R., India, and other multi-ethnic societies today. The merits of any particular secessionist argument have to be considered on its own terms, but Lincoln is right to warn that the logic of secessionism may lead to increasing fragmentation and endless conflict.

. . . I hold that, in contemplation of universal law and of the Constitution, the Union of these States is perpetual. Perpetuity is implied, if not expressed, in the fundamental law of all national governments. It is safe to assert that no government proper ever had a provision in its organic law for its own termination.

Continue to execute all the express provisions of our National Constitution, and the Union will endure forever—it being impossible to destroy it except by some action not provided for in the instrument itself.

Again, if the United States be not a government proper, but an association of States in the nature of contract merely, can it, as a contract, be peaceably unmade by less than all the parties who made it? One party to a contract may violate it—break it, so to speak; but does it not require all to lawfully rescind it?

Descending from these general principles, we find the proposition that, in legal contemplation the Union is perpetual confirmed by the history of the Union itself. The Union is much older than the Constitution. It was formed, in fact, by the Articles of Association in 1774. It was matured and continued by the Declaration of

Independence in 1776. It was further matured, and the faith of all the then thirteen States expressly plighted and engaged that it should be perpetual, by the Articles of Confederation in 1778. And, finally, in 1787 one of the declared objects for ordaining and establishing the Constitution was "to form a more perfect Union."

But if the destruction of the Union by one or by a part only of the States be lawfully possible, the Union is less perfect than before the Constitution, having lost the vital element of perpetuity. . . .

It follows from these views that no State upon its own mere motion can lawfully get out of the Union; that resolves and ordinances to that effect are legally void; and that acts of violence, within any State or States, against the authority of the United States, are insurrectionary or revolutionary, according to circumstances.

I therefore consider that, in view of the Constitution and the laws, the Union is unbroken; and to the extent of my ability I shall take care, as the Constitution itself expressly enjoins upon me, that the laws of the Union be faithfully executed in all the States. Doing this I deem to be only a simple duty on my part; and I shall perform it so far as practicable, unless my rightful masters, the American people, shall withhold the requisite means, or in some authoritative manner direct the contrary. I trust this will not be regarded as a menace, but only as the declared purpose of the Union that it will constitutionally defend and maintain itself. . . .

If by the mere force of numbers a majority should deprive a minority of any clearly written constitutional right, it might, in a moral point of view, justify revolution—certainly would if such a right were a vital one. But such is not our case. All the vital rights of minorities and of individuals are so plainly assured to them by affirmations and negations, guarantees and prohibitions, in the Constitution, that controversies never arise concerning them. But no organic law can ever be framed with a provision specifically applicable to every question which may occur in practical administration.

No foresight can anticipate, nor any document of reasonable length contain, express provisions for all possible questions. Shall fugitives from labor be surrendered by national or by State authority? The Constitution does not expressly say. *May* Congress prohibit slavery in the Territories? The Constitution does not expressly say. *Must* Congress protect slavery in the Territories? The Constitution does not expressly say.

From questions of this class spring all our constitutional controversies, and we divide upon them into majorities and minorities. If the minority will not acquiesce, the majority must, or the government must cease. There is no other alternative; for continuing the government is acquiescence on one side or the other.

If a minority in such case will secede rather than acquiesce, they make a precedent which in turn will divide and ruin them; for a minority of their own will secede from them whenever a majority refuses to be controlled by such minority. For instance, why may not any portion of a new confederacy a year or two hence arbitrarily secede again, precisely as portions of the present Union now claim to secede from it? All who cherish disunion sentiments are now being educated to the exact temper of doing this.

Is there such perfect identity of interests among the States to compose a new Union, as to produce harmony only, and prevent renewed secession?

Plainly, the central idea of secession is the essence of anarchy. A majority held in restraint by constitutional checks and limitations, and always changing easily with deliberate changes of popular opinions and sentiments, is the only true sovereign of a free people. Whoever rejects it does, of necessity, fly to anarchy or to despotism. Unanimity is impossible; the rule of a minority, as a permanent arrangement, is wholly inadmissible; so that, rejecting the majority principle, anarchy or despotism in some form is all that is left.

This country, with its institutions, belongs to the people who inhabit it. Whenever they shall grow weary of the existing government, they can exercise their constitutional right of amending it, or their revolutionary right to dismember or overthrow it. I cannot be ignorant of the fact that many worthy and patriotic citizens are desirous of having the National Constitution amended. While I make no recommendation of amendments, I fully recognize the rightful authority of the people over the whole subject, to be exercised in either of the modes prescribed in the instrument itself; and I should, under existing circumstances, favor rather than oppose a fair opportunity being afforded the people to act upon it. . . .

Why should there not be a patient confidence in the ultimate justice of the people? Is there any better or equal hope in the world? . . .

By the frame of the government under which we live, this same people have wisely given their public servants but little power for mischief; and have, with equal wisdom, provided for the return of that little to their own hands at very short intervals. While the people retain their virtue

and vigilance, no administration, by any extreme of wickedness or folly, can very seriously injure the government in the short space of four years.

In your hands, my dissatisfied fellow-countrymen, and not in mine, is the momentous issue of civil war. The government will not assail you. You can have no conflict without being yourselves the aggressors. You have no oath registered in heaven to destroy the government, while I shall have the most solemn one to "preserve, protect, and defend it."

I am loath to close. We are not enemies, but friends. We must not be enemies. Though passion may have strained, it must not break our bonds of affection. The mystic chords of memory, stretching from every battle-field and patriot grave to every living heart and hearthstone all over this broad land, will yet swell the chorus of the Union when again touched, as surely they will be, by the better angels of our nature.

Abraham Lincoln delivers his First Inaugural Address on the steps of the unfinished Capitol building.

GETTYSBURG ADDRESS

The battle of Gettysburg, in July of 1863, was a great turning point in the Civil War. For the first time the Union Army was able to administer a convincing defeat to the Confederate forces led by Robert E. Lee. It was the beginning of the end for the Confederacy. Lincoln's presence at the ceremonies to dedicate the graveyard there was an afterthought. The featured speaker was Edward Everett, the former Secretary of State and President of Harvard, who was thought to be the finest orator in the country. The officials in charge of national cemeteries doubted that President Lincoln had sufficient skills as a speaker to do justice to the occasion, but asked him to say a few words following Everett's address. Everett's torrent of high-blown rhetoric went on for two hours, not unusual in an age with few other sources of entertainment. Lincoln said more in his two minutes.

The Gettysburg Address interprets the war as a test of whether or not a government dedicated to the proposition that "all men are created equal" can long endure. In the earlier stages of the conflict, Lincoln had avoided making grand utterances about the equality of man and attacking slavery, out of fear of alienating opinion in the border slave states that had not joined the Confederacy. He had been careful to define the North's aims modestly as a simple restoration of the Union, not a social revolution that would destroy slavery. As the great black abolitionist leader Frederick Douglass said, in order to "free his country from the great crime of slavery," Lincoln first had to "save his country from dismemberment and ruin." To accomplish that essential task he had to have the "powerful cooperation of his loyal fellow-countrymen," who had strong prejudices against blacks. "Had he put the abolition of slavery before the salvation of the Union," Douglass argued, "he would inevitably have driven from him a powerful class of the American people and rendered resistance to rebellion impossible."

As the death toll mounted without any sign that the tide was turning, however, Lincoln came to believe that striking a blow against slavery would help his cause. In late 1862 he issued the Emancipation Proclamation, which set the slaves free on January 1, 1863, and ordered that black troops be accepted in the Union Army, a decision that shocked not only Confederates but a great many prejudiced Northern whites. He claimed that he did so out of military necessity, but he likely welcomed the necessity. The Gettysburg Address reveals the transformation of the Civil War from a war for the Union into a war for black freedom. Despite Lincoln's disclaimer, the world did "note" and "long remember" what he said there. It summed up central American political values in words for the ages.

Four score and seven years ago our fathers brought forth on this continent, a new nation, conceived in Liberty, and dedicated to the proposition that all men are created equal.

Now we are engaged in a great civil war, testing whether that nation, or any nation so conceived and so dedicated, can long endure. We are met on a great battle-field of that war. We

have come to dedicate a portion of that field, as a final resting place for those who here gave their lives that that nation might live. It is altogether fitting and proper that we should do this.

But, in a larger sense, we can not dedicate— we can not consecrate—we can not hallow— this ground. The brave men, living and dead, who struggled here, have consecrated it, far above our poor power to add or detract. The world will little note, nor long remember what we say here, but it can never forget what they did here. It is for us the living, rather, to be dedicated here to the unfinished work which they who fought here have thus far so nobly advanced. It is rather for us to be here dedicated to the great task remaining before us—that from these honored dead we take increased devotion to that cause for which they gave the last full measure of devotion—that we here highly resolve that these dead shall not have died in vain—that this nation, under God, shall have a new birth of freedom—and that government of the people, by the people, for the people, shall not perish from the earth.

SUSAN B. ANTHONY
WOMEN'S RIGHT TO VOTE

Women's suffrage advocates felt that the time was ripe for protest in the aftermath of the Civil War, when newly freed blacks won the right to vote in 1870 as a result of the Fifteenth Amendment to the Constitution. Their argument that the amendment barred electoral discrimination on the grounds of sex as well as "race, color, or previous condition of servitude" was never taken seriously. So Susan B. Anthony (1820–1906) and Elizabeth Cady Stanton (1815–1902) formed the National Woman Suffrage Association to crusade for another amendment guaranteeing the franchise to women, a drive that succeeded half a century later. Anthony engaged in civil disobedience on behalf of her cause by seeking to vote in the presidential election of 1872. Her defense of her actions here certainly does not reflect what the Framers meant by "we the people," "bill of attainder," or "ex post facto laws," but eventually the American public would come to agree with her on the substance of the issue.

Friends and Fellow Citizens:—I stand before you to-night under indictment for the alleged crime of having voted at the last presidential election, without having a lawful right to vote. It shall be my work this evening to prove to you that in thus voting, I not only committed no crime, but, instead, simply exercised my citizen's rights, guaranteed to me and all United States citizens by the National Constitution, beyond the power of any State to deny.

The preamble of the Federal Constitution says:

We, the people of the United States, in order to form a more perfect union, establish justice, insure domestic tranquility, provide for the common defense, promote the general welfare, and secure the blessings of liberty to ourselves and our posterity, do ordain and establish this Constitution for the United States of America.

It was we, the people; not we, the white male citizens; nor yet we, the male citizens; but we, the whole people, who formed the Union. And we formed it, not to give the blessings of liberty, but to secure them; not to the half of ourselves and the half of our posterity, but to the whole people—women as well as men. And it is a downright mockery to talk to women of their enjoyment of the blessings of liberty while they are denied the use of the only means of securing them provided by this democratic-republican government—the ballot.

For any State to make sex a qualification that must ever result in the disfranchisement of one entire half of the people is to pass a bill of at-

The aging Susan B. Anthony in her study, accompanied by portraits of fellow crusaders for women's rights. Closest to her hand is Elizabeth Cady Stanton, on the left, and Frances Wright, to the right.

tainder, or an *ex post facto* law, and is therefore a violation of the supreme law of the land. By it the blessings of liberty are for ever withheld from women and their female posterity. To them this government has no just powers derived from the consent of the governed. To them this government is not a democracy. It is not a republic. It is an odious aristocracy; a hateful oligarchy of sex: the most hateful aristocracy ever established on the face of the globe. An oligarchy of wealth, where the rich govern the poor; an oligarchy of learning, where the educated govern the igno-

rant; or even an oligarchy of race, where the Saxon rules the African, might be endured; but this oligarchy of sex, which makes father, brothers, husband, sons, the oligarchs over the mother and sisters, the wife and daughters of every household—which ordains all men sovereigns, all women subjects, carries dissension, discord and rebellion into every home of the nation.

Webster, Worcester and Bouvier all define a citizen to be a person in the United States, entitled to vote and hold office.

The only question left to be settled now

is: Are women persons? And I hardly believe any of our opponents will have the hardihood to say they are not. Being persons, then, women are citizens; and no State has a right to make any law, or to enforce any old law, that shall abridge their privileges or immunities. Hence, every discrimination against women in the constitutions and laws of the several States is to-day null and void, precisely as is every one against negroes.

ADDRESS TO THE AMERICAN MISSIONARY ASSOCIATION

Frederick Douglass (1817–1895) was born a slave in Maryland. He escaped and fled to the North, where he wrote his autobiography, *Narrative of the Life of Frederick Douglass*, edited his abolitionist paper, *The North Star*, and spoke on behalf of the black cause for the rest of his life.

In this selection—his last public address, given in Massachusetts in 1894—Douglass reviews what had happened to his people since Emancipation and the effort to reconstruct the South. Even in New England blacks were denied "fair play" in employment, and in the South, where nine out of ten of the country's blacks lived, things were much worse. During Reconstruction (1865–1877), the North had been able to force the southern states to grant the ballot to blacks, but formal political freedom, as Douglass stresses, was not enough to overcome the enormous handicaps left by a lifetime of enforced servitude. Given the immensity of the obstacles, Douglass saw remarkable progress in the first three decades of freedom.

However, he did not sufficiently appreciate—or perhaps optimistically chose to overlook—the alarming developments then underway in the South. In the 1890s and the opening decade of the twentieth century, the franchise was denied blacks throughout the South by legalistic devices that the Supreme Court failed to recognize for what they so obviously were—unconstitutional restrictions upon voting rights guaranteed by the Fifteenth Amendment. The faith of Douglass that "we have the organic law of the land on our side" proved to be sadly misplaced. The resistance to black patrons on southern railroads and steamboats and in hotels that Douglass cites as a sign of black progress was progress in the sense that there were then "educated, cultivated, and refined" blacks seeking access to such facilities, but the response of dominant whites to that progress was the building of an elaborate system of racial segregation that was designed to keep blacks "in their place" and to ensure white supremacy. That system of legally enforced racial segregation did not come under serious attack until World War II, and it was overturned only slowly and with great effort.

It has sometimes been thought and said that Northern benevolence has already done enough for the moral and religious improvement of the Negro, and that the time has arrived when such help is no longer needed, that the Negro should now be left to take care of himself, that the duty of the white people of the country was fully and fairly performed when they restored the Negro to his freedom.

In answer to this position, I have to say that

the claims of the Negro, viewed in the light of justice and fair play, are not so easily satisfied. The simple act of emancipation was indeed a great and glorious one, but it did not remove the consequences of slavery, nor could it atone for the centuries of wrong endured by the liberated bondman. It was a great and glorious thing to put an end to his physical bondage, but there was left to him a dreadful legacy of moral and intellectual deformity, which the abolition of physical bondage could not remove. . . .

In answer to the question as to what shall be done with the Negro, I have sometimes replied, "Do nothing with him, give him fair play and let him alone." But in reporting me, it has been found convenient and agreeable to place the emphasis of my speech on one part of my sentence. They willingly accepted my idea of letting the Negro alone, but not so my idea of giving the Negro fair play. It has always been easier for some of the American people to imitate the priest and the Levite, rather than the example of the good Samaritan; to let the Negro alone rather than to give him fair play. Even here in New England—the most enlightened and benevolent section of our country—the Negro has been excluded from nearly all profitable employments. I speak from experience. I came here from the South fifty-six years ago, with a good trade in my hands, and might have commanded by my trade three dollars a day, but my white brethren, while praying for their daily bread, were not willing that I should obtain mine by the same means open to them. I was compelled to work for one dollar a day, when others working at my trade were receiving three dollars a day.

But to return. When we consider the long years of slavery, the years of enforced ignorance, the years of injustice, of cruel strifes and degradation to which the Negro was doomed, the duty of the nation is not, and cannot be, performed by simply letting him alone.

If Northern benevolence could send a missionary to every dark corner of the South, if it could place a church on every hilltop in the South, a schoolhouse in every valley, and support a preacher in the one, and a teacher in the other,

for fifty years to come, they could not then even compensate the poor freedman for the long years of wrong and suffering he has been compelled to endure. The people of the North should remember that slavery and the degradation of the Negro were inflicted by the power of the nation, that the North was a consenting party to the wrong, and that a common sin can only be atoned and condoned by a common repentance. . . .

Under the whole heavens, there never was a people emancipated under conditions more unfavorable to mental, moral and physical improvement than were the slaves of our Southern States. They were emancipated not by the moral judgment of the nation as a whole; they were emancipated not as a blessing to themselves, but as a punishment to their masters; not to strengthen the emancipated, but to weaken the rebels, and, naturally enough, taking the emancipation in this sense, the old master class have resented it and have resolved to make his freedom a curse rather than a blessing to the Negro. In many instances they have been quite successful in accomplishing this purpose. Then the manner of emancipation was against the Negro. He was turned loose to the open sky without a foot of earth on which to stand; without a single farming implement; he was turned loose to the elements, to hunger, to destitution; without money, without friends; and to endure the pitiless storm of the old master's wrath. The old master had in his possession the land and the power to crush the Negro, and the Negro in return had no power of defence. The difference between his past condition and his present condition is that in the past the old master class could say to him, "You shall work for me or I will whip you to death"; in the present condition he can say to him, "You shall work for me or I will starve you to death." And to-day the Negro is in this latter condition.

No other nation ever treated a liberated people in such wise. When Russia emancipated her slaves to the number of twenty millions, she gave the head of each family three acres of ground, and implements with which to till the soil; that emancipation was merciful to the serf and honorable to a despotic government. It is to be regret-

An 1880s lithograph, "Heroes of the Colored Race," shows Frederick Douglass in the center and former U.S. Senators Bruce and Revels on either side. In the margins are other black leaders, Lincoln, Ulysses S. Grant, and John Brown.

ted that no such honor is to be accorded to this nation and government in its treatment of its emancipated slaves. They were turned loose, sick and well; strong and weak; young and old; in a state of utter destitution, hardly owning the clothes on their backs. . . .

When we consider the destitution in which the colored people of the United States were when emancipated, the wonder is not that they are so far in the rear of the white man's civilization, but that their advancement has been as rapid and complete as the evidence demonstrates. . . .

With all the discouraging circumstances that now surround what is improperly called the Negro problem, I do not despair of a better day. It is sometimes said that the condition of the colored man to-day is worse than it was in the time of slavery. To me this is simply an extravagance. We now have the organic law of the land on our side. We have thousands of teachers, and hundreds of thousands of pupils attending schools; we can now count our friends by the million. In many of the States we have the elective franchise; in some of them we have colored office-holders. It is no small advantage that we are citizens of this Republic by special amendment of the Constitution. The very resistance that we now meet on

Southern railroads, steamboats and hotels is evidence of our progress. It is not the Negro in his degradation that is objected to, but the Negro educated, cultivated and refined. The Negro who fails to respect himself, who makes no provision for himself or his family, and is content to live the life of a vagabond, meets no resistance. He is just where he is desired by his enemies. Perhaps you will say that this proves that education, wealth and refinement will do nothing for the Negro; but the answer to this is, "that the hair of the dog will cure the bite" eventually. All people suddenly springing from a lowly condition have to pass through a period of probation. At first they are denounced as "upstarts," but the "upstarts" of one generation are the élite of the next.

The history of the great Anglo-Saxon race should encourage the Negro to hope on and hope ever, and work on and work ever. They were once the slaves of the Normans; they were despised and insulted. They were looked upon as of coarser clay than the haughty Norman. Their language was despised and repudiated, but where to-day is the haughty Norman? What people and what language now rock the world by their power?

My hope for the Negro is largely based upon his enduring qualities. No persecutions, no proscriptions, no hardships are able to extinguish him. He neither dies out, nor goes out. He is here to stay, and while here he will partake of the blessings of your education, your progress, your civilization, and your Christian religion. His appeal to you to-day is for an equal chance in the race of life, and, dark and stormy as the present appears, his appeal will not go unanswered.

JOHN MARSHALL HARLAN
DISSENT FROM *PLESSY V. FERGUSON*

In theory, the three amendments to the Constitution passed during Reconstruction guaranteed full-fledged citizenship to American blacks. In time, one of these amendments—the Fourteenth—became the most litigated passage in the entire Constitution. No state shall "deprive any person of life, liberty, or property, without due process of law; nor deny to any person within its jurisdiction the equal protection of the law," it read in part. What did those broad and ambiguous phrases mean? The wording raised complicated questions about the nature of federalism, the power of the state, and the meaning of equality. Even today, more than a century later, such questions continue to split the Supreme Court into irreconcilable camps.

Equality was the issue in *Plessy v. Ferguson*. What sorts of state laws did the Fourteenth Amendment, with its reference to "equal protection," forbid? Homer Plessy, who was only one-eighth black (and looked white), challenged in court a Louisiana law that required separate railroad cars for black and white passengers. Was the state treating blacks and whites "equally" when it forced them to sit apart? The case wandered through the judicial system for quite some time, finally arriving at the Supreme Court in 1896, where Plessy lost. Justice Henry Billings Brown, for the majority, argued that integration—what he called the "enforced commingling of the two races"—was not necessary to civil and political equality between them. "Laws permitting, and even requiring their separation in places where they are liable to be brought into contact do not necessarily imply the inferiority of either race to the other," he wrote. Lousiana could recognize differences between the races without depriving blacks of the legal equality that is their right. Blacks could be "separate but equal."

In 1896, the court's opinion was not considered remarkable; indeed, it was hardly mentioned in the press. The views expressed in it were simply not controversial. Indeed, they were conventional wisdom. The unconventional thoughts were those of Justice John Marshall Harlan (1833–1911), whose dissenting opinion still remains the court's most eloquent plea for a color-blind Constitution.

The majority opinion in *Plessy* remained law until the separate-but-equal doctrine was rejected in 1954 in *Brown v. Board of Education*. *Plessy* had contained the seeds of its own destruction; gradually, over time, the stated commitment to equality came to assume more and more significance. On the other hand, Harlan's views have never been unequivocally embraced. The Constitution is still interpreted to allow color-conscious legislation—although that legislation now takes the form of laws and regulations that permit preferential treatment for blacks in an effort to compensate for past wrongs.

By the Louisiana statute, the validity of which is here involved, all railway companies (other than street railroad companies) carrying passengers in that State are required to have separate but equal accommodations for white and colored persons, "by providing two or more passenger coaches for each passenger train, *or* by dividing the passenger coaches by a *partition* so as to secure separate accommodations." Under this statute, no colored person is permitted to occupy a seat in a coach assigned to white persons; nor any white person, to occupy a seat in a coach assigned to colored persons. . . .

Thus the State regulates the use of a public highway by citizens of the United States solely upon the basis of race.

However apparent the injustice of such legislation may be, we have only to consider whether it is consistent with the Constitution of the United States. . . .

In respect of civil rights, common to all citizens, the Constitution of the United States does not, I think, permit any public authority to know the race of those entitled to be protected in the enjoyment of such rights. Every true man has pride of race, and under appropriate circumstances when the rights of others, his equals before the law, are not to be affected, it is his privilege to express such pride and to take such action based upon it as to him seems proper. But I deny that any legislative body or judicial tribunal may have regard to the race of citizens when the civil rights of those citizens are involved.

Indeed, such legislation, as that here in question, is inconsistent not only with that equality of rights which pertains to citizenship, National and State, but with the personal liberty enjoyed by every one within the United States.

The Thirteenth Amendment does not permit the withholding or the deprivation of any right necessarily inhering in freedom. It not only struck down the institution of slavery as previously existing in the United States, but it prevents the imposition of any burdens or disabilities that constitute badges of slavery or servitude. It decreed universal civil freedom in this country. This court has so adjudged. But that amendment having been found inadequate to the protection of the rights of those who had been in slavery, it was followed by the Fourteenth Amendment, which added greatly to the dignity and glory of American citizenship, and to the security of personal liberty, by declaring that "all persons born or naturalized in the United States, and subject to the jurisdiction thereof, are citizens of the United States and of the State wherein they reside," and that "no State shall make or enforce any law which shall abridge the privileges or immunities of citizens of the United States; nor shall any State deprive any person of life, liberty or property without due process of law, nor deny to any person within its jurisdiction the equal protection of the laws." These two amendments, if enforced according to their true intent and meaning, will protect all the civil rights that pertain to freedom and citizenship.

Finally, and to the end that no citizen should be denied, on account of his race, the privilege of participating in the political control of his country, it was declared by the Fifteenth Amendment that "the right of citizens of the United States to vote shall not be denied or abridged by the United States or by any State on account of race, color or previous condition of servitude."

These notable additions to the fundamental law were welcomed by the friends of liberty throughout the world. They removed the race line from our governmental systems. They had, as this court has said, a common purpose, namely, to secure "to a race recently emancipated, a race that through many generations have been held in slavery, all the civil rights that the superior race enjoy." They declared, in legal effect, this court has further said, "that the law in the States shall be the same for the black as for the white; that all persons, whether colored or white, shall stand equal before the laws of the States, and, in regard to the colored race, for whose protection the amendment was primarily designed, that no discrimination shall be made against them by law because of their color." . . .

It was said in argument that the statute of Louisiana does not discriminate against either race, but prescribes a rule applicable alike to white and colored citizens. But this argument does not meet the difficulty. Every one knows that the statute in question had its origin in the purpose, not so much to exclude white persons from railroad cars occupied by blacks, as to exclude colored people from coaches occupied by or assigned to white persons. Railroad corporations of Louisiana did not make discrimination among whites in the matter of accommodation for travellers. The thing to accomplish was, under the guise of giving equal accommodation for whites and blacks, to compel the latter to keep to themselves while travelling in railroad passenger coaches. No one would be so wanting in candor as to assert the contrary. The fundamental objection, therefore, to the statute is that it interferes with the personal freedom of citizens. . . .

If a white man and a black man choose to occupy the same public conveyance on a public highway, it is their right to do so, and no government, proceeding alone on grounds of race, can prevent it without infringing the personal liberty of each. . . .

The white race deems itself to be the dominant race in this country. And so it is, in prestige, in achievements, in education, in wealth and in power. So, I doubt not, it will continue to be for all time, if it remains true to its great heritage and holds fast to the principles of constitutional liberty. But in view of the Constitution, in the eye of the law, there is in this country no superior, dominant, ruling class of citizens. There is no caste here. Our Constitution is color-blind, and neither knows nor tolerates classes among citizens. In respect of civil rights, all citizens are equal before the law. The humblest is the peer of the most powerful. The law regards man as man, and takes no account of his surroundings or of his color when his civil rights as guaranteed by the supreme law of the land are involved. It is, therefore, to be regretted that this high tribunal, the final expositor of the fundamental law of the land, has reached the conclusion that it is competent for a State to regulate the enjoyment by citizens of their civil rights solely upon the basis of race. . . .

The destinies of the two races, in this country, are indissolubly linked together, and the interests of both require that the common government of all shall not permit the seeds of race hate to be planted under the sanction of law. What can more certainly arouse race hate, what more certainly create and perpetuate a feeling of distrust between these races, than state enactments, which, in fact, proceed on the ground that colored citizens are so inferior and degraded that they cannot be allowed to sit in public coaches occupied by white citizens? That, as all will admit, is the real meaning of such legislation as was enacted in Louisiana. . . .

The arbitrary separation of citizens, on the basis of race, while they are on a public highway, is a badge of servitude wholly inconsistent with the civil freedom and the equality before the law established by the Constitution. It cannot be justified upon any legal grounds.

If evils will result from the commingling of the two races upon public highways established for the benefit of all, they will be infinitely less than those that will surely come from state legislation regulating the enjoyment of civil rights upon the basis of race. We boast of the freedom enjoyed by our people above all other peoples. But it is difficult to reconcile that boast with a state of the law which, practically, puts the brand of servitude and degradation upon a large class of our fellow-citizens, our equals before the law. The thin disguise of "equal" accommodations for passengers in railroad coaches will not mislead any one, nor atone for the wrong this day done.

I am of opinion that the statute of Louisiana is inconsistent with the personal liberty of citizens, white and black, in that State, and hostile to both the spirit and letter of the Constitution of the United States. If laws of like character should be enacted in the several States of the Union, the effect would be in the highest degree mischievous. Slavery, as an institution tolerated by law would, it is true, have disappeared from our country, but there would remain a power in the States, by sinister legislation, to interfere with the full enjoyment of the blessings of freedom; to regulate civil rights, common to all citizens, upon the basis of race; and to place in a condition of legal inferiority a large body of American citizens, now constituting a part of the political community called the People of the United States, for whom, and by whom through representatives, our government is administered. Such a system is inconsistent with the guarantee given by the Constitution to each State of a republican form of government, and may be stricken down by Congressional action, or by the courts in the discharge of their solemn duty to maintain the supreme law of the land, anything in the constitution or laws of any State to the contrary notwithstanding.

For the reasons stated, I am constrained to withhold my assent from the opinion and judgment of the majority.

OLIVER WENDELL HOLMES, JR.

DISSENT FROM *ABRAMS V. UNITED STATES*

The First Amendment protects free speech, but it was not until the end of World War I that the Supreme Court began to shape an intricate body of laws protecting civil liberties. The coming of the war provoked a genuine radical anti-war movement that, in turn, prompted Congress to pass the sort of sweeping repressive legislation that was obviously open to constitutional challenge.

The statutes passed by Congress and challenged by dissidents were the Espionage Act of 1917 and the Sedition Act of 1918. Together they banned speech that might even remotely interfere with the war effort—speech that attacked, for instance, the Constitution.

In this wartime atmosphere many Americans—Germans, socialists, anarchists, and pacifists, among others—found themselves the targets of suspicion. In fact, that suspicion outlasted the war itself. In 1919 a wave of strikes, riots and bombings shook the nation. The bombings were thought to be the work of anarchists and, in combination with the strikes and the formation of an American Communist Party, they led to new panic—a "Red Scare," as it came to be called.

In the summer of 1918 a group of Russian immigrants, self-proclaimed socialists and anarchists, threw about 5,000 leaflets from the windows of a New York hat factory. The leaflets bitterly denounced actions that President Woodrow Wilson had taken against the

Bolsheviks and called for a general strike to prevent the production of arms which, they said, would be used against the fledgling Soviet Union. There was no evidence that anyone engaged in war work in fact read the leaflets, but the defendants were arrested for sedition.

Here is how one set of leaflets read, in part:

> Workers . . . must spit in the face of the false, hypocritic, military propaganda. . . . Workers in the ammunition factories, you are producing bullets, bayonets, cannon, to murder not only the Germans but also your dearest, best, who are in Russia and are fighting for freedom. . . . Workers, our reply . . . has to be general strike!

The men were tried and found guilty by a judge who (as one scholar has put it) viewed the defendants as "exhibits from a museum of un-American horrors." They received sentences ranging from three to twenty years in prison.

The Supreme Court upheld their convictions, but two members of the Court—Justices Oliver Wendell Holmes, Jr. and Louis D. Brandeis—dissented. Justice Holmes' dissent further develops the idea that freedom of speech is not absolute. The context must be taken into account. When words create "a clear and present danger" resulting in action that Congress has a right to prevent, the speech is not protected. When the nation is at war, things that might be said in a time of peace cannot be permitted; nonetheless, the government must take care not to restrict the freedom of speech without such cause.

. . . I do not doubt for a moment that by the same reasoning that would justify punishing persuasion to murder, the United States constitutionally may punish speech that produces or is intended to produce a clear and imminent danger that it will bring about forthwith certain substantive evils that the United States constitutionally may seek to prevent. The power undoubtedly is greater in time of war than in time of peace because war opens dangers that do not exist at other times.

But as against dangers peculiar to war, as against others, the principle of the right to free speech is always the same. It is only the present danger of immediate evil or an intent to bring it about that warrants Congress in setting a limit to the expression of opinion where private rights are not concerned. Congress certainly cannot forbid all effort to change the mind of the country. Now nobody can suppose that the surreptitious publishing of a silly leaflet by an unknown man, without more, would present any immediate danger that its opinions would hinder the success of the government arms or have any appreciable tendency to do so. . . .

Persecution for the expression of opinions seems to me perfectly logical. If you have no doubt of your premises or your power and want a certain result with all your heart you naturally express your wishes in law and sweep away all opposition. To allow opposition by speech seems to indicate that you think the speech impotent, as when a man says that he has squared the circle, or that you do not care wholeheartedly for the result, or that you doubt either your power or your premises. But when men have realized that time has upset many fighting faiths, they may come to believe even more than they believe the very foundations of their own conduct that the ultimate good desired is better reached by free trade in ideas—that the best test of truth is the power of the thought to get itself accepted in the competition of the market, and that truth is the only ground upon which their wishes safely can be carried out. That at any rate is the theory of our Constitution. It is an experiment, as all life is an experiment. Every year if not every day we have to wager our salvation upon some prophecy based upon imperfect knowledge. While that experiment is part of our system

I think that we should be eternally vigilant against attempts to check the expression of opinions that we loathe and believe to be fraught with death, unless they so imminently threaten immediate interference with the lawful and pressing purposes of the law that an immediate check is required to save the country. I wholly disagree with the argument of the Government that the First Amendment left the common law as to seditious libel in force. History seems to me against the notion. I had conceived that the United States through many years had shown its repentance for the Sedition Act of 1798, by repaying fines that it imposed. Only the emergency that makes it immediately dangerous to leave the correction of evil counsels to time warrants making any exception to the sweeping command, "Congress shall make no law … abridging the freedom of speech." Of course I am speaking only of expressions of opinion and exhortations, which were all that were uttered here, but I regret that I cannot put into more impressive words my belief that in their conviction upon this indictment the defendants were deprived of their rights under the Constitution of the United States.

Oliver Wendell Holmes, Jr. became known as the "Great Dissenter" for his controversial opinions in such cases as *Abrams v. United States.*

SIDNEY HOOK

BREAD AND FREEDOM

Sidney Hook (1902–1988) was one of the leading American philosophers of the twentieth century. An ardent disciple of John Dewey, Hook was a champion of pragmatism and democracy. Born in New York City, Hook taught for many years at New York University.

His celebrated essay "Bread and Freedom" was written in 1940, as Europe faced the twin totalitarian threats of Nazism and Communism. American intellectuals were quick to perceive the threat of fascist totalitarianism, but a significant minority embraced the Communist claim that people should not worry about "bourgeois freedoms" until they had achieved economic sufficiency. Although Hook had been a Marxist during the 1920s, he became one of the earliest and most outspoken anti-Marxists in the 1930s and after.

It was Hook's conviction that cultural and intellectual freedom was necessary in all societies, regardless of economic conditions. He prophetically warned that those who gave up their freedom in hopes of getting bread were likely to end up without either bread or freedom. His essay, excerpted here, appeared in a collection of his writings entitled *Political Power and Personal Freedom.*

. . . Freedoms, like rights, may limit as well as reinforce each other. Despite various doctrines of absolute and inalienable rights, no one can reasonably hold that any specific right or freedom should be gratified regardless of its consequences on the community and its bearings on other rights and freedoms. Some order of priority among freedoms must be recognized, and some method of determining that priority must be found. Freedoms may be ordered in relation to each other in the light of some encompassing value or ideal although the precise emphasis is a matter of degree dependent upon specific historical situations. In one sense of John Dewey's much misunderstood phrase that "each situation has its own unique good," we can also say that each situation has its own unique combination of freedoms which only intelligence can determine.

Perhaps the nearest we can come to a justifying principle for that complex of freedoms which we select as preferred in any situation is its tendency to maximize the amount of freedom for the individual. We want a world in which all individuals are as free as possible to develop their personalities in a peaceful community. Among the cultures of the West, different philosophical schools interpret and ground this value in the light of conflicting assumptions about the nature of man and the universe. But whatever else they would say about man, they would agree that to be human is to be capable of intelligence and moral choice, and that all freedoms are justified which enhance the capacity of intelligent moral choice.

Democracy is the fairest and most peaceful method that has been found to resolve the conflicts of interests underlying the conflicts of freedoms. Its central concept of freely given consent rests on the operation of a whole cluster of freedoms, here called political, not all of which are explicitly formulated in the Bill of Rights. The exercise of these political freedoms is what we should primarily mean by the American way of life. For these are the *strategic* freedoms; they enable us to win new freedoms and check the excesses of the old. So long as they prevail, modifications of and restrictions on other freedoms are reversible. Where they are undermined, no other freedom can be anything but an assertion of power by a privileged group. That is why every group that wishes to see conflicting interests resolved reasonably, or is wise about the conditions under which it enjoys its own freedom, must be profoundly concerned with the state of freedom of speech and assembly, freedom of inquiry and teaching, freedom of press and other forms of communication, freedom of cultural opportunity and development. For in large measure intelligent moral choice depends upon them.

Like other groups in American life, business has seldom given any indication that it is aware of the connection between these strategic freedoms. There has been a tendency to ignore them except when a direct relationship of a most immediate kind with the narrow group interest could be demonstrated. . . .

This comparative inactivity of the American businessman in the strengthening of the culture complex of freedom is surprising from the point of view of his own ideology. Although in theory he often interprets the American way of life as if it were identical with free enterprise, if not an outgrowth of it, in practice he has until recently left the actual defense of the specific freedoms which constitute the American way of life as it is actually lived and experienced largely to socialists and liberals who are vigorous critics of free enterprise. . . .

If we judge the American businessman not by what he says but by what he does and fails to do, then it sometimes seems as if he shared a common premise with his bitterest enemy, the doctrinaire, orthodox communist. Although they differ about what constitutes an economically sound basis of society, and in their conception of economic freedom, they both believe that once an economically sound system is established, cultural and political freedoms will take care of themselves. Both regard freedoms as by-products of, or superstructural additions to, the economic foundations. Both are caught in a kind of historical automatism from whose implications the businessman releases himself only by abandoning, rather inconsistently, the causal monism which rules out the role of ideas and ideals in redetermining the direction of history.

The orthodox communist is more consistent than any other believer in economic determinism, but he pays a terrible price for his consistency. He identifies freedom with the acceptance of historical necessity and its inevitabilities. What seem to be genuine alternatives of diminishing or increasing the amount of freedom in society appear to him to be nothing but ripples on an irresistible undertow carrying us to a more "progressive" economy which through the terror regime of a self-selected political elite guarantees freedom for all and luxuries for everyone....

This is, indeed, a far cry from the conscious ideology of the American businessman (to the extent that he has any). He assumes that the operation of natural laws in a free-enterprise system, provided that the government does not attempt to interfere with them, *necessarily* carries with it the structure of all our other freedoms. If we make explicit what follows from that assumption, a world view not dissimilar to that of dialectical materialism results.

If our argument is sound, then no matter what the character of the economic system, political and cultural freedom can never be taken for granted. They must always be fought for. A particular economic system may make certain political and cultural freedoms unlikely, but there is an entire spectrum of possibilities compatible with it whose realization involves moral choices and commitments. Belief in a free-market economy is not the same as belief in a free society.... In economics, as in every other aspect of human behavior, fundamental decisions are moral decisions—informed or uninformed, wise or foolish. The probability that they will be informed and wise is largely dependent on the extent to which the strategic freedoms pervade the social structure.

The businessman's commonly expressed conviction that freedom is rooted in free enterprise tends to paralyze him into inaction, or at least hopelessness, when he is confronted with the problem of strengthening freedom in depressed areas of the world. Because he so frequently believes that freedom (i.e., democracy) is impossible without an economic base similar to America's, he tends to have little confidence in *any* program for keeping Asia, for example, noncommunist. His opinion although grounded differently is not dissimilar to one expressed by certain delegates to the Indian Congress for Cultural Freedom. The delegates, who were generally quite sympathetic to the purposes of the Congress, asked: "What is the use of talking about cultural freedom to a starving man? Is there any point in discussing threats to intellectual and cultural life where poverty is so widespread that many people cannot begin to enjoy the freedoms of such life?"

The issues posed by these questions are relevant to the struggle for freedom, not merely in Asia, but everywhere in the world where economic hardships and misery abound. They are focused most sharply wherever Communist propaganda seizes upon existing economic conditions to dismiss democratic concern for freedom as a desire merely to perpetuate the cultural privileges of a leisured class. The fact is that Communist performance with respect to living conditions falls far short not only of Communist promises but also of democratic performance. But this, unfortunately, is usually discovered by those who have been seduced only after their freedoms have been destroyed. It therefore becomes important to clarify the issues, particularly since there is evidence that many Europeans and even more Asians have found the argument persuasive.

Is the antithesis between bread and freedom a legitimate one? Can more bread be produced and distributed by sacrificing cultural and intellectual freedom, by dismissing the latter as spiritual goods that will automatically be added to the human estate *after* first things have been provided for?

Let us begin with starving men. It is certainly futile to talk about cultural freedom to those who are starving. By the same token, it is just as futile to talk to them about education, hygiene, cruelty to women and children, social reform, or even love of God. The one thing to do about starving men is to feed them. But it is noteworthy to observe that those who protest against talking about freedom to men who are starving do not themselves feed them. Nor do they content themselves with advocating that they be fed by others. Instead they *talk* about other things, offer panaceas, and seek support for programs involving an apparent concern for many excellent matters except freedom. To be blunt, the argument against discussing freedom with starving men is usually not much more than an apology for some form of cultural tyranny. . . .

The basic problem consists of understanding the relationships between bread and freedom. But before discussing them a number of preliminary questions must be considered.

First, even if it were granted that bread is a necessary condition of freedom, this by itself would not be sufficient to justify any particular social program, or to justify indifference to the defense of freedom. For believers in free enterprise, collectivism, a welfare state, and a mixed economy are all equally convinced that only through the systems they espouse can bread be most effectively produced and distributed. Unless one is to make a claim to infallibility, the right of the people *freely to choose* which economic system is to minister to their material needs cannot be abridged. And this right freely to choose carries with it, as we have seen, a cluster of other rights which, if embodied in practice, constitute a considerable part of what we mean by cultural and intellectual freedom.

Second, in our complex world it is undoubtedly true that most social problems are interrelated. However, it does not follow that they can all be tackled at once or that there is no point in addressing ourselves to one particular problem at a time. Years ago when associations were organized to abolish child labor, some writers criticized these efforts on the ground that it was fruitless to agitate for abolition until the whole complex of conditions that produced child labor

was removed. Yet, although it is far from certain that the causes of child labor have been eliminated, child labor has in large measure been abolished by efforts directed to that specific end. The social causes of illiteracy, violation of civil liberties, and cruelty to children are many and complex, but it would be downright foolish to criticize efforts to extend literacy, protect civil liberties, and prevent inhumanity to children on the ground that until their fundamental causes are removed—causes about whose nature there is no universal agreement—nothing or little can be done. . . .

Our final preliminary point is necessary as a caution to those who naively believe that social reforms by themselves are sufficient to prevent cultural freedom from being destroyed by the aggressive expansion of Communist totalitarianism in its crusade for world domination. No one can deny the contributing role economic conditions played in bringing Hitler to power. But once he achieved power, not all the Point Four programs in the world would have prevented him from embarking upon his program of world conquest. If anything, they would have whetted his appetite. Social conditions in Denmark, Belgium, Norway, and other Western countries were definitely superior to those of Germany. Conditions in Finland and Poland and the Baltic countries were superior to those in the Soviet Union. But this did not deter Hitler or Stalin.

In the present state of international affairs, social reforms are certainly necessary whenever acute need and poverty exist. But those who say that freedom can take care of itself once the slums of London or Bombay are razed are ignorant of the nature of modern totalitarianism. The model housing projects of Socialist Vienna were no deterrent either to Dollfuss' Heimwehr or Hitler's S.S. troops.

It is not without significance that, except in certain situations of natural disaster such as drought and flood, higher standards of living seem to prevail in countries with greater cultural and intellectual freedom. This is of course a rough judgment, for standards of living may be a function of the presence or absence of natural resources, and comparisons, to be instructive, must be drawn between nations whose physical potentials are not too diverse. . . . But when all allowance is made, it seems clear that there is a very impressive correlation between freedom and bread. There may be dearth for some even in nations whose average is high. But the impressive fact is that the voluntary movement of populations in quest for a better material life is always towards countries in which a freer cultural and intellectual climate obtains.

When people suffer from want, immediate relief from suffering becomes focal in their minds. They may identify this relief with social progress somewhat in the same way that a man who suffers from toothache identifies health with sound teeth. In such circumstances they may not look too closely at the means proposed to bring them relief and may give credence to the exhortations of the demagogue and to the typical rhetorical questions; "When you are hungry can you eat freedom? Can you feed it to your children? Can it keep you warm?" It becomes relevant to inquire, therefore, whether, in fact, the economic conditions of the masses have ever actually been improved as a consequence of the destruction of their cultural and political freedoms. . . .

Sometimes those who counterpose bread and freedom suggest that it is entirely possible to surrender freedom for the security of a job and living quarters and the privileges of education and health insurance. But again a little reflection indicates the absurdity of such a separation of freedom and security. How can there be genuine security so long as arbitrary power, whether it be of an employer or a group, or especially of the *state as employer*, is not subject to the restraints of a freely operating democratic process?

The profoundest lesson of our era is the fact that without political freedom there can be no other freedoms, but only an uncertain and uneasy exercise of privileges which may be terminated abruptly without anybody's having to account to those who are affected by these decisions.

The notion that *first* one must strive to improve working conditions and *then* begin to be concerned with freedom is really foreign to the workers themselves whenever they are able to make voluntary choices. For they have learned from their own experience that without *free* trade unions, so-called improvements in their conditions can be snatched from them by arbitrary decrees. Without free trade unions, without the right to speak, assemble, and publish freely in opposition to their employers, whether the latter be private individuals or public officials, participation in determining the conditions and rewards of work is at best a farce, and usually nothing more than a legal device for imposing a system of forced labor. In all countries where political freedoms do not exist, the function of trade unions is not to protect the worker or to fight for his material interests but to increase his production—in the distribution of which, incidentally, he has no voice. The worker without political freedom, far from enjoying his security, becomes enslaved to the machinery of production regardless of the legal forms of ownership.

This suggests that it is a grave error to assume that freedom is a concern only of the cultured or professional groups whose task is the creation and dissemination of ideas. Even more mistaken is the view that freedom is something to be won only after sufficient leisure has been acquired in which to enjoy it. The truth is, even as the advertisements proclaim, that everyone has a stake in freedom in his every-day life and work. Although Marx is still one of the inconvenient minor deities in the Communist pantheon, his own writings deny in the most emphatic way the validity of the antithesis between bread and freedom. "The proletariat," he writes, "which will not allow itself to be treated as canaille, regards its courage, self-confidence, independence and sense of personal dignity as more necessary than its daily bread."

Whatever may be the historical facts, it is certainly conceivable that human beings may surrender their freedom for the comforts of a well-appointed jail including the right (not possessed by the citizens of Iron Curtain countries) to denounce their jailors. It is conceivable but psychologically extremely unlikely when they understand what they are committing themselves to. Who, indeed, would exchange the uncertainties of a life outside a jail and the right to work and fight as a free man for all the food, clothing, shelter, medical service, and even congenial occupational therapy that the most enlightened penal institution can provide? And to be offered this kind of security for life would hardly enhance its attractiveness.

It is not necessary to claim that there is a freedom reflex in the human psyche in order to recognize that the desire for freedom is not reducible *merely* to a desire for material goods and services, important as these are. There is an irreducible quality in the experience of uncoerced choice which leads men to risk their very lives in its behalf. Whether our choices are good or bad, wise or foolish, we feel diminished as human beings if we are prevented from making them. Denied freedom to make choices, we are denied responsibility, and to deny our responsibility is to deny our humanity. It is the unique glory of man that although he hopes and works for an abundant life, he is prepared to die in order to prove that he is human. . . .

FRANKLIN DELANO ROOSEVELT
THE FOUR FREEDOMS

The world picture looked gloomy when Franklin Delano Roosevelt (1882–1945) delivered his annual message to Congress in January, 1941, after winning the presidency for an unprecedented third time. Hitler's forces dominated the European continent, and in the Far East Japan was pursuing the aggressive expansionist course that led it to attack American forces at Pearl Harbor before the year was out. Roosevelt devoted the bulk of his message to a discussion of what the U.S. could do to aid the countries resisting the Axis Powers. In this excerpt he outlines his basic goals for America's "political and economic systems," and then sets forth the "four freedoms" that he hoped to see secured everywhere around the globe in the postwar world.

. . . There is nothing mysterious about the foundations of a healthy and strong democracy. The basic things expected by our people of their political and economic systems are simple. They are:

Equality of opportunity for youth and for others.

Jobs for those who can work.

Security for those who need it.

The ending of special privilege for the few.

The preservation of civil liberties for all.

The enjoyment of the fruits of scientific progress in a wider and constantly rising standard of living.

These are the simple and basic things that must never be lost sight of in the turmoil and unbelievable complexity of our modern world.

The inner and abiding strength of our economic and political systems is dependent upon the degree to which they fulfill these expectations. . . .

In the future days, which we seek to make secure, we look forward to a world founded upon four essential human freedoms.

The first is freedom of speech and expression everywhere in the world.

The second is freedom of every person to worship God in his own way everywhere in the world.

The third is freedom from want, which, translated into world terms, means economic understandings which will secure to every nation a healthy peacetime life for its inhabitants everywhere in the world.

The fourth is freedom from fear—which,

translated into world terms, means a worldwide reduction of armaments to such a point and in such a thorough fashion that no nation will be in a position to commit an act of physical aggression against any neighbor—anywhere in the world.

That is no vision of a distant millennium. It is a definite basis for a kind of world attainable in our own time and generation. That kind of world is the very antithesis of the so-called new order of tyranny which the dictators seek to create with the crash of a bomb.

To that new order we oppose the greater conception—the moral order. A good society is able to face schemes of world domination and foreign revolutions alike without fear.

Since the beginning of our American history we have been engaged in change—in a perpetual peaceful revolution—a revolution which goes on steadily, quietly adjusting itself to changing conditions—without the concentration camp or the quicklime in the ditch. The world order which we seek is the cooperation of free countries, working together in a friendly, civilized society.

Franklin Delano Roosevelt shakes hands with a West Virginia coal miner during the 1932 Presidential campaign.

ROBERT H. JACKSON

WEST VIRGINIA BOARD OF EDUCATION V. BARNETTE

Can public authorities insist that all school children salute the national flag? That was the question in two Supreme Court cases in the early 1940s. In *Minersville School District v. Gobitis* (1940), the elementary school principal in the town of Minersville, Pennsylvania, had insisted that Lillian and William Gobitis join their classmates in saluting the flag at the start of every school day. The Gobitis family, as members of the Jehovah's Witness sect, objected on religious grounds. The flag was a graven image, they said; they could not allow their children to bow down to it, for the Book of Exodus forbade them to. The Supreme Court ruled against them, however, arguing that the value of national unity—of which the flag was a symbol—outweighed the commitment to religious freedom contained in the First Amendment.

Just three years later, in the very similar case of *West Virginia Board of Education v. Barnette*, the Court reversed itself. The majority opinion in this case, written by Justice Robert H. Jackson (1892–1954), eloquently explored an issue basic to democratic government: how much enforced conformity does national unity demand?

There is no doubt that, in connection with the pledges, the flag salute is a form of utterance. Symbolism is a primitive but effective way of communicating ideas. The use of an emblem or flag to symbolize some system, idea, institution, or personality, is a short cut from mind to mind. Causes and nations, political parties, lodges and ecclesiastical groups seek to knit the loyalty of their followings to a flag or banner, a color or design. The State announces rank, function, and authority through crowns and maces, uniforms and black robes; the church speaks through the Cross, the Crucifix, the altar and shrine, and clerical raiment. Symbols of State often convey political ideas just as religious symbols come to convey theological ones. Associated with many of these symbols are appropriate gestures of acceptance or respect: a salute, a bowed or bared head, a bended knee. A person gets from a symbol the meaning he puts into it, and what is one man's comfort and inspiration is another's jest and scorn. . . .

. . . [T]he State . . . employs a flag as a symbol of adherence to government as presently organized. It requires the individual to communicate by word and sign his acceptance of the political ideas it thus bespeaks. Objection to this form of communication when coerced is an old one, well known to the framers of the Bill of Rights.

It is also to be noted that the compulsory flag salute and pledge requires affirmation of a belief and an attitude of mind. It is not clear whether the regulation contemplates that pupils forego any contrary convictions of their own and become unwilling converts to the prescribed ceremony or whether it will be acceptable if they simulate assent by words without belief and by a gesture barren of meaning. It is now a commonplace that censorship or suppression of expression of opinion is tolerated by our Constitution only when the expression presents a clear and present danger of action of a kind the State is empowered to prevent and punish. . . .

To sustain the compulsory flag salute we are required to say that a Bill of Rights which guards the individual's right to speak his own mind, left it open to public authorities to compel him to utter what is not in his mind. . . .

It was said that the flag-salute controversy confronted the Court with "the problem which

Lincoln cast in memorable dilemma: 'Must a government of necessity be too *strong* for the liberties of its people, or too *weak* to maintain its own existence?' " and that the answer must be in favor of strength. . . .

It may be doubted whether Mr. Lincoln would have thought that the strength of government to maintain itself would be impressively vindicated by our confirming power of the state to expel a handful of children from school. . . .

Government of limited power need not be anemic government. . . .

Without promise of a limiting Bill of Rights it is doubtful if our Constitution could have mustered enough strength to enable its ratification. To enforce those rights today is not to choose weak government over strong government. It is only to adhere as a means of strength to individual freedom of mind in preference to officially disciplined uniformity for which history indicates a disappointing and disastrous end. . . .

The very purpose of a Bill of Rights was to withdraw certain subjects from the vicissitudes of political controversy, to place them beyond the reach of majorities and officials and to establish them as legal principles to be applied by the courts. One's right to life, liberty, and property, to free speech, a free press, freedom of worship and assembly, and other fundamental rights may not be submitted to vote; they depend on the outcome of no elections. . . .

National unity as an end which officials may foster by persuasion and example is not in question. The problem is whether under our Constitution compulsion as here employed is a permissible means for its achievement.

Struggles to coerce uniformity of sentiment in support of some end thought essential to their time and country have been waged by many good as well as by evil men. Nationalism is a relatively recent phenomenon but at other times and places the ends have been racial or territorial security, support of a dynasty or regime, and particular plans for saving souls. As first and moderate methods to attain unity have failed, those bent on its accomplishment must resort to an ever increasing severity. As governmental pressure toward unity becomes greater, so strife becomes more bitter as to whose unity it shall be. Probably no deeper division of our people could proceed from any provocation than from finding it necessary to choose what doctrine and whose program public educational officials shall compel youth to unite in embracing. Ultimate futility of such attempts to compel coherence is the lesson of every such effort from the Roman drive to stamp out Christianity as a disturber of its pagan unity, the Inquisition, as a means to religious and dynastic unity, the Siberian exiles as a means to Russian unity, down to the fast failing efforts of our present totalitarian enemies. Those who begin coercive elimination of dissent soon find themselves exterminating dissenters. Compulsory unification of opinion achieves only the unanimity of the graveyard.

It seems trite but necessary to say that the First Amendment to our Constitution was designed to avoid these ends by avoiding these beginnings. There is no mysticism in the American concept of the State or of the nature or origin of its authority. We set up government by consent of the governed, and the Bill of Rights denies those in power any legal opportunity to coerce that consent. Authority here is to be controlled by public opinion, not public opinion by authority.

The case is made difficult not because the principles of its decision are obscure but because the flag involved is our own. Nevertheless, we apply the limitations of the Constitution with no fear that freedom to be intellectually and spiritually diverse or even contrary will disintegrate the social organization. To believe that patriotism will not flourish if patriotic ceremonies are voluntary and spontaneous instead of a compulsory routine is to make an unflattering estimate of the appeal of our institutions to free minds. We can have intellectual individualism and the rich cultural diversities that we owe to exceptional minds only at the price of occasional eccentricity and abnormal attitudes. When they are so harmless to others or to the State as those we deal with here, the price is not too great. But freedom to differ is not limited to things that do not matter much. That would be a mere shadow of freedom. The test of its substance is the right to differ as to things that touch the heart of the existing order.

If there is any fixed star in our constitutional constellation, it is that no official, high or petty, can prescribe what shall be orthodox in politics, nationalism, religion, or other matters of opinion or force citizens to confess by word or act their faith therein. If there are any circumstances which permit an exception, they do not now occur to us.

We think the action of the local authorities in compelling the flag salute and pledge transcends constitutional limitations on their power and invades the sphere of intellect and spirit which it is the purpose of the First Amendment to our Constitution to reserve from all official control. . . .

Love of country must spring from willing hearts and free minds, inspired by a fair admin-istration of wise laws enacted by the people's elected representatives within the bounds of express constitutional prohibitions. These laws must, to be consistent with the First Amendment, permit the widest toleration of conflicting viewpoints consistent with a society of free men.

Neither our domestic tranquillity in peace nor our martial effort in war depend on compelling little children to participate in a ceremony which ends in nothing for them but a fear of spiritual condemnation. If, as we think, their fears are groundless, time and reason are the proper antidotes for their errors. The ceremonial, when enforced against conscientious objectors, more likely to defeat than to serve its high purpose, is a handy implement for disguised religious persecution. As such, it is inconsistent with our Constitution's plan and purpose.

MARTIN LUTHER KING, JR.

STRIDE TOWARD FREEDOM

During World War II and its aftermath, the South's "Jim Crow" system of legally enforced racial segregation came under increasing attack. Blacks who fought in the armed services did so, by and large, in racially segregated units, but shortly after the war's end President Truman ordered integration of the military. Then in 1954 the Supreme Court ruled in *Brown v. Board of Education of Topeka, Kansas* that segregation of public school children by race violated the "equal protection of the laws" clause of the Fourteenth Amendment.

After *Brown* the action shifted from the courtroom to the street. In Montgomery, Alabama in 1955 blacks launched a mass protest against segregation by refusing to ride the buses. Leading the Montgomery bus boycott was a young minister, Martin Luther King, Jr. (1929–1968), who had only recently returned to his native South after taking a doctorate in divinity from Boston University. In his 1958 book *Stride Toward Freedom* he outlined his strategy for toppling Jim Crow by means of nonviolent mass resistance, a campaign of "civil disobedience." The United States, he perceived, had long had a "schizophrenic personality on the question of race," with the ideal of equality embodied in the Declaration its better half and the brutal realities of slavery and segregation as the other, darker half. He rejected both the natural response of passive resignation to oppression and the equally natural path of bitter and violent resistance, calling for nonviolent resistance as a middle way, a kind of higher Hegelian synthesis of these opposites.

It is noteworthy, in light of subsequent developments in the black protest movement, that King was insistent that his aim was racial integration, not black power; equal treatment for all regardless of the color of their skin, not reverse discrimination as a

compensation for past injustices. As he put it, "God is not interested merely in the freedom of black men, and brown men, and yellow men. God is interested in the freedom of the whole human race."

Along with the Negro's changing image of himself has come an awakening moral consciousness on the part of millions of white Americans concerning segregation. Ever since the signing of the Declaration of Independence, America has manifested a schizophrenic personality on the question of race. She has been torn between selves—a self in which she has proudly professed democracy and a self in which she has sadly practiced the antithesis of democracy. The reality of segregation, like slavery, has always had to confront the ideals of democracy and Christianity. Indeed, segregation and discrimination are strange paradoxes in a nation founded on the principle that all men are created equal. This contradiction has disturbed the consciences of whites both North and South, and has caused many of them to see that segregation is basically evil. . . .

History has thrust upon our generation an indescribably important destiny—to complete a process of democratization which our nation has too long developed too slowly, but which is our most powerful weapon for world respect and emulation. How we deal with this crucial situation will determine our moral health as individuals, our cultural health as a region, our political health as a nation, and our prestige as a leader of the free world. The future of America is bound up with the solution of the present crisis. The shape of the world today does not permit us the luxury of a faltering democracy. The United States cannot hope to attain the respect of the vital and growing colored nations of the world unless it remedies its racial problems at home. If America is to remain a first-class nation, it cannot have a second-class citizenship.

A solution of the present crisis will not take place unless men and women work for it. Human progress is neither automatic nor inevitable. Even a superficial look at history reveals that no social advance rolls in on the wheels of inevitability. Every step toward the goal of justice

requires sacrifice, suffering, and struggle, the tireless exertions and passionate concern of dedicated individuals. Without persistent effort, time itself becomes an ally of the insurgent and primitive forces of irrational emotionalism and social destruction. This is no time for apathy or complacency. This is a time for vigorous and positive action. . . .

There is no such thing as the freedom of exhaustion. Some people are so worn down by the yoke of oppression that they give up. A few years ago in the slum areas of Atlanta, a Negro guitarist used a sing almost daily: "Ben down so long that down don't bother me." This is the type of negative freedom and resignation that often engulfs the life of the oppressed.

But this is not the way out. To accept passively an unjust system is to co-operate with that system; thereby the oppressed become as evil as the oppressor. Non-cooperation with evil is as much a moral obligation as is cooperation with good. The oppressed must never allow the conscience of the oppressor to slumber. Religion reminds every man that he is his brother's keeper. To accept injustice or segregation passively is to say to the oppressor that his actions are morally right. It is a way of allowing his conscience to fall asleep. At this moment the oppressed fails to be his brother's keeper. So acquiescence—while often the easier way—is not the moral way. It is the way of the coward. The Negro cannot win the respect of his oppressor by acquiescing; he merely increases the oppressor's arrogance and contempt. Acquiescence is interpreted as proof of the Negro's inferiority. The Negro cannot win the respect of the white people of the South or the peoples of the world if he is willing to sell the future of his children for his personal and immediate comfort and safety.

A second way that oppressed people sometimes deal with oppression is to resort to physical violence and corroding hatred. Violence often brings about momentary results. Nations have frequently won their independence in battle. But in spite of temporary victories, violence never brings permanent peace. It solves no social problem; it merely creates new and more complicated ones.

Violence as a way of achieving racial justice is both impractical and immoral. It is impractical because it is a descending spiral ending in destruction for all. The old law of an eye for an eye leaves everybody blind. It is immoral because it seeks to humiliate the opponent rather than win his understanding; it seeks to annihilate rather than to convert. Violence is immoral because it thrives on hatred rather than love. It destroys community and makes brotherhood impossible. It leaves society in monologue rather than dialogue. Violence ends by defeating itself. It creates bitterness in the survivors and brutality in the destroyers. A voice echoes through time saying to every potential Peter, "Put up your sword." History is cluttered with the wreckage of nations that failed to follow this command.

If the American Negro and other victims of oppression succumb to the temptation of using violence in the struggle for freedom, future generations will be the recipients of a desolate night of bitterness, and our chief legacy to them will be an endless reign of meaningless chaos. Violence is not the way.

The third way open to oppressed people in their quest for freedom is the way of nonviolent resistance. Like the synthesis in Hegelian philosophy, the principle of nonviolent resistance seeks to reconcile the truths of two opposites— acquiescence and violence—while avoiding the extremes and immoralities of both. The nonviolent resister agrees with the person who acquiesces that one should not be physically aggressive toward his opponent; but he balances the equation by agreeing with the person of violence that evil must be resisted. He avoids the nonresistance of the former and the violent resistance of the latter. With nonviolent resistance, no individual or group need submit to any

wrong, nor need anyone resort to violence in order to right a wrong.

It seems to me that this is the method that must guide the actions of the Negro in the present crisis in race relations. Through nonviolent resistance the Negro will be able to rise to the noble height of opposing the unjust system while loving the perpetrators of the system. The Negro must work passionately and unrelentingly for full stature as a citizen, but he must not use inferior methods to gain it. He must never come to terms with falsehood, malice, hate, or destruction.

Nonviolent resistance makes it possible for the Negro to remain in the South and struggle for his rights. The Negro's problem will not be solved by running away. He cannot listen to the glib suggestion of those who would urge him to migrate en masse to other sections of the country. By grasping his great opportunity in the South he can make a lasting contribution to the moral strength of the nation and set a sublime example of courage for generations yet unborn.

By nonviolent resistance, the Negro can also enlist all men of good will in his struggle for equality. The problem is not a purely racial one, with Negroes set against whites. In the end, it is not a struggle between people at all, but a tension between justice and injustice. Nonviolent resistance is not aimed against oppressors but against oppression. Under its banner, consciences and not racial groups are enlisted.

If the Negro is to achieve the goal of integration, he must organize himself into a militant and nonviolent mass movement. All three elements are indispensable. The movement for equality and justice can only be a success if it has both a mass and militant character; the barriers to be overcome require both. Nonviolence is an imperative in order to bring about ultimate community.

A mass movement of a militant quality that is not at the same time committed to nonviolence tends to generate conflict, which in turn breeds anarchy. The support of the participants and the sympathy of the uncommitted are both inhibited by the threat that bloodshed will engulf the community. This reaction in turn encourages the opposition to threaten and resort to force. When, however, the mass movement repudiates violence while moving resolutely toward its goal, its opponents are revealed as the instigators and practitioners of violence if it occurs. Then public support is magnetically attracted to the advocates of nonviolence, while those who employ violence are literally disarmed by overwhelming sentiment against their stand. . . .

Nonviolence can touch men where the law cannot reach them. When the law regulates behavior it plays an indirect part in molding public sentiment. The enforcement of the law is itself a form of peaceful persuasion. But the law needs help. The courts can order desegregation of the public schools. But what can be done to mitigate the fears, to disperse the hatred, violence, and irrationality gathered around school integration, to take the initiative out of the hands of racial demagogues, to release respect for the law? In the end, for laws to be obeyed, men must believe they are right.

Here nonviolence comes in as the ultimate form of persuasion. It is the method which seeks to implement the just law by appealing to the conscience of the great decent majority who through blindness, fear, pride, or irrationality have allowed their consciences to sleep.

The nonviolent resisters can summarize their message in the following simple terms: We will take direct action against injustice without waiting for other agencies to act. We will not obey unjust laws or submit to unjust practices. We will do this peacefully, openly, cheerfully because our aim is to persuade. We adopt the means of nonviolence because our end is a community at peace with itself. We will try to persuade with our words, but if our words fail, we will try to persuade with our acts. We will always be willing to talk and seek fair compromise, but we are ready to suffer when necessary and even to risk our lives to become witnesses to the truth as we see it.

The way of nonviolence means a willingness to suffer and sacrifice. It may mean going to jail. If such is the case the resister must be willing to fill the jail houses of the South. It may even mean physical death. But if physical death is the price that a man must pay to free his children and his white brethren from a permanent death of the spirit, then nothing could be more redemptive.

What is the Negro's best defense against acts of violence inflicted upon him? As Dr. Kenneth Clark has said so eloquently, "His only defense is to meet every act of barbarity, illegality, cruelty and injustice toward an individual Negro with the fact that 100 more Negroes will present themselves in his place as potential victims." Every time one Negro school teacher is fired for believing in integration, a thousand others should be ready to take the same stand. If the oppressors bomb the home of one Negro for his protest, they must be made to realize that to press back the rising tide of the Negro's courage they will have to bomb hundreds more, and even then they will fail.

Faced with this dynamic unity, this amazing self-respect, this willingness to suffer, and this refusal to hit back, the oppressor will find, as oppressors have always found, that he is glutted with his own barbarity. Forced to stand before the world and his God splattered with the blood of his brother, he will call an end to his self-defeating massacre.

American Negroes must come to the point where they can say to their white brothers, paraphrasing the words of Gandhi: "We will match your capacity to inflict suffering with our capacity to endure suffering. We will meet your physical force with soul force. We will not hate you, but we cannot in all good conscience obey your unjust laws. Do to us what you will and we will still love you. Bomb our homes and threaten our children; send your hooded perpetrators of violence into our communities and drag us out on some wayside road, beating us and leaving us half dead, and we will still love you. But we will soon wear you down by our capacity to suffer. And in winning our freedom we will so appeal to your heart and conscience that we will win you in the process."

Realism impels me to admit that many Negroes will find it difficult to follow the path of nonviolence. Some will consider it senseless; some will argue that they have neither the strength nor the courage to join in such a mass demonstration of nonviolent action. As E. Franklin Frazier points out in *Black Bourgeoisie*, many Negroes are occupied in a middle-class struggle for status and prestige. They are more concerned about "conspicuous consumption" than about the cause of justice and are probably not prepared for the ordeals and sacrifices involved in nonviolent action. Fortunately, however, the success of this method is not dependent on its unanimous acceptance. A few Negroes in every community, unswervingly committed to the nonviolent way, can persuade hundreds of others at least to use nonviolence as a technique and serve as the moral force to awaken the slumbering national conscience. Thoreau was thinking of such a creative minority when he said:

> I know this well, that if one thousand, if one hundred, if ten men whom I could name—if ten honest men only—aye, if one honest man, in the state of Massachusetts, ceasing to hold slaves were actually to withdraw from the co-partnership, and be locked up in the county jail therefore, it would be the abolition of slavery in America. For it matters not how small the beginning may seem to be, what is once well done is done forever.

Mahatma Gandhi never had more than one hundred persons absolutely committed to his philosophy. But with this small group of devoted followers, he galvanized the whole of India, and through a magnificent feat of nonviolence challenged the might of the British Empire and won freedom for his people.

This method of nonviolence will not work miracles overnight. Men are not easily moved from their mental ruts, their prejudiced and irrational feelings. When the underprivileged demand freedom, the privileged first react with bitterness and resistance. Even when the demands are couched in nonviolent terms, the initial response is the same. Nehru once remarked that the British were never so angry as when the Indians resisted them with nonviolence, that he never saw eyes so full of hate as those of the British troops to whom he turned the other cheek when they beat him with lathis. But nonviolent resistance at least changed the minds and hearts of the Indians, however impervious the British may have appeared. "We cast away our fear," says Nehru. And in the end the British not only granted freedom to India but came to have a new respect for the Indians. Today a mutual friendship based on complete equality exists between these two peoples within the Commonwealth.

In the South, too, the initial white reaction to Negro resistance has been bitter. I do not predict that a similar happy ending will come to Montgomery in a few months because integration is more complicated than independence. But I know that the Negroes of Montgomery are already walking straighter because of the protest. And I expect that this generation of Negro children throughout the United States will grow up stronger and better because of the courage, the dignity, and the suffering of the nine children of Little Rock, and their counterparts in Nashville, Clinton, and Sturgis. And I believe that the white people of this country are being affected too, that beneath the surface this nation's conscience is being stirred.

The nonviolent approach does not immediately change the heart of the oppressor. It first does something to the hearts and souls of those committed to it. It gives them new self-respect, it calls up resources of strength and courage that they did not know they had. Finally it reaches the opponent and so stirs his conscience that reconciliation becomes a reality.

I suggest this approach because I think it is the only way to re-establish the broken community. Court orders and federal enforcement agencies will be of inestimable value in achieving desegregation. But desegregation is only a partial, though necessary, step toward the ultimate goal which we seek to realize. Desegregation will break down the legal barriers, and bring men together physically. But something must happen so to touch the hearts and souls of men that they will come together, not because the law says it, but because it is natural and right. In other words, our ultimate goal is integration which is genuine intergroup and interpersonal living. Only through nonviolence can this goal be attained for the aftermath of nonviolence is reconciliation and the creation of the beloved community.

It is becoming clear that the Negro is in for a season of suffering. As victories for civil rights mount in the federal courts, angry passions and deep prejudices are further aroused. The mountain of state and local segregation laws still stands. Negro leaders continue to be arrested and harassed under city ordinances, and their homes continue to be bombed. State laws continue to be enacted to circumvent integration. I pray that, recognizing the necessity of suffering, the Negro will make of it a virtue. To suffer in a righteous cause is to grow to our humanity's full stature. If only to save himself from bitterness, the Negro needs the vision to see the ordeals of this generation as the opportunity to transfigure himself and American society. If he has to go to jail for the cause of freedom, let him enter it in the fashion Gandhi urged his countrymen, "as the bridegroom enters the bride's chamber"— that is, with a little trepidation but with great expectation.

Nonviolence is a way of humility and self-restraint. We Negroes talk a great deal about our rights, and rightly so. We proudly proclaim that three-fourths of the people of the world are colored. We have the privilege of watching in our generation the great drama of freedom and independence as it unfolds in Asia and Africa. All of these things are in line with the work of providence. We must be sure, however, that we accept them in the right spirit. In an effort to achieve freedom in America, Asia, and Africa we must not try to leap from a position of disadvantage to one of advantage, thus subverting justice. We must seek democracy and not the substitution of one tyranny for another. Our aim must never be to defeat or humiliate the white man. We must not become victimized with a philosophy of black supremacy. God is not interested merely in the freedom of black men, and brown men, and yellow men. God is interested in the freedom of the whole human race.

The nonviolent approach provides an answer to the long debated question of gradualism *versus* immediacy. On the one hand it prevents one from falling into the sort of patience which is an excuse for do-nothingism and escapism, ending up in standstillism. On the other hand it saves one from the irresponsible words which estrange without reconciling and the hasty judgment which is blind to the necessities of social process. It recognizes the need for moving toward the goal of justice with wise restraint and calm reasonableness. But it also recognizes the immorality of slowing up in the move toward justice and capitulating to the guardians of an unjust status quo. It recognizes that social change cannot come overnight. But it causes one to work as if it were a possibility the next morning. . . .

MARTIN LUTHER KING, JR.

LETTER FROM BIRMINGHAM CITY JAIL

The civil disobedience campaigns Dr. King called for spread through the South following the Montgomery Bus Boycott. Mass noncompliance with segregation ordinances attained its ends in some places, and in others it failed in its immediate objectives but attained the larger end of mobilizing national opinion on behalf of black rights by provoking such brutal repression that it attracted national publicity.

The 1963 campaign in Birmingham, the most segregated big city in America, was a classic instance of the latter. After King led a march on City Hall after having been refused a proper permit by the authorities, he and other demonstrators were tossed into jail, where he wrote this stirring letter. The demonstrations continued, and the city's police forces attacked demonstrators ruthlessly with police dogs, fire hoses, and cattle prods. The climax of the hideous spectacle was the bombing of a church that left four young black girls dead. The Birmingham tragedy was the single most important catalyst for the passage of the sweeping Civil Rights Act of 1964 and the Voting Rights Act of 1965, which struck down every vestige of legally enforced segregation and provided federal protection against discrimination in employment and public facilities.

King's letter from the Birmingham jail came at an early stage of the affair, and was a response to a public statement by a group of Birmingham's white liberal clergymen who supported integration but attacked the demonstrations as "unwise and untimely." Such "extreme measures," they said, though "technically peaceful," served only to "incite hatred and violence" and thus to impede "the resolution of our local problems." King was surprised and disappointed at criticism from that quarter, and scribbled his response in the margins of a newspaper in his cell. His answer includes a sentence of over three hundred words that sums up the evils of segregation as movingly as anyone ever has. Perhaps most striking is King's passionate sense that "the goal of America is freedom," that the destiny of his people is "tied up with America's destiny," that "the sacred heritage of our nation" was embodied in "our echoing demands."

. . . I am in Birmingham because injustice is here. Just as the prophets of the eighth century B.C. left their villages and carried their "thus saith the Lord" far beyond the boundaries of their home towns, and just as the Apostle Paul left his village of Tarsus and carried the gospel of Jesus Christ to the far corners of the Greco-Roman world, so am I compelled to carry the gospel of freedom beyond my own home town. Like Paul, I must constantly respond to the Macedonian call for aid.

Moreover, I am cognizant of the interrelatedness of all communities and states. I cannot sit idly by in Atlanta and not be concerned about what happens in Birmingham. Injustice anywhere is a threat to justice everywhere. We are caught in an inescapable network of mutuality, tied in a single garment of destiny. Whatever affects one directly, affects all indirectly. Never again can we afford to live with the narrow, provincial "outside agitator" idea. Anyone who lives inside the United States can never be considered an outsider anywhere within its bounds.

You deplore the demonstrations taking place

in Birmingham. But your statement, I am sorry to say, fails to express a similar concern for the conditions that brought about the demonstrations. . . .

Birmingham is probably the most thoroughly segregated city in the United States. Its ugly record of brutality is widely known. Negroes have experienced grossly unjust treatment in the courts. There have been more unsolved bombings of Negro homes and churches in Birmingham than in any other city in the nation. These are the hard, brutal facts of the case. On the basis of these conditions, Negro leaders sought to negotiate with the city fathers. But the latter consistently refused to engage in good-faith negotiation.

Then, last September, came the opportunity to talk with leaders of Birmingham's economic community. In the course of the negotiations, certain promises were made by the merchants— for example, to remove the stores' humiliating racial signs. . . . [But a] few signs, briefly removed, returned; the others remained.

As in so many past experiences, our hopes

had been blasted, and the shadow of deep disappointment settled upon us. We had no alternative except to prepare for direct action, whereby we would present our very bodies as a means of laying our case before the conscience of the local and the national community. Mindful of the difficulties involved, we decided to undertake a process of self-purification. We began a series of workshops on nonviolence, and we repeatedly asked ourselves: "Are you able to accept blows without retaliating?" "Are you able to endure the ordeal of jail?" . . .

You may well ask: "Why direct action? Why sit-ins, marches and so forth? Isn't negotiation a better path?" You are quite right in calling for negotiation. Indeed, this is the very purpose of direct action. Nonviolent direct action seeks to create such a crisis and foster such a tension that a community which has constantly refused to negotiate is forced to confront the issue. It seeks so to dramatize the issue that it can no longer be ignored. My citing the creation of tension as part of the work of the nonviolent-resister may sound rather shocking. But I must confess that I am not afraid of the word "tension." I have earnestly opposed violent tension, but there is a type of constructive, nonviolent tension which is necessary for growth. Just as Socrates felt that it was necessary to create a tension in the mind so that individuals could rise from the bondage of myths and half-truths to the unfettered realm of creative analysis and objective appraisal, so must we see the need for nonviolent gadflies to create the kind of tension in society that will help men rise from the dark depths of prejudice and racism to the majestic heights of understanding and brotherhood.

The purpose of our direct-action program is to create a situation so crisis-packed that it will inevitably open the door to negotiation. I therefore concur with you in your call for negotiation. Too long has our beloved Southland been bogged down in a tragic effort to live in monologue rather than dialogue. . . .

My friends, I must say to you that we have not made a single gain in civil rights without determined legal and nonviolent pressure. Lamentably, it is an historical fact that privileged groups seldom give up their privileges voluntarily. Individuals may see the moral light and voluntarily give up their unjust posture; but, as Reinhold Niebuhr has reminded us, groups tend to be more immoral than individuals.

We know through painful experience that freedom is never voluntarily given by the oppressor; it must be demanded by the oppressed. Frankly, I have yet to engage in a direct-action campaign that was "well timed" in the view of those who have not suffered unduly from the disease of segregation. For years now I have heard the word "Wait!" It rings in the ear of every Negro with piercing familiarity. This "Wait" has almost always meant "Never." We must come to see, with one of our distinguished jurists, that "justice too long delayed is justice denied."

We have waited for more than 340 years for our constitutional and God-given rights. The nations of Asia and Africa are moving with jet-like speed toward gaining political independence, but we still creep at horse-and-buggy pace toward gaining a cup of coffee at a lunch counter. Perhaps it is easy for those who have never felt the stinging darts of segregation to say, "Wait." But when you have seen vicious mobs lynch your mothers and fathers at will and drown your sisters and brothers at whim; when you have seen hate-filled policemen curse, kick and even kill your black brothers and sisters; when you see the vast majority of your twenty million Negro brothers smothering in an airtight cage of poverty in the midst of an affluent society; when you suddenly find your tongue twisted and your speech stammering as you seek to explain to your six-year-old daughter why she can't go to the public amusement park that has just been advertised on television, and see tears welling up in her eyes when she is told that Funtown is closed to colored children, and see ominous clouds of inferiority beginning to form in her little mental sky, and see her beginning to distort her personality by developing an unconscious bitterness toward white people; when you have to concoct an answer for a five-year-old son who is asking: "Daddy, why do white people treat colored people so mean?"; when you take a cross-country drive and find it necessary to sleep night after night in the uncomfortable corners of your automobile because no motel will accept you; when you are humiliated day in and day out by nagging signs reading "white" and "colored"; when your first name becomes "nigger," your middle name becomes "boy" (however old you are) and your last name becomes "John," and your wife and mother are never given the respected title "Mrs."; when you are harried by day and haunted by night by the fact that you are a Negro, living constantly at tiptoe stance, never quite knowing what to expect next, and are plagued with inner fears and outer resentments; when you are forever fighting a degenerating sense of "nobodiness"—then you will understand why we find it difficult to wait. There comes a time when the cup of endurance runs over, and men are no longer willing to be plunged into the abyss of despair. I hope, sirs, you can understand our legitimate and unavoidable impatience.

You express a great deal of anxiety over our willingness to break laws. This is certainly a legitimate concern. Since we so diligently urge people to obey the Supreme Court's decision of 1954 outlawing segregation in the public schools, at first glance it may seem rather paradoxical for us consciously to break laws. One may well ask: "How can you advocate breaking some laws and obeying others?" The answer lies in the fact that there are two types of laws: just and unjust. I would be the first to advocate obeying just laws. One has not only a legal but a moral responsibility to obey just laws. Conversely, one has a moral responsibility to disobey unjust laws. I would agree with St. Augustine that "an unjust law is no law at all."

Now, what is the difference between the two? How does one determine whether a law is just or unjust? A just law is a man-made code that squares with the moral law or the law of God. An unjust law is a code that is out of harmony with the moral law. To put it in the terms of St. Thomas Aquinas: An unjust law is a human law that is not rooted in eternal law and natural law.

Any law that uplifts human personality is just. Any law that degrades human personality is unjust. All segregation statutes are unjust because segregation distorts the soul and damages the personality. It gives the segregator a false sense of superiority and the segregated a false sense of inferiority. Segregation, to use the terminology of the Jewish philosopher Martin Buber, substitutes an "I—it" relationship for an "I—thou" relationship and ends up relegating persons to the status of things. Hence segregation is not only politically, economically and sociologically unsound, it is morally wrong and sinful. Paul Tillich has said that sin is separation. Is not segregation an existential expression of man's tragic separation, his awful estrangement, his terrible sinfulness? Thus it is that I can urge men to obey the 1954 decision of the Supreme Court, for it is morally right; and I can urge them to disobey segregation ordinances, for they are morally wrong.

Let us consider a more concrete example of just and unjust laws. An unjust law is a code that a numerical or power majority group compels a minority group to obey but does not make binding on itself. This is *difference* made legal. By the same token, a just law is a code that a majority compels a minority to follow and that it is willing to follow itself. This is *sameness* made legal.

Let me give another explanation. A law is unjust if it is inflicted on a minority that, as a result of being denied the right to vote, had no part in enacting or devising the law. Who can say that the legislature of Alabama which set up that state's segregation laws was democratically elected? Throughout Alabama all sorts of devious methods are used to prevent Negroes from becoming registered voters, and there are some counties in which, even though Negroes constitute a majority of the population, not a single Negro is registered. Can any law enacted under such circumstances be considered democratically structured?

Sometimes a law is just on its face and unjust in its application. For instance, I have been arrested on a charge of parading without a permit. Now, there is nothing wrong in having an ordi-

Reverend Martin Luther King, Jr. stares pensively out of his cell in Birmingham, Alabama in November, 1967, five months before his assassination in Memphis.

nance which requires a permit for a parade. But such an ordinance becomes unjust when it is used to maintain segregation and to deny citizens the First-Amendment privilege of peaceful assembly and protest.

I hope you are able to see the distinction I am trying to point out. In no sense do I advocate evading or defying the law, as would the rabid segregationist. That would lead to anarchy. One who breaks an unjust law must do so openly, lovingly, and with a willingness to accept the penalty. I submit that an individual who breaks a

law that conscience tells him is unjust, and who willingly accepts the penalty of imprisonment in order to arouse the conscience of the community over its injustice, is in reality expressing the highest respect for law.

Of course, there is nothing new about this kind of civil disobedience. It was evidenced sublimely in the refusal of Shadrach, Meshach and Abednego to obey the laws of Nebuchadnezzar, on the ground that a higher moral law was at stake. It was practiced superbly by the early Christians, who were willing to face hungry lions and the excruciating pain of chopping blocks rather than submit to certain unjust laws of the Roman Empire. To a degree, academic freedom is a reality today because Socrates practiced civil disobedience. In our own nation, the Boston Tea Party represented a massive act of civil disobedience.

We should never forget that everything Adolf Hitler did in Germany was "legal" and everything the Hungarian freedom fighters did in Hungary was "illegal." It was "illegal" to aid and comfort a Jew in Hitler's Germany. Even so, I am sure that, had I lived in Germany at the time, I would have aided and comforted my Jewish brothers. If today I lived in a Communist country where certain principles dear to the Christian faith are suppressed, I would openly advocate disobeying that country's antireligious laws. . . .

Like a boil that can never be cured so long as it is covered up but must be opened with all its ugliness to the natural medicines of air and light, injustice must be exposed, with all the tension its exposure creates, to the light of human conscience and the air of national opinion before it can be cured.

In your statement you assert that our actions, even though peaceful, must be condemned because they precipitate violence. But is this a logical assertion? Isn't this like condemning a robbed man because his possession of money precipitated the evil act of robbery? Isn't this like condemning Socrates because his unswerving commitment to truth and his philosophical inquiries precipitated the act by the misguided populace in which they made him drink hemlock? Isn't this like condemning Jesus because his unique God-consciousness and never-ceasing devotion to God's will precipitated the evil act of crucifixion? We must come to see that, as the federal courts have consistently affirmed, it is wrong to urge an individual to cease his efforts to gain his basic constitutional rights because the quest may precipitate violence. Society must protect the robbed and punish the robber. . . .

Oppressed people cannot remain oppressed forever. The yearning for freedom eventually manifests itself, and that is what has happened to the American Negro. Something within has reminded him of his birthright of freedom, and something without has reminded him that it can be gained. Consciously or unconsciously, he has been caught up by the *Zeitgeist*, and with his black brothers of Africa and his brown and yellow brothers of Asia, South America and the Caribbean, the United States Negro is moving with a sense of great urgency toward the promised land of racial justice. If one recognizes this vital urge that has engulfed the Negro community, one should readily understand why public demonstrations are taking place. The Negro has many pent-up resentments and latent frustrations, and he must release them. So let him march; let him make prayer pilgrimages to the city hall; let him go on freedom rides—and try to understand why he must do so. If his repressed emotions are not released in nonviolent ways, they will seek expression through violence; this is not a threat but a fact of history. So I have not said to my people: "Get rid of your discontent." Rather, I have tried to say that this normal and healthy discontent can be channeled into the creative outlet of nonviolent direct action. And now this approach is being termed extremist.

But though I was initially disappointed at being categorized as an extremist, as I continued to think about the matter I gradually gained a measure of satisfaction from the label. Was not Jesus an extremist for love: "Love your enemies, bless them that curse you, do good to them that hate you, and pray for them which despitefully use you, and persecute you." Was not Amos an extremist for justice: "Let justice roll down like waters and righteousness like an ever-flowing stream." Was not Paul an extremist for the Christian gospel: "I bear in my body the marks of the Lord Jesus." Was not Martin Luther an extremist: "Here I stand; I cannot do otherwise, so help me God." And John Bunyan: "I will stay in jail to the end of my days before I make a butchery of my conscience." And Abraham Lincoln: "This nation cannot survive half slave and half free." And Thomas Jefferson: "We hold these truths to be self-evident, that all men are created equal . . ." So the question is not whether we will be extremists, but what kind of extremists we will be. Will we be extremists for hate or for love? Will we be extremists for the preservation of injustice or for the extension of justice? In that dramatic scene on Calvary's hill three men were crucified. We must never forget that all three were crucified for the same crime—the crime of extremism. Two were extremists for immorality, and thus fell below their environment. The other, Jesus Christ, was an extremist for love, truth and goodness, and thereby rose above his environment. Perhaps the South, the nation and the world are in dire need of creative extremists. . . .

I have no fear about the outcome of our struggle in Birmingham, even if our motives are at present misunderstood. We will reach the goal of freedom in Birmingham and all over the nation, because the goal of America is freedom. Abused and scorned though we may be, our destiny is tied up with America's destiny. Before the pilgrims landed at Plymouth, we were here. Before the pen of Jefferson etched the majestic words of the Declaration of Independence across the pages of history, we were here. For more than two centuries our forebears labored in this country without wages; they made cotton king; they built the homes of their masters while suffering gross injustice and shameful humiliation—and yet out of a bottomless vitality they continued to thrive and develop. If the inexpressible cruelties of slavery could not stop us, the opposition we now face will surely fail. We will win our freedom because the sacred heritage of our nation and the eternal will of God are embodied in our echoing demands. . . .

Over the past few years I have consistently preached that nonviolence demands that the means we use must be as pure as the ends we seek. I have tried to make clear that it is wrong to use immoral means to attain moral ends. But now I must affirm that it is just as wrong, or perhaps even more so, to use moral means to preserve immoral ends. . . .

I wish you had commended the Negro sit-inners and demonstrators of Birmingham for their sublime courage, their willingness to suffer and their amazing discipline in the midst of great provocation. One day the South will recognize its real heroes. They will be the James Merediths, with the noble sense of purpose that enables them to face jeering and hostile mobs, and with the agonizing loneliness that characterizes the life of the pioneer. They will be old, oppressed, battered Negro women, symbolized in a seventy-two-year-old woman in Montgomery, Alabama, who rose up with a sense of dignity and with her people decided not to ride segregated buses, and who responded with ungrammatical profundity to one who inquired about her weariness: "My feets is tired, but my soul is at rest." They will be the young high school and college students, the young ministers of the gospel and a host of their elders, courageously and nonviolently sitting in at lunch counters and willingly going to jail for conscience' sake. One day the South will know that when these disinherited children of God sat down at lunch counters, they were in reality standing up for what is best in the American dream and for the most sacred values in our Judaeo-Christian heritage, thereby bringing our nation back to those great wells of democracy which were dug deep by the founding fathers in their formulation of the Constitution and the Declaration of Independence. . . .

If I have said anything in this letter that overstates the truth and indicates an unreasonable impatience, I beg you to forgive me. If I have said anything that understates the truth and indicates my having a patience that allows me to settle for anything less than brotherhood, I beg God to forgive me.

I hope this letter finds you strong in the faith. I also hope that circumstances will soon make it possible for me to meet each of you, not as an integrationist or a civil-rights leader but as a fellow clergyman and a Christian brother. Let us all hope that the dark clouds of racial prejudice will soon pass away and the deep fog of misunderstanding will be lifted from our fear-drenched communities, and in some not too distant tomorrow the radiant stars of love and brotherhood will shine over our great nation with all their scintillating beauty.

In April 1989, Chinese students spontaneously converged on Tiananmen Square in response to news of the death of former Communist Party leader Hu Yaobang, bearing wreaths in his honor. As their numbers grew, the gathering turned into a political protest, because Hu had been purged from his office two years earlier for failing to stifle student dissent. This photograph, taken on April 17, shows students gathered at the Monument of the Chinese People, where they copied the latest bulletins that had been posted there by leaders of the democracy movement.

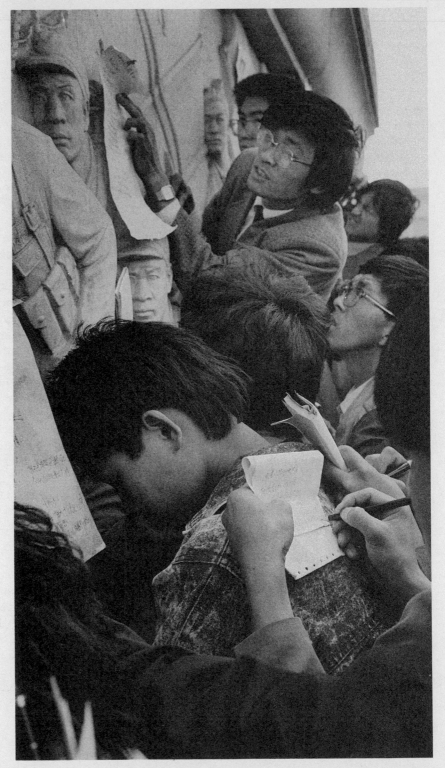

CONTEMPORARY
INTERNATIONAL
DEMOCRATIC IDEAS

INTERNATIONAL DECLARATION OF HUMAN RIGHTS

Before the mid-twentieth century, there were no restraints on what a state could do to its citizens; the relationship between a state and its citizens was thought to be a domestic, internal matter, of no concern to the rest of the world. However, the unprecedented genocides committed during World War II spurred the creation of the United Nations, one of whose basic purposes was international cooperation "in promoting and encouraging respect for human rights and for fundamental freedoms for all without distinction as to race, sex, language, or religion" (Article 1, 55c). To make those references in the U.N. Charter explicit, a commission was authorized to draft an international charter of human rights. The chairwoman of the commission was Anna Eleanor Roosevelt, wife of the late U.S. President, Franklin Delano Roosevelt.

During a two-and-a-half year period, representatives from all of the United Nations negotiated the wording of the Declaration. Those from Western democracies insisted on the primacy of the political and civil rights of individuals; those from socialist countries wanted to emphasize the social and economic rights that were owed citizens by the state. The Declaration incorporated both sets of demands, but not to the satisfaction of the socialist countries, which abstained when the Declaration was put to a vote.

On December 10, 1948, the Declaration of Human Rights was adopted by the United Nations. The vote was 48 for, none against. Eight nations abstained: Byelorussian S.S.R., Czechoslovakia, Poland, Saudi Arabia, Ukrainian S.S.R., U.S.S.R., Union of South Africa, and Yugoslavia. Saudi Arabia objected to the Declaration's affirmation of freedom of religion. South Africa objected to the Declaration's commitment to racial equality and freedom from discrimination.

Although it was not intended to be a binding covenant, the Declaration was eventually accepted as a statement of universal aspirations by which to assess the behavior of all nations. Although the specific provisions of the Declaration have been repeatedly violated over the years by many members of the United Nations, the Declaration has nonetheless served as a useful gauge. In every nation, human rights organizations and dissidents refer to the Declaration as a consistent standard of human rights and freedoms.

Virtually every national constitution reiterates the major provisions of the Declaration, regardless of the actual nature of the government. Even tyrannical states that strictly regulate the press, limit their citizens' freedom of movement, prohibit free trade unions, and abuse every other aspect of the Declaration, nonetheless pay it obeisance, either by endorsing it or by incorporating parts of it into their constitution. No nation repudiates the Declaration; instead, those who violate it deny doing so.

In view of the fact that so many members of the United Nations regularly ignore the letter and spirit of the Declaration, it may appear that the Declaration of Human Rights has little force or validity. Yet its very existence serves as a standard by which people judge the conditions of their lives and as a continuing inspiration to people who live in nations that make unkept promises.

PREAMBLE

*W*hereas recognition of the inherent dignity and of the equal and inalienable rights of all members of the human family is the foundation of freedom, justice and peace in the world.

Whereas disregard and contempt for human rights have resulted in barbarous acts which have outraged the conscience of mankind, and the advent of a world in which human beings shall enjoy freedom of speech and belief and freedom from fear and want has been proclaimed as the highest aspiration of the common people.

Whereas it is essential, if man is not to be compelled to have recourse, as a last resort, to rebellion against tyranny and oppression, that human rights should be protected by the rule of law.

Whereas it is essential to promote the development of friendly relations between nations.

Whereas the peoples of the United Nations have in the Charter reaffirmed their faith in fundamental human rights, in the dignity and worth of the human person and in the equal rights of men and women and have determined to promote social progress and better standards of life in larger freedom.

Whereas Member States have pledged themselves to achieve, in co-operation with the United Nations, the promotion of universal respect for and observance of human rights and fundamental freedoms.

Whereas a common understanding of these rights and freedoms is of the greatest importance for the full realization of this pledge.

Now, Therefore,

THE GENERAL ASSEMBLY PROCLAIMS

This universal declaration of human rights as a common standard of achievement for all peoples and all nations, to the end that every individual and every organ of society, keeping this Declaration constantly in mind, shall strive by teaching and education to promote respect for these rights and freedoms and by progressive measures, national and international, to secure their universal and effective recognition and ob-

servance, both among the peoples of Member States themselves and among the peoples of territories under their jurisdiction.

Article 1

All human beings are born free and equal in dignity and rights. They are endowed with reason and conscience and should act towards one another in a spirit of brotherhood.

Article 2

Everyone is entitled to all the rights and freedoms set forth in this Declaration, without distinction of any kind, such as race, colour, sex, language, religion, political or other opinion, national or social origin, property, birth or other status.

Furthermore, no distinction shall be made on the basis of the political, jurisdictional or international status of the country or territory to which a person belongs, whether it be independent, trust, non-self-governing or under any other limitation of sovereignty.

Article 3

Everyone has the right to life, liberty and security of person.

Article 4

No one shall be held in slavery or servitude; slavery and the slave trade shall be prohibited in all their forms.

Article 5

No one shall be subjected to torture or to cruel, inhuman or degrading treatment or punishment.

Article 6

Everyone has the right to recognition everywhere as a person before the law.

Article 7

All are equal before the law and are entitled without any discrimination to equal protection of the law. All are entitled to equal protection against any discrimination in violation of this Declaration and against any incitement to such discrimination.

Article 8

Everyone has the right to an effective remedy by the competent national tribunals for acts violating the fundamental rights granted him by the constitution or by law.

Article 9

No one shall be subjected to arbitrary arrest, detention or exile.

Article 10

Everyone is entitled in full equality to a fair and public hearing by an independent and impartial tribunal, in the determination of his rights and obligations and of any criminal charge against him.

Article 11

1. Everyone charged with a penal offence has the right to be presumed innocent until proved guilty according to law in a public trial at which he has had all the guarantees necessary for his defence.
2. No one shall be held guilty of any penal offence on account of any act or omission which did not constitute a penal offence, under national or international law, at the time when it was committed. Nor shall a heavier penalty be imposed than the one that was applicable at the time the penal offence was committed.

Article 12

No one shall be subjected to arbitrary interference with his privacy, family, home or correspondence, nor to attacks upon his honour and reputation. Everyone has the right to the protection of the law against such interference or attacks.

Article 13

1. Everyone has the right to freedom of movement and residence within the borders of each state.
2. Everyone has the right to leave any country, including his own, and to return to his country.

Eleanor Roosevelt, widow of President Franklin Delano Roosevelt, played a leading role in the drafting and adoption of the Universal Declaration of Human Rights. Deeply interested in social issues, particularly women's rights and racial equality, she represented the United States at the United Nations after her husband's death in 1945 and was chairperson of its Commission on Human Rights.

Article 14

1. Everyone has the right to seek and to enjoy in other countries asylum from persecution.
2. This right may not be invoked in the case of prosecutions genuinely arising from non-political crimes or from acts contrary to the purposes and principles of the United Nations.

Article 15

1. Everyone has the right to a nationality.
2. No one shall be arbitrarily deprived of his nationality nor denied the right to change his nationality.

Article 16

1. Men and women of full age, without any limitation due to race, nationality or religion, have the right to marry and to found a family. They are entitled to equal rights as to marriage, during marriage and at its dissolution.
2. Marriage shall be entered into only with the free and full consent of the intending spouses.
3. The family is the natural and fundamental group unit of society and is entitled to protection by society and the State.

Article 17

1. Everyone has the right to own property alone as well as in association with others.
2. No one shall be arbitrarily deprived of his property.

Article 18

Everyone has the right to freedom of thought, conscience and religion; this right includes freedom to change his religion or belief, and freedom, either alone or in community with others and in public or private, to manifest his religion or belief in teaching, practice, worship and observance.

Article 19

Everyone has the right to freedom of opinion and expression; this right includes freedom to hold opinions without interference and to seek, receive and impart information and ideas through any media and regardless of frontiers.

Article 20

1. Everyone has the right to freedom of peaceful assembly and association.
2. No one may be compelled to belong to an association.

Article 21

1. Everyone has the right to take part in the government of his country, directly or through freely chosen representatives.
2. Everyone has the right of equal access to public service in his country.
3. The will of the people shall be the basis of the authority of government; this will shall be expressed in periodic and genuine elections which shall be by universal and equal suffrage and shall be held by secret vote or be equivalent free voting procedures.

Article 22

Everyone, as a member of society, has the right to social security and is entitled to realization, through national effort and international cooperation and in accordance with the organization and resources of each State, of the economic, social and cultural rights indispensable for his dignity and the free development of his personality.

Article 23

1. Everyone has the right to work, to free choice of employment, to just and favourable conditions of work and to protection against unemployment.
2. Everyone, without any discrimination, has the right to equal pay for equal work.
3. Everyone who works has the right to just and favourable remuneration ensuring for himself and his family an existence worthy of human dignity, and supplemented, if necessary, by other means of social protection.
4. Everyone has the right to form and to join trade unions for the protection of his interests.

Article 24

Everyone has the right to rest and leisure, including reasonable limitation of working hours and periodic holidays with pay.

Article 25

1. Everyone has the right to a standard of living adequate for the health and well-being of him-

self and of his family, including food, clothing, housing and medical care and necessary social services, and the right to security in the event of unemployment, sickness, disability, widowhood, old age or other lack of livelihood in circumstances beyond his control.

2. Motherhood and childhood are entitled to special care and assistance. All children, whether born in or out of wedlock, shall enjoy the same social protection.

Article 26

1. Everyone has the right to education. Education shall be free, at least in the elementary and fundamental stages. Elementary education shall be compulsory. Technical and professional education shall be made generally available and higher education shall be equally accessible to all on the basis of merit.

2. Education shall be directed to the full development of the human personality and to the strengthening of respect for human rights and fundamental freedoms. It shall promote understanding, tolerance and friendship among all nations, racial or religious groups, and shall further the activities of the United Nations for the maintenance of peace.

3. Parents have a prior right to choose the kind of education that shall be given to their children.

Article 27

1. Everyone has the right freely to participate in the cultural life of the community, to enjoy the arts and to share in scientific advancement and its benefits.

2. Everyone has the right to the protection of the moral and material interests resulting from any scientific, literary or artistic production of which he is the author.

Article 28

Everyone is entitled to a social and international order in which the rights and freedoms set forth in this Declaration can be fully realized.

Article 29

1. Everyone has duties to the community in which alone the free and full development of his personality is possible.

2. In the exercise of his rights and freedoms, everyone shall be subject only to such limitations as are determined by law solely for the purpose of securing due recognition and respect for the rights and freedoms of others and of meeting the just requirements of morality, public order and the general welfare in a democratic society.

3. These rights and freedoms may in no case be exercised contrary to the purposes and principles of the United Nations.

Article 30

Nothing in this Declaration may be interpreted as implying for any State, group or person any right to engage in any activity or to perform any act aimed at the destruction of any of the rights and freedoms set forth herein.

BORIS PASTERNAK
NOBEL PRIZE

Boris Pasternak (1890–1960) was born in a small town near Moscow. He published his first volume of poems in 1913; by 1922, with the publication of his third volume of poetry, he was recognized as a major poet. From 1933 to 1943, Pasternak was unable to publish because his lyrical style of poetry was out of favor with government authorities. During this time, he supported himself as a translator. When Pasternak submitted his novel *Doctor Zhivago* to a Moscow literary magazine, it was rejected as "libelous" because of its depiction of the Russian Revolution. The novel was published in the West in 1957, where it became a best-seller and was translated into 18 languages. While the novel received international acclaim, Pasternak was subjected to a campaign of abuse in the Soviet press and was ousted from the translators' union, thus cut off from his income. In 1958, as the Soviet press printed demands for his expulsion from the country, Pasternak was awarded the Nobel Prize for Literature. Stung by the attacks on him, he declined the honor; he wrote the following poem in 1959.

Like a beast in a pen, I'm cut off
From my friends, freedom, the sun,
But the hunters are gaining ground.
I've nowhere else to run.

Dark wood and the bank of a pond,
Trunk of a fallen tree.
There's no way forward, no way back.
It's all up with me.

Am I gangster or murderer?
Of what crime do I stand
Condemned? I made the whole world weep
At the beauty of my land.

Even so, one step from my grave,
I believe that cruelty, spite,
The powers of darkness will in time
Be crushed by the spirit of light.

The beaters in a ring close in
With the wrong prey in view.
I've nobody at my right hand,
Nobody faithful and true.

And with such a noose on my throat
I should like for one second
My tears to be wiped away
By someone at my right hand.

Boris Pasternak, Russian poet and novelist, won the Nobel Prize for Literature in 1958, when this photograph was taken at his country home.

ALEKSANDR SOLZHENITSYN

LIVE NOT BY LIES

Born in 1918, Aleksandr Solzhenitsyn has been acknowledged as one of the greatest writers of the twentieth century. As a boy he was thoroughly steeped in the history and literature of Russia; he studied at the University of Rostov and later taught mathematics and astronomy at a secondary school in southern Russia. After the Nazi attack on the Soviet Union he served in the Red Army. In 1945, he was arrested for a critical reference to Stalin in a private letter and was sentenced without a hearing to eight years in a labor camp. His prison term ended on the day of Stalin's death in 1953, but he was placed in "perpetual exile" in Kazakhstan rather than given his freedom.

Nikita Khrushchev's accession to power in 1957 brought a period of relative liberalization, marked by efforts to banish the Stalinist cult of personality. Like many other victims of the Stalin era, Solzhenitsyn was released from exile, and his conviction was voided. In 1962, Solzhenitsyn's *One Day in the Life of Ivan Denisovich*, a fictionalized portrayal of life in a prison camp, was published with Khrushchev's explicit approval. The novel won worldwide acclaim and was translated into every major European language.

When Khrushchev was ousted in 1964, the de-Stalinization program abruptly ended, and Solzhenitsyn and his work fell out of favor with the authorities. His archives and a new novel, *The First Circle*, were seized by the police. Solzhenitsyn's celebrity as a writer and his courageous resistance to attempts to silence him brought him international attention. In 1970, after being dropped by the Union of Soviet Writers the previous year, he won the Nobel Prize for Literature.

His books continued to be published in the West, to the embarrassment of Soviet authorities. Solzhenitsyn was expelled from the Soviet Union in February 1974, shortly after the publication of the first volume of *The Gulag Archipelago*, an exposé of Soviet prison camps. He settled in the United States, in a small town in Vermont.

On February 18, 1974, days after Solzhenitsyn's expulsion, *The Washington Post* published this appeal to his countrymen.

At one time we dared not even to whisper. Now we write and read *samizdat*, and sometimes when we gather in the smoking room at the Science Institute we complain frankly to one another: What kind of tricks are they playing on us, and where are they dragging us? Gratuitous boasting of cosmic achievements while there is poverty and destruction at home. Propping up remote, uncivilized regimes. Fanning up civil war. And we recklessly fostered Mao Tse-tung at our expense—and it will be we who are sent to war against him, and will have to go. Is there any way out? And they put on trial anybody they want, and they put sane people in asylums—always they, and we are powerless.

Things have almost reached rock bottom. A universal spiritual death has already touched us all, and physical death will soon flare up and consume us both and our children—but as before we still smile in a cowardly way and mumble without tongues tied: But what can we do to stop it? We haven't the strength.

We have been so hopelessly dehumanized that for today's modest ration of food we are willing to abandon all our principles, our souls, and all the efforts of our predecessors and all the opportunities for our descendants—but just don't disturb our fragile existence. We lack staunchness, pride and enthusiasm. We don't even fear universal nuclear death, and we don't fear a third world war. We have already taken refuge in the crevices. We just fear acts of civil courage.

We fear only to lag behind the herd and to take a step alone—and suddenly find ourselves without white bread, without heating gas and without a Moscow registration.

We have been indoctrinated in political courses and in just the same way was fostered the idea to live comfortably, and all will be well for the rest of our lives. You can't escape your environment and social conditions. Everyday life defines consciousness. What does it have to do with us? We can't do anything about it.

But we can—everything. But we lie to ourselves for assurance. And it is not they who are to blame for everything—we ourselves, only we. One can object. But actually you can think anything you like. Gags have been stuffed into our mouths. Nobody wants to listen to us, and nobody asks us. How can we force them to listen? It is impossible to change their minds.

It would be natural to vote them out of office—but there are no elections in our country. In the West people know about strikes and protest demonstrations—but we are too oppressed and it is a horrible prospect for us: How can one suddenly renounce a job and take to the streets? Yet the other fatal paths probed during the past century by our bitter Russian history are nevertheless not for us, and truly we don't need them.

Now that the axes have done their work, when everything which was sown has sprouted anew, we can see that the young and presumptuous people who thought they would make our country just and happy through terror, bloody rebellion and civil war were themselves misled. No thanks, fathers of education! Now we know that infamous methods breed infamous results. Let our hands be clean!

The circle—is it closed? And is there really no way out? And is there only one thing left for us to do—to wait without taking action? Maybe something will happen by itself? It will never happen as long as we daily acknowledge, extoll, and strengthen—and do not sever ourselves from—the most perceptible of its aspects: Lies.

When violence intrudes into peaceful life, its face glows with self-confidence as if it were carrying a banner and shouting: "I am violence. Run away, make way for me—I will crush you." But violence quickly grows old. And it has lost confidence in itself, and in order to maintain a respectable face it summons falsehood as its ally—since violence can conceal itself with nothing except lies and the lies can be maintained only by violence. And violence lays its ponderous paw not every day and not on every shoulder. It demands from us only obedience to lies and daily participation in lies—all loyalty lies in that.

And the simplest and most accessible key to our self-neglected liberation lies right here: Personal non-participation in lies. Though lies conceal everything, though lies embrace everything, we will be obstinate in this smallest of matters: Let them embrace everything, but not with any help from me.

This opens a breach in the imaginary encirclement caused by our inaction. It is the easiest thing to do for us, but the most devastating for the lies. Because when people renounce lies it simply cuts short their existence. Like an infection, they can exist only in a living organism.

We do not exhort ourselves. We have not sufficiently matured to march into the squares and shout the truth out loud or to express aloud what we think. It's not necessary.

It's dangerous. But let us refuse to say that which we do not think.

This is our path, the easiest and most accessible one which takes into account our inherent cowardice, already well rooted. And it is much easier—it's dangerous even to say this—than the sort of civil disobedience which Gandhi advocated.

Our path is not to give conscious support to lies about anything whatsoever! And once we realize where lie the perimeters of falsehood—each sees them in his own way.

Our path is to walk away from this gangrenous boundary. If we did not paste together the dead bones and scales of ideology, if we did not sew together rotting rags we would be astonished how quickly the lies would be rendered helpless and subside.

That which should be naked would then really appear naked before the whole world.

So in our timidity, let each of us make a choice: Whether consciously to remain a servant of falsehood—of course, it is not out of inclination, but to feed one's family, that one raises his children in the spirit of lies—or to shrug off the lies and become an honest man worthy of respect both by one's children and contemporaries.

And from that day onward he:

- Will not henceforth write, sign or print in any way a single phrase which in his opinion distorts the truth.
- Will utter such a phrase neither in private conversation nor in the presence of many people, neither on his own behalf nor at the prompting of someone else, neither in the role of agitator, teacher, educator, nor in a theatrical role.
- Will not depict, foster or broadcast a single idea which he can see is false or a distortion of the truth, whether it be in painting, sculpture, photography, technical science or music.
- Will not cite out of context, either orally or written, a single quotation so as to please someone, to feather his own nest, to achieve success in his work, if he does not share completely the idea which is quoted, or if it does not accurately reflect the matter at issue.
- Will not allow himself to be compelled to attend demonstrations or meetings if they are contrary to his desire or will, will neither take into hand nor raise into the air a poster or slogan which he does not completely accept.
- Will not raise his hand to vote for a proposal with which he does not sincerely sympathize; will vote neither openly nor secretly for a person whom he considers unworthy or of doubtful abilities.
- Will not allow himself to be dragged to a meeting where there can be expected a forced or distorted discussion of a question.
- Will immediately walk out of a meeting, session, lecture, performance or film showing if he hears a speaker tell lies, or purvey ideological nonsense or shameless propaganda.
- Will not subscribe to or buy a newspaper or magazine in which information is distorted and primary facts are concealed. . . .

Russian novelist Aleksandr Solzhenitsyn, winner of the Nobel Prize for Literature in 1970, settled in the United States after being forced into exile by the Soviet Union in 1974. This photograph captures his arrival in the U.S.

Of course, we have not listed all of the possible and necessary deviations from falsehood. But a person who purifies himself will easily distinguish other instances with his purified outlook.

No, it will not be the same for everybody at first. Some, at first, will lose their jobs. For young people who want to live with the truth, this will, in the beginning, complicate their young lives very much, because the required recitations are stuffed with lies, and it is necessary to make a choice.

But there are no loopholes for anybody who wants to be honest: On any given day, any one of us will be confronted with at least one of the above-mentioned choices even in the most secure of the technical sciences. Either truth or falsehood: Toward spiritual independence, or toward spiritual servitude.

And he who is not sufficiently courageous even to defend his soul—don't let him be proud of his "progressive" views, and don't let him boast that he is an academician or a people's artist, a merited figure, or a general—let him say to himself: I am in the herd, and a coward. It's all the same to me as long as I'm fed and warm.

Even this path, which is the most modest of all paths of resistance, will not be easy for us. But it is much easier than self-immolation or a hunger strike: The flames will not envelope your body, your eyeballs will not burst from the heat, and brown bread and clean water will always be available to your family.

A great people of Europe, the Czechoslovaks, whom we betrayed and deceived: Haven't they shown us how a vulnerable breast can stand up even against tanks if there is a worthy heart within it?

You say it will not be easy? But it will be the easiest of all possible resources. It will not be an easy choice for a body, but it is the only one for a soul. No, it is not an easy path. But there are already people, even dozens of them, who over the years have maintained all these points and live by the truth.

So you will not be the first to take this path, but will join those who have already taken it. This path will be easier and shorter for all of us if we take it by mutual efforts and in close rank. If there are thousands of us, they will not be able to do anything with us. If there are tens of thousands of us, then we would not even recognize our country.

If we are too frightened, then we should stop complaining that someone is suffocating us. We ourselves are doing it. Let us then bow down even more, let us wait, and our brothers the biologists will help to bring nearer the day when they are able to read our thoughts.

And if we get cold feet, even taking this step, then we are worthless and hopeless, and the scorn of Pushkin should be directed to us:

"Why should cattle have the gifts of freedom?

"Their heritage from generation to generation is the belled yoke and the lash."

ANDREI SAKHAROV

PEACE, PROGRESS, AND HUMAN RIGHTS

As a successful nuclear physicist, Andrei Sakharov (1921–1989) could have enjoyed all the blandishments that the Soviet system had to offer its most valued members, but he rejected a life of comfort for the life of a heretic. In 1968, he became the leading champion of democracy and human rights in the Soviet Union. Soviet officials treated him as a pariah. As his fortunes fell in his own country, his international stature grew.

The son of a physics teacher, Sakharov was exempt from military service during World War II in order to complete his university studies; by 1948 he was at work on a project to develop a hydrogen bomb. At 32, he was elected to the U.S.S.R. Academy of Sciences, the youngest full member ever chosen. He was showered with honors and lived a life of ease, with a chauffeured car, special housing, shopping privileges, and a bodyguard.

In the late 1950s Sakharov became concerned about the ill effects of radioactive fallout from nuclear explosions. He pleaded with political leaders to stop testing programs, to no avail. Gradually, he became more outspoken on behalf of the intellectual freedom of writers and scientists. His underground manifesto, "Progress, Coexistence, and Intellectual Freedom," was published in the West in 1968, and he helped to form the Committee for Human Rights in 1970.

His life of privilege ended, he was ostracized by his former colleagues and hounded by the Soviet intelligence agency, the KGB. The harassment continued even after he won the Nobel Peace Prize in 1975. When he denounced the Soviet invasion of Afghanistan in 1980, Sakharov and his wife Yelena Bonner were banished to internal exile in Gorky, a city that was closed to the Western press. Not until 1986 were they released, by order of Mikhail Gorbachev, the head of state.

Sakharov was elected to the Congress of People's Deputies at the first free election in Soviet history in 1989. He became a leader of a faction demanding an end to the Communist party's monopoly of political power. On the day of his death, December 14, 1989, he urged the Congress to abolish Article Six of the Soviet Constitution, which made the Communist Party the only legitimate political party. Trying to slow the pace of reform, Gorbachev dismissed him from the podium. As *The New Republic* commented: "It was typical of Sakharov to embarrass power even in death."

What follows is an edited version of Sakharov's Nobel Peace Prize lecture of 1975. It was delivered by Bonner; Sakharov himself had been refused an exit visa "for reasons of security" because of his knowledge of "important state and military secrets."

Peace, progress, human rights—these three goals are indissolubly linked: it is impossible to achieve one of them if the others are ignored. This idea provides the main theme of my lecture.

I am deeply grateful that this great and significant award, the Nobel Peace Prize, has been given to me, and that I have the opportunity of addressing you here today. I was particularly gratified at the Committee's citation, which stresses the defense of human rights as the only sure basis for genuine and lasting international cooperation. This idea is very important to me; I am convinced that international trust, mutual understanding, disarmament, and international security are inconceivable without an open society with freedom of information, freedom of conscience, the right to publish, and the right to travel and choose the country in which one wishes to live. I am also convinced that freedom of conscience, together with other civic rights, provides both the basis for scientific progress and a guarantee against its misuse to harm mankind, as well as the basis for economic and social progress, which in turn is a political guarantee making the effective defense of social rights possible. At the same time I should like to defend the thesis of the original and decisive significance of civic and political rights in shaping the destiny of mankind. This view differs essentially from the usual Marxist theory, as well as from technocratic opinions, according to which only material factors and social and economic conditions are of decisive importance. (But in saying this, of course, I have no intention of denying the importance of people's material welfare.) . . .

There is a great deal to suggest that mankind, at the threshold of the second half of the twentieth century, entered a particularly decisive and critical historical era.

Nuclear missiles exist capable in principle of annihilating the whole of mankind; this is the greatest danger threatening our age. Thanks to economic, industrial, and scientific advances, so-called "conventional" arms have likewise grown incomparably more dangerous, not to mention chemical and bacteriological instruments of war.

There is no doubt that industrial and technological progress is the most important factor in overcoming poverty, famine, and disease. But this progress leads at the same time to ominous changes in the environment in which we live and to the exhaustion of our natural resources. Thus, mankind faces grave ecological dangers.

Rapid changes in traditional forms of life have resulted in an unchecked demographic explosion which is particularly noticeable in the developing countries of the Third World. The growth in population has already created exceptionally complicated economic, social, and psychological problems and will in the future inevitably pose still more serious problems. In many countries, particularly in Asia, Africa, and Latin America, the lack of food will be an overriding factor in the lives of many hundreds of millions of people, who from the moment of birth are condemned to a wretched existence on the starvation level. Moreover, future prospects are menacing, and in the opinion of many specialists, tragic, despite the undoubted success of the "green revolution."

But even in the developed countries, people face serious problems. These include the pressure resulting from excessive urbanization, all the changes that disrupt the community's social and psychological stability, the incessant pursuit of fashion and trends, overproduction, the frantic, furious tempo of life, the increase in nervous and mental disorders, the growing number of people deprived of contact with nature and of normal human lives, the dissolution of the family and the loss of simple human pleasures, the decay of the community's moral and ethical principles, and the loss of faith in the purpose of life. Against this background there is a whole host of ugly phenomena: an increase in crime, in alcoholism, in drug addiction, in terrorism, and so forth. The imminent exhaustion of the world's resources, the threat of overpopulation, the constant and deep-rooted international, political,

and social problems are making a more and more forceful impact on the developed countries too, and will deprive—or at any rate threaten to deprive—a great many people who are accustomed to abundance, affluence, and creature comforts.

However, in the pattern of problems facing the world today a more decisive and important role is played by the global political polarization of mankind, which is divided into the so-called First World (conventionally called the Western world), the Second (socialist), and the Third (the developing countries). Two powerful socialist states, in fact, have become mutually hostile totalitarian empires, in which a single party and the state exercise immoderate power in all spheres of life. They possess an enormous potential for expansion, striving to increase their influence to cover large areas of the globe. One of these states—the Chinese People's Republic—has reached only a relatively modest stage of economic development, whereas the other—the Soviet Union—by exploiting its unique natural resources, and by taxing to the utmost the powers of its inhabitants and their ability to suffer continued privation, has built up a tremendous war potential and a relatively high—though one-sided—economic development. But in the Soviet Union, too, the people's standard of living is low, and civic rights are more restricted than in less socialist countries. Highly complicated global problems also affect the Third World, where relative economic stagnation goes hand in hand with growing international political activity.

Moreover, this polarization further reinforces the serious dangers of nuclear annihilation, famine, pollution of the environment, exhaustion of resources, overpopulation, and dehumanization.

If we consider this complex of urgent problems and contradictions, the first point that must be made is that any attempt to reduce the tempo of scientific and technological progress, to reverse the process of urbanization, to call for isolationism, patriarchal ways of life, and a renaissance based on ancient national traditions, would be unrealistic. Progress is indispensable, and to halt it would lead to the decline and fall of our civilization.

Not long ago we were unfamiliar with artificial fertilizers, mechanized farming, chemical pesticides, and intensive agricultural methods. There are voices calling for a return to more traditional and possibly less dangerous forms of agriculture. But can this be accomplished in a world in which hundreds of millions of people are suffering from hunger? On the contrary, there is no doubt that we need increasingly intensive methods of farming, and we must spread modern methods all over the world, including the developing countries.

We cannot reject the idea of a spreading use of the results of medical research or the extension of research in all its branches, including bacteriology and virology, neurophysiology, human genetics, and gene surgery, no matter what potential dangers lurk in their abuse and the undesirable social consequences of this research. This also applies to research in the creation of artificial intelligence systems, research involving behavior, and the establishment of a unified system of global communication, systems for selecting and storing information, and so forth. It is quite clear that in the hands of irresponsible bureaucratic authorities operating secretly, all this research may prove exceptionally dangerous, but at the same time it may prove extremely important and necessary to mankind, if it is carried out under public supervision and discussion and socio-scientific analysis. We cannot reject wider application of artificial materials, synthetic food, or the modernization of every aspect of life; we cannot obstruct growing automation and industrial expansion, irrespective of the social problems these may involve.

Nuclear physicist Andrei Sakharov was the conscience of the world for nearly two decades. He won the Nobel Peace Prize in 1975 as a result of his relentless activism on behalf of human rights and intellectual freedom in the Soviet Union.

We cannot condemn the construction of bigger nuclear power stations or research into nuclear physics, since energetics is one of the bases of our civilization. . . .

We cannot cease interplanetary and intergalactic space research, including the attempts to intercept signals from civilizations outside our own earth. The chance that such experiments will prove successful is probably small, but precisely for this reason the results may well be tremendous.

I have mentioned only a few examples. In actual fact all important aspects of progress are closely interwoven; none of them can be discarded without the risk of destroying the entire structure of our civilization. Progress is indivisible. But intellectual factors play a special role in the mechanism of progress. Underestimating these factors is particularly widespread in the socialist countries, probably due to the populist-ideological dogmas of official philosophy, and may well result in distortion of the path of progress or even its cessation and stagnation.

Progress is possible and innocuous only when it is subject to the control of reason. The important problems involving environmental protection exemplify the role of public opinion, the open society, and freedom of conscience. The partial liberalization in our country after the death of Stalin made it possible to engage in public debate on this problem during the early 1960s. But an effective solution demands increased tightening of social and international control. The military application of scientific results and controlled disarmament are an equally critical area, in which international confidence depends on public opinion and an open society. The example I gave involving the manipulation of mass psychology is already highly topical, even though it may appear farfetched.

Freedom of conscience, the existence of an informed public opinion, a pluralistic system of education, freedom of the press, and access to other sources of information—all these are in very short supply in the socialist countries. This situation is a result of the economic, political, and ideological monism which is characteristic

of these nations. At the same time these conditions are a vital necessity, not only to avoid all witting or unwitting abuse of progress, but also to strengthen it.

An effective system of education and a creative sense of heredity from one generation to another are possible only in an atmosphere of intellectual freedom. Conversely, intellectual bondage, the power and conformism of a pitiful bureaucracy, acts from the very start as a blight on humanistic fields of knowledge, literature, and art and results eventually in a general intellectual decline, the bureaucratization and formalization of the entire system of education, the decline of scientific research, the thwarting of all incentive to creative work, stagnation, and dissolution.

In the polarized world the totalitarian states, thanks to détente, today may indulge in a special form of intellectual parasitism. And it seems that if the inner changes that we all consider necessary do not take place, those nations will soon be forced to adopt an approach of this kind. If this happens, the danger of an explosion in the world situation will merely increase. Cooperation between the Western states, the socialist nations, and the developing countries is a vital necessity for peace, and it involves exchanges of scientific achievements, technology, trade, and mutual economic aid, particularly where food is concerned. But this cooperation must be based on mutual trust between open societies, or—to put it another way—with an open mind, on the basis of genuine equality and not on the basis of the democratic countries' fear of their totalitarian neighbors. If that were the case, cooperation would merely involve an attempt at ingratiating oneself with a formidable neighbor. But such a policy would merely postpone the evil day, soon to arrive anyway and, then, ten times worse. . . . Détente can only be assured if from the very outset it goes hand in hand with continuous openness on the part of all countries, an aroused sense of public opinion, free exchange of information, and absolute respect in all countries for civic and political rights. In short: in addition to détente in the material sphere, with disarmament and trade, détente should take place in the intellectual and ideological sphere. . . .

I should also emphasize that I consider it particularly important for United Nations armed forces to be used more generally for the purpose of restricting armed conflicts between states and ethnic groups. I have a high regard for the United Nations role, and I consider the institution to be one of mankind's most important hopes for a better future. Recent years have proved difficult and critical for this organization. I have written on this subject in *My Country and the World*, but after it was published, a deplorable event took place: the General Assembly adopted—without any real debate—a resolution declaring Zionism a form of racism and racial discrimination. Zionism is the ideology of a national rebirth of the Jewish people after two thousand years of diaspora, and it is not directed against any other people. The adoption of a resolution of this kind has damaged the prestige of the United Nations. But despite such motions, which are frequently the result of an insufficient sense of responsibility among leaders of some of the UN's younger members, I believe nevertheless that the organization may sooner or later be in a position to play a worthy role in the life of mankind, in accordance with its Charter's aims.

Let me now address one of the central questions of the present age, the problem of disarmament. . . . It is imperative to promote confidence between nations, and carry out measures of control with the aid of international inspection groups. This is only possible if détente is extended to the ideological sphere, and it presupposes greater openness in public life. I have stressed the need for international agreements to limit arms supplies to other states, special agreements to halt production of new weapons systems, treaties banning secret rearmament, the elimination of strategically unbalancing factors, and in particular a ban on multi-warhead nuclear missiles. . . .

Regarding the problem of human rights, I should like to speak mainly of my own country. During the months since the Helsinki Conference there has been no real improvement in this

direction. In fact there have been attempts on the part of hard-liners to "give the screw another turn," in international exchange of information, the freedom to choose the country in which one wishes to live, travel abroad for studies, work, or health reasons, as well as ordinary tourist travel. To illustrate my assertion, I should like to give you a few examples—chosen at random and without any attempt to provide a complete picture.

You all know, even better than I do, that children from Denmark can get on their bicycles and cycle off to the Adriatic. No one would ever suggest that they were "teenage spies." But Soviet children are not allowed to do this! I am sure you are familiar with analogous examples.

The UN General Assembly, influenced by the socialist states, has imposed restrictions on the use of satellites for international TV transmissions. Now that the Helsinki Conference has taken place, there is every reason to deal afresh with this problem. For millions of Soviet citizens this is an important and interesting matter.

In the Soviet Union there is a severe shortage of artificial limbs and similar aids for invalids. But no Soviet invalid, even though he may have received a formal invitation from a foreign organization, is allowed to travel abroad in response to such an invitation.

Soviet newsstands rarely offer non-Communist newspapers, and it is not possible to buy every issue of Communist periodicals. Even informative magazines like *Amerika* are in very short supply. They are on sale only at a small number of newsstands, and are immediately snapped up by eager buyers.

Any person wishing to emigrate from the Soviet Union must have a formal invitation from a close relative. For many this is an insoluble problem—for 300,000 Germans, for example, who wish to go to West Germany. (The emigration quota for Germans is 5,000 a year, which means that one might be forced to wait for sixty years!) The situation for those who wish to be reunited with relatives in Socialist countries is particularly tragic. There is no one to plead their case, and in such circumstances the arbitrary behavior of the authorities knows no bounds.

The freedom to travel and the freedom to choose where one wishes to work and live are still violated in the case of millions of collective-farm workers, and in the situation of hundreds of thousands of Crimean Tatars, who thirty years ago were cruelly and brutally deported from the Crimea and who to this day have been denied the right to return to their homeland.

The Helsinki Accord confirms the principle of freedom of conscience. However, a relentless struggle will have to be carried on if the provisions of this agreement are to be realized in practice. In the Soviet Union today many thousands of people are both judicially and extrajudicially persecuted for their convictions: for their religious faith and their desire to bring up their children in a religious spirit, or for reading and disseminating—often only to a few acquaintances—literature of which the state disapproves, but which from the standpoint of ordinary democratic practice is absolutely legitimate. On the moral plane, there is particular gravity in the persecution of persons who have defended other victims of unjust treatment, who have worked to publish and, in particular, to distribute information regarding both the persecution and trials of persons with deviant opinions and the conditions in places of imprisonment.

It is unbearable to consider that at the very moment we are gathered together in this hall on this festive occasion hundreds and thousands of prisoners of conscience are suffering from undernourishment, as the result of year-long hunger, of an almost total lack of proteins and vitamins in their diet, of a shortage of medicines (there is a ban on the sending of vitamins and medicines to inmates), and of over-exertion. They shiver from cold, damp, and exhaustion in ill-lit dungeons, where they are forced to wage a ceaseless struggle for their human dignity and to maintain their convictions against the "indoctrination machine," in fact against the destruction of their souls. The special nature of the concentration-camp system is carefully concealed. The sufferings a handful have undergone,

because they exposed the terrible conditions, provide the best proof of the truth of their allegations and accusations. Our concept of human dignity demands an immediate change in this system for all imprisoned persons, no matter how guilty they may be. But what about the sufferings of the innocent? Worst of all is the hell that exists in the special psychiatric clinics in Dnepropetrovsk, Sytchevka, Blagoveshchensk, Kazan, Chernyakhovsk, Orel, Leningrad, Tashkent. . . .

A final solution to persecutions can be based on international agreement—amnesty for political prisoners, for prisoners of conscience in prisons, internment camps, and psychiatric clinics as set forth in a UN General Assembly resolution. This proposal involves no intervention in the internal affairs of any country. It would apply to every state on the same basis—to the Soviet Union, to Indonesia, to Chile, to the Republic of South Africa, to Spain, to Brazil, and to every other country. Since the protection of human rights has been proclaimed in the United Nations Declaration of Human Rights, there can be no reason to call this issue a matter of purely internal or domestic concern. In order to achieve this goal, no efforts can be too great, however long the road may seem. And that the road is long was clearly shown during the recent session of the United Nations, in the course of which the United States moved a proposal for political amnesty, only to withdraw it after attempts had been made by a number of countries to expand the scope of the amnesty. I much regret what took place. A problem cannot be removed from circulation. I am profoundly convinced that it would be better to liberate a certain number of people—even though they might be guilty of some offense or other—than to keep thousands of innocent people locked up and exposed to torture.

Without losing sight of an overall solution of this kind, we must fight against injustice and the violation of human rights for every individual person separately. Much of our future depends on this.

In struggling to defend human rights we ought, I am convinced, first and foremost to protect the innocent victims of regimes installed in various countries, without demanding the destruction or total condemnation of these regimes. We need reform, not revolution. We need a flexible, pluralist, tolerant society, which selectively and experimentally can foster a free, undogmatic use of the experiences of all kinds of social systems. What is détente? What is rapprochement? We are concerned not with words, but with a willingness to create a better and more decent society, a better world order.

Thousands of years ago human tribes suffered great privations in the struggle to survive. It was then important not only to be able to handle a club, but also to possess the ability to think intelligently, to take care of the knowledge and experience garnered by the tribe, and to develop the links that would provide cooperation with other tribes. Today the human race is faced with a

similar test. In infinite space many civilizations are bound to exist, among them societies that may be wiser and more "successful" than ours. I support the cosmological hypothesis which states that the development of the universe is repeated in its basic characteristics an infinite number of times. Further, other civilizations, including more "successful" ones, should exist an infinite number of times on the "preceding" and the "following" pages of the Book of the Universe. Yet we should not minimize our sacred endeavors in this world, where, like faint glimmers in the dark, we have emerged for a moment from the nothingness of dark unconsciousness into material existence. We must make good the demands of reason and create a life worthy of ourselves and of the goals we only dimly perceive.

SERGEI GRIGORYANTS

WHY MUST WE BE GRATEFUL?

An integral part of recent efforts to initiate reform in the Soviet Union was the policy of *glasnost*—a greater openness in the examination of social and political issues. After seven decades of imposed conformity and political orthodoxy, the Soviet intellectual community came to life. Writers who had previously been banned, or whose writings had been published only underground as *samizdat*, began to speak out. New magazines appeared, dedicated to widening the range of public discourse and to speaking honestly about politics, society, literature, and history.

One of the bravest of the new publications was a magazine called *Glasnost*, edited by Sergei Grigoryants (1941–   ). In it Grigoryants continually pressed the outer limits of the new policy of openness in pursuit of political and intellectual freedom. From time to time the magazine was shut down, even in the era of *glasnost*, and Grigoryants was periodically arrested for the views expressed in the magazine.

Unable to leave the Soviet Union, Grigoryants sent the following essay to be read to the international conference on human rights in Krakow, Poland in August 1988, the first such conference ever convened in a Communist country.

Why, like one of Chekhov's heroes, must we always remind ourselves that the human rights situation could be even worse than it is? Why,

when we remember the millions of people who have been shot, must we console ourselves that there are no executions now? Why, if a cigarette lighter explodes in my pocket, must I be grateful that the explosion did not happen in an ammunition dump? And why, if your wife has betrayed you, must you be grateful that it was you, and not your country, she betrayed?

The evils that continue to plague us make it impossible to understand what the world we live in is really like. Political prisoners continue to languish in prisons throughout the world, especially in the Soviet Union. Individuals continue to be deported from the Soviet Union without trial while national democratic movements are stifled, as in Armenia. The country's leaders persist in behaving as if they owned the country outright, and they demonstrate their disregard for everyone and everything in their use of the media.

What, then, is really happening in the Soviet Union? Without question, the will of the people is paralyzed. What we see happening in one part of the country is akin to simple movements of the fingers on one hand in an attempt to overcome that paralysis. Elsewhere, however, active movements are in evidence. For example, the Estonians have reclaimed their fallen heroes, their national flag, and their national anthem. They are also restoring the monuments built in memory of those who died during the 1918–1920 War of Independence and, in addition, are building monuments to commemorate the heroes of the 1940 resistance. The foxholes of the Forest Brethren are presently being restored as a museum.

It must be clearly understood that nationalist movements and democratic movements, especially in the Soviet Union, are one. The two cannot be separated for the simple reason that man, a social animal, is only human when he remembers his nationality. This is precisely why the Estonians and Armenians are so right to pursue their causes.

Will human rights be respected? And what, if anything, can we do to ensure that they will continue to be respected? We can hardly expect those who pilot the ship of state to take up the cause of human rights; after all, these helmsmen have no need of something that simply gets in their way. Human rights can only be attained by the people through democratic movements. Meanwhile, independent publications along with women's and youth groups—in short, all organizations that are not tied to state authority and that do not enjoy the state's protection and benevolence—must be fully supported. And, it should be noted, such organizations are slowly coming into existence.

It is no longer necessary to live under the terror that reigned in 1917, when Russia became the most repressed, most servile country in the world—at the same time Lenin proclaimed Russia the world's freest country. We should not conclude that, since there had been no tradition or experience of democracy in Russia when the revolution occurred, the Soviet peoples are incapable of creating democratic institutions for themselves now. What started as a negative experience can ultimately be transformed into a positive one. At present, we are reevaluating our own history and assessing our own mistakes in order not to repeat them. We call upon those countries that already enjoy the fruits of democracy to support and assist us in our efforts. We are firm in our conviction that each nation has the right to self-determination and, moreover, the right to exercise that self-determination. And as for freedom, all nations should unite in striving to achieve it.

JAKUB KARPÍNSKI

THE OFFICIAL POLISH PRESS ON THE EVENTS OF MARCH 1968

Jakub Karpínski (1940–   ) was a leader of student demonstrations at the University of Warsaw against the Polish government in March 1968. For his role he was imprisoned from 1968 to 1971. He became a professor of sociology and eventually taught at the University of Warsaw, the London School of Economics, and the State University of New York at Albany. The following excerpt is from Karpínski's *Mowa do Ludu (Speaking to the People)*, published in London in 1984.

Who Did It?

certain well-defined groups

small, irresponsible groups of young people

an insignificant reactionary group

a group of provokateurs

a few irresponsible firebrands

groups of dirty, long-haired firebrands

not our working-class children

the spoiled sons of parents holding high government posts

people who want to sneak on stage through the back door

centers of anti-communist diversion

continuers of the sort of imperialism that produced Hitler

International Zionism

enemies of People's Poland

revisionists and bankrupt Zionists

What Happened?

an insignificant reactionary group of writers attacked the Party's political line and was applauded by hostile, anti-Polish organizations abroad

groups of students blocked traffic

a provocation

youth allowed itself to be drawn into a dirty political power-play

students were cut off from their studies

Polish society was thrown into turmoil

on the healthy body of the working class a boil appeared which had to be removed

Society's Response

disapproval

open indignation

the whole nation absolutely condemns the instigators of the wild excesses

workers tell the firebrands: NO

we stand by the Party

we're with you, Comrade Wieslaw [Gomulka]

Warsaw protests against Israel's treacherous assault

the nation is engaged in the building of socialism

What Is To Be Done?

it is necessary to separate the wheat from the chaff

we demand the punishment of the instigators

we demand the punishment of the parents

we condemn revisionists and reformers

children should be raised with more discipline

expell the Zionists from the Party

send the Zionists to Israel

we are determined to chop off every hand raised against our beloved Fatherland

ADOLF JUZWÉNKO

THE RIGHT TO HISTORICAL TRUTH

In Poland, as in other Communist-controlled nations, it was not possible to write honestly about the past. Historians and other scholars were not permitted to write about episodes that reflected badly on the Communist authorities. Official textbooks omitted or distorted important historical facts, as did other official publications. Yet the Polish people knew about the Nazi–Soviet pact of 1939; they knew about the mass deportations of Poles to Russia in 1940 and 1941; they knew that the Soviets, not the Nazis, were responsible for the Katyn Forest massacres in 1940; they knew that the Communist regime in Poland had been imposed by Soviet power, not by the will of the people.

Adolf Juzwénko, (1949–   ) a Polish historian, wrote the following article for the magazine *Res Publica* in 1987. During this period, when the union Solidarity was banned yet actively publishing newspapers, books, and magazines, *Res Publica* operated in a gray area. It was tolerated by the authorities on condition that it accept official censorship. Juzwénko's article was totally banned by the censors. It was eventually published in the West.

During the winter of 1989 and the spring of 1990, each of the nations in eastern Europe that gained its freedom from Communist domination insisted upon an honest accounting of its history. The Poles demanded official acknowledgment of the Katyn murders; the Hungarians demanded a ceremonial acknowledgment of the heroes of the 1956 revolution; and the Czechoslovaks demanded and received an apology for the Warsaw Pact invasion of 1968. It was a remarkable demonstration of the importance of truth in history.

. . . After the war people in Poland were subjected to a peculiar form of education. The aim was to make everyone believe that communism and the Polish People's Republic were the fruits of a historical process nurtured by generations of the most enlightened and right-thinking people. Since it was impossible to prove this hypothesis by conscientious research, it was accepted that the science of history "if it is to be a real academic discipline . . . must primarily be concerned with the history of material goods, the history of the labouring masses, the history of the working classes." Historians were encouraged to assess the past "from the point of view of the development and struggle of the working class—that is the point of view of communism, of the future."

Not all historians obeyed these instructions. But it would be ingenuous to suggest that they left no trace on the attitudes of the Polish historical community or that they did not have a grave effect on the quality of Polish historiography.

The demand for reliable works on the 19th and 20th centuries has recently intensified among those with a general interest in history. As they search through the shelves of bookshops or libraries many Poles ask for the names of writers who do not conceal the truth, or for trustworthy accounts. Such demands can be troublesome. It is impossible to satisfy them without taking into account the political climate in which historical outlines were written in post-war Poland.

Writers, literary critics, historians of literature, historians and philosophers have all spoken out about the enslavement of the Polish humanities by communism after the Second World War. A lot of attention has been paid particularly to those whom one could class as being tainted by

Marxism. These included historians. I do not, however, wish to deal primarily with them. They were not a significant group either in terms of numbers or importance. Doctrinarians cannot be good historians; they cannot be historians at all. Historians soon realised that.

In his preface to *The Captive Mind*, Czeslaw Milosz wrote about his motives for remaining in the service of the Polish People's Republic's government after the war: "Let's imagine a scientist who has a laboratory in one of the towns of Eastern Europe and for whom that laboratory is crucial. Would it be easy for him to give it up or would he not rather agree to pay a high price so as not to lose that which plays such an important role in his life? My mother's tongue was that laboratory to me. As a poet my public was only in my country and only there could I publish my works."

Historians can say the same about themselves. They are tied to their native laboratories to an even greater extent. In every country, and especially in one whose history is as complex as Poland's, historians do their research primarily on their own nation and write their books primarily for their countrymen. It is not surprising, therefore, that, like Milosz, they decided to play with the Communist authorities the game of "surrenders and public avowals of loyalty, subterfuge and labyrinthine movements in defence of certain values." Within a few years, however, Milosz withdrew from this game. He realised that he had no chance in it. Those who continued to play did not even notice how they'd become its victims. It was inevitable that this should happen, because the rules of the game were dictated by one side only: the one-party authorities.

In 1951, during a conference in Otwock, historians were humiliated and forced to accept absurd instructions which pushed Polish historiography down the blind alley of "the only correct" methodology.

Particularly vitriolic attacks were directed in Otwock against Henryk Wereszycki's *The Political History of Post-Uprising Poland, 1864–1918*, published in 1948. The fate of this outstanding historian's book draws attention to a key fact in any discussion of the development of Polish historiography after the Second World War. Some forty years after its first publication, Wereszycki's textbook can still be considered the best academic study of the post-Uprising period. Despite this, Wereszycki's book has not been reprinted since 1948 by any of the country's top publishing houses, though I happen to know that attempts to do so have been made. Only in the last few years have the facts and assessments presented in Wereszycki's book been allowed to go outside the narrow confines of academic monographs and specialist periodicals.

History dealing with the post-1918 period has suffered even more. In the last three decades not a single book has been published by any of the top houses on the history of the labour movement, or of the state's political systems, or of Poland's place in Europe and her relations with neighbouring states, whose author could state with a clear conscience that it had been printed without any intervention by the censor—even if it was written without the constraints of self-censorship.

While historians of ancient and medieval history were allowed far greater freedom after 1956, historians of the 19th and even more so of the 20th centuries were still forced to work within imposed limits. Because here, to cite Tadeusz Manteuffel, "the repositioning of the study of history within a Marxist methodology was tied in with the class warfare which the enemy is also conducting in a subversive way on the historical sector of the ideological front."

From 1956 to the present day a significant section of the historical community has been struggling to recover the rights lost after 1948: the right to historical truth, the right to comparatively unfettered opportunities to practise the profession of historian, the right to publish the full results of their research. Thanks to this struggle Polish historiography of the most recent past contains some of the most interesting and sound works in Eastern Europe. Nevertheless one cannot be completely satisfied with it, still less fail to see that it, too, is the fruit of manipulation.

After the Stalinist night historians behaved a little like the man in the Jewish joke who was advised by his rabbi to fill his apartment with animals. Then, still following his rabbi's advice, he moved one animal out every day, and each time was delighted to see that he had more room in his apartment. After 1956 historians could publish texts they'd never dreamt of being allowed to publish before, and they were satisfied with the thought that, in time, they'd be allowed to publish even more. With this faith in the future they themselves limited the extent of their research, doctored their assessments, adapted the shape of their own books to the prevailing political climate. They tried to bypass the recommendations and regulations which were in force. It was hard to have any academic existence without being published, and nothing was published without first going through various filters.

These tactics have often been effective. One cannot deny that some good historical work has been published in the controlled publishing market. But the majority of it has consisted of works on very specialised subjects. Attempts to fool the censor have generally been abysmal failures when the author has dealt with a large theme requiring an extensive canvas: for example, when writing the biography of an outstanding politician. In such cases the background has had to be revamped because it was necessary to show that socialist thought and the labour movement, even when in error, were generally correct; that the Soviet Union always wanted to do what was right and if sometimes it turned out otherwise then that was for reasons beyond its control, and so on.

Many historians have agreed to this revamping out of what they profoundly believed to be necessity, but over the years they have done so with ever-increasing reluctance. During the '80s many of them have tried to dissociate themselves from their earlier academic work. Some have gone to the other extreme. Many of them no longer have the strength to go back again to a fundamental examination of the sources, and it would be hard to criticise them for that. This research will have to be taken up by the next generation of historians and we can only hope that they will eventually produce an original, uncensored general history of the period.

There are, however, a fair number of historians in the community who have readily sacrificed historical truth in return for large print runs of their books and larger payments, or even tried to win over the political decision-makers with their works.

The publishing market, thanks to manipulation of the size of print runs, has been flooded with just such works. It is to these books that readers have had easiest access and it is to them that teachers at all levels must refer their pupils or students.

This long manipulation of history has deformed not only the nation's historical awareness, but has seriously demoralised a significant part of the historical community, undermined its authority, and deprived its work of credibility. As a result, society's historical consciousness has inevitably been filled with artificial half-truths, and often simply untruths, about the history of the last two centuries. Moreover, a great number of people have become historically confused, unable often to distinguish truth from half-truth or a conformist compilation from an honest historical monograph. Such people are easier to manipulate. And it is to such people that woolly discussions on the new subject set by the manipulators are addressed—the subject of history's "blank spots."

These discussions are undertaken by writers who are renowned for always writing what they were told to. Today they hopefully await the moment when they will be the first to be instructed to tell the truth about the Ribbentrop-Molotov pact, or about Katyn. So they write countless articles, dodging and weaving and counting on the possibility that in the meantime something will change that will allow them triumphantly to cry: "Eureka!"

During the discussions which have taken place recently, with the participation of historians, I have noticed a great deal of optimism, a belief that in the not too distant future these so-called "blank spots" will disappear. I'd like it to happen, too, but I'm not so optimistic. Besides which, I see these "blank spots" slightly differently.

In a radio interview broadcast in August 1987, Colonel Marek Tarczynski was asked: "have there been any studies of the Polish–Soviet war of 1920 undertaken in the Polish People's Republic?" His reply was as follows; "There have been studies, there have been doctoral and post-doctoral theses written about it. The published literature on the subject, however, is confined only to more general textbooks and is contained in general works on Polish history. There has been no monograph work devoted to the 1920 war and the Battle of Warsaw. Political considerations have been responsible for this."

From this one can deduce that the events of 1920 have been researched by historians but that the results have not been published and that the assessments of the 1920 war contained in the text-books are essentially honest and justified.

But can one really accept this? Considerations which the Colonel called "political" required (can one use the past tense here?) that in writing about 1920, or indeed about any other piece of Polish–Soviet relations, one had to indicate the party responsible for all that was bad in these relations. The guilty party could never be the Soviet side. And that is how the matter is treated in the text-books the Colonel mentions. Monographs based on source evidence would not have supported such a thesis and so could not be written. Their absence made it easier to operate in half-truths and lies. And that is where the root of the "blank spots" problem can be found. Paradoxically, the poor quality of general works on the subject is not the result of their being "blank spots"; rather it is the "blank spots" which have come into being as a result of the *a priori* acceptance of certain general values and the forcing of historical facts to fit in with these.

The truth about 1920, or about August and September 1939, or even about Katyn, loses its full meaning when it is presented in a falsified historical context. For its true significance can only be seen against a broad background of historical events. Marxist historical literature claims that in 1920 it was not Russia that intervened in Poland's internal affairs but Poland that intervened in Russia's; it acts as if it were ignorant of the programme of the leadership of the Communist Workers' Party of Poland which was active in Russia at the time; as if it were ignorant of the way in which the Provisional Revolutionary Committee of Poland, with Marchlewski and Dzierzynski at its head, came into being in Bialystok; as if, indeed, it were unaware of the fact that a Poland deeply rooted in the Christian tradition was unsuited to the provision of a bridgehead between the Communist revolutions in Russia and Germany. Nor does it mention that in this situation the Communists resolved that force must be used to turn Poland into a Soviet republic. The same applies to the events of 1939 and to Katyn. If the whole truth about 17 September were revealed then it would transpire that the "theory of two enemies" wasn't created in Poland but that Poland did indeed have two enemies. If the Russians accepted responsibility for the Katyn massacre then the behaviour of the Polish government in April 1943 could not be called provocative, but the actions of the Soviet government would have to be so termed.

A very interesting exhibition of photographs taken from Alain Jaubert's *Le Commisariat aux archives: Les photos qui falsifient l'histoire* was shown at Wroclaw's Archdiocese Museum in September 1987. Jaubert shows how history can be manipulated by using retouched photographs. One of the pictures was of Lenin speaking to the Red Army troops on 5 May 1920 as they were leaving for the Polish front. On the steps next to the platform, waiting for their turn to speak, are Trotsky and Kamenev. In the '30s these two were rubbed out of this photo since they were regarded as "enemies of the people." Today, one can surmise, in the drive to remove the "blank spots," it would be better for propaganda purposes if Lenin could be rubbed out of the picture leaving only Trotsky, who could be held responsible for Russia's policy towards Poland at that time.

For if you rub something out of a picture, if you rub it out of all pictures, you do it in order to be able to make false generalisations later without fear of reproof. It is harder for those historians who know what's been rubbed out of the picture to write a dishonest general history.

Today, Polish historiography of the most recent past is to a significant extent a victim of this kind of manipulation of history. Thousands of historical books and articles have been written in Poland since the war. They have all had to go through the censor's filters, placed at various points. As a result many of them have been disfigured. Can the author of a general history of Poland who uses detailed studies which have been prepared in this way protect his or her own work from similar disfigurement? The answer is yes; but it is difficult and demands a sense of responsibility from the author and a willingness to undertake such work.

Yet many authors of general histories act as if they did not know that the monographs and articles which they refer to have been censored before appearing in print. I sometimes get the impression that it's more comfortable for them to pretend ignorance.

An honest, full, general work on Poland's most recent political history cannot be passed by the censor. And that is the greatest and saddest of the "blank spots." A current example of this is the fate of Tadeusz Lepkowski's projected general history of Poland from the 18th to the 20th century. It transpires that, just like Wereszycki's book before it, Lepkowski's manuscript is suitable only for the *samizdat* and émigré publishing circuit. The Warsaw historian's paper "Polish society between the 18th and 20th centuries: rhythms of development and dynamics of change," read at the 13th General Conference of Polish Historians at Poznan in September 1984, was not included in the *Documents* of the conference published by Ossolineum. It is not difficult to see why. The editor of the *Documents* dismisses Lepkowski's contribution with the laconic note: "Was submitted to the editor." And nothing else.

What is surprising, however, is that the discussion on the paper, judging from the report published in the *Documents*, seemed to evade the issues raised in it. The participants were not ready for it. Too much would have had to be turned upside down in their own minds, and for that more time is needed.

The characteristic trait of Polish historical writing is that it breaks off at the year 1945. Between 1944 and 1948 the rhythm of development imposed on the Poles by their history was interrupted for the second time; but historians are expected to demonstrate that the very opposite happened. In this situation the majority of historians in Poland avoid analysing the post-war history of their country. And this at a time when, in the rest of the world general histories are increasingly being written with a view to tying in the past with the present.

The outstanding French historian Fernand Braudel gave a lecture at Warsaw University in April 1967 entitled "History and the study of the Present." In it he looked at the sources of history's vital strength and the usefulness to us now of studying the past. Braudel is categorically opposed to the treatment of history as a study of a dead world. "For a historian," he says, "what is apparent are not just the things that have happened. History is not imprisoned in the world of dead things, and thus a historian may express his views, and fully justified views at that, about the present." In Braudel's work, the past interacts with the present: "History," he says, "is the study of former and present societies with one particular variable which the historian employs—continuity."

No such general history of the country exists in Poland. And this is because a historical analysis carried out in the way suggested by Braudel would have to be cut off, at the latest, in the 1970s or '80s. That is, before the emergence of the labour movement and other political mass movements. Probably the only historian who has presented Poland's history from its beginning to

During the heyday of Communist rule in the Soviet Union and Eastern Europe, historical accounts were routinely rewritten to reflect the current Communist Party line. When a party leader was purged, the official press transformed him from a hero to a scapegoat. Even photographs were "revised" to change history. The photographs portray a meeting held in Prague on June 27, 1948, to announce the "unification" of the Communist Party of Czechoslovakia and the Czechoslovak Social Democratic Party. In the original, Rudolf Slansky, the Secretary General of the Czechoslovak Communist Party, appears second from the right. Slansky was a leading figure in the Communist takeover of Czechoslovakia in February 1948, but in 1952, he was executed on trumped-up charges of treason. After Slansky's disgrace, his image was removed from the official photograph. Long after Slansky was officially absolved in 1963, the only reminder of his presence in the official photograph was the bottle of mineral water at his place.

the present in this way is Norman Davies of London University. That is why—despite the fact that they have not been translated—there is such widespread interest in his works throughout the world, including Poland.

One Polish historian who applies Braudel's methodological principles in practice is Lepkowski. In his Poznan paper he looked at Polish society as a changing structure, in motion. He tied in the history of the forty post-war years with the history of Poland from almost three centuries ago and came to the conclusion that the essential problem determining our development over a period of 250 years (from the 18th century to the present) is that of the Poles' political dependence.

The censor did not allow Lepkowski's text to be published. Once again it was proved that any full picture of the past is unacceptable to political state systems based on doctrine. Such systems want to see reality not as it is, but as it is imagined to be by the creator of the doctrine. That is why they use history, to quote Marc Bloch, "not in order to explain the present, but rather for a more accurate justification or accusation of it."

After forty years of history's being treated in this way, can one be surprised by our people's poor knowledge of their own history and by their confusion in the labyrinthine meanderings of the country's past?

At the same time historians (and not only historians) frequently show irritation at the low level of Polish historical awareness. They are particularly irritated by the statements and behaviour of those Poles who, when considering the future perspectives of their country, draw inaccurate conclusions from the past and thereby align themselves with little understood and falsely interpreted political currents.

We should bear in mind that, because of the lack of political plurality in post-war Poland, contemporary Poles, having nothing to choose from, not having their own experience of an independent political life from which to draw conclusions, have tended to refer back to their historical experiences and especially to the experiences of the 2nd Republic. We must remember that those experiences come from Poland's only period of full independence in virtually the last 300 years, apart from the four years of the Great Sejm. So interest in Pilsudski, Dmowski, Witos, the interwar Socialists, Nationalists, Liberals, People's Party, and Christian–Democratic thought has grown apace. This widespread excitement, particularly among the young people, has to some extent been a form of replacement interest, a preparation supposedly for the practice of politics.

The frequently uncritical assessments made by many journalists writing about history in *samizdat* publications (though not only there) have similar roots, especially when the subject is the 2nd Republic. There are frequent attempts made to transfer anachronistic political divisions wholesale from the past into the present, divisions which, as it happens, are socially shallow and intellectually barren.

Unfortunately all this is fostered by a lack of real knowledge about the interwar years, and for this Polish historiography must take its share of the blame. Historians cannot blame the readers of their works for this because the readers, searching for knowledge about the 20th century, most often come across schematic essays which have been tainted by the absence of freedom and plurality. It is understandable, therefore, that they do not believe even accurate assessments contained in those works. Looking for different perspectives they are most likely to come across uncritical apologies written by authors who are ideologically and organisationally connected with specific political currents.

Historians could contribute to a change in the existing state of affairs by writing well-documented and critical books to satisfy the public's interest in history and not, as often happens, by expressing outrage at the general lack of knowledge about the country's past.

The '80s have liberated many Poles from the fear of participating in politics. History has stopped being merely a substitute for politics. It seems that there has been a decline in the interest in history among would-be politicians. The ruling circles of the Polish People's Republic are also attaching less importance to it. Let us hope that all this will create a much calmer climate in which historians can do their research, will give them a greater opportunity to treat history as an academic pursuit and not mainly as an auxiliary to politics.

At present the principal duty of historians in Poland is not to allow themselves and their works to be manipulated. "If history is to fulfil its duty as the *magister vitae*," wrote Stanislaw Kutrzeba in 1916, "then historians must do their professional duty. History can be a good teacher only when historiography gives men of action who study their nation's life all the information which it can and ought to give: above all, gives them an overall view of their nation's history . . .

a view which is critical." Politicians cannot use a history which "gives them only fragments instead of the whole," which is only a shallow presentation of facts "without a deeper view of them and placing them within the context of historical development. For what conclusions could they draw from that? How can they avoid making errors?" Historiography fulfills its social duties, Kutrzeba goes on, when it is academically sound. "Because if it provides a complete historical picture seen from all sides . . . then it gives statesmen and all those who think about the life and future of their nation what they need."

These remarks by a great historian of the Polish state and of Polish law are just as valid now as they were more than seventy years ago.

ARTUR MIEDZYRZECKI

WHAT DOES THE POLITICAL SCIENTIST KNOW?

This poem was written in the early 1980s by the Polish poet Artur Miedzyrzecki (1922–   ) at a time when the fate of the Solidarity trade union was uncertain. Solidarity was briefly granted legitimacy by the government in 1980. Opponents to the Communist regime clustered around Solidarity and the Catholic Church. But in 1981 martial law was imposed, Solidarity was declared illegal and its leaders were arrested. What the poet saw clearly was that the Communist government had lost its ability to control the people of Poland; the usual combination of threats, bribes, and coercion was no longer working.

Indeed, after eight years of trying to eliminate Solidarity, the government finally acknowledged that it could not govern without recognizing this independent labor organization. In 1989 the government negotiated with Solidarity to reconstruct the Polish government, and Solidarity was soon swept to power by the votes of the people. It was the first time that a Communist regime had admitted that it could not function without some attempt to gain the consent of the people. The victory of the Solidarity movement in Poland gave heart to opposition groups in other Eastern European nations controlled by the Communists.

What does the political scientist know?
The political scientist knows the latest trends
The current states of affairs
The history of doctrines

What does the political scientist not know?
The political scientist doesn't know about
     desperation
He doesn't know the game that consists
Of renouncing the game

It doesn't occur to him
That no one knows when
Irrevocable changes may appear
Like an ice-floe's sudden cracks

And that our natural resources
Include knowledge of venerated laws
The capacity for wonder
And a sense of humor

ZBIGNIEW HERBERT

REPORT FROM THE BESIEGED CITY and THE POWER OF TASTE

Zbigniew Herbert (1924–   ) is widely regarded as one of the best contemporary European poets. Born in Lvov, Poland, Herbert was a teenager when the city was annexed by the Soviet Union as a result of the Molotov-Ribbentrop pact of 1939. Two years later, when the Nazis invaded the Soviet Union, they also seized Lvov. When the war ended in 1945, Lvov was retaken by the Soviet Union and incorporated into its territory. Herbert moved to central Poland after the war; at no time since his adolescence did he know an existence free of totalitarian rule.

Although Herbert was well educated, he spurned the official patronage of the state and was consigned to menial jobs. His first book of poetry was published during a period of political thaw. Other collections followed, and Herbert won numerous literary prizes in the West. His poems have been translated into almost every European language.

He never spoke on behalf of any organized group; only for the plight of the individual conscience trapped in a totalitarian state. The following poems appeared in *Report from the Besieged City*, which was first published in 1983.

Report from the Besieged City

Too old to carry arms and fight like the
        others—

they graciously gave me the inferior role of
        chronicler
I record—I don't know for whom—the history
        of the siege

I am supposed to be exact but I don't know
        when the invasion began
two hundred years ago in December in
        September perhaps yesterday at dawn
everyone here suffers from a loss of the sense
        of time

all we have left is the place the attachment to
        the place
we still rule over the ruins of temples specters
        of gardens and houses
if we lose the ruins nothing will be left

I write as I can in the rhythm of interminable
        weeks
monday: empty storehouses a rat became the
        unit of currency

tuesday: the mayor murdered by unknown
        assailants
wednesday: negotiations for a cease-fire the
        enemy has imprisoned our messengers
we don't know where they are held that is the
        place of torture
thursday: after a stormy meeting a majority of
        voices rejected
the motion of the spice merchants for
        unconditional surrender
friday: the beginning of the plague
        saturday: our invincible defender
N.N. committed suicide sunday: no more
        water we drove back
an attack at the eastern gate called the Gate of
        the Alliance

all of this is monotonous I know it can't move
        anyone

I avoid any commentary I keep a tight hold on
        my emotions I write about the facts
only they it seems are appreciated in foreign
        markets

yet with a certain pride I would like to inform the world
that thanks to the war we have raised a new species of children
our children don't like fairy tales they play at killing
awake and asleep they dream of soup of bread and bones
just like dogs and cats

in the evening I like to wander near the outposts of the City
along the frontier of our uncertain freedom
I look at the swarms of soldiers below their lights
I listen to the noise of drums barbarian shrieks
truly it is inconceivable the City is still defending itself
the siege has lasted a long time the enemies must take turns
nothing unites them except the desire for our extermination
Goths the Tartars Swedes troops of the Emperor regiments of the Transfiguration
who can count them
the colors of their banners change like the forest on the horizon
from delicate bird's yellow in spring through green through red to winter's black

and so in the evening released from facts I can think
about distant ancient matters for example our

friends beyond the sea I know they sincerely sympathize
they send us flour lard sacks of comfort and good advice
they don't even know their fathers betrayed us
our former allies at the time of the second Apocalypse
their sons are blameless they deserve our gratitude therefore we are grateful
they have not experienced a siege as long as eternity
those struck by misfortune are always alone
the defenders of the Dalai Lama the Kurds the Afghan mountaineers

now as I write these words the advocates of conciliation
have won the upper hand over the party of inflexibles
a normal hesitation of moods fate still hangs in the balance

cemeteries grow larger the number of defenders is smaller
yet the defense continues it will continue to the end
and if the City falls but a single man escapes
he will carry the City within himself on the roads of exile
he will be the City
we look in the face of hunger the face of fire face of death
worst of all—the face of betrayal

and only our dreams have not been humiliated

The Power of Taste

It didn't require great character at all
our refusal disagreement and resistance
we had a shred of necessary courage
but fundamentally it was a matter of taste
                Yes taste
in which there are fibers of soul the cartilage of conscience

Who knows if we had been better and more attractively tempted
sent rose-skinned women thin as a wafer

or fantastic creatures from the paintings of Hieronymus Bosch
but what kind of hell was there at this time
a wet pit the murderers' alley the barrack called a palace of justice
a home-brewed Mephisto in a Lenin jacket
sent Aurora's grandchildren out into the field
boys with potato faces
very ugly girls with red hands

Verily their rhetoric was made of cheap sacking

(Marcus Tullius kept turning in his grave)
chains of tautologies a couple of concepts like
	flails
the dialectics of slaughterers no distinctions in
	reasoning
syntax deprived of beauty of the subjunctive

So aesthetics can be helpful in life
one should not neglect the study of beauty

Before we declare our consent we must
	carefully examine
the shape of the architecture the rhythm of the
	drums and pipes
official colors the despicable ritual of funerals

Our eyes and ears refused obedience
	the princes of our senses proudly chose
		exile

It did not require great character at all
we had a shred of necessary courage
but fundamentally it was a matter of taste
		Yes taste
that commands us to get out to make a wry
	face draw out a sneer
even if for this the precious capital of the body
	the head
		must fall

LECH WALESA
NOBEL PEACE PRIZE LECTURE

Soon after World War II, the nations of Eastern Europe were imprisoned—as Winston Churchill described it—behind an "Iron Curtain." In each of these countries, the Communist Party controlled all political, social, cultural, and economic life, and the Party's rule was supported by Soviet military might. Spontaneous uprisings erupted—in East Germany in 1953, Poland in 1956 and 1970, Hungary in 1956, and Czechoslovakia in 1968—but they were suppressed by Soviet bloc troops and tanks.

The first rupture of the Iron Curtain occurred in Gdansk, Poland, when shipyard workers organized the Solidarity union, the first free trade union in Eastern Europe. Its leader was Lech Walesa (1943–   ), an electrician who first became a union activist in 1976. In August 1980, having been dismissed for his organizing activities, Walesa climbed over the wall of the Lenin Shipyard in Gdansk to urge 17,000 workers to strike. He was elected head of the strike committee, and the shipyard strike spread to become a general strike. Its success established Solidarity as a union, with Walesa as its chairman. The Polish government raised wages, promised greater political and religious freedom, and recognized the union's right to organize workers.

These remarkable gains were suddenly withdrawn on December 13, 1981, when the Polish government declared martial law, outlawed Solidarity, and arrested most of its leaders. Walesa spent nearly a year under arrest, and many other Solidarity activists created an underground society, with its own newspapers, books, and lectures. During the next five years, Solidarity remained underground. In 1983 Walesa received the Nobel Peace Prize for his valiant defense of freedom in Poland.

In 1989 the deepening economic crisis caused the Polish Communist Party to legalize Solidarity. Negotiations produced the nation's first free elections since World War II. Solidarity was permitted to contest only 35 percent of the seats in the Parliament, but won such a sweeping victory that it was invited to form a coalition government with the Communists.

The legitimation of Solidarity and its entry into the political process encouraged anti-Communist opposition groups in other Eastern European countries. When Soviet Premier Mikhail Gorbachev made clear that the U.S.S.R. would not interfere in the internal affairs of its Warsaw Pact allies, every Communist regime in Eastern Europe except Albania collapsed in the autumn of 1989, in response to popular demands for free elections and a multi-party system. In some countries, like Bulgaria, the Communist Party changed its name and won at the polls, but most others elected opposition parties to power. In 1990, Walesa was elected President of Poland.

What follows is Lech Walesa's Nobel Peace Prize lecture, delivered by his wife Danuta in 1983. At the time, Solidarity was still illegal, and Walesa feared that he would not be permitted to reenter the country if he left it to accept his award in person.

. . . I belong to a nation which over the past centuries has experienced many hardships and reverses. The world reacted with silence or with mere sympathy when Polish frontiers were crossed by invading armies and the sovereign state had to succumb to brutal force. Our national history has so often filled us with bitterness and the feeling of helplessness. But this was, above all, a great lesson in hope. Thanking you for the award I would like, first of all, to express my gratitude and my belief that it serves to enhance the Polish hope. The hope of the nation which throughout the 19th century had not for a moment reconciled itself with the loss of independence, and fighting for its own freedom, fought at the same time for the freedom of other nations. The hope whose elations and downfalls during the past forty years—i.e., the span of my own life—have been marked by the memorable and dramatic dates: 1944, 1956, 1970, 1976, 1980.

And if I permit myself at this juncture and on this occasion to mention my own life, it is because I believe that the prize has been granted to me as to one of many.

My youth passed at the time of the country's reconstruction from the ruins and ashes of the war in which my nation never bowed to the enemy paying the highest price in the struggle. I belong to the generation of workers who, born in the villages and hamlets of rural Poland, had the opportunity to acquire education and find employment in industry, becoming in the course conscious of their rights and importance in society. Those were the years of awakening aspirations of workers and peasants, but also years of many wrongs, degradations and lost illusions. I was barely 13 years old when, in June 1956, the desperate struggle of the workers of Poznan for bread and freedom was suppressed in blood. Thirteen also was the boy Romek Strzalkowski—who was killed in the struggle. It was the "Solidarity" union which 25 years later demanded that tribute be paid to his memory. In December 1970 when workers' protest demonstrations engulfed the towns of the Baltic coast, I was a worker in the Gdansk Shipyard and one of the organizers of the strikes. The memory of my fellow-workers who then lost their lives, the bitter memory of violence and despair has become for me a lesson never to be forgotten.

Few years later, in June 1976, the strike of the workers at Ursus and Radom was a new experience which not only strengthened my belief in the justness of the working people's demands and aspirations, but has also indicated the urgent need for their solidarity. This conviction brought me, in the summer of 1978, to the Free Trade Unions—formed by a group of courageous and dedicated people who came out in the defence of the workers' rights and dignity. In July and August of 1980 a wave of strikes has swept throughout Poland. The issue at stake was then something much bigger than only material conditions of existence. My road of life has, at the time of the struggle, brought me back to the shipyard in Gdansk. The whole country has joined forces with the workers of Gdansk and

Szczecin. The agreements of Gdansk, Szczecin and Jastrzebie were eventually signed and the "Solidarity" union has thus come into being.

The great Polish strikes, of which I have just spoken, were events of a special nature. Their character was determined on the one hand by the menacing circumstances in which they were held and, on the other, by their objectives. The Polish workers who participated in the strike actions, in fact represented the nation.

When I recall my own path of life I cannot but speak of the violence, hatred and lies. A lesson drawn from such experiences, however, was that we can effectively oppose violence only if we ourselves do not resort to it.

In the brief history of those eventful years, the Gdansk Agreement stands out as a great charter of the rights of the working people which nothing can ever destroy. Lying at the root of the social agreements of 1980 are the courage, sense of responsibility, and the solidarity of the working people. Both sides have then recognized that an accord must be reached if bloodshed is to be prevented. The agreement then signed has been and shall remain the model and the only method to follow, the only one that gives a chance of finding a middle course between the use of force and a hopeless struggle. Our firm conviction that ours is a just cause and that we must find a peaceful way to attain our goals gave us the strength and the awareness of the limits beyond which we must not go. What until then seemed impossible to achieve has become a fact of life. We have won the right to association in trade unions independent from the authorities, founded and shaped by the working people themselves.

Our union—the "Solidarity"—has grown into a powerful movement for social and moral liberation. The people freed from the bondage of fear and apathy, called for reforms and improve-

Lech Walesa, an electrician at the Gdansk shipyards in Poland and leader of the Solidarity trade union, talking to steelworkers at the gate of the Lenin Shipyards in Gdansk. In a historic agreement in August 1980, the Communist government agreed to a settlement that recognized the union's right to strike. Although the government tried to destroy the union by declaring martial law, Solidarity survived as a political and social force and revealed the regime's inability to govern.

ments. We fought a difficult struggle for our existence. That was and still is a great opportunity for the whole country. I think that it marked also the road to be taken by the authorities, if they thought of a state governed in cooperation and participation of all citizens. "Solidarity," as a trade union movement, did not reach for power, nor did it turn against the established constitutional order. During the 15 months of "Solidarity's" legal existence nobody was killed or wounded as a result of its activities. Our movement expanded by leaps and bounds. But we were compelled to conduct an uninterrupted struggle for our rights and freedom of activity while at the same time imposing upon ourselves the unavoidable self-limitations. The programme of our movement stems from the fundamental moral laws and order. The sole and basic source of our strength is the solidarity of workers, peasants and intelligentsia, the solidarity of the nation, the solidarity of people who seek to live in dignity, truth, and in harmony with their conscience.

Let the veil of silence fall presently over what happened afterwards. Silence, too, can speak out.

One thing, however, must be said here and now on this solemn occasion: the Polish people have not been subjugated nor have they chosen the road of violence and fratricidal bloodshed.

We shall not yield to violence. We shall not be deprived of union freedoms. We shall never agree with sending people to prison for their convictions. The gates of prisons must be thrown open and persons sentenced for defending union and civic rights must be set free. The announced trials of eleven leading members of our movement must never be held. All those already sentenced or still awaiting trials for their union activities or their convictions—should return to their homes and be allowed to live and work in their country.

The defence of our rights and our dignity, as well as efforts never to let ourselves to be overcome by the feeling of hatred—this is the road we have chosen.

The Polish experience, which the Nobel Peace Prize has put into limelight, has been a difficult, a dramatic one. Yet, I believe that it looks to the future. The things that have taken place in human conscience and reshaped human attitudes cannot be obliterated or destroyed. They exist and will remain.

We are the heirs of those national aspirations thanks to which our people could never be made into an inert mass with no will of their own. We want to live with the belief that law means law and justice means justice, that our toil has a meaning and is not wasted, that our culture grows and develops in freedom.

As a nation we have the right to decide our own affairs, to mould our own future. This does not pose any danger to anybody. Our nation is fully aware of the responsibility for its own fate in the complicated situation of the contemporary world.

Despite everything that has been going on in my country during the past two years, I am still convinced that we have no alternative but to come to an agreement, and that the difficult problems which Poland is now facing can be resolved only through a real dialogue between state authorities and the people.

During his latest visit to the land of his fathers, Pope John Paul II had this to say on this point:

Why do the working people in Poland—and everywhere else for that matter—have the right to such a dialogue? It is because the working man is not a mere tool of production, but he is the subject which throughout the process of production takes precedence over the capital. By the fact of his labour, the man becomes the true master of his workshop, of the process of labour, of the fruits of his toil and of their distribution. He is also ready for sacrifices if he feels that he is a real partner and has a say in the just division of what has been produced by common effort.

It is, however, precisely this feeling that we lack. It is hardly possible to build anything if frustration, bitterness and a mood of helplessness prevail. He who once became aware of the power of solidarity and who breathed the air of freedom will not be crushed. The dialogue is possible and we have the right to it. The wall raised by the course of events must not become an unsurmountable obstacle. My most ardent desire is that my country will recapture its historic opportunity for a peaceful evolution and that Poland will prove to the world that even the most complex situations can be solved by a dialogue and not by force. . . .

I think that all nations of the world have the right to life in dignity. I believe that, sooner or later, the rights of individuals, of families, and of entire communities will be respected in every corner of the world. Respect for civic and human rights in Poland and for our national identity is in the best interest of all Europe. For, in the interest of Europe is a peaceful Poland, and the Polish aspirations to freedom will never be stifled. The dialogue in Poland is the only way to achieving internal peace and that is why it is also an indispensable element of peace in Europe. . . .

May I repeat that the fundamental necessity in Poland is now understanding and dialogue. I think that the same applies to the whole world: we should go on talking, we must not close any doors or do anything that would block the road to an understanding. And we must remember that only peace built on the foundations of justice and moral order can be a lasting one.

In many parts of the world the people are searching for a solution which would link the two basic values: peace and justice. The two are like bread and salt for mankind. Every nation and every community have the inalienable right to these values. No conflicts can be resolved without doing everything possible to follow that road. Our times require that these aspirations which exist the world over must be recognized.

Our efforts and harsh experiences have revealed to the world the value of human solidarity. Accepting this honourable distinction I am thinking of those with whom I am linked by the spirit of solidarity.

—first of all, of those who in the struggle for the workers' and civic rights in my country paid the highest price—the price of life;

—of my friends who paid for the defence of "Solidarity" with the loss of freedom, who were sentenced to prison terms or are awaiting trial;

—of my countrymen who saw in the "Solidarity" movement the fulfilment of their aspirations as workers and citizens, who are subjected to humiliations and ready for sacrifices, who have learn[ed] to link courage with wisdom and who persist in loyalty to the cause we have embarked upon;

—of all those who are struggling throughout the world for workers' and union rights, for the dignity of a working man, for human rights.

Inscribed on the monument erected at the entrance to the Gdansk Shipyard in memory of those who died in December 1970 are the words of the Psalm: "The Lord will give power to His people, the Lord will give His people the blessing of peace."

Let these words be our message of brotherhood and hope.

CHARTER 77 DECLARATION

In 1975 35 nations signed the Helsinki Accords, which recognized the permanency of the borders of postwar Europe and which bound the signatories to respect basic human and political rights and to promote international exchanges. All of the nations of Europe except Albania signed, as did the United States and Canada. The agreement had been eagerly sought by the Soviet Union, in order to gain international recognition for the postwar status quo and agreement on noninterference in the internal affairs of states; the West hoped that the Helsinki agreement would promote respect for human rights and increase communication between East and West.

In each of the countries that signed the Accords, Helsinki Watch committees were formed. Members of these committees in Soviet bloc countries were harassed and often arrested. One of the most determined and embattled committees was established in Czechoslovakia by a group that issued a statement called Charter 77, which called on the government of Czechoslovakia to honor the human rights provisions of the Helsinki Accords. The statement was released in January 1977 and was signed by Jan Patocka, Vaclav Havel, and Jiri Hajek. Over 200 people added their signatures to the original declaration.

Intolerant of dissent, the Communist authorities sentenced the leaders of Charter 77, and of its offshoot VONS (the Committee for the Defense of the Unjustly Persecuted), to jail. Nonetheless, Charter 77 proved to be a resilient organization. The dissident community was small, but each year three new representatives stepped forward to represent Charter 77, even though public identification with the dissident movement exposed them to arrest and loss of employment. Over the years, Charter 77 released hundreds of documents, and its statement was signed by nearly 1,500 people. Always embattled, it was an effective rallying point for the dissident movement of Czechoslovakia.

On 13 October 1976 the Collection of Laws of the C.S.S.R. (no. 120) published the "International Pact on Civil and Political Rights" and the "International Pact on Economic, Social and Cultural Rights" which had been signed in the name of our Republic in 1968, confirmed in Helsinki in 1975, and which acquired validity here on 23 March 1976. From that day our citizens have the right and our State the duty to be guided by them.

The freedoms and rights of people which are guaranteed by these pacts are important values of civilisation for which the efforts of many progressive forces have been directed in history and their statement in law can significantly assist human development in our society.

We therefore welcome the fact that the Czechoslovak Socialist Republic has entered into these pacts.

Their publication, however, reminds us with new urgency how many fundamental civil rights remain, unfortunately, only on paper in our country.

Quite illusory, for instance, is the right to freedom of expression, guaranteed by Article 19 of the first pact: tens of thousands of citizens are prevented from working in their occupations merely because they hold views differing from the official views. At the same time they are often

subjected to all kinds of discrimination and harassment by the authorities and public organisations; deprived of all means to defend themselves, they are, in effect, the victims of a type of apartheid.

Hundreds of thousands of further citizens are denied "freedom from fear" (preamble to the first pact) because they are obliged to live in permanent danger of losing the opportunity to work, and other opportunities, if they voice their views.

In conflict with Article 13 of the second pact, ensuring the right to education for all, numerous young people are prevented from studying purely on account of their views, or even the views of their parents. Countless citizens have to live in fear that if they were to express themselves in accordance with their convictions, they or their children could be denied the right to education.

Exercising the right "to seek, receive and spread information and ideas of all kinds, regardless of frontiers, orally, in writing or in print" or "through art" (point 2, Article 19 of the first pact) is attacked not only extrajudicially, but also judicially, often in the guise of criminal prosecution (witness to this are, for instance, the trials of young musicians now proceeding).

Freedom of public expression is suppressed

by the central control over all communications media and publishing and cultural facilities. No political, philosophical, scientific or artistic expression which however slightly deviates from the official ideological or aesthetic bounds can be published; public criticism of crisis symptoms in society is barred; there is no opportunity for public defence against false and offensive accusations by official propaganda (the legal protection against "attacks on honour and reputation," explicitly guaranteed by Article 17 of the first pact, does not exist in practice); false accusations cannot be refuted and every attempt to get restitution through the courts is in vain; open debate in the area of intellectual and cultural work is excluded. Many scholars and cultural workers and other citizens are discriminated against merely because in earlier years they legally or openly voiced opinions which are condemned by the present political power.

The freedom of religious confession, emphatically guaranteed by Article 18 of the first pact, is systematically restricted by arbitrary authority: by curtailing the activities of priests, who are permanently threatened by the possibility that state consent to the performance of their office may be refused or withdrawn; by job or other sanctions against those who express their religious beliefs in word or deed; by suppressing religious teaching etc.

As an instrument for restricting, and often completely suppressing, many civil rights we have the system whereby, in effect, all institutions and organisations of state are subordinated to the political directives from the apparatus of the ruling party and to the decisions of individuals influential in the power structure. The Constitution of the C.S.S.R. and the other laws and legal norms give no authority either for the content and form, nor for the making and application of such decisions; they are often purely verbal, entirely unknown to citizens, and uncontrollable by them; their originators are responsible to none but themselves and their hierarchy, yet they exert a decisive influence on the legislative and executive organs of state administration, the judiciary, the trade unions, organisations around

special interest and other public organisations, other political parties, enterprises, factories, institutes, offices, and other establishments, and their orders take precedence over the law. When an organisation or individual comes into conflict with such an order in their interpretation of their rights and duties, they cannot turn to an impartial institution, because none exists. All this gravely limits the rights deriving from Articles 21 and 22 of the first pact (the right of association and the prohibition of any restriction on implementing it) and Article 25 (the equal right to share in managing public affairs), Article 26 (excluding all discrimination before the law). The present situation also prevents workers and other employees from establishing, without restriction trade union and other organisations to protect their economic and social interests and freely to exercise the right to strike (point 1, Article 8 of the second pact).

Other civil rights, including the explicit prohibition of "arbitrary interference in private life, in the family, home or correspondence" (Article 17 of the first pact), are also gravely infringed by the many ways in which the Ministry of the Interior controls citizens' lives, for instance by tapping telephones, listening devices in homes, checking on mail, personal surveillance, house searches, forming a network of informers from among the public (often won over by impermissible threats, or promises) etc. The Ministry also frequently intervenes in employers' decisions, inspires discriminatory actions by official bodies and organisations, campaigns in the media. This activity is not regulated by law, it is secret and the citizen has no defence against it.

In cases of politically motivated prosecution, the examining and judicial organs infringe the rights of the accused and of their defence, although these are guaranteed by Article 14 of the first pact and Czechoslovak law. People convicted in this manner are treated in prison in a way which denies their human dignity, endangers their health and attempts to break them morally.

There is also a general infringement of point 2 of Article 12 of the first pact, which guarantees the right of the citizen to leave his country; under the pretext of "protecting national security" (point 3), this right is tied to various impermissible conditions. Arbitrary procedure is also employed in issuing entry visas to foreign nationals, many of whom are unable to visit Czechoslovakia merely because they have had working or friendly contacts with people who are discriminated against here.

Some citizens call attention to the constant infringement of human rights and democratic freedoms—either privately at their places of work, or publicly, which is possible in practice only through the foreign media—and demand remedy in concrete cases; but their voices usually get no response, or they become the subjects of investigation.

The responsibility for maintaining civil rights in the land belongs, of course, to the political and state power. But not to it alone. Everyone bears their share of responsibility for public matters, and hence also for the observance of pacts valid in law, which are, in any case, binding not only on governments but on all citizens.

The sense of this coresponsibility, the belief in the meaning of the citizens' commitment, the will for it, and the common need to seek a new and more effective expression of it, has led us to think of drawing up CHARTER 77, the origin of which we are publicly announcing today.

CHARTER 77 is a free, informal and open association of people of varied opinions, varied beliefs and professions, who are united by the will individually and jointly to work for the respecting of civil and human rights in our country and in the world—the rights which both the international pacts recognise for man, the final act of the Helsinki conference, various other international documents against war, force and social and spiritual oppression, and which are stated in sum in the United Nations General Declaration on Human Rights.

CHARTER 77 is rooted in the solidarity and friendship of people who share a concern for the ideals which they have seen, and still see, as part of their lives and work.

CHARTER 77 is not an organisation, it has no statutes, no permanent bodies or formally organised membership. Anyone who agrees with its ideas, takes part in its work and supports it belongs to it.

CHARTER 77 is not a basis for activity as a political opposition. It aims to serve the general interest as do many similar initiatives by citizens in various countries in the West and the East. Thus it is not intended to put forward its own programmes of political or social reform or changes, but to conduct in its sphere a constructive dialogue with the political and state power, especially by calling attention to various cases where human and civil rights are infringed, to propose solutions, submit more general proposals aimed at strengthening these rights and their guarantees, to act as an intermediary in possible conflict situations which may be caused by the lack of political rights, etc.

By its symbolical name CHARTER 77 stresses its origin on the threshold of a year declared as the year of political prisoners and in which the Belgrade conference is to examine how the Helsinki undertakings have been implemented.

As signatories to this declaration, we empower Prof. Dr. Jan Patocka, Dr. h.c. Vaclav Havel and Prof. Jiri Hajek DrSc to be spokesmen for CHARTER 77. These spokesmen are authorised to represent the Charter both in relation to state and other organisations, and to the public here and abroad, and they guarantee by their signatures the authenticity of the documents. In us, and in other citizens who join in, they will have their associates who will take part with them in any necessary negotiations, will undertake specific tasks and will share all responsibility with them.

We believe that CHARTER 77 will contribute to enabling all Czechoslovak citizens to live and work as free people.

VACLAV HAVEL

THE POWER OF THE POWERLESS

Born in 1936 into a prosperous family, Vaclav Havel had the misfortune to come of age under a Communist regime. He was denied a high school or university education because of his bourgeois origins. Nonetheless, he enrolled in night school, read voraciously, worked in a chemical laboratory by day, and educated himself. In 1956, not yet 20 years old, he stood up at a literary conference to demand official recognition for dissident writers, the "forgotten poets." Havel's brashness was harshly criticized but made him the main topic of the conference.

During the 1960s, Havel worked at a small avant-garde theater called the Theatre on the Balustrade; he began as a stagehand, but later became its resident playwright. There he wrote two plays, *The Garden Party* and *The Memorandum*, which established his reputation. During the Prague Spring in 1968, Havel played an active part in articulating the need for political freedom and a legal opposition to the Communist regime. Even after the Soviet-led invasion of Czechoslovakia that ended the brief period of liberalization, Havel never compromised his resistance to the dictatorship.

Havel was arrested in 1969 for subversion because he signed a petition opposing the "normalization" imposed by the Communist leader Gustav Husak. Although the trial was adjourned, Havel's books were banned, his works removed from all libraries, and his plays barred from being performed. While banned, he wrote several plays, none of which could be staged in his native land. His works were read and performed outside of Czechoslovakia, however, and his international reputation grew.

Havel became widely known inside and outside Czechoslovakia as the nation's leading dissident. In 1977 he was one of the founders of Charter 77, the organization created by Czechoslovakian dissidents to monitor the promises made in the Helsinki Accords, which was endorsed by the Czechoslovak government. His international fame did not protect him from harassment and arrest. He was arrested three times, and spent nearly four years in jail from 1979 to 1983. The letters he wrote to his wife while in prison were later collected and published as *Letters to Olga*; they are an outstanding example of dissident literature.

Havel achieved a special place in Czechoslovak letters because of his commitment to democratic and humane principles at a time when those principles were cause for arrest rather than celebration. He stubbornly clung to his convictions, and he lived and wrote as though the repressive state did not exist. The ouster of the Communist regime in 1989 brought him a political and moral vindication that was more fantastic than anything in his plays: He was elected President of Czechoslovakia.

In a famous 1978 essay called "The Power of the Powerless," Havel wrote eloquently of the responsibility each person bears for perpetuating the dictatorship through their daily compliance. What was needed, he argued, was personal commitment to "living in truth." An excerpt follows.

A spectre is haunting eastern Europe: the spectre of what in the West is called "dissent." This spectre has not appeared out of thin air. It is a natural and inevitable consequence of the present historical phase of the system it is haunting. It was born at a time when this system, for a thousand reasons, can no longer base itself on the unadulterated, brutal, and arbitrary application of power, eliminating all expressions of nonconformity. What is more, the system has become so ossified politically that there is practically no way for such nonconformity to be implemented within its official structures.

Who are these so-called "dissidents"? Where does their point of view come from, and what importance does it have? What is the significance of the "independent initiatives" in which "dissidents" collaborate, and what real chances do such initiatives have of success? Is it appropriate to refer to "dissidents" as an opposition? If so, what exactly is such an opposition within the framework of this system? What does it do? What role does it play in society? What are its hopes and on what are they based? Is it within the power of the "dissidents"—as a category of sub-citizen outside the power establishment—to have any influence at all on society and the social system? Can they actually change anything? . . .

. . . [I]f an atmosphere of revolutionary excitement, heroism, dedication, and boisterous violence on all sides characterizes classical dictatorships, then the last traces of such an atmosphere have vanished from the Soviet bloc. For some time now this bloc has ceased to be a kind of enclave, isolated from the rest of the developed world and immune to processes occurring in it. To the contrary, the Soviet bloc is an integral part of that larger world, and it shares and shapes the world's destiny. This means in concrete terms that the hierarchy of values existing in the developed countries of the West has, in essence, appeared in our society (the long period of coexistence with the West has only hastened this process). In other words, what we have here is simply another form of the consumer and industrial society, with all its concomitant social, intellectual, and psychological consequences. It is impossible to understand the nature of power in our system properly without taking this into account.

The profound difference between our system—in terms of the nature of power—and what we traditionally understand by dictator-ship, a difference I hope is clear even from this quite superficial comparison, has caused me to search for some term appropriate for our system, purely for the purposes of this essay. If I refer to it henceforth as a *post-totalitarian* system, I am fully aware that this is perhaps not the most precise term, but I am unable to think of a better one. I do not wish to imply by the prefix "post-" that the system is no longer totalitarian; on the contrary, I mean that it is totalitarian in a way fundamentally different from classical dictatorships, different from totalitarianism as we usually understand it. . . .

The manager of a fruit and vegetable shop places in his window, among the onions and carrots, the slogan: "Workers of the World, Unite!" Why does he do it? What is he trying to communicate to the world? Is he genuinely enthusiastic about the idea of unity among the workers of the world? Is his enthusiasm so great that he feels an irrepressible impulse to acquaint the public with his ideals? Has he really given more than a moment's thought to how such a unification might occur and what it would mean?

I think it can safely be assumed that the overwhelming majority of shopkeepers never think about the slogans they put in their windows, nor do they use them to express their real opinions. That poster was delivered to our greengrocer from the enterprise headquarters along with the onions and carrots. He put them all into the window simply because it has been done that way for years, because everyone does it, and because that is the way it has to be. If he were to refuse, there could be trouble. He could be reproached for not having the proper "decoration" in his window; someone might even accuse him of disloyalty. He does it because these things must be done if one is to get along in life. It is one of the thousands of details that guarantee him a relatively tranquil life "in harmony with society," as they say.

Obviously the greengrocer is indifferent to the semantic content of the slogan on exhibit; he does not put the slogan in his window from any personal desire to acquaint the public with the ideal it expresses. This, of course, does not mean that his action has no motive or significance at all, or that the slogan communicates nothing to anyone. The slogan is really a *sign*, and as such it contains a subliminal but very definite message. Verbally, it might be expressed this way: "I, the greengrocer XY, live here and I know what I must do. I behave in the manner expected of me. I can be depended upon and am beyond reproach. I am obedient and therefore I have the right to be left in peace." This message, of course, has an addressee: it is directed above, to the greengrocer's superior, and at the same time it is a shield that protects the greengrocer from potential informers. The slogan's real meaning, therefore, is rooted firmly in the greengrocer's existence. It reflects his vital interests. But what are those vital interests?

Let us take note: if the greengrocer had been instructed to display the slogan, "I am afraid and therefore unquestioningly obedient," he would not be nearly as indifferent to its semantics, even though the statement would reflect the truth. The greengrocer would be embarrassed and ashamed to put such an unequivocal statement of his own degradation in the shop window, and quite naturally so, for he is a human being and thus has a sense of his own dignity. To overcome this complication, his expression of loyalty must take the form of a sign which, at least on its textual surface, indicates a level of disinterested conviction. It must allow the greengrocer to say, "What's wrong with the workers of the world uniting?" Thus the sign helps the greengrocer to conceal from himself the low foundations of his obedience, at the same time concealing the low foundations of power. It hides them behind the façade of something high. And that something is *ideology*. . . .

Between the aims of the post-totalitarian system and the aims of life there is a yawning abyss—while life, in its essence, moves towards plurality, diversity, independent self-constitution and self-organization, in short, towards the fulfilment of its own freedom, the post-totalitarian system demands conformity, uniformity, and discipline. While life ever strives to create new and "improbable" structures, the post-totalitarian system contrives to force life into its most probable states. The aims of the system reveal its most essential characteristic to be introversion, a movement towards being ever more completely and unreservedly *itself*, which means that the radius of its influence is continually widening as well. This system serves people only to the extent necessary to ensure that people will serve it. Anything beyond this, that is to say, anything which leads people to overstep their predetermined roles is regarded by the system as an attack upon itself. And in this respect it is correct: every instance of such transgression is a genuine denial of the system. It can be said, therefore, that the inner aim of the post-totalitarian system is not mere preservation of power in the hands of a ruling clique, as appears to be the case at first sight. Rather, the social phenomenon of self-preservation is subordinated to something higher, to a kind of blind *automatism* which drives the system. No matter what position individuals hold in the hierarchy of power, they are not considered by the system to be worth anything in themselves, but only as things intended to fuel and serve this automatism. For this reason, an individual's desire for power is admissible only in so far as its direction coincides with the direction of the automatism of the system.

Ideology, in creating a bridge of excuses between the system and the individual, spans the abyss between the aims of the system and the aims of life. It pretends that the requirements of the system derive from the requirements of life. It is a world of appearances trying to pass for reality.

The post-totalitarian system touches people at every step, but it does so with its ideological gloves on. This is why life in the system is so thoroughly permeated with hypocrisy and lies: government by bureaucracy is called popular government; the working class is enslaved in the name of the working class; the complete degradation of the individual is presented as his or her ultimate liberation; depriving people of information is called making it available; the use of power to manipulate is called the public control of power, and the arbitrary abuse of power is called observing the legal code; the repression of culture is called its development; the expansion of imperial influence is presented as support for the oppressed; the lack of free expression becomes the highest form of freedom; farcical elections become the highest form of democracy; banning independent thought becomes the most scientific of world views; military occupation becomes fraternal assistance. Because the regime is captive to its own lies, it must falsify everything. It falsifies the past. It falsifies the present, and it falsifies the future. It falsifies statistics. It pretends not to possess an omnipotent and unprincipled police apparatus. It pretends to respect human rights. It pretends to persecute no one. It pretends to fear nothing. It pretends to pretend nothing.

Individuals need not believe all these mystifications, but they must behave as though they did, or they must at least tolerate them in silence, or get along well with those who work with them. For this reason, however, they must *live within a lie*. They need not accept the lie. It is enough for them to have accepted their life with it and in it. For by this very fact, individuals confirm the system, fulfil the system, make the system, *are* the system. . . .

. . . [I]t is impossible to talk about what in fact "dissidents" do and the effect of their work without first talking about the work of all those who, in one way or another, take part in the independent life of society and who are not necessarily "dissidents" at all. They may be writers who write as they wish without regard for censorship or official demands and who issue their work—

In 1968, Soviet troops and troops from other Communist bloc countries invaded Czechoslovakia and ended a brief period known as "Prague Spring," when a reform government tried to liberalize society and introduce "socialism with a human face." After the invasion, euphemistically called "normalization," Czechoslovakia reverted to hardline, anti-democratic Communism until 1989's "velvet revolution."

when official publishers refuse to print them—as *samizdat*. They may be philosophers, historians, sociologists and all those who practise independent scholarship and, if it is impossible through official or semi-official channels, who also circulate their work in *samizdat* or who organize private discussions, lectures and seminars. They may be teachers who privately teach young people things that are kept from them in the state schools; clergymen who either in office or, if they are deprived of their charges, outside it, try to carry on a free religious life; painters, musicians and singers who practise their work regardless of how it is looked upon by official institutions; everyone who shares this independent culture and helps to spread it; people who, using the means available to them, try to express and defend the actual social interests of workers, to put real meaning back into trade unions or to form independent ones; people who are not afraid to call the attention of officials to cases of injustice and who strive to see that the laws are observed; and the different groups of young people who try to extricate themselves from manipulation and live in their own way, in the spirit of their own hierarchy of values. The list could go on.

Very few would think of calling all these people "dissidents." And yet are not the well-known "dissidents" simply people like them? Are not all these activities in fact what "dissidents" do as well? Do they not produce scholarly work and publish it in *samizdat*? Do they not write plays and novels and poems? Do they not lecture to students in private "universities?" Do they not struggle against various forms of injustice and attempt to ascertain and express the genuine social interests of various sectors of the population?

After having tried to indicate the sources, the inner structure and some aspects of the "dissident" attitude as such, I have clearly shifted my viewpoint from outside, as it were, to an investigation of what these "dissidents" *actually* do, how their initiatives are manifested and where they lead.

The first conclusion to be drawn, then, is that the original and most important sphere of activity, one that predetermines all the others, is simply an attempt to create and support the "independent life of society" as an articulated expression of "living within the truth." In other words, serving truth consistently, purposefully and articulately, and organizing this service. This is only natural, after all: if living within the truth is an elementary starting point for every attempt made by people to oppose the alienating pressure of the system, if it is the only meaningful basis of any independent act of political import, and if, ultimately, it is also the most intrinsic existential source of the "dissident" attitude, then it is difficult to imagine that even manifest "dissent" could have any other basis than the service of truth, the truthful life and the attempt to make room for the genuine aims of life. . . .

 # A FEW REMARKS

The repressive government of Czechoslovakia was openly challenged on June 29, 1989 with the release of a statement called "A Few Remarks." By late August, an estimated 20,000 people had signed the brief declaration.

Others had written open letters to the government before, but this was the first to attract supporters beyond the relatively small number of known dissidents. The Communist authorities launched a propaganda campaign against the statement and threatened leading signatories. The four who had published their names under the statement were charged with incitement. The four were the playwright Vaclav Havel; Stanislav Devdry (a well-known dissident who suffered several arrests and was sentenced to 20 months in prison for dissident activity); Jiri Krizan (a screenwriter); and Sasa Vondra (a spokesman for the dissident group Charter 77).

When people recount the events that mobilized public opinion against the Communist regime, "A Few Remarks" is noted as a document that encouraged many to step forward and be counted for the first time.

The events of early 1989 clearly demonstrate once again that the Czechoslovak leadership, for all its talk of *perestroika* and democratization, is desperately resisting anything that promotes, or even faintly resembles, democracy. The leadership has rejected citizens' petitions and independent initiatives as "acts of coercion." It condemns divergent political opinions as "anti-socialist" and "hostile." It breaks up peaceful public assemblies. And it allows the public no say whatsoever in the creation of new laws.

The early months of 1989 also demonstrate, however, that the citizenry is stirring from its lethargy. More and more people now have the courage to express their longing for social change publicly.

The growth of social activity is thus increasingly on a collision course with the inflexibility of the authorities. Social tensions are on the rise, and there is the danger of an open crisis.

None of us wants such a crisis.

We are therefore calling upon the leadership of our country to realize that the time has come for genuine and comprehensive systemic change and, moreover, that such change is possible and can succeed only if preceded by truly free and democratic discussion. A first step toward effecting meaningful change—from rewriting the constitution to reforming the economy—must be a fundamental change in the social climate of our country: it must recover its spirit of freedom, confidence, tolerance, and pluralism.

In our view, this requires:

- the immediate release of all political prisoners;
- ending restrictions on freedom of assembly;
- ending the persecution of independent initiatives and the treatment of such groups as criminal organizations: the government must understand that these initiatives are a natural part of public life and a legitimate expression of its diversity, as indeed the public has long perceived them to be. Similarly, no obstacles should be placed in the way of the formation of new civic movements, including independent trade unions, clubs and associations;
- freeing the media and all cultural activity from all forms of political manipulation and from all censorship. They must be open to a free exchange of ideas, and the existing independent media should be legalized;
- respect for the justified demands of all citizens who are religious;
- the presentation to both experts and the general public, without delay, of all proposed and completed projects that might have permanent effects on the environment of our country and thus affect future generations;
- the initiation of free discussion on not only the events of the 1950s, but also of the Prague Spring, the Warsaw Pact invasion, and the subsequent period of "normalization." It is sad to see that whereas serious discussion of these topics is now possible in the countries that participated in the invasion, this part of our history remains taboo here—because those responsible for Czechoslovakia's decline over the past two decades don't want to relinquish their party and government posts.

Anyone who is in agreement with us is welcome to express their support by adding his or her signature.

We call upon the government not to respond to this appeal in the manner it usually responds to inconvenient opinions; that would be a fatal blow to the hopes that guide us, namely the hope for a genuine dialogue within our society. Such dialogue is the only feasible way out of the blind alley in which Czechoslovakia finds itself today.

VACLAV HAVEL
NEW YEAR'S ADDRESS

On January 1, 1990, Vaclav Havel spoke to the people of Czechoslovakia—and the world. Only three days earlier, he had been elected President of Czechoslovakia by the nation's legislature. As recently as the spring of 1989 he had been in jail for his dissident activities. His ascension to the presidency was the crowning achievement of Czechoslovakia's "velvet revolution," a peaceful rebellion during November and December of 1989 in which the people of Czechoslovakia forced the capitulation of their Communist rulers through massive demonstrations, work stoppages, and protest marches. Because political opposition had been illegal for more than four decades, there were no organized political parties and few national figures of opposition. Havel was the man of the hour. In a few short weeks, Havel was transformed from Czechoslovakia's leading dissident to its president.

For forty years on this day you heard from my predecessors the same thing in a number of variations: how our country is flourishing, how many millions of tons of steel we produce, how happy we all are, how we trust our government, and what bright prospects lie ahead of us.

I assume you did not propose me for this office so that I, too, should lie to you.

Our country is not flourishing. The enormous creative and spiritual potential of our nations is being wasted. Entire branches of industry produce goods that are of no interest to anyone, while we lack the things we need. The state, which calls itself a workers' state, humiliates and exploits workers. Our outmoded economy wastes what little energy we have. A country that once could be proud of the educational level of its citizens now spends so little on education that it ranks 72nd in the world. We have polluted our land, rivers, and forests, bequeathed to us by our ancestors; we now have the most contaminated environment in all of Europe. People in our country die sooner than in the majority of European countries.

Allow me a small personal observation: when I recently flew to Bratislava, I found some time during various discussions to look out of the window of the plane. I saw the industrial complex of the Slovnaft chemical plant and the giant Petrzalka housing project right behind it. The view was enough for me to understand that for decades our statesmen and political leaders did not look or did not want to look out the windows of their airplanes. No study of statistics available would have enabled me faster and better to understand the situation we have gotten ourselves into.

But all this is not even the main problem. The worst thing is that we live in a contaminated moral environment. We have fallen morally ill because we became used to saying one thing and thinking another. We have learned not to believe in anything, to ignore each other, to care only about ourselves. Notions such as love, friendship, compassion, humility, or forgiveness have lost their depth and dimensions; for many of us, they represent nothing more than psychological idiosyncrasies, or appear to be some kind of relic from times past, rather comical in the era of computers and spaceships. Only a few of us managed to cry out loud that the powers-that-be should not be all-powerful; that special farms producing uncontaminated, top-quality food just for the powerful should send their produce to schools, children's homes, and hospitals. The previous regime, armed with its arrogant and intolerant ideology, reduced man to a means of production and nature to a tool of production. Thus it attacked both their very essence and their mutual relationship. It reduced gifted and autonomous people to nuts and bolts in some monstrously huge, noisy, and stinking machine, whose real purpose is not clear to anyone. Such a machine can do nothing but slowly and inexorably wear itself out along with all its nuts and bolts.

When I talk about the contaminated moral atmosphere, I am not talking only about the gentlemen who eat organic vegetables and do not look out the windows of their planes. I mean all of us. We have all become used to the totalitarian system and accepted it as an immutable fact, thus helping to perpetuate it. In other words, we are all—though naturally to various degrees—responsible for the creation of the totalitarian machinery. None of us is just its victim; we are all also responsible for it.

Why do I say this? It would be very unwise to think of the sad legacy of the last forty years as something alien or something inherited from a distant relative. On the contrary, we have to accept this legacy as something we have inflicted on ourselves. If we accept it as such, we will understand that it is up to all of us, and only us, to do something about it. We cannot blame the previous rulers for everything—not only because it would be untrue, but also because it could weaken our sense of duty, our obligation to act independently, freely, sensibly, and quickly. Let us not be mistaken: even the best government in the world, the best parliament, and the best president cannot do much on their own. And in any case, it would be wrong to expect a cure-all from them alone. Freedom and democracy, after all, require everyone to participate and thus to share responsibility.

If we realize this, then all the horrors that the new Czechoslovak democracy has inherited will cease to appear so horrific. If we realize this, hope will return to our hearts.

In the effort to rectify matters of common concern we have something to build on. The recent past—and in particular, the last six weeks of our peaceful revolution—has shown the enormous human, moral, and spiritual potential: the civic culture that has slumbered in our society beneath the mask of apathy. Whenever someone categorically claimed that we were this or that, I always objected that society is a very mysterious creature and that it is not wise to trust the face it chooses to show you. I am happy I was not mistaken. People all around the world wondered how those meek, humiliated, cynical citizens of Czechoslovakia, who seemed to believe in nothing, found the strength to cast off the totalitarian system in several weeks, and do it in a decent and peaceful manner. And let us ask: Where did young people who never knew another system get their longing for truth, their love of free thought, their political imagination, their civic courage, and their civic prudence? How did their parents—precisely the generation thought to be lost—join them? How is it possible that so many people immediately grasped what had to be done, without needing anyone else's advice or instructions?

I think there are two main reasons: First of all, people are never merely a product of the external world—they are always able to respond to something superior, however systematically the external world tries to snuff out that ability. Second, humanistic and democratic traditions, about which there had been so much idle talk, did after all slumber in the subconscious of our nations and national minorities. These traditions were inconspicuously passed from one generation to another, so that each of us could discover them at the right time and transform them into deeds.

Of course we had to pay for our present freedom. Many citizens died in prison in the 1950s. Many were executed. Thousands of human lives were destroyed. Hundreds of thousands of talented people were forced to leave the country. Those who defended the honor of our nations during World War II, those who rebelled against totalitarian rule, those who simply managed to remain themselves and think freely—all were persecuted. We should not forget any of those who paid for our present freedom in one way or another. Independent courts should consider the possible guilt of those who were responsible for the persecutions, so that the whole truth about our recent past is fully revealed.

We must also bear in mind that other nations have paid even more dearly for their present freedom, and that indirectly they have also paid for ours. The rivers of blood that flowed in Hungary, Poland, Germany, and not long ago in such a horrific manner in Romania, and the sea of blood shed by the nations of the Soviet Union, must not be forgotten, because all human suffering concerns every human being. But the sacrifices of these peoples must not be forgotten also because their suffering forms the tragic background to our own new-found freedom and to the gradual emancipation of the nations of the Soviet bloc. Without the changes in the Soviet Union, Poland, Hungary, and East Germany, what happened here could scarcely have taken place, and certainly not in such a calm and peaceful manner.

The fact that we enjoyed optimal international conditions does not mean that someone has directly supported us during the recent weeks. In fact, after hundreds of years, both our nations have raised their heads high without relying on the help of stronger countries. It seems to me that this constitutes the great moral asset of the present moment. This moment holds within itself the hope that in the future we will no longer suffer from the complexes of those indebted to someone else. Now it is solely up to us whether the promise of this moment will be fulfilled, and whether our civic, national, and political self-respect will be revived.

Self-respect is not pride.

Quite the contrary: only a person or a nation with self-respect, in the best sense of the word, is capable of listening to others while accepting them as equals, of forgiving enemies while expiating their own sins. Let us try to infuse our communities with this kind of self-respect; let our country's behavior on the international stage be marked by this kind of self-respect. Only then will we restore our self-confidence, our respect for one another, and our respect for other nations.

Our state should never again be an appendage or a poor relative of any other state. While it is true that we must accept and learn many things from other countries, we must do so as an equal partner who has something to offer.

Our first president, T. G. Masaryk, wrote: Jesus, not Caesar. Thus he followed our philosophers Chelcicky and Comenius. I dare to say that we may even have an opportunity to spread this idea abroad, to introduce a new element into European and global politics. Our country, if that is what we want, can now permanently radiate love, understanding, and the power of the spirit and of ideas. It is precisely this glow that we can offer as our contribution to international politics.

Masaryk rooted his politics in morality. Let us try—in a new era and in a new way—to restore this conception of politics. Let us teach ourselves and others that politics should be animated by the desire to contribute to the community, rather than by the need to cheat or rape the community. Let us teach ourselves and others that politics can be not only the art of the possible—especially if this means speculations, calculations, intrigues, secret deals, and pragmatic maneuvering—but also the art of the impossible, namely, the art of improving ourselves and the world.

We are a small country, yet at one time we were the spiritual crossroads of Europe. Is there any reason why we could not regain that distinction? Would it not be a way to repay those whose help we are going to need?

Our home-grown mafia—those who do not look out of the windows of their planes and eat specially fed pigs—may still linger in our midst, muddying the waters from time to time. But it is no longer our main enemy. The international mafia of which it is a part is even less our enemy. Our main enemy today is our own bad habits: indifference to the common good, vanity, personal ambition, selfishness, and envy. The main struggle will have to be fought against these foes.

Free elections and an election campaign lie ahead of us. Let us not allow this struggle to dirty the clean face of our gentle revolution. Let us not allow the world's sympathy, which we won so quickly, to be lost with equal speed in the coming skirmishes for power. Let us not allow selfish desires to bloom once again under the noble veil of the desire to serve the common good. It is not really important which party, club, or group will prevail in the elections. The important thing is that the winners will be the best of us—in the moral, civic, political, and professional sense—regardless of the winner's political affiliations. The future policies and prestige of our state will depend on the personalities that we shall select and later elect to our representative bodies.

My dear fellow citizens!

Three days ago the deputies of the Federal Assembly, expressing your will, elected me president of the republic. You therefore rightly expect that I should mention the tasks that I as president see before me.

The first of these is to use all my powers and influence to ensure that we shall soon step up to ballot boxes in free elections, and that our path toward this historic event will be dignified and peaceful.

My second task is to guarantee that we approach these elections as two genuinely self-governing nations, which mutually respect their interests, national identity, religious traditions, and symbols. As a Czech who swore his presidential oath to an eminent and personally close Slovak, I feel a special obligation, knowing the various bitter experiences that Slovaks have gone through in the past, to see to it that the interests of the Slovak nation are respected, and that the way to any state office, including the highest one, will never be closed to Slovaks in the future.

My third task is to do everything in my power to improve the lot of children, old people, women, the sick, national minorities, and all citizens who for any reason are worse off than others. The best food or hospitals must no longer be prerogatives of the powers-that-be: they must first be offered to those who need them most.

As the supreme commander of the armed forces, I want to ensure that the defense capability of our country will no longer serve as a pretext for anyone to thwart peace initiatives, including the reduction of military service, the

Vaclav Havel, Czechoslovakia's leading dissident and playwright, was a key figure in "the velvet revolution" of 1989, first as a unifying figure in the dissident movement, then as a successful candidate for president.

establishment of alternative military service, and the general humanization of military life.

In our country, there are many prisoners who were convicted of serious crimes and are being punished for them. However, they had to undergo—in spite of the good will of some investigators, judges, and, above all, defense lawyers—a debased judiciary process that curtailed their rights. Now they live in prisons that, rather than attempting to awake the better qualities that inhere in every human being, humiliate people and destroy them physically and mentally. In view of this fact, I have decided to declare a relatively extensive amnesty. I ask the prisoners to understand that the damage caused by forty years of unjust interrogations, trials, and imprisonments cannot be repaired overnight, and that all the changes that are being speedily prepared will nonetheless still require a certain amount of time. By rebelling, the prisoners will neither help society nor themselves. I also call upon the public not to fear the prisoners after they are released, not to make their lives difficult, and to help them in a Christian spirit to seek within themselves that which the prisons did not help them to find: the ability to repent and the desire to live an upright life.

My honourable task is to strengthen the authority of our country in the world. I would be glad if other countries respected us for showing understanding, tolerance, and love of peace. I would be happy if Pope John Paul II and the Dalai Lama of Tibet could visit our country before the elections, if only for one day. I would be happy if our friendly relations with all nations were strengthened. I would be happy if we succeeded before the elections in establishing diplomatic relations with the Vatican and Israel. I would also like to contribute to peace by my brief visit tomorrow to our close neighbors, namely, the German Democratic Republic and the Federal Republic of Germany. Nor shall I forget our other neighbors—Poland, Hungary, and Austria.

In conclusion, I would like to say that I want to be a president who will speak less and work more. To be a president who will not only look out the windows of his airplane, but who will always be among his fellow citizens and listen to them attentively.

You may ask what kind of republic I dream of. Let me reply: I dream of a republic that is independent, free, and democratic; a republic with economic prosperity yet social justice; a humane republic that serves the individual and therefore hopes that the individual will serve it in turn; a republic of well-rounded people, because without such people, it is impossible to solve any of our problems, whether they be human, economic, ecological, social, or political.

The most distinguished of my predecessors opened his first speech with a quote from Comenius [the great Czech educator of the 17th century]. Allow me to end my first speech with my own paraphrase of the same statement: My People, your Government has returned to you!

VIKTOR ORBÁN
THE REBURIAL OF IMRE NAGY

Hungary has a long history of repression and rebellion; it is a country that has endured occupation by foreign powers for centuries. Dismembered after World War I, Hungary hoped to regain some of its lost territory by joining forces with the Germans against the Russians during World War II. At the end of the war, Soviet forces occupied Hungary, and in 1949 a pro-Soviet government was formed. A revolution against the Communists broke out in 1956, but it was crushed by Soviet tanks and troops. The premier of the anti-Soviet government was Imre Nagy. Nagy had served as premier from 1953 until 1955, when he was forced out. After the failure of the uprising, Nagy was executed, and his body was dumped in an unmarked grave with hundreds of others who had participated in the events of 1956.

Over the years, the authorities insisted that the 1956 uprising was a counterrevolution, the work of riffraff and traitors, but the liberalizing trends in Europe in the 1980s affected Hungary, and its leaders began to tell the truth about the revolution. In early 1989, the government acknowledged that the uprising was a genuine rejection of the Stalinist system and a plea for democracy and freedom.

On June 16, 1989 the remains of Imre Nagy and other leaders of the 1956 revolution were reburied with state honors. More than 300,000 Hungarians attended the ceremony in Budapest. Five coffins bore names, and the sixth coffin symbolized the known and unknown victims of the system. Some of the victims were 18-year-olds, executed as late as 1960; the government had waited until they were old enough to receive the death penalty.

At the reburial ceremony, the leaders of Hungary turned out to pay tribute to Nagy and his colleagues. Government officials, parliamentary leaders, dignitaries from every Hungarian church, and representatives from organizations across the country participated. Among several speakers, the only one whose presentation was interrupted by applause was Viktor Orbán, (1963–   ) who spoke for FIDESZ, the Federation of Young Democrats, a militant student group. At age 26, Orbán was the youngest speaker on that solemn occasion.

Citizens!

In the forty years since the beginning of the communist dictatorship and the Soviet occupation, Hungary has only once had the chance, only once had the strength and the courage, to attain her ambitions of 1848: national independence and political liberty. Our aims haven't changed; we will not renounce any of the goals of 1848, as we cannot renounce 1956, either.

The young Hungarians now struggling for de-

At a meeting of a Hungarian democratic party in the spring of 1990, Hungarians proudly displayed their national flag with a hole where the symbol of Communism—the hammer and sickle—had been ripped out.

mocracy bow their heads before the communist Imre Nagy and his companions for two reasons.

We appreciate that these statesmen identified themselves with the wishes of the Hungarian nation, that they broke with the sacred tenets of communism—that is, with blind obedience to the Russian empire and with the dictatorship of a single party.

In 1956, the Hungarian Socialist Workers' Party (MSZMP) seized our future. Thus, there in the sixth coffin, alongside the massacred youth, lay our prospects for years to come.

Friends! We young people fail to understand many things that are obvious to the older generations. We are puzzled that those who were so eager to slander the Revolution and Imre Nagy have suddenly become the greatest supporters of the former prime minister's policies. Nor do we understand why the party leaders who saw to it that we were taught from books that falsified the Revolution are now rushing to touch the coffins as if they were good-luck charms. We need not be grateful for their permission to bury our martyrs after thirty-one years; nor do we have to thank them for allowing our political organizations to function. Hungary's leaders are not to be praised because they have refrained from using weapons against those striving for democracy and free elections, because they have not adopted, as well they could, the methods of Li Peing, Pol Pot, Jaruzelski, and Rákosi.

Citizens! Thirty-three years after the Hungarian Revolution was crushed and thirty-one years after the execution of the last legitimate prime minister, we may now have a chance to achieve peacefully the goals that the revolutionaries briefly attained through bloody combat. If we trust our souls and our strength, we can put an end to the communist dictatorship; if we are determined enough, we can force the party to submit to free elections; and if we do not lose sight of the ideals of 1956, then we will be able to elect a government that will immediately begin negotiations on the swift withdrawal of the Russian troops. We can fulfill the will of the Revolution if—and only if—we are brave enough. We cannot trust the party-state to change of its own accord. Remember: on October 6, 1956, on the very day László Rajk was reburied, the party's daily declared in bold letters: "Never Again!" Three weeks later, the communist party ordered its security forces to shoot and kill defenseless people. Before two years had passed, the MSZMP had hundreds of innocent people, even party members, sentenced to death on trumped-up charges. We will never accept the empty promises of communist leaders; our goal is to prevent the ruling party from ever using force against us again. This is the only way to avoid new coffins— new burials like today's. Imre Nagy, Miklós Gimes, Géza Losonczy, Pál Maléter, and József Szilágyi gave their lives for Hungarian independence and liberty. These values are still cherished by Hungary's youth: we bow to your memory.

Requiseat in pacem!

HELMUT FRAUENDORFER

ROMANIA: THE GRIM ISLAND OF SOUTH-EASTERN EUROPE

In August 1988, a year before massive political changes occurred in Eastern Europe and the Soviet Union, a conference on human rights was convened in Krakow, Poland. It was the first human rights conference ever to be independently organized in a communist country. More than 700 Poles from various opposition groups were joined by almost 300 representatives of human rights organizations and trade unions from Western Europe, the

Americas, and Communist bloc nations. The meeting was held at Nowa Huta, a drab cinderblock "new town" of high-rise apartment buildings. Organized in secret, until the conference actually began it was uncertain whether the authorities would permit it to proceed.

Among the most moving presentations to the conference was Helmut Frauendorfer's harrowing description of life in Communist Romania under the dictator Nicolae Ceauşescu. Frauendorfer, an ethnic German, fled Romania not long before the conference began. Sixteen months later, Ceauşescu and his wife were arrested and executed in the midst of a revolution against his tyrannous rule.

In my country, the words "human rights" are among the most hated by its ruler, Nicolae Ceauşescu. His people can shiver in the cold, starve, be imprisoned, be beaten, be shot or murdered in other ways, but they have no right to defend themselves, to live in dignity.

And this is happening right now, here in Europe.

The violation of human rights is a well-established practice in Romania. That is, if we assume that all men have a right to food and warmth; that women have the right to decide how many children to bear whenever and wherever they choose; and that all people have the right to decent medical care. None of these rights is recognized in Romania; in fact, the list of rights that are not recognized is virtually endless. I am no expert in this field: I am only a writer who has seen and heard what is happening in his country. With your permission, ladies and gentlemen, I will give you a firsthand account of the state of affairs in my country.

The violation of human rights begins in Romania when life itself begins, or, more precisely, before it begins. Women are forced to give birth whether they want to or not. In order to realize his "magnificent vision," Ceauşescu wants every woman to have at least four children. Thus, the most intimate sphere of human life, the womb, is violated. Women who work suffer forced gynecological examinations. My wife, a village schoolteacher, was ordered to see a doctor because of her failure to produce children. The doctor wanted to know what we did, for instance, during power outages. "We munch on pumpkin seeds," my wife replied. He was nice enough not to force my wife to undergo an examination, but she didn't dare tell him that we use Yugoslav contraceptives obtained on the black market. Contraception in any form is strictly prohibited. Abortion is a crime punishable by many years' imprisonment. If a woman unsuccessfully attempts to abort her pregnancy, she receives no medical care until the public prosecutor has questioned her. In the meantime, she may bleed to death. And our doctors have assented to this practice.

On the other hand, if a woman wants to have a baby, she is not at all certain whether it will survive, since, in Romania, not even hospitals are immune to power outages. Newborns die in incubators. In fact, they are not even given birth certificates until a few weeks after they are born. That way, if an infant dies in the interim, neither the birth nor the death are recorded. Thus, the real infant mortality rate is much higher than the official statistics indicate. And if a mother's offspring dies during the first few weeks, she is not given credit for having had one of her compulsory four children; she must produce another to replace the one that perished.

If a newborn survives its stay in the hospital, the ordeal is not over. The whole family, even distant relatives, must struggle to find proper nourishment for the infant, standing in line all night long if necessary to buy food for the baby.

In recent years, the West has been flooded by letters from Romania's sick begging for the medicines they need. Ceauşescu has reduced the import of medicine to a minimum. You must fight your disease on your own—though if you become a patient in a hospital, you will have to do

In the midst of the Romanian revolution of December 1989, a group of happy Romanians drive around the streets of Bucharest, displaying a hangman's noose superimposed over a drawing of the hated dictator Nicolae Ceausescu.

so with someone lying right next to you because there are so few beds. Old people are no longer even hospitalized.

Enough about hospitals. Let's assume that the child survives his stay there and, in turn, the privations of his infancy. He is now old enough to go to school. Let me describe the conditions at the village school where I taught for three years. It is winter: teachers and students sit in the classroom wearing their overcoats, mittens, and wool caps, shivering in the cold. They can't write—their hands are too stiff. There is no power in the village from Monday morning to Saturday afternoon. Austerity measures. No buses. Austerity measures. A number of children walk two and a half miles twice a day to get to school; teachers who live in the next village have to walk five miles. Children often faint in class; at first they don't want to say anything, but later they admit that they haven't eaten anything all day. At home, the children continue to shiver because if their parents use too much gas—or electricity when it's available—they are fined.

In the spring and autumn schools are closed, and the students go out into the fields. Whether it's raining or snowing, the students—who range in age from eight to seventeen—are forced to work ten hours a day, seven days a week. The number who have been injured or who have died because of illness or accident will never be made public. Nobody talks about the beatings that take place in the schools and on the farms alike. Teachers are not the only ones to administer the beatings: the First Secretary of the Party Committee for the Arges region, for example, beat several exhausted children who had sat down to rest in a field where they were working.

Our rural inhabitants—genuine peasants no longer exist—are obligated to give milk, cheese, eggs, wood, and one hog a year to the state. The village policeman dutifully collects all this. He also confiscates any bread that appears to have been bought in town and arrests those who have illegally slaughtered livestock. After the harvest, workers on collective farms never receive the produce and grain they were promised the spring before. And the village policeman makes sure they go back to work the following spring.

Industrial workers are cheated just like agricultural workers are. They usually only receive half their promised wages, or they spend months at a time on unpaid lay-offs. Discussing unemployment is taboo in Romania. But the unemployed do indeed exist, though they do not receive any kind of benefits. At least people have time to stand in line during these "unpaid vacations." What do they find for sale? A few basic items, all rationed. I myself saw bones for sale that had already been stripped clean of meat.

Besides destroying the population's standard

of living, Ceauşescu is engaged in the destruction of Romanian culture. In the late 1960s, culture was given some respect—but that period did not last long. Real culture was replaced by a combination of the cult of the proletariat and the cult of the leader's personality. All cultural institutions exist only to praise Ceauşescu and his wife, and the censors take great pains to insure that they do nothing else. Officially, however, the office of censor has been abolished. Whether or not that's true makes little difference, since any text is first of all censored by the writer himself, then by the cultural committee to which he belongs, and then by the editor of the journal in which the text is to appear.

But it is not only texts intended for publication that suffer from censorship. In 1984, while I was being interrogated by officers of the Romanian security service, passages from a letter which I wrote to a friend living abroad were quoted to me. Of course, the letter never made it through. That mail disappears, that telephone lines are tapped, are facts of life.

Although almost nothing works anymore in Romania, there is one ministry which functions flawlessly: the Ministry of Internal Affairs. With the help of the police and security services, President Ceauşescu wages war against his own people. Informants play an important role: in the small town where I live, two of the local school's eleven teachers are known informants. Beatings and torture are common in prisons and wherever detainees are held. Very often people just disappear from the streets. After a while, they turn up dead in some prison. In the majority of such cases, no explanations are given, and the families of the deceased are usually too terrified to enquire any further into the matter.

Those hounded on account of their political and religious convictions frequently end up in psychiatric hospitals. Even if they are lucky enough to be discharged, they are never the same again. In the town of Petru Groza I saw such a hospital; with its guards and towering fence, it looked more like a prison.

The national minorities suffer from particularly acute oppression. Romania is home to

Hungarians, Germans, Jews, Gypsies, Serbians, Slovaks, Bulgarians, Czechs, and Ukrainians. Since nationalism, chauvinism and even anti-Semitism have been propagated from the highest level of government, the problems of the various minorities have been impossible to solve. The few minority cultural institutions that still exist are all but meaningless. They only serve to further the propaganda interests of the Ceauşescu regime in the various languages of the national minorities. Schools where the language of instruction is not Romanian have been abolished; only language courses in the minority tongues are offered. Television programs in Hungarian and German have been discontinued. I could go on and on.

The authorities do allow Germans and Jews to emigrate—though only after subjecting them to all sorts of harassment. But they have a strong incentive to do so: West Germany and Israel pay for every immigrant they receive from Romania.

Ceauşescu's campaign against the more concrete expression of culture, namely architecture, is more widely known. He hadn't even finished his demolition of Bucharest when he announced plans to destroy 8,000 villages across the country. This plan is aimed primarily at the hated minorities; it began, in fact, with a village which lies in a German district, Gottlob. Ceauşescu's plans, however, uproot not only the national minorities, but his own people as well. These plans violate the most basic human right by forcing people to move out of their ancestral homes and into giant concrete boxes.

Nature, too, is under attack in Ceauşescu's Romania. Enormous sums have been poured into the construction of a canal that connects the Danube river with the Black Sea. The canal—built with the help of soldiers, convicts, and students—has been used for little besides Ceauşescu's royal jaunts with which he tries to impress foreign dignitaries. Now he has construction projects in store which would devastate the environmentally unique Danube River delta.

It is no wonder that the entire population of

Romania would emigrate if it could. Since this is impossible, the Romanian people can only resign themselves to their fate. Attempts to counter this predominant attitude—such as the workers' rebellion in Brasov, the actions of a few intellectuals, and occasional protests—receive little support from the general population, which has been terrorized into obedience. There are individuals who try to escape, but it is a daunting task to cross the borders without a passport—even though Romania does not share a border with any Western country. Some succeed; others are returned to their families in coffins; and others still are caught, tortured, and thrown in prison. For ten years, border guards have been ordered to shoot at Romanians trying to cross into Yugoslavia. According to the latest information, they shoot at those who try to cross into Hungary—and even into the Soviet Union!

How can all this happen in Europe, at a time of international detente, reforms, *glasnost* and *perestroika*? Primarily because of restrictions on the free flow of information. Western politicians have turned a blind eye toward the reality of Ceaușescu's regime, preferring instead to see him as a thorn in Moscow's side. Private contacts with foreigners are forbidden. Even Romanian tourists abroad say nothing about the situation in their homeland because they have been ordered not to.

The time has come to break this silence. Both the East and the West must be told about what is going on in Romania. Public pressure from all sides must be brought to bear on this tyrant, whose dog is treated better than the vast majority of Romanians. (That's right, his dog. Last winter, I happened to be on a street in Bucharest which Ceaușescu's motorcade often takes. Sure enough, traffic was suddenly halted, and policemen flooded the area. Motorcycle escorts appeared, followed by two police cars and then Ceaușescu's car itself, with the rest of the convoy behind it. The only occupant of the presidential car besides the driver was Ceaușescu's dog.)

At the beginning, I stated that the violation of human rights begins when life begins, and even earlier. Unfortunately, I can't say that it ends with death. What will Ceaușescu do with the graves of the dead after he razes the villages in which they lived? He'll liquidate the cemeteries as well. Under Ceaușescu, there is no peace for the living—nor for the dead.

 ANA BLANDIANA
A STAR IN MY STREET

Among the most repressive of Communist regimes was Nicolae Ceaușescu's Romania. Ceaușescu permitted no opposition and no criticism. The country was desperately poor, and Ceaușescu's economic austerity policies, coupled with the inefficiency of state control of the economy, made matters worse; any hint of criticism enraged the maximum leader. One of Romania's most prominent poets, Ana Blandiana, published a book of poetry for children entitled *Events in My Street*. Ceaușescu concluded that one of the poems, a poem about a cat, was really about him. (He may have been right; artists and writers in totalitarian countries often veil their criticisms in coded language.)

Blandiana promptly lost her right to publish in Romanian newspapers and magazines, all of which were controlled by the state. At the same time, her books were being published in East Germany, the Soviet Union, Italy, and England. Soon after she issued a public appeal to the president protesting her innocence, an anthology of her earlier poems was published in Romania, but the rest of her works remained banned until the revolution at the end of 1989.

The poem that follows is the one that enraged President Ceauşescu. (Translated by Peter Jay.)

Before I go any further,
There's a bracket I must open
(A chapter, that's to say,
In a story or a book)—
About someone who's not
A local down my way,
In fact, in his case,
Adjectives explain
Nothing, so I'd better say
That I'm talking of SCALLION.
And when I've said SCALLION
I think that's quite enough
And I need explain no more,
For you all know at once
Who this character is,
Whom I permit myself
To style the most renowned
Tomcat in the town,
To whom poems have been written
And whose portraits have been drawn
As is usual with stars.
And what's more, they have shown
Cartoons about him, full
Of thrills and full of fun,
Even on television.
Well, after such successes
So incontestable
And incredible
It's no wonder at all
That when he goes out to stroll
The whole street's in a spin
And rushes out to see him.
Windows are flung wide open,
Schoolbooks are forgotten by children,
Branches lean out over the fence,
The crush is dense
As a high street's.
Cars are forced
To slow right down.
Admiring glances are cast
In a catlike fashion.
He's given flowers,
Bread and salt,

A letter or two
In an envelope,
And everyone shouts
"SCALLION,"
He proceeds with importance and with
                                    cool,
Gives a piece of advice, hears a louder
Protest (like that of a hen with chicks
Against a tomcat marauder),
Distributes simpers, paw-shakes,
Here and there a fine
Or rather
A rebuke
And everyone's attentive
And full of gratitude.
Even (believe it or not) the scraps
Between the female alley-cats
And the tomcats are suspended!
And (to top it all) I've heard tell
That a little mouse
Waiting to be snatched
By His Highness
Whined in a high pitch
Between his sighs:
"Oh, what a privilege
To be swallowed just by Him!"
In this uncanny situation
I find it only normal
That Scallion's grown too big for his fur
And thinks he's phenomenal.
So I'm amazed as a result
That he answers when I call him
(Offering him, admittedly, out of
                                    gratitude,
A poem).
It's probable that in his mind,
The mind of a celebrity
At its apogee,
There comes from time to time,
With difficulty,
Like an erratum,
The memory
That he's a character of mine.

VYTAUTAS LANDSBERGIS

REJECTING HATRED

In 1940, Nazi Germany and the Soviet Union agreed to abrogate the national independence of the three Baltic republics, Lithuania, Estonia, and Latvia. Without a popular referendum or any other kind of consent, the three republics were absorbed into the Soviet Union. For nearly five decades, the Baltic republics were known as "captive nations," and their loss of independence seemed irreversible.

Then, in the mid-1980s, nationalist movements began to organize in all three Baltic states. The most assertive of these was Lithuania's, where a nationalist movement called *Sajudis* gained widespread popular support. Taking advantage of the liberalized political situation introduced by Soviet leader Mikhail Gorbachev, the Sajudis movement challenged the Communist party. When elections were held in February 1990, the Sajudis candidates won control of the Lithuanian parliament.

On March 11, 1990 the Lithuanian parliament declared its independence. The Lithuanians insisted that they were not trying to break away from the Soviet Union because Lithuania did not belong to the Soviet Union. They were merely reasserting the sovereignty that had been illegally destroyed by two lawless dictators.

The Soviet Union refused to accept the declaration of independence and imposed an economic blockade on Lithuania to force its submission to Moscow's authority. Lithuania appealed to the West for support, but the West was more interested in supporting Mikhail Gorbachev's ambitious political reforms than in defending tiny Lithuania.

Vytautas Landsbergis (1932–), the president of Lithuania, carried his nation's plea to anyone who would listen. On his side was the solid mandate of the Lithuanian people; against him was the military and economic might of the Soviet Union. Lithuania's example did not go unheeded; almost every other republic in the Soviet Union adopted a declaration of sovereignty following Lithuania's path. In 1991, with the collapse of Communist power in the Soviet Union, the three Baltic states won recognition of their independence.

The dramatically changed political situation in 1990 unleashed dangerous nationalist and ethnic tensions throughout Eastern and Central Europe, threatening the democratic movement. It was this topic that President Landsbergis addressed at a conference in Oslo, Norway in August 1990, where he reaffirmed the will of his people to pursue a peaceful, democratic future.

I doubt whether any one person has more personally felt the constantly shifting ethnic patchwork of Eastern Europe than the Noble Laureate Czeslav Milosz, a Lithuanian-born Pole, now residing in America. His "native Europe," particularly its eastern half, has been inhabited from ancient times by nations and ethnic communities, whose territories never seemed to conform to old and new political borders. Such a place, said the poet, could only live in endless conflict, or in the false tranquility of a "Pax Ruthena." Maybe for this very reason, the Western democracies embraced and tolerated a "Russian Peace": let the Soviets dominate these conquered lands and satellite protectorates; let them torture and deport their peoples . . . Better to close one's eyes to this huge, this continuing war-like conflict, the largest of all wars, than to witness the smaller battles that could arise there.

And maybe this is why Western Europe, even now, appears strangely, maybe even unethically concerned, when it interprets Eastern Europe's Spring as a Winter of frightening instability.

Lithuania is an ancient land, formed ethnically over 5,000 years ago, and first unified as a political entity, a Kingdom or Grand Duchy, in the 13th century—finally evolving into a democratic Republic, with its own place on the map of Europe. For two hundred years, she fought against Christian Europe, and later, defending her right to self-determination, freely accepted and embraced Western Christianity. She was an example of tolerance, of acceptance, offering haven to Jews and Tartars, and granting universal guarantees and privileges to merchants and apprentices. Already in the 14th century, the ruler of Lithuania, . . . Gediminas, while considering baptism, explained to Pope John XXII: "We allow the Christians to honor their God according to their own traditions, the Russians according to their customs, the Poles according to theirs, and we, the Lithuanians, honor God accordingly to our rituals, and yet, we all have one God." The humane values of this Pagan King evolved into the very political and cultural traditions of the state later established by the Lithuanian people. These traditions flourished with the expansion of Christian Lithuania's influence and control into lands bordering the Black Sea and to the very gates of Moscow in the 15th century, and later, in the 16th century, when her cultural ties spanned the distance to Italy and Spain.

Lithuania would soon see harder times: war, disease, invasion and political collapse, until finally, at the close of the 18th century, the Lithuanian Grand Duchy, already stripped of much of its territory, was completely and finally vanquished and absorbed into the Russian Empire, with western Lithuanian lands remaining under Prussian control. A long night of injustice and injury, rebellions in the name of freedom, and horrible repression swept over the land.

The Phoenix would soon rise from the ashes with the end of the First World War and the collapse of the empires of Central and Eastern Europe. Lithuania waged a continuous political and armed struggle for control of her ethnic lands. Success did not always grace her efforts, as

Vytautas Landsbergis, chairman of the Supreme Council of the Lithuanian Republic, casts his ballot for independence of February 9, 1991. In an effort to separate peacefully from the Soviet Union, Lithuania tried to show that its population wanted self-government. The independence initiative passed overwhelmingly, but the Soviet Union rejected the Lithuanian appeal.

even Lithuania's capital, Vilnius, was lost to foreign control for nineteen years. Yet the state reestablished on February 16, 1918 was recognized and respected by her European family, becoming a fellow-member in the League of Nations, and which, even after the rise of authoritarian power in Lithuania, continued to seek guarantees of its citizens' basic rights and provide for their well-being.

1940. Lithuania was swept in to a storm of aggression and violence. Massacres and deportations began; her children fled or were removed from their homes and their familiar neighborhoods, bringing about ... unprecedented confrontation and confusion. Unfortunately, this process of destruction continued in various forms and methods, and only a small part of Nazi and repeated Soviet crimes in Lithuania are known, let alone understood, by the rest of the world.

The Soviet system was based on fear. A fear not only of the outside world, but fear of one's neighbors, one's own family. Domestic policies were directed at one goal: to take away the personal values and principles of peoples and nations, and to break the spirit and morality of each and every man and woman through humiliation and degradation. The so-called "public" life was oriented toward total alienation and adherence to some sort of metaphysical horror called the "system." The greatest obstacle to such a complete dehumanization of society—love—was to be destroyed, leaving a new man, a crude slave to primitive rationalization, prepared to take over the entire world.

This hatred instilled in the people by the Soviets was purported to follow a theory of a class system: the "people" were encouraged to despise "enemies of the people," and this hatred, like a 20th century Moloch, demanded more and more sacrifices to survive and grow. For this reason not only the rich "bourgeois" were subject to suspicion, but all people became potential enemies.

Because hatred destroys the very essence of humane values, nothing is left to redirect or control it: it spreads like a flood, eating away at the spirit like the water that erodes the land, pouring into and feeding its strength from old scars in the earth—the historical injustice suffered by nations.

For more than two years now, rumors have been actively spread in the Soviet Union that Lithuanians hate Russians. These rumors, in turn, breed certain reactions and responses. Upon arrival in Lithuania, however, many Russian tourists and guests do not find any strong antagonism directed toward them—on the contrary, they are surprised that, in reality, such an air of antagonism does not exist.

Moreover, when the people of Moscow began bringing their own sugar rations to the Lithuanian Legation in the Soviet Capital as a gift to the children of Lithuania during the hard months of the economic blockade directed against our country, we were overjoyed that the old Soviet propaganda machine proved itself no longer able to undermine basic humanitarian values.

It would seem that every newly endured or remembered injustice should only breed more hatred and desire for revenge. To our good fortune, it is not always so. Perhaps excessive or continuous injustice makes any further vendettas meaningless and strengthens an overriding desire for *justice* only—a justice that would save both parties: the victim as well as the oppressor. This is the way to democracy which, after all, is not an abstract value meant for debate, but a real path for a nation to follow and live by.

When I hear the claim that ethnic hatred poses a threat to democracy, I immediately feel a need to disagree with such a narrow, maybe even pragmatic, political view. . . .

The threat to our nations comes from undemocratic and anti-democratic social forces who, for their own purposes, or perhaps due to their own imperfect nature, foster fear, mistrust and hatred.

We see this threat very clearly in Lithuania today: frightening rumors and provocations should (if they were successful, if evil were to triumph over reason), create barriers between peoples, particularly between Lithuanians and Russians, between Lithuanians and Poles. And then each [group] would stand on its side of the barrier, preparing to "defend" itself, all the while believing in their hearts that they are merely defending themselves and not preparing for confrontation.

These imperial policies have been more successful in the Caucasus region, while in Lithuania we have been able to resist them, neutralize them.

At this point I could, of course, cite from horrible hate letters written in Russian, and sometimes in Lithuanian, sent to the former leadership of the Lithuanian Reform Movement "Sajudis" and the current leadership of the Republic of Lithuania; I could comment on them with words of sympathy for the authors, but that is not very important.

Our world is extremely diverse, and for this reason, spiritually rich and dynamic. The total unification of vanquished neighbors with victorious empires sought in earlier times could today be best called spiritual and cultural genocide. But it also brought on a spiritual slavery to fear, which these empires condemned themselves to endure, like the very prison chains they forged for their victims. Today the last Eurasian empire continues to suffer from this slavery. The only way to help it is not to fear it, to reject fear. As I see it, Western Europe is still afraid, and therefore has much work to do.

Fear of strangers, and in the face of this, the discomfort brought on by humiliation, and the resulting hatred—perhaps this complex reflects ancient feelings of civilization's first tribes.

But should a stranger be hated? Does different necessarily mean strange?

For if a person is identified as a "stranger," this is certainly not his own inherent state or characteristic, but a feeling generated by one's surroundings, which, unfortunately, often are of a negative nature, confining the "stranger" in a foreign atmosphere, and thereby instilling fear into him.

Christianity brought with it the idea of *brotherhood*, and spoke no longer merely of love between a man and a woman, but of love for all people, a love for the world.

Indeed, it would be distressing to find humanity standing at a crossroads, deciding whether to follow the path towards love for one's neighbor, or the path leading to hatred of all that is foreign.

Perhaps, in the lives of people, nations and states, we are faced with an eternal, maybe even metaphysical struggle between that which is foreign and that which is known and understood. Not having found a closeness, we withdraw from a "strange" alien world. Then, out of our hopelessness, we either take revenge upon the first person we may happen upon, or, we may find the strength to love him, to call him brother. And even some, having found the grace of the Lord, may grow to love the world, to love the Lord.

What have we learned over these 2,000 years? Are we only now learning our ABC's, or are we moving from a world of strangers to a world of brothers?

We have experienced terrible lessons, this is true. Yet we have all been given a fortunate assignment: some of us must emerge from the practice of inhumane behavior, while others must wade out from the swamp of indifference.

My small country, Lithuania, has an extremely varied historical experience; based on this, she chose her path and goals, which may, to some, appear impossible to achieve: confronted by so many obstacles and suffering from such deep wounds, to establish a state of social concord, a state of peace.

But Lithuania continues on her path. Let this be her contribution to a community of nations, to the Europe of the future. Though rejected and unwelcome, we will continue on our path, because we believe that such is the only path for all nations: to triumph over fear, eliminate mistrust, not give in to hatred, to nurture the centuries-old tradition of tolerance, damaged but certainly not forgotten, and preserve the trusty tools of tillers of the soil: patience and tenacity.

Lithuanians, and other inhabitants of Lithuania, must defend themselves together, as one. Our enemies are not nations, but inhumanity, injustice, the toleration of injustice around us and within us. Our enemy is fear and the fostering of fear. One should be ashamed if someone fears him. Yet we can draw strength from what we have experienced and what we have seen in less than one year, what many should see and experience: the Baltic way, where we stood, all one million of us, hand in hand, not looking to see whether we stood next to a Lithuanian, a Jew or a Pole: the play "Family Songbook," directed by the Polish director A. Hanuskevic, in three languages, on the stage of the Russian Theater of Lithuania; the unanimous votes of deputies of all nationalities and views in Lithuania's Supreme Council in favor of that, which is so important to all of us; the commemorations of the tragic suffering endured by Lithuania's Jews and of those who tried to help them; Ludwig von Beethoven's 9th Symphony and the "Peace Children" in Vilnius' Cathedral Square; the crosses carried from that square throughout all of Lithuania; the farewell, in that same square, to a man who set himself aflame in the name of his country; the return of remains of those deported to distant Siberia and their reburial in their holy, native land, blessed by tears of grief.

May they rest in peace, and may the living be blessed with hope. For even in rebirth there is suffering, which must be completely and wholly endured.

WEI JINGSHENG
THE FIFTH MODERNIZATION

After the Communist revolution in China in 1949, the Communist party established rigid control of economic, social, political, and cultural life. The party and the government spoke with one voice, eliminating all opposition. In the 1950s, the party collectivized agriculture, imposed "thought reform" on the urban intelligentsia, and required adherence to the party line. As in the Soviet Union, where a "cult of personality" was created to deify Joseph Stalin, the Chinese Communist party established a cult of personality to worship Chairman Mao Zedong. Over the years, the party alternated between long periods of intense ideological orthodoxy and brief periods of liberalization. A series of political campaigns was aimed at crushing counterrevolutionaries, spies, traitors, "capitalist roaders," and intellectuals with bourgeois family origins.

In 1956, Chairman Mao encouraged a measure of intellectual freedom by saying "Let a hundred flowers bloom, let a hundred schools contend." A year later, however, the regime launched an "anti-rightist campaign" to stamp out opposition to the party line. In 1966, Mao proclaimed a Cultural Revolution, ostensibly to rekindle revolutionary fervor; during this period, the Red Guards beat up teachers, burned books, and killed potential opponents of the regime. Thousands, perhaps hundreds of thousands, of intellectuals, teachers and students were sent to the countryside to live and work with peasants.

After Mao died in 1976, the elite group known as the "Gang of Four" (led by Mao's widow) was arrested, tried, and convicted for leading the Cultural Revolution. During the brief period of liberalization that followed, a small number of Chinese demanded democracy. Wall posters appeared, explaining the need for greater democracy in China. The regime hesitated, then cracked down on the democracy campaigners.

The most prominent dissident arrested during this period was Wei Jingsheng (1950–   ). Wei, an electrician, wrote wall posters and edited *Exploration Magazine*. Wei wrote several articles during the "democracy spring" of 1978–1979. The most famous of his essays was "The Fifth Modernization," a commentary on the government's policy of "four modernizations." Wei argued that modernization of any country—whether in the

Journals, magazines and radios no longer play up themes on dictatorship of the proletariat and class struggle. One reason is that this line of propaganda was used as some magical power by the "gang of four" who have been overthrown. Another reason, which is even more important, is that the people have had enough of it so that it can no longer deceive anybody.

According to the laws of history, the new will not come until the old is gone. Now that the old is gone, the people are rubbing their eyes in eager expectation. Finally, with God's blessing, they got a great promise—the "four modernizations." Chairman Hua, the wise leader, and Vice Chairman Deng, an even wiser and greater leader in the people's minds, have defeated the "gang of four," and the very eager hope for democracy and prosperity by those who had shed their blood at Tiananmen Square seemed soon to materialize.

However, to the people's regret, the hated old political system has not changed and even any talk about the much hoped for democracy and freedom is forbidden.

Now do people have democracy? No. Do they want to be masters of their own destiny? Definitely yes. This was the reason for the Communist Party's victory over the Kuomintang. But what has happened to the promise of democracy when victory was already won? The slogan of people's democratic dictatorship was followed by that of the dictatorship of the proletariat.

There is no need now to determine the ratio of Mao Tse-tung's merits and shortcomings. He first spoke about this as a self-defense. People should now think for a while and see if, without Mao Tse-tung's autocracy, China would be in its present backward state. Are Chinese people stupid, or lazy, or unwilling to enjoy wealth? Are they expecting too much? Quite the opposite. Then why?

The answer is quite obvious. Chinese people should not have taken this road. Then why did they take it? Only because they were led by that self-exalting autocrat. If they did not take this road, he would exercise dictatorship over them. The people could see no other road, and therefore had no choice. Is this not deception? Can there be any merit in deception?

What road is that? It is called the "socialist road." According to the definition of the Marxist ancestors, socialism means that the people, or the proletariat, are their own masters. Let me ask the Chinese workers and peasants: "With the meager wages you get every month, whose master and what kind of master can you be?" Sad to relate, you are "mastered" by somebody else.

What is true democracy? It means the right of the people to choose their own representatives to work according to their will and in their interest. Only this can be called democracy. Furthermore, the people must also have the power to replace their representatives any time so that these representatives cannot go on deceiving others in the name of the people. This is the kind of democracy enjoyed by people in European and American countries. In accordance with their will, they could run such people as Nixon, de Gaulle and Tanaka out of office. They can reinstate them if they want, and nobody can interfere with their democratic rights.

In China, however, if people even comment on the already dead "Great Helmsman Mao Tse-tung" or the "Great Man" without peers in history, the jail will be ready for him with open doors and various unpredictable calamities may befall him.

Will there be great disorder across the land and defiance of laws human and divine once people enjoy democracy? Do not recent periodicals show that just because of the absence of democracy, dictators, big and small, were defying laws human and divine? How to maintain democratic order is the domestic problem requiring solution

During democracy demonstrations in Beijing's Tiananmen Square, students erected a thirty-foot statue that they called the "Goddess of Democracy," directly facing the portrait of Mao Tse-Tung. Less than a week later, on June 4, 1989, Chinese troops smashed the protest, destroyed the statue, and killed numerous demonstrators.

by the people themselves, and there is no need for the privileged overlords to worry about it. Therefore, judging from past history, a democratic social system is the major premise or the prerequisite for all developments—or modernizations. Without this major premise or prerequisite, it would be impossible not only to continue further development but also to preserve the fruits of the present stage of development. The experiences of our great motherland over the past 30 years have provided the best evidence.

Why must human history take the road toward prosperity or modernization? The reason is that human beings need a prosperous society to produce realistic fruits and to provide them with maximum opportunity to pursue their first goal of happiness, namely freedom. Democracy means the maximum attainable freedom so far known by human beings. It is quite obvious that democracy has become the goal in contemporary human struggles.

Is the struggle for democracy what the Chinese people really want? The Cultural Revolution was the first occasion for them to demonstrate their strength, and all reactionary forces trembled before them. Because the people had then no clear orientation and the democratic forces did not play the main role in the struggle, the majority of them were bought over by the autocratic tyrant, led astray, divided, slandered and finally violently suppressed. Thus these forces came to an end.

Today, 12 years later, the people have finally learned where their goal is. They have a clear orientation and a real leader—the democratic banner. The Xidan Democracy Wall has become their first battlefield in their fight against reactionaries and their struggle will certainly be victorious, or, as so often talked about, the people will certainly be liberated. This is a slogan with new significance. There will still be bloodshed and sufferings, and we may be covertly plotted against. However, the democratic banner cannot be obscured by the miasmal mists. Let us unite under this great and real banner and march toward modernization for the sake of the people's peace, happiness, rights and freedom!

TRIAL OF WEI JINGSHENG

Wei Jingsheng was arrested for counterrevolutionary activities in March 1979 and convicted in October. He was sentenced to 15 years in prison. Other champions of democracy in China were imprisoned, but Wei was the first and most daring. He was widely known among Chinese students and dissidents as the man who challenged the full power of the state—and lost. According to press reports, Wei was kept in complete isolation in a tiny cell, denied family visits, and allowed only two meals a day. As a result, he grew sick, toothless, and broken. Yet the government has refused to show any leniency to him, because "Wei Jingsheng has refused to reform himself, and he does not regret his crimes." What Wei probably did not know, in his isolation cell, is that he became a hero to the democracy movement in China in 1989 and that his name—and the memory of his heroism—survives.

A transcript of Wei Jingsheng's trial was published in the Chinese dissident magazine *April Fifth Forum* in October 1979. The indictment by the public prosecutor and Wei Jingsheng's defense speech are printed here.

The accused is Wei Jengsheng, pen-name Jin Sheng. A student, male, 29 years of age, place of birth Zhao County in Anhui Province. Now a worker at the administrative office of Peking Municipal Parks. Resident at No. 2, Lane 4, off Bu Wai North Street, in Xicheng district, Peking. After notification by Peking People's Procuratorate, the accused was arrested by the Peking Public Security Bureau on a charge of counter-revolutionary crimes and is now in custody. This case of counterrevolution on the part of the accused Wei Jingsheng was presented by Peking Public Security Bureau to the Procuratorate who examined the evidence and confirmed that there was a case to answer on the following charges:

1. He provided foreigners with our nation's military intelligence. In February 1979 the accused supplied foreigners with military information when our nation launched a defensive counterattack against Vietnam and had just commenced military action in defense of our national border areas. This military intelligence included the name of our nation's commander-in-chief of the forces committed in the action, the numbers of troops taking part in the action, the progress of the fighting as well as the number of casualties. Wei Jingsheng betrayed his fatherland

by providing foreigners with such information and committed the crime of counter-revolution stipulated in Article 6 of the Regulations Regarding the Punishment of Counterrevolutionaries.

2. He spread counterrevolutionary propaganda and agitation. The accused Wei Jingsheng did this through the medium of writing counter-revolutionary articles and by supervising the editing of the counterrevolutionary publication *Exploration*. Between the months of December 1978 and February 1979 he wrote such articles as "Democracy: The Fifth Modernization" and "Human Rights, Equality and Democracy," etc., propagating and inciting the overthrow of the dictatorship of the proletariat and our socialist system. He distributed these publications in both the cities of Peking and Tianjin.

Article 2 of the Constitution stipulates that Marxism-Leninism and Mao Zedong Thought are the guiding ideology of the People's Republic of China. However, Wei Jingsheng slandered Marxism-Leninism and Mao Zedong Thought when he said that it was an "even more brilliant piece of quackery than any of the old itinerant pox-doctors' panaceas." The first article of our Constitution stipulates: "The People's Republic of China is a socialist state under the Dictatorship of the Proletariat led by the working classes with the alliance of worker and peasant as its basis"; article 56 stipulates that all citizens must support the Communist Party's leadership, uphold the socialist system, safeguard the unity of the fatherland and national unity, and abide by the Constitution and law. Wei Jingsheng, however, vilified our country's system of proletarian dictatorship by saying that it is a system of feudal monarchism in the guise of socialism. He incited the masses no longer to trust the stability and unity of dictatorship, nor to serve as tools for modernization or of dictators' ambitious aggrandizement. Further, he told the masses not to cherish illusions about their rulers but called upon the people to focus their fury on the evil system responsible for the masses' miserable lot, and to wrest the reins of government from the hands of their lords and masters.

Article 2 of the Act for the Punishment of Counterrevolution stipulates: "All counterrevolutionary criminals whose goal is to overthrow the people's democratic regime or to undermine the people's democratic cause shall be punished in accordance with this Act." Our people's democratic regime is none other than the dictatorship of the proletariat and according to the law all actions which have as their aim the overthrow of the socialist system and the political power of dictatorship of the proletariat and thereby harm the People's Republic of China constitute counterrevolutionary acts. . . .

It is hoped that the defendant will be punished according to the law.

[After cross-examination by the prosecutor and presentations by witnesses, Wei was called upon by the judge to deliver his defense address.]

WEI: I see as unfounded and unsubstantiated the charges in the indictment brought by the People's Procuratorate of Peking's Municipality. My editing of publications and my writing of posters were both in accordance with Article 45 of the constitution: "Citizens enjoy freedom of speech, correspondence, the press, assembly, association, procession, demonstration and the freedom to strike, and have the right to 'speak out freely air their views fully, hold great debates and write big-character posters.' " Our reasons for producing our publication were simply to attempt a tentative exploration of the path along which China could advance this objective. Our activities, motivated by the principles I have just mentioned, are described as counterrevolutionary by the Public Security Department and the Procuratorate. We cannot accept such a description. I shall now go on to express substantiated views on each of the charges listed in the indictment.

THE FIRST CHARGE. The indictment states that I provided foreigners with national military information and committed the crime of counterrevolution . . . the wording of the new penal code and of the old Act for the Punishment of Counterrevolution reads alike: providing military information to *the enemy* constitutes the crime of treason. Yet, in the eyes of the Public Prosecutor, my discussions with English and French foreign correspondents are seen as treasonable conduct. Is this not as good as describing the English and French journalists as the enemy? I would like to draw the attention of the prosecution to the fact that when Hua Gofeng received the journalists of four Western European nations, he quite clearly addressed each correspondent from each nation as "my friend."

The constitution stipulates that it is the duty of all citizens to *keep national secrets*. Yet here, where the wording of the constitution is quite explicit on this aspect of the citizen's duties, the indictment uses the vague and hazy term *military intelligence*. It is common knowledge that a lot of what passes for military intelligence or information is obtainable by an analysis of what is stated in the public media of any nation's newspapers, radio and television news reports, etc. It is clear then that the term military information or intelligence is an over-generalized concept. Since it is the duty of all citizens to keep national secrets, this presupposes that the citizens know in the first place what the secrets are that they are supposed to keep. That is to say, this secret must be recognizable from the outset as a piece of classified information. It must be clearly indicated or marked down as a national or military secret. Only then do the citizens have the duty to maintain its secrecy. Never once in the period that followed the outbreak of the Sino-Vietnamese War did I come into contact with anything whatsoever marked as a classified secret. Thus, there is no question of my furnishing anyone with anything that can be described as secret by the terms of the legal definition. When I chatted with reporters and foreign diplomats from friendly nations it was difficult for me not to mention every aspect of the internal situation in our country. . . .

JUDGE: Talk slower, Wei Jingsheng.

WEI: Whether or not the news I mentioned in my conversations with foreigners was news which the government preferred not to divulge I had no means of knowing. Since I am just an ordinary citizen, my sources of information remain the grapevine and rumor, not official documents from a government source. Whether or not my information might have happened to coincide quite fortuitously with points of information marked as classified secrets in government documents I likewise have no means of telling, because I have never set eyes on any classified documents. But the news I discussed could not have had any harmful effect on the front-line situation. That was something to which I gave some thought before I said anything. In the instance of my mention of the name of the Commander-in-Chief at the front, whoever has heard of a victory being won because the Commander-in-Chief's name was not revealed? Conversely, whoever has heard of defeat being suffered simply because the enemy knew the name of one's own Commander-in-Chief? No cases of either kind exist, so in what way can my mention of his name have had an adverse effect on the front-line situation? Throughout the whole gamut of ancient and modern history, I

have never heard of knowledge of the Commander-in-Chief's name proving to be a vital factor in the final outcome of hostilities. Such a theory just doesn't hold water.

Naturally, the public prosecutor may state that, according to established custom and practice in our nation, anything that comes into the authorities' heads may be considered a national secret. At the time when the "Gang of Four" was in power, when the isolationist policy held sway and the nation was sealed off from the outside world behind closed doors, anything that appealed to the authorities became a national secret, and just to say a few words to a foreigner could, if the powers wished, be construed as having illicit relations with a foreign country. Perhaps the public prosecutor wants all citizens to abide by the established practices of the "Gang of Four" era? Or does he just want them to adhere to the law? In this respect the Department of Public Security has already spoken, when it said I must abide by the rules and regulations governing the maintenance of official secrets. I do not know what these rules and regulations are. I do know that in themselves they refer to keeping things secret; but, because they are not publicly promulgated for ordinary citizens to abide by, they can only be something laid down by some internal bureau. The ordinary citizen, therefore, may be obliged to abide by the constitution and the law, but he is under no obligation to abide by rules and regulations about which he knows nothing, since they were made by some internal bureau.

To sum up. Firstly, I had no intention of betraying the fatherland. Secondly, I supplied the enemy with nothing at all. Thirdly, I gave my friends no official secrets—either national or military. Thus the prosecution's accusation that I committed treason is quite unfounded. If the prosecution considers the content of my discussions with foreigners as things the government would rather I had not mentioned, and that I made a mistake by so doing, I am perfectly willing to accept that. Moreover, I am perfectly willing to accept that, in response to the government's reasonable demands hereafter, it is the duty of every citizen to maintain secrecy about matters the government feels should be kept secret. But, in turn, I trust the government will be able to be more explicit in its stipulation of the actual scope of those secrets it expects its citizens to maintain, and not leave them in a state of perplexed bewilderment; nor will it directly prevent Chinese nationals from having friendly relations with the nationals of other countries, since all this will only further confuse the administration of justice and have adverse effects upon the nation and its people.

THE SECOND CHARGE. The indictment states that I carried out counterrevolutionary propaganda and agitation, and describes my essays, "Democracy: The Fifth Modernization," etc., as reactionary articles. Likewise our publication *Exploration* is referred to as reactionary. In view of this, we must first make it clear what is meant by such terms as "reactionary," "counterrevolutionary" and "revolutionary."

As a result of the influence of all those years of cultural autocracy, and the obscurantist policy of keeping the people in a state of blind ignorance in the "Gang of Four" era, there are even now people whose outlook is that if one does things exactly in accordance with the will of the leadership currently in power, this is what is meant by being "revolutionary" whereas to run counter to the will of those currently in power is counterrevolutionary. I cannot agree with such a vulgar debasement of the concept of revolution. The term "revolutionary" entails following a course of action whereby one moves with the current of historical development, and strives to remove all that is old and conservative blocking and impeding the onward flow of history. Revolution is the struggle of new phenomena against old phenomena. To attach the label of perpetual revolution to the will and ambition of those currently in power is tantamount to stifling all diversity of thought; "Power is Truth." Such a vulgarization of the concept of revolution served as one of the most effective tools with which the "Gang of Four" suppressed anything remotely revolution-

ary and crushed the people into the ground for more than twenty years.

Now allow me to turn to the term "counterrevolutionary," and its valid and proper frame of reference. Strictly speaking, the term implies a historical approach to the examination of the political concept to be applied to a given problem. In the realm of politics there is no immutable concept, and at different historical periods, because the revolutionary trends or currents are different, each conception of the word counterrevolutionary differs, as indeed do the phenomena to which the term is applied. If one particular conception of the term (valid for one particular period) is made the norm, the result can only be the arbitrary attaching of labels to the wrong people. Even in times of revolution itself, because of the limits of the levels of understanding among the populace, there arise a number of conflicting interpretations of this one word counterrevolutionary. To use this term as an immutable political concept for assessing the guilt of those charged with crimes is like using the willow catkins floating in the breeze as a device for assessing altitude. This is the reason behind the great number of injustices, wrongs, and misjudged cases which have arisen in this country over the past 30 years. It is also one of the reasons why the "Gang of Four" were able to gain power in the very teeth of popular resentment. The inevitable result of making the current political concept the legal norm or standard is an open invitation to be taken in and deceived by such terms as counterrevolutionary.

Next we come to the connection between my articles and the present revolutionary trend. The present historical trend or current is a democratic one. At this stage in the development of Chinese society, her population is confronted with the following problem: Unless there is a reform of the social system, accompanied by the eradication of the social origins of the dictatorial fascist autocracy, together with a thorough implementation of democracy and a guarantee of the people's democratic rights, then Chinese society will be unable to advance and the socialist modernization of the country be incapable of achievement. Thus, the democratic trend is this age's revolutionary current, while those autocratic conservatives who stand in opposition to the democratic trend are the real counterrevolutionaries of the age.

The central argument of those articles of mine, such as "Democracy: The Fifth Modernization," is that without democracy there will be no Four Modernizations; without the *fifth* modernization, or democracy, any talk of modernization will remain an empty lie. How does such an argument constitute counterrevolution? Surely it is those very people who oppose democracy who should be included in the counterrevolutionary category? Naturally I do not claim that the grounds of my argument and its thesis are always perfectly correct. They too must await the ultimate test of historical practice. They too must undergo all manner of criticism from every quarter, for only then can they be made more accurate. But even if the grounds of my argument and the underlying thesis are not completely accurate, this in no way impairs the revolutionary nature of my topic, which is clear in its argument.

THE THIRD CHARGE. The indictment states I slandered Marxism-Leninism and Mao Zedong Thought by likening it to an even more brilliant piece of quackery than any of the old itinerant pox-doctors' panaceas and poultices. My understanding of the term slander is that it refers to a person being groundlessly charged with a crime he has not committed. The manufacture of poultices and panaceas is no crime. By quoting me out of context and giving a garbled version of what I said, the prosecutor can hardly be said to have made out a case for slander.

The Marxism I attacked in my essays is in no way the Marxism of more than a hundred or so years ago, but rather the form of Marxism favored by that school of political con men such as Lin Biao and the "Gang of Four." I recognize nothing in this world as constantly immutable, nor any theory as absolutely correct. All ideological theory is relative, for within its existing context it contains elements of relative truth and,

conversely, elements of relative absurdity. At one given time and in one given situation it may be a relatively accurate theory, whereas at another given time and situation it can be relatively preposterous. In the face of certain data it may be a correct theory, while in the face of different data it may appear absurd. Certain theories in themselves share at one and the same time the possibility of being correct and the possibility of being absurd. Marxism is in no way an exception. Marxism, over a hundred years of development, has been successively transformed into a number of divergent schools—Kautskyism, Leninism, Trotskyism, Stalinism, Mao Zedong Thought, Eurocommunism, etc. While these different theories all abide by the basic tenets of Marxism, or do so in part, they have also carried out partial modifications and revisions of Marxism as a system. Thus, though they are called Marxist, none of them is the original Marxist system. To a considerable extent the theoretical core of original Marxism is in part centered around a description of a proper society, an idealistic state which is by no means unique in its conception to Marxism alone. For such a society was a widespread aspiration, shared by the working classes and intellectuals alike in their hope for liberty and equality, public ownership of property, and social justice. The method Marxism advocated for the achievement of this ideal society was the fusing of common democracy with a dictatorship in which power had been centralized. It is this fusion which is the most striking characteristic of the Marxist tenets.

Following a hundred years of actual practice, those governments which have emerged from this method of dictatorship, where power has been concentrated—such as those of the Soviet Union, Vietnam, and China before smashing of the "Gang of Four"—have without exception deteriorated into fascist regimes, where a small leading faction imposes its autocracy over the large mass of ordinary laboring people. Moreover, the fascist dictators, in whose grasp the government has come to rest, have long since ceased to use the dictatorship of the proletariat as a tool of implementing the old ideals of Communism itself. Precisely the opposite is the case. For without exception these rulers have used the ideals of Communism to reinforce the so-called dictatorship of the proletariat so that it may function as a tool for the benefit of those in power.

Thus, Marxism's fate is common to that of several religions. After the second or third generation of transmission, its revolutionary substance is quietly removed, while its doctrinal ideals are partially taken over by the rulers, to be used as an excuse to enslave the people and as a tool to deceive and fool them. By this stage, the nature of its teachings has also undergone a basic change, in that the ideals become, respectively, the excuse and tool of enslavement and deception. Thus, the nature of the teachings has been fundamentally changed. I call the practice of using ideals to mislead and enslave people "idealism." (Others think of it as a matter of faith.) The feudal fascist dictatorship of the "Gang of Four" represented the culmination of such a development. When these forms of fascism make use of fine and glorious ideals to set up a blind faith in some modern superstition, so that the people may be the easier cheated and deceived, is this not a modern form of charlatanism? Is it not an even more brilliant panacea or poultice than those of the old nostrum-mongering pox-doctors?

Here I should point out that it was by basing my studies on the course of the historical development of Marxism that I reached these conclusions, and that any possible inaccuracies can be resolved by further theoretical inquiry. Though I welcome anyone's criticism of these conclusions of mine, regardless of their accuracy, according to the principle of the freedoms of discussion and publication, it does not constitute a crime to promote tentative theoretical inquiry and exchange such ideological conclusions with others. We should always adopt a critical approach to past ideological theory that still survives in actuality in the present age, and since this is the Marxist approach to pursuing studies, why can't we treat Marxism critically as well? Those who forbid the critical treatment of Marx-

ism are engaged in the very process of transforming Marxism into a religious faith. Any man has the right to believe and adhere to the theories he holds to be correct, but he should not use legally binding stipulations to impose on others the theories he has faith in, otherwise he is interfering with the liberties of his fellow men.

THE FOURTH CHARGE. The indictment claims that, by flaunting the banner of so-called free speech for democracy and human rights, I incited the overthrow of the socialist system and the political power of the dictatorship of the proletariat. First of all, allow me to point out there is nothing whatsoever "so-called" about free speech. On the contrary, it is stipulated by the constitution as a right to be enjoyed by all citizens. The Public Prosecutor's choice of such a term in discussing rights granted citizens by the constitution not only shows his prejudice when thinking on such matters, but further illustrates that he has forgotten his responsibility to protect the rights of his fellow citizens. He makes the rights of the citizens in this country of ours the object of ridicule.

I feel there is no need for me to refute item by item the public prosecutor's method of quoting me out of context when he is listing the charges against me. I would merely like to point out his carelessness and his negligence. In the indictment there appear the following words: "a system of feudal monarchism in the guise of socialism." Was not the "Gang of Four's" fascist dictatorship simply feudal monarchism in the guise of socialism? Again there appears this expression of mine, "nor serve as tools for the modernization of the ambitious aggrandizement by the dictatorship," which was followed in my original by, "we want the modernization of the people's lives." Don't tell me the prosecutor wants the modernization of ambitious aggrandizement by the dictatorship but does not want a real modernization of the people's lives? I don't think the prosecutor can be like that. I am also unwilling to believe that the prosecutor will forbid criticism of the "Gang of Four's" feudal fascism. Yet why then did I quote in evidence those illustrations? I do not desire to make improper comments. I merely know that those remarks of the prosecutor are in no way able to illustrate that I wanted to overthrow the government and the socialist system, nor are they able to illustrate that I was harming the democratic cause.

In the cause of the publication of our magazine *Exploration*, we never once joined up with any conspiratorial organization, nor did we ever take part in the activities of any violent organization. *Exploration* was on sale to the public as a publication designed to explore and probe theoretical problems; never did it make the overthrow of political power its aim, nor could it ever have been engaged in activities aimed at overthrow of the government. It saw itself as a part of the democratic cause, nor could it ever have harmed that cause. When people ask us if we were ever prepared to participate in armed struggle, or carry out actions aimed at the overthrow of the government, I have already supplied them a precise answer to such a question. I recognize legitimate propaganda and the democratic movement as the indispensable means to foster democratic government. Only when it has been understood by the majority will democratic government gradually come into being, through the reform of the old political system. This viewpoint was one of the basic aims of our publication. Yang Guang, Lu Lin, Zhao Nan, and Liu Qing can all bear witness to this fact. They have all heard what I have to say on this subject.

The public prosecutor's accusation that I wanted to overthrow the socialist system is even more at odds with the facts. The prosecutor claims to have examined my essays, so he should have noticed that section within the article, "Democracy: The Fifth Modernization," called "Socialism and Democracy," which deals with my attitude toward socialism. On the many occasions that the prosecutor had talks with me, I also mentioned this same question, so he cannot say he does not know. Of course in the eyes of the prosecutor, his interpretation of a socialist system may possibly differ enormously from my conception of that system. I recognize that in reality the socialist system may take many different forms and not be one stereotype. In the light of their most obvious distinction, I would classify socialist systems into two large categories. The first is the Soviet-style of dictatorial socialism, with its chief characteristic of having its power concentrated in the hands of the minority in authority. The second category is democratic socialism, with the power reinvested in the whole people organized on a democratic footing. The majority of people in our nation all wish for the implementation of this kind of socialism. The aim of our exploratory inquiry was to seek the way to attain such a socialist system. My taking part in the democratic movement was with the aim of implementing this form of democratic socialism.

I consider that without carrying out a reform of the social system, without a true establishment of popular democratic power, and if there is no democratic system of government to act as a guarantee, then our nation's economic modernization cannot be attained. A democratic system of government is the prerequisite for our country's total modernization. This was the idea behind the title of my article "Democracy: The Fifth Modernization"; it was the central idea expounded in the same essay. Perhaps the members of the Office of the Procuratorate do not agree with my theory, but their disagreement with my theories does not brand me as someone wanting to overthrow the socialist system.

THE FIFTH CHARGE. There is no need for me to refute item by item in the list of charges in the indictment those places where the prosecution quotes me out of context. I would only point out two things. First, the constitution grants citizens the right to criticize their leaders, because these leaders are not gods. It is only through the people's criticism and supervision that those leaders will make fewer mistakes, and only in this way that the people will avoid the misfortune of having their lords and masters ride roughshod over them. Then, and only then, will the people be able to breathe freely. Secondly, if we wish to carry out the reform of our nation's socialist system we must base this on the entire population using the methods of criticism and discussion to find out the defects in the present system; otherwise reforms cannot be successfully carried out.

It is the people's prerogative, when faced by unreasonable people and unacceptable matters, to make criticisms. Indeed, it is also their unshirkable duty so to do and this is a sovereign right with which no individual or government organization has a right to interfere.

Criticism may not be beautiful or pleasant to hear, nor can it always be completely accurate. If one insists on criticism being pleasant to hear, and demands its absolute accuracy on pain of punishment, this is as good as forbidding criticism and banning reforms. In such a situation one might just as well deify the leadership outright. Surely we are not expected to retread that old path of blind faith in the leadership advocated by the "Gang of Four"? Naturally criticism should have substantial factual basis, nor should we tolerate personal attacks and malicious slandering. This taboo was one of the principles adhered to by our publication, as our introductory opening statement to our readers demonstrates. If the prosecution feels that in this respect I did not do enough, I am willing to accept the criticism put forward by the prosecution or anyone else.

That concludes my defense address. . . .

[After Wei's speech, the public prosecutor delivered a refutation. The court recessed, then the judge spoke.]

VERDICT AND SENTENCE

JUDGE: Wei Jingsheng betrayed his fatherland by supplying a foreigner with state military information. He violated the constitution by his writing of reactionary articles and, by his furtherance of counterrevolutionary propaganda and agitation, he endangered the basic national and popular interests. All of this constitutes a serious counterrevolutionary crime of a most heinous nature.

In order to safeguard the socialist system and consolidate the dictatorship of the proletariat, to guarantee the smooth progress of the buildup of our socialist modernization, and to suppress destructive counterrevolutionary activity in accordance with the stipulations of Article 2, Article 6 paragraph 1, Article 10 paragraphs 2 and 3 and Articles 16 and 17 of the Act of the People's Republic of China for the Punishment of Counterrevolution, we sentence Wei Jingsheng to fifteen years of imprisonment, with the deprivation of all political rights for a period of three years on completion of his prison sentence.

The prisoner may appeal to the Higher People's Court of Peking within ten days of the second day of receiving this sentence.

BEI DAO
THE ANSWER and DECLARATION

Bei Dao is the pen name of Zhao Zhenkai (1949–   ), one of China's best-known poets. Born in Beijing in 1949, he grew up under Communism and joined the Red Guards during the Cultural Revolution. Disillusioned, he turned to poetry, where he sought individual freedom and honesty. Bei Dao took part in demonstrations in Tiananmen Square on April 5, 1976 to mourn the death of premier Chou Enlai and to protest the dictatorship of the Gang of Four; several of his poems were read to the demonstrators, including "The Answer," which became well-known. The demonstration ended violently, and the date "April Fifth," became important in the history of the democracy movement. Bei Dao was one of the editors of *Jintian* (*Today*), one of the score or more underground publications that appeared in 1978. The magazine was banned in 1979, and more than 20 writers and editors were jailed for counterrevolutionary activities, including Wei Jingsheng, editor of

Exploration, and Xu Wenli, editor of *April Fifth Forum*, who were given 15-year sentences. Although his magazine was closed, Bei Dao was not arrested. During the years of liberalization, some of his poems appeared in official publications. The following poems appeared in his collection, *The August Sleepwalker*, translated by Bonnie McDougall.

The Answer

Debasement is the password of the base,
Nobility the epitaph of the noble,
See how the gilded sky is covered
With the drifting twisted shadows of the dead.

The Ice Age is over now.
Why is there ice everywhere?
The Cape of Good Hope has been discovered.
Why do a thousand sails contest the Dead Sea?

I came into this world
Bringing only paper, rope, a shadow,
To proclaim before the judgment
The voice that has been judged:

Let me tell you, world.
I—do—not—believe!
If a thousand challengers lie beneath your feet,
Count me as number one thousand and one.

I don't believe the sky is blue;
I don't believe in thunder's echoes;
I don't believe that dreams are false;
I don't believe that death has no revenge.

If the sea is destined to breach the dikes
Let all the brackish water pour into my heart;
If the land is destined to rise
Let humanity choose a peak for existence again.

A new conjunction and glimmering stars
Adorn the unobstructed sky now:
They are the pictographs from five thousand
        years,
They are the watchful eyes of future
        generations.

Declaration

Perhaps the final hour is come
I have left no testament
Only a pen, for my mother
I am no hero
in an age without heroes
I just want to be a man

The still horizon

Divides the ranks of the living and the dead
I can only choose the sky
I will not kneel on the ground
Allowing the executioners to look tall
The better to obstruct the wind of freedom

From star-like bullet holes shall flow
A blood-red dawn

FANG LIZHE

APPEAL TO DENG XIAOPING

On January 6, 1989 Fang Lizhe (1936–   ) sent an open letter to China's leader, Deng Xiaoping, urging the release of Wei Jingsheng and other political prisoners. This was a gesture of extraordinary courage, for it was the first time in the history of Communist China that a dissident had directly and openly challenged the leader of the state. Fang, however, was no ordinary dissident. He began to criticize Maoism in the 1950s. He was ousted from the Communist party in 1957, 1966, and 1987. An astrophysicist with an international reputation for his work in cosmology, Fang was appointed Vice-Chancellor of Keda, the University of Science and Technology of Hefei in Anhui Province in 1985. Following student protests on behalf of democracy and human rights in December 1986, Fang was accused of encouraging the students; he was dismissed from his job and expelled from the Chinese Communist party. He quickly became known as the nation's leading political dissident and was even called the "Chinese Sakharov."

Fang's appeal soon galvanized others to speak out on behalf of amnesty for political prisoners. Within weeks leading Chinese scholars, artists, and writers signed three other open letters to the government. Never before had Chinese intellectuals been so bold in presenting their demands to the head of state.

Fang's appeal to President Deng follows.

Dear President Deng,

This year marks the fortieth anniversary of the founding of the People's Republic and the seventieth anniversary of the May the Fourth Movement. People today are more concerned than ever before about the present and the future, and are looking forward to these two anniversaries as occasions for [renewed] hope. Therefore, I wish to suggest to you with all frankness that you mark this occasion with an announcement of a general amnesty in China, and in particular, the release of Wei Jingsheng and all

other political prisoners. However one may judge Wei Jingsheng, he has already served ten years of detention and his release, in my view, would be a humanitarian gesture beneficial to social morality. This year also marks the bicentenary of the French Revolution, a symbol of Liberty, Equality and Fraternity which, whatever one's overall view of it, has bequeathed to humanity an enduring respect for the rights of man. It is in this spirit that I beg you to consider my request in order to give a new value at the dawn of our future.

 ## THE MAY 19 PETITION

In December 1986, Chinese students demonstrated for democracy at the Chinese University of Science and Technology in Hefei, where Fang Lizhe was vice-chancellor. The demonstrations were a response to the government's arbitrary decision to void the students' election of representatives to the Peoples' Congress. College students from more than a dozen cities joined the protest.

The Communist party's response to the student demonstrations was to oust Hu Yaobang, the general secretary of the party, who was suspected of sympathizing with the students, and to fire a few intellectuals, including Fang, who were charged with supporting "bourgeois liberalization."

The student democracy movement was quiet for a time, then flared again when Hu Yaobang suddenly died on April 15, 1989. The next day, thousands of students congregated in Tiananmen Square to mourn his death. Their spontaneous gesture quickly turned into a mass demonstration for democracy and freedom. By April 18, there were over 100,000 students massed on the square demanding democracy, an end to corruption, and freedom of the press. On April 27, more than 1,000,000 citizens marched in the streets to support the democracy movement. On May 13, more than 2,000 students joined in a fast to pressure the government on behalf of their demands; the fasters wore white headbands with "Fasting" or "Give me freedom or give me death" written on them. Teachers, journalists, and workers marched in support of the students.

On May 19, the following petition was signed by Yan Jiaqi, a prominent political scientist; Su Xiaokang, a well-known writer and film producer; and Wang Juntao, a noted journalist.

We, as intellectuals, in the name of our personal integrity and all our moral rectitude, with our body and mind, with all our dignity as individuals, solemnly swear never to retreat in the quest for democracy pioneered by the students with their blood and lives, never under any pretext to disengage ourselves because of cowardice, never to allow again the humiliations of the past, never to sell out our moral integrity, never to submit ourselves to dictatorship, never to pledge allegiance to the last emperors of the China of the '80s.

At the height of the 1989 democracy protests, thousands of students gathered in Tiananmen Square—the traditional gathering place for mass Communist party demonstrations—with banners that read "Long Live Freedom, Long Live Democracy."

★ POEMS FROM TIANANMEN SQUARE

The following poems were written by anonymous demonstrators for democracy in Tiananmen Square in Beijing during the spring of 1989.

We have awakened the people
We have seeded democracy
We will win
Our next generation
Will continue
It doesn't matter
If we don't succeed

Even if the din
   reaches the clouds
Can it match the sound
   of the golden bell?
Even if your loudspeaker
   reaches the end of the world
Can the lies become the truth?

★ STATEMENT OF THE FEDERATION FOR A DEMOCRATIC CHINA

After the brutal repression of the Chinese democracy movement in June 1989, the Chinese government arrested thousands of people who had participated in the protest in Tiananmen Square. Some were executed, others given long prison sentences. An unknown number of Chinese dissidents managed to flee the country. In September 1989, more than 150 delegates from Chinese communities around the world met in Paris, where they established the Federation for a Democratic China (FDC). The FDC elected as its chairman Yan Jiaqi, formerly director of Beijing's Institute of Political Science and an adviser to Zhao Ziyang, the deposed general secretary of the Chinese Communist party; the student leader, Wuer Kaixi, was chosen as vice chairman of the organization.

The FDC issued a statement, which is excerpted here.

. . . The Chinese people have reached the limits of their patience with the dictatorship of the Communist Party. History shows that the defects inherent in a system of one-party dictatorship can only be overcome by the disappearance of this system. The single party will never yield its position without a democratic awakening of all social groups, the appearance of an independent political force, and an unswerving and ever-growing democratic movement. The FDC has been established to accomplish these historic tasks.

The June 4 massacre has raised the consciousness of Chinese people all over the world, and has brought about the unification of Chinese democratic forces. The FDC is an independent political organization of Chinese people throughout the globe dedicated to the advance of democracy in China. Its principal objectives are to safeguard basic human rights, to uphold social justice, to develop a private enterprise economy, and to end one-party dictatorship.

The FDC upholds the following propositions:

Men are born with certain fundamental and inalienable rights: the rights to life and development, to the pursuit of happiness, and to human dignity and security. These rights are the basis of a civilized, modern society and the *sine qua non* of democratic politics.

All members of society are equal and are entitled to equal opportunity, regardless of sex, race, profession, and family origin. Healthy and stable social development is impossible without the elimination of privileges and the maintenance of justice.

Every citizen has the right to own and dispose of the tools and fruits of his labor. The deprivation of individual property rights in the name of the state is an important cause of the economic stagnation and political tyranny found in countries ruled by a communist party. Returning social wealth to the people and developing private enterprise are the sole path to solving China's economic problems and to achieving its modernization.

To end dictatorship and institute democracy, it is necessary to safeguard the citizen's basic rights—freedom of religion, speech, press, as-

sembly, and association. The armed forces must be controlled only by the state. The judiciary must be independent. Schooling should be freed from ideological control by the government so that academic and educational autonomy is assured. . . .

Adhering to the principles of peace, rationality, and nonviolence, the FDC strongly denounces the terrorist practices employed by the totalitarian regime against the people. . . .

The FDC is convinced that the days of China's dictatorship are numbered. The creation of a democratic China and the reawakening of the Chinese nation are near. . . .

The 21st century will be the century of democracy in China.

Long live a free and democratic China!

On June 4, 1989, when the Chinese army recaptured Tiananmen Square from the democracy demonstrators, this photograph of a lone dissident captured the imagination of the world. The young man stood in front of a line of tanks, bringing them briefly to a halt, until friends pulled him away.

FANG LIZHE

HUMAN RIGHTS IN CHINA

In 1989 Fang Lizhe was the recipient of the Robert F. Kennedy Human Rights Award. During the Chinese democratic uprising in May and June 1989, Fang was an inspiration to the students but he never joined their demonstrations. He knew that if he were present in Tiananmen Square, the government would accuse him of masterminding the protests and would deny that the students' protest was authentic. When the government crushed the democratic movement on June 4, 1989, Fang Lizhe and his wife took refuge in the American Embassy in Beijing. That winter Fang was informed that he had received the Kennedy Award for his devotion to the cause of human rights. Of course, he was unable to leave the country to receive the award. His acceptance speech is reprinted here.

A year later, Fang Lizhe and his wife were permitted to leave China. They went into exile in the United States, where both were able to pursue their careers as scientists.

I am very proud, and deeply moved, to have this opportunity to speak with you today; at the same time, I am filled with a sense of sorrow and shame. I am moved because you have chosen to honor me with the 1989 Robert F. Kennedy Human Rights Award. It attests to the fact that I have not been, and am not now, alone. The source of my sorrow is that in this land of my birth, human dignity has once again been trampled upon. Having had my own basic rights stripped away, I am more acutely aware than ever that we are still far from accomplishing what we must in the cause of advancing respect for all human beings.

The values underlying human dignity are common to all peoples. They are comprised of universally applicable standards of human rights that hold no regard for race, language, religion, or other belief. These universal standards, symbolized by the United Nations Declaration of Human Rights, have increasingly earned the acceptance and respect of the world at large. When a commemorative gathering was held last November in Beijing to honor the fortieth anniversary of the Declaration, many of us were delighted, because it seemed to us at the time that the principles of human rights were finally starting to take root in our ancient land.

However, time after time these fond dreams have been shattered by harsh reality. In the face of the bloody tragedy of last June, we must admit to having been far too optimistic. Some of those who were responsible for this repression have recently attempted to defend their behavior by declaring that "China has its own standards of human rights." They have completely rejected the world's condemnation by refusing to admit the universal nature of human rights. They appear to think that as long as they can dub something a "household affair," to be dealt with internally, that they can ignore the laws of human decency and do whatever they please. But this is the worst kind of feudalistic logic. During China's long period of isolation from the rest of the world, this ideology of purporting to be "master of all under heaven" may have been an effective means of controlling the country. But in the latter part of the 20th century, declarations about "household affairs" only serve to expose those who make them as feudal dictators. Such statements have lost their capacity either to intimidate or deceive.

Nowadays, a growing number of Chinese believe that for China to catch up with the modern world, we must change our own society by absorbing those aspects of more modern civilization that have proven progressive and universal, especially science and democracy. From the movement for science and democracy of 1919 to the rising tide of demand for intellectual freedom of 1957, and from the protest marches of 1926 that were met with swords and guns to the demonstrations of 1989 that were confronted with tanks, we can see how passionately the Chinese people want a just, rational, and prosperous society. Although China has some very deep-seated problems that cause it to lag behind the developed countries, our history clearly shows that the Chinese people have sought the same kind of progress and development as people everywhere, no matter their race or nationality. When it comes to such common aspirations, Chinese people are no different from any other. Like all members of the human race, the Chinese are born with a body and a brain, with passions and with a soul. Therefore they can and must enjoy the same inalienable rights, dignity, and liberty as other human beings.

Allow me to draw an historical analogy. Recent propaganda to the effect that "China has its own standards for human rights" bears an uncanny similarity to pronouncements made by our 18th century rulers when they declared that "China has its own astronomy." The feudal aristocracy of 200 years ago opposed the notion of an astronomy based on science. They refused to acknowledge the universal applicability of modern astronomy, or even that it might be of some use in formulating the Chinese calendar. The reason they opposed modern astronomy was that the laws of astronomy, which pertain everywhere, made it quite clear that the "divine right to rule" claimed by these people was a fiction. By the same token, the principles of human rights which also pertain everywhere, make it clear that the "right to rule" claimed by some today is just as baseless. This is why rulers from every era, with their special privileges, have opposed the equality inherent in such universal ideas.

The advance of civilization has largely followed from the discovery and development of universally applicable concepts and laws; those who rejected the idea that science applied everywhere were in fact demonstrating their fear of modern civilization. The feudal aristocrats of two centuries past saw astronomy as a bearer of modern culture, and as a result ruthlessly persecuted those engaged in its study and practice. Indeed, in one instance of repression during the early Qing dynasty, five astronomers of the Beijing Observatory were put to death. Far from demonstrating the might of the perpetrators, such brutality only demonstrated their fear. Equally terrified by the implications of universal human rights, modern-day dictators also resort to murder. But no more than in the case of their predecessors should this be construed as an indication of their strength.

Some people say that the terror that has filled Beijing since June can't help but make one feel pessimistic. And, I must admit to such feelings of pessimism myself. But I would also like to offer a small bit of encouragement. Remember that in the current climate of terror, it may well be that those who are most terrified are those who have just finished killing their fellow human beings. We may be forced to live under a terror today, but we have no fear of tomorrow. The murderers, on the other hand, are not only fearful today, they are even more terrified of tomorrow. Thus, we have no reason to lose faith. Ignorance may dominate in the short term through the use of violence, but it will eventually be unable to resist the advance of universal laws. And this will come to pass just as surely as the earth turns.

Of course, it takes time for the earth to turn, and for China things could take even longer. With this in mind, I would like to say a few things to the young Chinese in the audience. I know that many of you have dedicated your lives to building our country anew. Since the road to rebirth will be a long one, I fervently hope that you will not discontinue your education, but instead will work even harder to deepen and enrich your knowledge. We are all disciples of non-violence. What power can non-violence summon as a means of resisting the armed violence of guns the world over? There are many strategies of non-violence, but what is most basic is the force of knowledge. Without knowledge, non-violence can deteriorate into begging, and history is unmoved by begging. It is only when we stand on the shoulders of the giant of knowledge that we will truly be able to change the course of history. Only with knowledge will we be able to overcome the violence of ignorance at its very roots. Only with knowledge will we have the compassion necessary to deliver from their folly those with superstitious faith in the omnipotence of violence. As Ibsen said, "if you want to be of value to society, there is no better way than to forge yourself into a vessel for its use." I hope that all of us will strive to forge ourselves into such vessels.

Many friends have expressed great concern about my current situation, and from the bottom of our hearts my wife and I want to take this opportunity to thank both those we already know and those we have not yet met. Because of the extraordinary circumstances under which we now live, I am unable to tell you any of the details of our lives. But there is perhaps one bit of news that may somewhat lighten your hearts. I am doing my best to exercise to their fullest extent two of my remaining rights, namely the right to think and the right to inquire. I am continuing my research in astrophysics, and since June of this year I have already written two research papers and am now in the midst of a third.

In the field of modern cosmology, the first principle is called "the Cosmological Principle." It says that the universe has no center, that it has the same properties throughout. Every place in the universe has, in this sense, equal rights. How can the human race, which has evolved in a universe of such fundamental equality, fail to strive for a society without violence and terror? How can we fail to build a world in which the rights due to every human being from birth are respected?

May the blessings of the universe be upon us all.

NYEIN CHAN

THE DREAM OF A PEOPLE and I AM A CHILD OF BURMA

Burma gained its independence from Great Britain in 1948. Its parliamentary system was overthrown in 1962 by a military coup led by Ne Win, who proclaimed Burma a socialist state and assumed dictatorial powers. After promising to establish "the Burmese Way to Socialism," Ne Win turned Burma into one of the most repressive dictatorships in the world. He encouraged hatred of foreigners, particularly Chinese and Indians, whose properties were expropriated. Although rich in natural resources, Burma soon became one of the poorest nations in Asia.

In 1988 massive anti-government demonstrations took place throughout the country. Hundreds of thousands of Burmese joined a general strike. More than 1,000,000 people went to the streets to demand democracy and an end to one-party rule. On September 19, 1988 the military attacked the demonstrators, and at least 3,000 unarmed people, mainly students, were killed.

After the bloody repression of the Burmese democracy movement, thousands of students and working people fled to camps along the Burmese-Thailand border where they sought refuge. The military regime renamed the country Myanmar and excluded the international press from its territory. Far from the gaze of the world media, the student rebels languished in their jungle camps, all but forgotten in their lonely crusade for democracy.

In 1990 the military regime allowed a multi-party election. It was widely expected that the election would be a farce, because the opposition was harassed. Publications critical of the government were banned; meetings of more than five people were prohibited without a permit. Opposition figures were placed under house arrest. Nonetheless, the people turned out to vote and anti-government candidates won by an overwhelming landslide. However, long after the election, the military government showed no signs of relinquishing power.

Nyein Chan is the pseudonym of a Burmese poet who edited a collection entitled *Voices from the Jungle: Burmese Youth in Transition*, which was published in Japan in 1989.

The Dream of a People

You who demand power!

Do you not know
that
even your greatest demonstrations of authority
can not take away
the dream of the people?

To suddenly lose a dream

just within grasp,
does not destroy
the will of the people,
but drives it deeper into the soul
and even deeper underground.

It will continue to surface
until it becomes a reality.

I Am a Child of Burma

If anyone asks you who I am
Just tell them, "I am a child of Burma."

My sweat mingles with its soil and waters.
With the peasants, I have tilled the earth
planted, nurtured and harvested the rice
and carried the produce to every village
so my brothers and sisters will be nourished.
I have fished its waters and hunted its forests
and I know every inch of its rich resources.
The dusty paths which crisscross my
            motherland
have been marked by my footprints
and its mountains, valleys and rivers
have heard my voice.

If anyone asks you who I am,
just tell them, "I am a child of Burma."

My tears have flowed for those who suffer
My arms have held the children
whose hungry bodies cry for their mother's
            breast.
With the peasants I have watched in grief

as the rice withered in the hot sun
and the officials took the meager crop for tax.
I have cried for my brothers and sisters,
locked away in prisons, with no voice of
            defence,
and death their only liberation.
We have labored hard and long to build life
and yet, each day, the hope of our hearts has
            faded into
poverty.

If any one asks you who I am,
just tell them, "I am a child of Burma."

My blood now returns to its rivers and soil
and flows with that of many other heroes of
            days past.
No longer can I sit silently and enjoy the sweet
            breezes
nor laugh with friends as though life were free
            and good.
The sweat and tears of days past
require that my blood also be offered.

For one day, the wrong must be righted,
the poor empowered and the imprisoned set
    free.
I have given my sweat and my tears,

now take my blood as well, so life can grow,
for I am a child of Burma,
yes,
I am a child of Burma.

NGUYEN CHI THIEN
APE AND MAN

According to Vietnamese emigre groups, as many as 500,000 people were confined to prisons and reeducation camps after the takeover of Vietnam by the Communists in 1975. Tens of thousands had been imprisoned in the Communist north long before then. One of them was Nguyen Chi Thien (1933–   ), a writer who was first arrested in North Vietnam in 1959 for his role in creating a literary review called *Vi Dan* (*For the People*). The young writer, a member of the Vietnamese Hundred Flowers movement, was imprisoned until 1978. In the months after his release, he wrote down 377 poems that he had composed and memorized while in prison. He traveled to Hanoi, where he managed to throw the book of poems through the gates of a Western embassy before the police seized him.

A letter from the poet was attached to the book of poems. It began: "Sir: In the name of the millions of innocent victims of dictatorship, of those who have already fallen and of those who are still dying a slow and painful death in Communist prisons, I beg you to publish these poems in your free country . . ." The poems were published in France under the title *Flowers of Hell*. Twenty of them were set to music by Vietnamese composer Pham Duy. The fate of Nguyen Chi Thien is unknown. As he predicted, "All perishes/Only poetry remains."

From ape to man, the process took
    millions of years
from man to ape, will it take so
    many?
People of the world, come and visit
    concentration camps in the heart
    of distant jungles!
Naked prisoners, bathing together
    in herds
living in stinking darkness with lice
    and mosquitoes,
fighting each other for one piece
of manioc root or sweet potato,
chained, shot, dragged, beaten

torn up at the will of their
    captors,
thrown away for the rats to
    gnaw.
These apes are not swift,
they are slow in their movements
unlike the apes that descend from
    ancient times.
These apes are hungry and thin as
    toothpicks,
Yet they produce the nation's wealth
    all year long
People of the world, please come and
    visit.

SALMAN RUSHDIE

IN GOOD FAITH

It caused an international sensation in the spring of 1989 when the leader of Iran, the Ayatollah Ruhollah Khomeini, called on Muslims to kill Salman Rushdie (1947–   ) because his novel, *The Satanic Verses*, insulted the Islamic faith. The novel was banned in most of the Arab world, as well as in India, Pakistan, France, and West Germany. Many American booksellers removed the book from their shelves for fear of reprisals. In fact, several bookstores in the United States and elsewhere that did sell the book were targets of terrorist bombings, and the book was publicly burned by angry mobs in various countries.

Born in Bombay to a well-to-do Muslim family, Salman Rushdie was educated at British boarding schools and at Cambridge University. After graduating from Cambridge in 1968, he went to Karachi, Pakistan, where his family had moved. His various literary efforts, including a play he produced and an article he wrote, were censored, and he soon returned to live and write in London. After the publication of his novels *Midnight's Children* and *Shame*, he was recognized as a major literary figure. *The Satanic Verses* dealt directly with issues of cultural exile and personal identity in a world where people like Rushdie have multiple and plural cultural identities.

After the threat to his life, Rushdie went into hiding. A year after he disappeared from public view, he published a reflection on his personal ordeal, which he called "In Good Faith." Excerpts from this essay follow.

It has been a year since I last spoke in defence of my novel *The Satanic Verses*. I have remained silent, though silence is against my nature, because I felt that my voice was simply not loud enough to be heard above the clamour of the voices raised against me.

I hoped that others would speak for me, and many have done so eloquently, among them an admittedly small but growing number of Muslim readers, writers and scholars. Others, including bigots and racists, have tried to exploit my case (using my name to taunt Muslim and non-Muslim Asian children and adults, for example) in a manner I have found repulsive, defiling and humiliating.

At the centre of the storm stands a novel, a work of fiction, one that aspires to the condition of literature. It has often seemed to me that people on all sides of the argument have lost sight of this simple fact. *The Satanic Verses* has been described, and treated, as a work of bad history, as an anti-religious pamphlet, as the product of an

international capitalist-Jewish conspiracy, as an act of murder ("he has murdered our hearts"), as the product of a person comparable to Hitler and Attila the Hun. It felt impossible, amid such a hubbub, to insist on the fictionality of fiction.

Let me be clear: I am not trying to say that *The Satanic Verses* is "only a novel" and thus need not be taken seriously, even disputed with the utmost passion. I do not believe that novels are trivial matters. The ones I care most about are those which attempt radical reformulations of language, form, and ideas, those that attempt to do what the word *novel* seems to insist upon: to see the world anew. I am well aware that this can be a hackle-raising, infuriating attempt.

What I have wished to say, however, is that the point of view from which I have, all my life, attempted this process of literary renewal is the result not of the self-hating, deracinated uncle-Tomism of which some have accused me, but precisely of my determination to create a literary language and literary forms in which the experience of formerly colonized, still-disadvantaged peoples might find full expression. If *The Satanic Verses* is anything, it is a migrant's-eye view of the world. It is written from the very experience of uprooting, disjuncture and metamorphosis (slow or rapid, painful or pleasurable) that is the migrant condition, and from which, I believe, can be derived a metaphor for all humanity.

Standing at the centre of the novel is a group of characters most of whom are British Muslims, or not-particularly-religious persons of Muslim background, struggling with just the sort of great problems that have arisen to surround the book, problems of hybridization and ghettoization, of reconciling the old and the new. Those who oppose the novel most vociferously today are of the opinion that intermingling with a different culture will inevitably weaken and ruin their own. I am of the opposite opinion. *The Satanic Verses* celebrates hybridity, impurity, intermingling, the transformation that comes of new and unexpected combinations of human beings, cultures, ideas, politics, movies, songs. It rejoices in mongrelization and fears the absolutism of the Pure. Mélange, hotch-potch, a bit of this and a bit of that is *how newness enters the world*. It is the great possibility that mass migration gives the world, and I have tried to embrace it. *The Satanic Verses* is for change-by-fusion, change-by-conjoining. It is a love-song to our mongrel selves.

Throughout human history, the apostles of purity, those who have claimed to possess a total explanation, have wrought havoc among mere mixed-up human beings. Like many millions of people, I am a bastard child of history. Perhaps we all are, black and brown and white, leaking into one another, as a character of mine once said, *like flavours when you cook*.

The argument between purity and impurity, which is also the argument between Robespierre and Danton, the argument between the monk and the roaring boy, between primness and impropriety, between the stultifications of excessive respect and the scandals of impropriety, is an old one; I say, let it continue. Human beings understand themselves and shape their futures by arguing and challenging and questioning and saying the unsayable; not by bowing the knee, whether to gods or to men.

The Satanic Verses is, I profoundly hope, a work of radical dissent and questioning and reimagining. It is not, however, the book it has been made out to be, that book containing "nothing but filth and insults and abuse" that has brought people out on to streets across the world.

That book simply does not exist.

This is what I want to say to the great mass of ordinary, decent, fair-minded Muslims, of the sort I have known all my life, and who have provided much of the inspiration for my work: to be rejected and reviled by, so to speak, one's own characters is a shocking and painful experience for any writer. I recognize that many Muslims have felt shocked and pained, too. Perhaps a way forward might be found through the mutual recognition of that mutual pain. Let us attempt to believe in each other's good faith.

I am aware that this is asking a good deal. There has been too much name-calling. Muslims have been called savages and barbarians and worse. I, too, have received my share of invective. Yet I still believe—perhaps I must—that understanding remains possible, and can be achieved without the suppression of the principle of free speech.

What it requires is a moment of good will; a moment in which we may all accept that the other parties are acting, have acted, in good faith. . . .

How is freedom gained? It is taken: never given. To be free, you must first assume your right to freedom. In writing *The Satanic Verses*, I wrote from the assumption that I was, and am, a free man.

What is freedom of expression? Without the freedom to offend, it ceases to exist. Without the freedom to challenge, even to satirize all orthodoxies, including religious orthodoxies, it ceases to exist. Language and the imagination cannot be imprisoned, or art dies, and with it, a little of what makes us human. *The Satanic Verses* is, in

Censorship, east and west: The urge to purge appears to be as universal as the yearning for freedom.

part, a secular man's reckoning with the religious spirit. It is by no means always hostile to faith. "If we write in such a way as to pre-judge such belief as in some way deluded or false, then are we not guilty of élitism, of imposing our world-view on the masses?" asks one of its Indian characters. Yet the novel does contain doubts, uncertainties, even shocks that may well not be to the liking of the devout. Such methods have, however, long been a legitimate part even of Islamic literature.

What does the novel dissent from? Certainly not from people's right to faith, though I have none. It dissents most clearly from imposed orthodoxies *of all types*, from the view that the world is quite clearly This and not That. It dissents from the end of debate, of dispute, of dissent. Hindu communalist sectarianism, the kind of Sikh terrorism that blows up planes, the fatuousnesses of Christian creationism are dissented from as well as the narrower definitions of Islam. . . .

He did it on purpose is one of the strangest accusations ever levelled at a writer. Of course I did it on purpose. The question is, and it is what I have tried to answer: what is the "it" that I did?

What I did not do was conspire against Islam;

or write—after years and years of anti-racist work and writing—a text of incitement to racial hatred; or anything of the sort. My golem, my false Other, may be capable of such deeds, but I am not.

Would I have written differently if I had known what would happen? Truthfully, I don't know. Would I change any of the text now? I would not. It's too late. As Friedrich Dürrenmatt wrote in *The Physicists*: "What has once been thought cannot be unthought. . . ."

I am not the first writer to be persecuted by Islamic fundamentalism in the modern period; among the greatest names so victimized are the Iranian writer Ahmad Kasravi, stabbed to death by fanatics, and the Egyptian Nobel laureate Naguib Mahfouz, often threatened but still, happily, with us. I am not the first artist to be accused of blasphemy and apostasy; these are, in fact, probably the most common weapons with which fundamentalism has sought to shackle creativity in the modern age. . . .

As for the British Muslim "leaders," they cannot have it both ways. Sometimes they say I am entirely unimportant, and only the book matters; on other days they hold meetings at mosques across the nation and endorse the call for my killing. They say they hold to the laws of this country, but they also say that Islamic law has moral primacy for them. They say they do not wish to break British laws, but only a very few are willing openly to repudiate the threat against me. They should make their position clear: are they democratic citizens of a free society or are they not? Do they reject violence or do they not?

After a year, it is time for a little clarity.

To the Muslim community at large, in Britain and India and Pakistan and everywhere else, I would like to say: do not ask your writers to create *typical* or *representative* fictions. Such books are almost invariably dead books. The liveliness of literature lies in its exceptionality, in being the individual, idiosyncratic vision of one human being, in which, to our delight and great surprise, we may find our own image reflected. A book is a version of the world. If you do not like it, ignore it; or offer your own version in return.

And I would like to say this: life without God seems to believers to be an idiocy, pointless, beneath contempt. It does not seem so to non-believers. To accept that the world, here, is all there is; to go through it, towards and into death, without the consolations of religion seems, well, at least as courageous and rigorous to us as the espousal of faith seems to you. Secularism and its works deserve your respect, not your contempt.

A great wave of freedom has been washing over the world. Those who resist—in China, in Romania—find themselves bathed in blood. I should like to ask Muslims—that great mass of ordinary, decent, fair-minded Muslims to whom I have imagined myself to be speaking for most of this piece—to choose to ride the wave; to renounce blood; not to let Muslim leaders make Muslims seem less tolerant than they are. *The Satanic Verses* is a serious work, written from a non-believer's point of view. Let believers accept that, and let it be. . . .

NELSON MANDELA

STATEMENT AT THE RIVONIA TRIAL

Nelson Mandela (1918–   ) became a symbol of the struggle for racial equality and democracy in South Africa during the 27 years he spent in prison. He was born in Qunu, a small town in the Transkei in South Africa. His father was a leader of the Tembu tribe. He entered Fort Hare College in 1938 and was expelled two years later for participating in a student strike. Mandela studied law at the University of the Witwatersrand in Johannesburg, and in 1944, with Oliver Tambo and Walter F. Sisulu, he formed the Youth League of the African National Congress (ANC). In 1952, Mandela and Tambo opened the first black law office in South Africa.

During the 1950s Mandela was arrested on several occasions but was acquitted or received a suspended sentence each time. Then, in 1960 the African National Congress was declared illegal, and Mandela was convicted for incitement and leaving the country illegally. While Mandela was serving a 5-year prison sentence, police raided the ANC's headquarters at Rivonia, outside Johannesburg, and found documents describing a guerrilla campaign. Mandela and eight others were accused of sabotage and conspiracy to overthrow the government. Eight of the defendants, including Mandela, were sentenced to life in prison.

In 1980 the United Nations Security Council called for Mandela's release from prison, and the South African government was isolated by other governments because of its policy of apartheid, or enforced racial segregation. In 1985 the government offered to free Mandela if he would renounce violence; he refused to do so unless the government ended apartheid and granted full political rights to blacks. Mandela refused to leave prison until the government met his terms. In early 1990 President F. W. De Klerk legalized the African National Congress and dozens of other banned organizations and freed hundreds of political prisoners. In February 1990 Mandela too was released from prison and embarked on a triumphant international tour to celebrate not only his freedom but the beginning of the end of apartheid.

Following are excerpts from his speech at the Rivonia trial in 1964.

At the outset, I want to say that the suggestion made by the state in its opening that the struggle in South Africa is under the influence of foreigners or Communists is wholly incorrect. I have done whatever I did, both as an individual and as a leader of my people, because of my experience in South Africa and my own proudly felt African background, and not because of what any outsider might have said.

In my youth in the Transkei I listened to the elders of my tribe telling stories of the old days. Amongst the tales they related to me were those of wars fought by our ancestors in defense of the fatherland. . . . I hoped then that life might offer me the opportunity to serve my people and make my own humble contribution to their freedom struggle. . . .

We felt that without violence there would be no way open to the African people to succeed in their struggle against the principle of white supremacy. All lawful modes of expressing opposition to this principle had been closed by the legislation, and we were placed in a position in which we had to either accept a permanent state of inferiority or to defy the Government. . . . We first broke the law in a way which avoided any recourse to violence; when this form was legislated against, and when the Government resorted to a show of force to crush opposition to its policies, only then did we decide to answer violence with violence.

But the violence we chose to adopt was not terrorism. We who formed Umkonto were all members of the African National Congress, and had behind us the ANC tradition of nonviolence and negotiations as a means of solving political disputes. We believed that South Africa belonged

to all the people who lived in it, and not to one group, be it black or white. We did not want an interracial war, and tried to avoid it to the last minute. . . .

This then was the plan: Umkonto was to perform sabotage, and strict instructions were given to its members, right from the start, that on no account were they to injure or kill people in planning or carrying out operations. . . .

I have denied that I am a Communist; and I think that in the circumstances I am obliged to state exactly what my political beliefs are. I have always regarded myself . . . as an African patriot. . . .

Today, I am attracted by the idea of a classless society, an attraction which springs in part from Marxist reading and in part from my admiration of the structure and organization of early African societies in this country. The land, then the main means of production, belonged to the tribe. There were no rich or poor and there was no exploitation.

It is true, as I have already stated, that I have been influenced by Marxist thought. But this is also true of many of the leaders of the new independent states. Such widely different persons as Gandhi, Nehru, Nkrumah and Nasser all acknowledge this. . . .

Indeed, for my own part, I believe that it is open to debate whether the Communist Party has any specific role to play at this particular stage of our political struggle. The basic task at the present moment is the removal of race discrimination and the attainment of democratic rights on the basis of the Freedom Charter. Insofar as that party furthers this task, I welcome its assistance. . . .

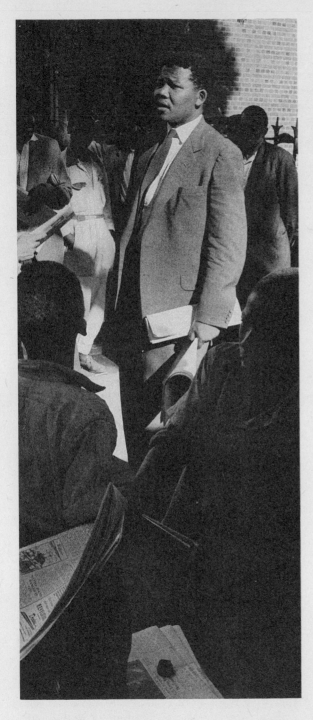

Nelson Mandela is pictured here at his trial in 1964, when he was sentenced to life in prison for sabotage and conspiracy to overthrow the government.

From my reading of Marxist literature and from conversations with Marxists, I have gained the impression that Communists regard the parliamentary system of the West as undemocratic and reactionary. But on the contrary, I am an admirer of such a system.

Magna Carta, the Petition of Rights and the Bill of Rights are documents held in veneration by democrats throughout the world.

I have great respect for British political institutions, and for the country's system of justice. I regard the British Parliament as the most democratic institution in the world, and the independence and impartiality of its judiciary never fail to arouse my admiration.

The American Congress, that country's doctrine of separation of powers, as well as the independence of its judiciary, arouse in me similar sentiments.

I have been influenced in my thinking by both West and East. All this has led me to feel that in my search for a political formula, I should be absolutely impartial and objective. I should tie myself to no particular system of society other than that of socialism. I must leave myself free to borrow the best from the West and from the East. . . .

The Government often answers its critics by saying that Africans in South Africa are economically better off than the inhabitants of the other countries in Africa. I do not know whether this statement is true and doubt whether any comparison can be made without having regard to the cost-of-living index in such countries.

But even if it is true, as far as the African people are concerned it is irrelevant. Our complaint is not that we are poor by comparison with people in other countries, but that we are poor by comparison with the white people in our own country, and that we are prevented by legislation from altering this imbalance.

The lack of human dignity experienced by Africans is the direct result of the policy of white supremacy. White supremacy implies black inferiority. Legislation designed to preserve white supremacy entrenches this notion.

Menial tasks in South Africa are invariably

performed by Africans. When anything has to be carried or cleaned the white man will look around for an African to do it for him, whether the African is employed by him or not.

Because of this sort of attitude, whites tend to regard Africans as a separate breed. They do not look upon them as people with families of their own; they do not realize that they have emotions, that they fall in love like white people do, that they want to be with their wives and children like white people want to be with theirs, that they want to earn enough money to support their families properly, to feed and clothe them and send them to school. . . .

Africans want to be paid a living wage. Africans want to perform work they are capable of doing, and not work the Government declares them to be capable of. Africans want to be allowed to live where they obtain work, and not be endorsed out of an area because they were not born there.

Africans want to be allowed to own land in places where they work, and not be obliged to live in rented houses they can never call their own. Africans want to be part of the general population, and not confined to living in their own ghettos. . . .

Above all, we want equal political rights, because without them our disabilities will be permanent. I know this sounds revolutionary to the whites in this country, because the majority of voters will be Africans. This makes the white man fear democracy.

But this fear cannot be allowed to stand in the way of the only solution which will guarantee racial harmony and freedom for all. It is not true that the enfranchisement of all will result in racial domination. Political division, based on color, is entirely artificial, and when it disappears, so will the domination of one color group by another. The ANC has spent half a century fighting against racialism. When it triumphs it will not change that policy.

This then is what ANC is fighting. Their struggle is a truly national one. It is a struggle of the African people, inspired by their own suffering and their own experience. It is a struggle for the right to live.

During my lifetime I have dedicated myself to this struggle of the African people. I have fought against white domination, and I have fought against black domination. I have cherished the ideal of a democratic and free society in which all persons live together in harmony and with equal opportunities. It is an ideal I hope to live for and to achieve. But if needs be, it is an ideal for which I am prepared to die.

 # AN OPEN LETTER TO CITIZEN MOBUTU SESE SEKO

Zaire was a Belgian colony, the Belgian Congo, until 1960 when it gained its independence and was renamed the Democratic Republic of the Congo. In 1965 a military coup led by General Mobutu Sese Seko overthrew the government and embarked on a campaign of nationalization and nationalism. The name of the country was changed to Zaire in 1971. Under Mobutu no opposition was permitted to his party, the Popular Movement of the Revolution (MPR); the press was rigidly controlled; and those who criticized the president were subject to imprisonment.

In December 1980, 13 members of Zaire's Parliament published an open letter to President Mobutu comparing his promises of reform to the actual state of affairs. They castigated him for failing to democratize the political system, for mismanaging the economy, for tolerating widespread corruption in government, and for permitting the deterioration of the health and welfare of the people of Zaire, noting that Zaire is a nation of immense natural resources whose people are malnourished and impoverished.

Soon after the letter was released, all 13 signatories were arrested and stripped of their parliamentary immunity. All were deprived of their civil and political rights for periods of one to five years and were banished to the interior of the country, where some were held under house arrest. In June 1982 12 of the signatories were retried for attempting to form a new political party. A month later they were sentenced to 15 years in prison.

In May 1990 President Mobutu announced that he would lift the 20-year ban on opposition political parties and begin planning for an election. However, a political rally by a new group was attacked by government forces less than a week later, and several people were killed. Dissidents in Zaire, including some of those who signed the letter excerpted below, did not believe that Mobutu was prepared to permit opposition or open criticism of his one-party, one-man rule.

CITIZEN PRESIDENT-FOUNDER,

In your July first, 1977 address at the City of the Party at N'Sele, after having seen that the voice of the people was often hushed up and that it ran the risk of being heard too late, you added the following:

The Popular Movement of the Revolution is a democratic party and not a dictatorial one. The people of Zaire must also be able to voice constructive criticism, for it is my belief that any objective criticism is part of the exercise of democracy. Criticism becomes subversive only when it is covert, underhanded, and destructive.

For the first time, allow us to make use of this democratic freedom which you have publicly recognized. And allow us to use it by appealing directly to you. As the problems raised here are of a public nature, we have thought it good to give them the attention which they deserve.

Citizen President-Founder, the comments which follow constitute neither a satire nor a trial. They are simply the results of our daily preoccupations, of the questions which naturally arise in the confrontation between our present life and your public declarations. . . .

Citizen President-Founder, on November 24, 1965, by a coup d'etat, you took the serious decision of personally assuming the supreme magistrature of our country. The justifications given at that time, as long as they did not take away from the people their primeval role, convinced us of your patriotic sentiment and your desire to lead our young and great nation toward happiness and prosperity.

On December 12, 1965, . . . in front of the Nation gathered at the 20th of May Stadium, you made a severe indictment, followed by a crucial analysis of the political, economic, financial and social situation. Your words did not fail to move sensitive hearts and earned you the trust and enthusiasm of a people just liberated from long colonial domination. Legitimate new hope was born.

Since then, fifteen years have passed . . .

Citizen President-Founder, even though we have, at the end of these fifteen years of a rule which you have not shared, known periods of prosperity (between 1967 and 1970) for which we congratulate you, we must nevertheless recognize that since that time, the state of Zaire has become more and more alarming on all fronts . . . .

While calling itself a democratic Party, the first action set by the MPR was to disregard one of the most fundamental and natural rights belonging to the people: freedom of choice. The MPR is a Party which recruits its followers by force. One of its slogans makes this coercive aspect clear: "Like it or not, you are a member of the MPR." ("Olinga olinga te, ozali MPR.")

And this first blow to freedom was unfortunately institutionalized. One knows that freedom is man's most cherished possession, an innate gift which no temporal leader has the right to take away, which no people have the right to give up. Did not John Milton write:

> Our liberty is not Caesar's. It is a blessing we have received from God himself. It is what we are born to. To lay this down at Caesar's feet, which we derive not from him, which we are not beholden to him for, were an unworthy action, and a degrading of our very nature.

In your Regime, Citizen President-Founder, the press is nationalized. Many efforts seeking to obtain its liberalization have fallen short of being heard and understood. The foreign press entering the country is censured. This censure, however, is far from being effective, since the security services which seize the newspapers or magazines that criticize Zaire (or give information which is accurate but embarrassing to the leadership) end up selling them for a fortune. Those who get hold of them ensure a large circulation by making photocopies. . . .

Citizen President-Founder, as an experienced politician, you well know that it is unthinkable that 25 million Zairians all be MPR militants by conviction. The obligation that they be members of the MPR even before birth, whether they want to be or not, turns them into slaves, not free men. It is first a violation of divine will. And it is a violation of the N'Sele Manifesto as well as a flagrant contradiction of all your statements, be they on democracy or freedom.

Now, we can assure you that a considerable contingent of our population does not allege to the MPR and with good reason. And we doubt very much that all your colleagues, taking into account the way in which you recruit them, are more convinced than the others.

Also, if you are convinced that the majority of the people of Zaire belong to the MPR, which we concede, then you may as well govern with the majority and agree to recognize the minority's right to exist, to voice its opinions freely and above all to enjoy the protection of the State. And you will have thus conformed to the democratic ideal which you have time and time again called for. As long as you do not allow dissenting opin-

ions, all your efforts will remain fruitless and peace in Zaire will not be truly present in the hearts of men.

In the past, you have said that one man by himself could not see everything. Even today, the mass media continues to cry, not without scruples, that "The President-Founder is not a magician. Alone he can do nothing . . ." You can sense that the people's support is missing. And that support will never be yours as long as you insist on being the "Lone Man," who considers the people of Zaire as a flock of sheep; and as long as you continue to think as the Belgian colonizers did, and much more than they, that you can succeed in providing the people's happiness and contentment despite themselves.

Indeed, the people of Zaire, who have paid a hefty price for freedom and democracy, continue to believe that their country should be administered through democratic institutions . . . .

To say today and to proclaim to the world, that this concept of the State and of these institutions is not feasible in Zaire, is to preach the theory of the difference in nature, to follow the steps of the reactionaries of the good old colonial days who supported the idea that blacks were incapable of learning mathematics or abstract sciences, for example . . .

Citizen President-Founder, it happens that you improvise in public; which you do brilliantly, moreover. But as a politician, you are under obligation to take into account the psychology of the masses. The use of demagogy in arousing the crowds is too tempting for you to pass up in such circumstances. You have made slips of the tongue on occasion. How can all these statements constitute the Party doctrine without some discriminatory criteria? How can you expect all you say to be word of law?

Also, it can not be accepted that you continue changing the laws and the Constitution by speeches. Subalterns are coerced into recognizing the authority of presidential statements as law, even if they endanger general interests. And these statements come into effect before legal clauses are even modified. And this is justified by saying that the Revolution runs better than its textual counterparts!

These concepts are arbitrary. And as long as they remain, the State of Law advocated by the MPR will be long in coming . . . .

We prefer to mention, since it is more eloquent than any other statement, your own confirmation of the situation, made after 12 years of unshared rule:

It cannot be allowed that a foreigner or a Zairian citizen feel more terrorized than secure in seeing a magistrate or a policeman. And too often, many innocent people suffer injustices while the real culprits roam about freely and arrogantly.

And this situation endures. Judicial decisions condemning the State or State bodies, in separation of wrongdoings made to private citizens, are not carried out. Is that a good administration of justice? Is the State not bound by moral and legal rules as is any private citizen? Otherwise, who must lead the way?

Also, for some time on the international level with good reason, Zaire has been listed among the countries who violate human rights. We have been blamed for whimsical trials, lack of procedure, third party rights violations, disregard for corporal integrity, arbitrary arrests, inhuman jail conditions, and more. . . .

[Corruption] is one of the grievances you had with the political leaders of the First Republic. And which probably tipped the scales in favor of the coup d'etat of November 24, 1965.

We are not trying to absolve those political leaders. Their wrongdoings will someday be pointed out by historians. What we do remember is that opposition in those days was so vigilant and unbending, that it was not just satisfied with denouncing but also with inflicting censure so that public morality could be safeguarded.

Today, on the other hand, it can be said that corruption, misappropriation of funds, embezzlement, and greed, have reached their peak. It could even be said that they have been institutionalized. Never has the country been robbed so much and the people exploited so much. From

time to time, the foreign media are sufficiently scandalized to give alarming details. In spite of banking secrecy and censure of the press, the average citizen knows that today political leaders hold some of the largest fortunes in the world. . . .

Citizen President-Founder, we note, coming from you, that not only are you a democrat, but that the people, tied to democracy, are opposed to the mere concept of a lifelong term . . .

As we examine the current structure of the MPR, it is honestly impossible not to attribute to you a desire for a life-long term as president, or at least, the possibility of a mandate by succession.

Let us consider your personal statute only. Either you are above the Constitution, and by a ripple effect, undisputed leader with unlimited power to create or destroy institutions and men; or you give up these powers to comply with the Constitution but maintain nevertheless the presidency of the MPR, of the Congress, of the Political Bureau, of the Executive Council, of the Judiciary Council and, by delegation, of the Legislative Council. After all this, are you still a democrat?

With the recent restructuring of the MPR, and after taking back what you had once given, you have become "Man-Organization" or better yet "Central Branch of decision-making" and are thus above any other section of the Party, and have far greater decision-making authority (if not more dangerous authority), because of Party supremacy over the State. Some powers, and we are wondering which, you have considered yourself unable to exercise and have handed them over to the Central Committee. But the President of the Central Committee is you. This Committee, one of the functions of which is to nominate the candidate for President of the Republic, is composed of members who are themselves nominated and recalled by you. Before holding office, they have to swear allegiance not to the Party, not to the Constitution, but to you . . . .

During the Political Bureau meeting held on Monday, August 11, 1980, a new branch of the Party was created: the Executive Committee of the MPR. From now on, Zaire will have two Executive branches, one in the Party and one in the Government. Already being the President of the Executive Council of Government, you cannot be anything less than that in the Party Executive Committee. In short, you are Head of State, President-Founder of the MPR, President of Congress, President of the Man-Organization, President of the Central Committee, President of the Party Executive Committee, President of the Political Bureau, President of the Legislative Council by proxy, and more.

Don't you think that it is too much power to hold and too many duties for one man to perform at the same time? . . .

We know how much you are allergic to honesty and truth. But having freely taken the responsibility of assuming the leadership of our country, you obviously had to expect some day this kind of reaction. We have been obeying you for fifteen years. What have we not done, during that time, for your use and pleasure? Singing, dancing, liveliness; in short we have gone through all kinds of humiliations and degradation, that even foreign colonization had not subjected us to. All this so that you could follow through on your fight for the fulfillment, even in part, of the social model which you had planned and proposed. Did you succeed? Alas no!

After these fifteen years of unshared rule, we find ourselves in the presence of two absolutely distinct factions. On one side a few privileged people, scandalously rich. On the other, the mass of the people wallowing in misery and counting only on international relief to survive as best they can. And when relief reaches Zaire, the rich manage to embezzle the goods for their own profit!

Yes, this off-handedness has gone so far that some did not think twice about appropriating for themselves the rations destined for our own men fighting in Shaba. You publicly acknowledged this in a meeting at the 20th of May Stadium.

Taking all this into account, we wish to reaffirm our opposition to violence, and our belief in the possibility of finding, in talks, with mutual respect, peaceful solutions which can safeguard national unity, national peace, the integrity of our territory and especially solutions which favour and stimulate feelings of brotherhood without which it is impossible to build this large nation at the heart of Africa.

Throughout this letter, we have attempted to show how you have, without apparent motive and without forewarning, gone back on the promises made in your declaration of faith stated during the coup d'etat of November 24, 1964.

From this demonstration, it appears that the socioeconomic diseases, which for good reasons led to your coup d'etat, have not been fought. On the contrary, the situation has worsened to the point that today, it is considered desperate. And this, in spite of regained peace, in spite of the absence of political unrest, and despite the important internal and external means that were at your disposal . . . .

Citizen President-Founder, to conclude, let us say that it is illusory and self-defeating to want to create an immortality forcefully and using any means, by confiscating power, by surrounding yourself with a divine image, by naming our avenues and stadiums after yourself or yours, etc.

Indeed, only history can truly and durably consecrate a man's immortality, as the wisdom of the Bible teaches us. (Ecclesiastes Ch. 2).

In fifteen years of unshared rule, surrounded most of the time by other "men-alone" named by you, often representing only themselves, sometimes strangers to our country, you have taken us through a tunnel the end of which only you can see, through an abyss.

Worse, by systematically refusing all sorts of stratagems designed to truly democra[t]ize the country and its institutions, by imposing a facade of unanimity which hides unrest, you have denied our people the necessary apprenticeship of democracy, of free and peaceful interaction of different ideas in a spirit of constructive emulation.

The most visible consequence so far has been exile or taking arms for a good many of our fellow-countrymen as the only means of political expression. But the worst consequence of your regime which smothers democracy is that, according to you, the country runs the risk of living political and social chaos even worse than the one to which your accession put an end, because the people are no longer used to taking part in debates and the elite has hardly learned to hold a conversation and peacefully discuss its views with the people.

Maybe you still have time to change the course of events to a favorable direction.

Citizen President-Founder, Zaire belongs to 25 million Zairians. The millions that we believe to be legitimately representing, or that sympathize with our cause, agree that an immediate and major change must be made in our society, before it is too late.

This change implies the complete transformation of the country's structures and, in effect, the enjoyment of all political and democratic rights, mainly the freedom of opinion and of the press.

To be worthwhile and durable, these reforms can only occur after a national debate bringing together not only those elected by the people, but also representatives of different political opinion groups, whatever they may be, designated freely by the groups which delegate them.

But at this point, we are already convinced that if the authorities allow them to express themselves freely, the great majority of our fellow-countrymen will demand, through their delegates, far-reaching political reform with the following features:

1. The *raison d'etre* of the Zairian State is: prosperity and happiness not for a handful of men, but for all Zairians.
2. Every Zairian and his property must have protection from arbitrary power.
3. The Constitution and the laws of Zaire must apply effectively to each and everyone, without regard to their function or social rank.
4. The political organization of our country must rest upon the true (and not just claimed) consensus of our people and fulfill the deep aspirations of our masses. This is only possible with the establishment of an effective democracy in Zaire.
5. Democracy will be effective in Zaire only if the representatives of our people in the political branches of the State are freely elected by the people.
6. A stop must be put to outright centralization and to the concentration of power in the hands of one person.
7. Power must be distributed, with precision, among the different political branches of the State, in the framework determined by the Constitution.
8. From the bottom to the highest level, the control of all State branches must be organized so that it be effective and efficient.
9. The Executive branch must be completely subject to the true control of the Legislative Council, a branch whose members are elected by the people.
10. The real democratization of the regime and the effective guarantee of the rights of man postulate freedom in the mass media. The Zairian newspapers, radio and television must serve all Zairians. For them to stop serving an oligarchy there must be pluralism in mass media. Besides, lies can only be fought by their contradictions, and that also justifies the need for pluralism.

GIBSON KAMAU KURIA

THE UNIVERSALITY OF BASIC RIGHTS

Gibson Kamau Kuria (1947–   ), the most prominent human rights lawyer in Kenya, was a leading advocate of political pluralism, an independent judiciary, freedom of the press, and respect for the rule of law. Kamau Kuria was born in Nyeri District of Kenya, the son of parents who had no formal education. He graduated from the University of East Africa in

Dar es Salaam in 1971 and studied law at Wadham College, Oxford University. From 1974 until 1987 he taught law at the University of Nairobi, then formed a private law practice. Many of his clients were political dissidents. In 1987 he was arrested and detained for associating with people who were charged with subverting public security—his clients.

In 1988 the Robert F. Kennedy Memorial Foundation bestowed its Human Rights Award on Gibson Kamau Kuria. He was not permitted to leave Kenya to accept the award, so members of the Kennedy family brought the award to Kenya in March 1989. The speech he delivered is excerpted below.

In 1990 the Kenyan police physically attacked leading political opponents, and a number of opposition journalists and lawyers were detained without charges. Kamau Kuria took refuge in the American Embassy and eventually went into exile in the United States.

. . . This evening I will assume that I am having a dialogue with all my fellow human beings in the world. Whatever I say about Kenya is an application to our situation of truths which are valid everywhere. I wish to use John Rawls's concept of "original position" in his *A Theory of Justice*.

- to argue that human rights can be and are protected in a society where most people obey either God's laws or man's just laws
- that the individual as either a citizen of a particular state or as a citizen of God's Kingdom on earth is under a moral duty to act in a way which advances or better secures enjoyment of human rights—the human situation in the world today is as sorry as it is because of the individual's breach of that duty
- that where the breach occurs to a small extent in a democratic state a mean spirit emerges and the enjoyment suffers—where the breach is on a large scale the results are either a civil war or a dictatorship in which human rights cannot be enjoyed
- in the contemporary world the lawyer, like the Christian, following Cicero of Rome or Jeremiah and Daniel of the *Old Testament* is under a moral duty to draw the attention of his society to the dangers he sees and to refuse to participate in activities which would undermine the constitutional order and
- breaches in Kenya of both the citizen's and Christian's duties are such that the country must go back to its 1963 democratic values if great danger which looms is to be avoided.

The expression "original position" firstly refers to a civil society with a democratic system of government in which enjoyment of rights is secured by a constitution, a political tradition, an independent judiciary, legislature, executive, and the individual has an unfettered right to choose his governors and to remove them from authority. The concept is loose enough to include many countries in the world which either have had such a constitutional order or have one today. Even where there is such a constitutional order, its ideals are rarely adhered to strictly.

Because of this reason I am making an appeal that even in such countries there be a return to the original position. Where there has been such a constitutional order which has been departed from the appeal is to return to both former constitutional position and ideal. Where a country has never had such a constitutional order the argument is that such a society has a capacity to attain such an order and the present sorry situation represents man's fall from his ideal. Even in such a society there can be a notional return to the original position. In each case the return is to be through obedience to God's or man's just laws. I being a Christian lawyer and this function coming as it does shortly after the Holy Week, I cannot help drawing on Biblical truths today.

When living in my cell at Naivasha Prison as a detained person in 1987 I found and even today find great encouragement from *Psalm 27* and *Daniel* Chapter 6. The *Psalm* indicates what happens to one who obeys God's laws. Daniel in my judgement was an ideal citizen and many can emulate him with advantage. Recently I argued amongst Christians inter alia that:

- the idea of human rights is rooted in a universal belief that the human being has a dignity or worth which puts a limit as to what fellow human beings acting through such institutions as the state may do to him
- that that vision of man is identical to the one Christ had at the time he taught his followers how to live on earth and
- that the Christian cannot follow Christ truly or faithfully and fail to defend any attack of his human rights and that of human beings anywhere else in the world. Today I will adopt those arguments.

The expression "human rights" refers to certain basic rights which the international community believes man needs or are essential for him to live in dignity. They are based on the international community's view of what it is to be a human being. Those rights include among others:

- the right not to have one's life taken without compliance with the law
- the right to liberty
- the right not to be treated like a slave or be tortured or subjected to degrading or inhuman treatment
- the right to hold property
- the right to the protection of the law to a lawyer to assist him in securing the protection of the law and to a fair trial
- freedom of worship
- freedom of association
- freedom of movement
- the right not to be discriminated against and
- the right to privacy and family life.

These rights lay down for all men every where a standard of morality below which a society acting through a government cannot be allowed to fall.

As constitutional experience in India in 1973 and the *South West African Cases* before the World Court in early 1970s showed, it is not appreciated by many people who accept the idea of human rights, that inherent in it is the view that no human institution, be it the legislature, the executive or the judiciary has or can in reason have the power to depart from the principle of human equality from which the rights spring. The contemporary world is one where one sees the pretence that such power to derogate from human equality exists. Men everywhere have a duty to eradicate this heresy. The International Community's statement of human rights which I intend to use as a basis is the one contained in the *United Nations Universal Declaration of Human Rights.*

The making of the award to me today reminds me of Jesus' instructions to his disciples the day he had the Last Supper with them. He commanded them to do certain things both as a way of keeping in mind what obedience to him entailed and as a means of bringing to fellow men God's own Kingdom to earth. I do not know how today's award was established. I know that the recipients need not be religious people. But it would appear that what the founders did is somewhat analogous to carrying out Jesus' instructions which I have referred to. St. Luke's record of those instructions reads as follows:

And he took the cup, and gave thanks and said, Take this and divide among yourselves. For I say unto you I will not drink of the fruit of wine until the Kingdom of God shall come. And he took bread and gave thanks and broke it and gave unto them saying This is my body which is given for you; this do in remembrance of me. Likewise also the cup after supper saying This cup is the new testament in my blood which is shed for you. (Chapter 22 verses 17–20.)

... In my judgement the passage requires anyone who obeys it and other teachings to be prepared to go all the way Christ went up to the Calvary. Many Christians largely pay lip service to those instructions. As a Christian I have tried to be faithful to it. Presumably it is because of that attempt that we have this function today....

I will review the human rights situation briefly. For this purpose I divide all the countries of the world into three classes. On the basis of this classification it can be said that the human community today falls into three classes:

First there is the class where even though the *Universal Declaration of Human Rights* is accepted, the essential institutions such as the rule of law, an independent judiciary, an independent legislature to which everyone has freedom to elect representatives of his political persuasions, an independent executive which does not discriminate against its citizens, and an independent press have never emerged at any time in its political history. The struggle for human rights among such people faces a conceptual problem as the institution cannot be said to have been accepted. The second class is that of countries which have in their political history subscribed to the *Universal Declaration of Human Rights* soon after the attainment of their independence and established institutions designed to ensure that human rights would be enjoyed. Many African, Caribbean and Asian countries fall into this category. India, most Caribbean countries and a few African countries apart, one sees in those countries either the abolition or weakening of democratic institutions. The struggle for human rights is in the nature of an endeavour to get the country to return to its original position of innocence. The third class of mankind lives in societies which have subscribed to the *Universal Declaration of Human Rights* and have old institutions which safeguard democracy and human rights. The Western countries belong to this class.

The award which is made to people in all the three classes will advance the respect for human rights. Irrespective of the class in which a country is, human experience is that:

- because of man's capacity for freedom to choose, there is a perpetual contest between good and evil; there is an era during which

Led by Archbishop Desmond Tutu and the mayor of Cape Town, thirty thousand people marched through the center of that South African city in a 1989 parade against violence and apartheid.

liberty is generally respected which era is followed by one where it is not respected; the guarantee against great violation of human rights is therefore institutions which ensure that power is distributed fairly between individuals and institutions; the countries which have fairly good institutions do not claim to have solved the political theory's problem of evolving a truly just society. The protection of human rights must include ensuring that the institutions which are essential for the enjoyment of human rights are not abolished or weakened;

- everywhere in the world irrespective of the constitution the executive branch of the government tends to exercise more power than it should in reason or according even to a very good constitution exercise; John Locke's observation that the civil society can be endangered by governors themselves is borne out by recent experience in the countries in both the second and the third classes; where the judiciary is independent, the institution of judicial review is being perfected to ensure that the executive remains in its legal territory; the protection of human rights entails strengthening the judiciary;

- inherent in the acceptance of the *Universal Declaration of Human Rights* is the acceptance of the legal and political fact that everyone must to use Bracton's own words be "under God and the law"; the sad reality of the contemporary world is that many countries which profess to respect human rights do not give effect to that proposition; human rights cannot be enjoyed where Bracton's law is not followed;

- although the international machinery for the protection of human rights is always being improved upon, a lot remains to be done to ensure that the international standards are maintained; the draft European convention which will permit states mutual inspection of institutions enforcing human rights is most welcome; one hopes that other countries will adopt similar conventions;

- the concept of sovereignty in international law and relations is in great need of refinement to ensure that human rights are better protected; it is unfortunate that for many years, the world community took no action against Hitler and Idi Amin who enforced dangerous concepts of sovereignty of nations;

- it is because of the realisation of the inadequacies of the international and national machineries for the enforcement of human rights that many associations and foundations have grown up in some countries; it is a sad commentary of the international situation that it is in the countries where human rights are protected least that either there are no private associations supporting human rights or no strong associations; there is an urgent need for such associations to be founded where they do not exist and for those there are to exchange their experiences;

- everywhere the struggle for human dignity is and has always been a struggle against vested interests which thrive from the violation of human rights; the trials and deaths of Socrates, Christ, St. Joan of Arc, and Sir Thomas More indicate how those vested interests can react; the 1988 *Human Rights Watch's Worldwide Survey* states that last year, thirty human rights monitors or activists were killed or died in custody; in this country, in the 1950s much blood was shed and many sacrifices made so that man may live in dignity; a just constitution was sought to ensure that the colonial violations of human rights might not recur in this country; my understanding of Greek and Roman history and institutions tells me that the changes which this country has effected in the institutions it inherited at independence are such that the latter have in essence disappeared and that unless we restore them, Kenya may suffer the same fate which befell these two states;

- unless the human being obeys either God's or man's just laws he is condemned to live in misery and without dignity; man's laws themselves must be based on a recognition of the human needs of everyone; no individual can in fact or reason authorise another to make laws or administer or execute laws in a manner oppressive to him; it is only the laws there is authority to make that there is obligation to obey; obedience to "laws" where is no authority to make leads to great suffering and bloodshed; another sad commentary on the human rights situation is that the universally accepted ideas have not been published as much as they should; in many countries false doctrines as to the extent of the authority of the civil government exist;

- the obedient citizen of God's state has something in common with the obedient citizen of the modern state; both are under a duty to act in ways which promote humanity; the fact that this is not being done by many people in the world does not render the proposition invalid. . . .

Today I would like to perform roles akin to the ones which Jeremiah and Cicero performed. In my capacity as both a Christian lawyer and a citizen I have:

- found that as a country we have the not too good distinction of being a place where a citizen has not been able to secure liberty through the process known as *habeas corpus*; in 1984 in a case where I was arguing a *habeas corpus* application I submitted that the court decision which was being relied upon in support of an argument for refusal of release of detained persons was from Uganda which after the decision witnessed calamities and that the history of that country was not a happy one; our court elected to follow that decision instead of those from India and the Caribbean countries where democracy is strong; the institution of *habeas corpus* protects human rights; we ought to make it work;
- found that it is very rarely that a person charged with political offence gets acquitted even where his defence appears strong; the time probably has come for Kenya to borrow from the old democracies the institution of jury where the verdict is given by one's twelve

peers as opposed to one official as is the case in this country today;

- found that in too many cases the courts have been reluctant to exclude confession made under circumstances that suggest that force had been used on the accused persons; cases of the mistreatment of suspects in custody have been such that the state has found it necessary to state that it is not its policy that the suspects in custody be mistreated; there may be a link between these two;
- come across many cases where allegations of abuse of power are made; I have seen great delay following the filing of cases in which abuse of power is alleged;
- witnessed changes in constitutional and statutory provisions dealing with the nature of the legislature, the right of the individual to participate in the political process, the nature of the judiciary, the nature of the executive, and the nature of liberty which mark a radical departure from democratic assumptions made at independence in 1963;
- witnessed a situation where the citizen's right to secure the protection of law through a lawyer of his choice has been greatly endangered;
- witnessed a general decline in tolerance for the different views held in the society;
- witnessed a move to curtail the professional independence which professional bodies have enjoyed and are entitled to enjoy;
- witnessed constitutional curtailment of the freedom of association in the political field; there is no freedom to belong to a political party other than the ruling one; non-party citizens have no political rights;
- witnessed the loss of the constitutional right to leave Kenya which is not preceded by compliance with rules of natural justice or due process; it is because I could not travel to Washington last November that we meet here today. The making of today's award will according to my moral reasoning remain incomplete as long as I cannot exercise my human and constitutional right to visit Washington where the award is normally made. . . .

My view is that our success as a nation has come from substantial adherence during the greater part of our nationhood to the institutions we adopted in 1963. Greater prosperity can only come from maintenance and strengthening of these. It cannot be said that we have been strengthening our institutions. Although it is getting very late, it is not too late to repent our sins and recapture our lost innocence as a nation. . . .

GITOBU IMANYARA
PROTEST AGAINST HIS ARREST

One of the boldest publications in Africa in the late twentieth century was *The Nairobi Law Monthly*, published and edited by Gitobu Imanyara (1955–   ). Launched in October 1987, the magazine became an outspoken voice for democracy and human rights in Kenya. The government of Kenya had little tolerance for criticism by the press. In March 1988 the government banned *Beyond*, a magazine published by the National Christian Council of Kenya, after it published accounts of election rigging; in April and May 1989 it banned *Financial Review* and *Development Agenda* for criticizing the government's economic and political policies; in June 1989 reporters from the Nation Group of Newspapers were barred from covering parliamentary proceedings for having expressed critical views.

In this climate of repression, it was not entirely unexpected when government ministers began to complain about *The Nairobi Law Monthly*. In March 1990 police agents paid a visit to the newspaper's offices; Imanyara refused then to leave with them, but prepared a statement for the inevitable time when they would return to arrest him. Imanyara's foresight proved accurate. He was arrested and jailed three months later in a government crackdown on political dissidents. Imanyara was released, then jailed again in 1991 because of the ideas expressed in his editorials. Excerpts from his statement are printed here.

. . . I will accompany these agents of terror because I have no physical power to resist them. I go knowing that there are millions of Kenyans who are silent and painfully bearing it out with me. . . . The Kenya Constitution does not empower policemen to accost a Kenyan and say: "Come let us go." The Kenya Constitution does not allow those in power to intimidate and terrorize those whom they rule. Sections 78 and 79 of the Kenya Constitution protect the freedom of every Kenyan to receive and hold ideas and beliefs without interference. Section 82 of the Constitution outlaws discrimination against any Kenyan on grounds of political opinion. . . . Those charged with the task of defending, upholding and preserving the Constitution should not be agents of destroying and undermining of the very Constitution they have sworn to defend and uphold. Those responsible for destruction of our Constitution will one day answer for their crimes. I refuse to be intimidated by the threat of the ban of *The Nairobi Law Monthly*, detention or further imprisonment following trumped charges or a manipulated trial. . . .

MWENI MWANGEKA AND MWELU MUTUKU

TODAY THE SOMALIS, TOMORROW . . . and 200 VS. 20,000,000

As the leading magazine in Kenya for proponents of democracy and human rights, *The Nairobi Law Monthly* regularly opened its pages to correspondence from readers. One of the features of the magazine was poetry sent in by readers, reflecting on their aspirations for Kenya. In issue #16, May 1989, Mweni Mwangeka contributed "Today the Somalis, Tomorrow . . ." and Mwelu Mutuku wrote "200 vs. 20,000,000."

Today the Somalis, Tomorrow . . .

Today it's the Somalis
and many are heard to say
"it concerns me not
for it's a Somali affair"
Tomorrow it might be the Pokot
and many will declare
"that's all right
for Pokot I sure am not"
The next day may be the Asians
and many will proclaim "it serves
them right"
The day after if it's the Luos
the voices will be heard

"they asked for it"
If the new week brings
the turn of the Kikuyus
those not affected so far
will worriedly whisper
"I hope it'll end there"
But will it?
Oppression of any Kenyan
is the oppression of all.
The time to say "no"
is now.

—*Mweni Mwangeka*

200 vs. 20,000,000

We the twenty million
are the ones who
gave the right to
the two hundred
the right to represent us
the privilege to
act on our behalf

The two hundred
were to carry out
this function according
to the rules in force
at the time of their election
they did not have the mandate

to force the change of rules

The two hundred
were to be the voice
of the twenty million
did not surrender
their own voice
did not forfeit
their own right
to speak

The two hundred
were meant to safeguard
life and liberty
of the twenty million

not to deprive them
of this inalienable right

If the original contract
is broken
then the twenty million
have the right
no, the duty
to say to the mere
two hundred
with one thunderous
voice
"No!"

—*Mwelu Mutuku*

WOLE SOYINKA
RELIGION AND HUMAN RIGHTS

Born in Abeokuta, Nigeria, Wole Soyinka (1934–   ) was awarded the Nobel Prize for Literature in 1986. As an undergraduate at University College in Ibadan he campaigned against tribalism and injustice; as a student and playwright in London he opposed colonialism, racial prejudice and apartheid. After Nigeria gained its independence, Soyinka frequently had to resist efforts by Nigerian government officials to censor his work. He wrote in an autobiographical statement in 1975, "I have one abiding religion— human liberty." Playwright, poet, essayist, and novelist, Soyinka was not only the leading literary figure on the African continent, but an outspoken critic of government brutality and champion of human rights. The following is the text of a speech delivered by Soyinka to a "Nobel Conference" in Paris in 1988.

A historic irony: we find ourselves in a period where "revisionist" tendencies, of far-reaching consequences for once sacrosanct social structures as well as human rights, have become the norm rather than the exception. Yet it is this same era of infectious, ideological rethinking that has unleashed on us what is probably the most virulent strain of religious zealotry— globally manifested—that this century has yet experienced. As a state instrument of internal control, and even in the conduct of foreign policies (including terrorism), it is possible to suggest that religious fanaticism has once again attained prime position as the most implacable enemy of the basic rights of humanity.

The events which capture our attention today, rendering us impotent recipients of global danger signals, largely involve the escalating aggression of religious will. Comparatively, the strictures of ideological systems on human thought, and even social options, begin to appear tame. For it is a paradox that, the greater the claims to absolute definitiveness of any political ideology, the less predictable have been its practical operations within society. For the citizens over whom it holds sway therefore, the possibility of a less repressive direction does provide a few crumbs of optimism. An overstatement perhaps, especially as the same "unpredictability" requires an ability to anticipate the "wind of change" and bend to its currents. Not all human-

ity, alas, is endowed with such dexterity of scent.

Yet even this desperate consolation of possible, humane deviations within a crushing social system is denied the inmates of the "holy state." They find themselves trapped within a mindless hermeticism whose sole claim to methodological pursuit is a consistent, structured dehumanisation. And such a state becomes a seeding-bed for undiscriminating dissemination, utilising all machinery at its disposal—including diplomatic pouches—for the sole task of elevating its creed of intolerance to universalist heights. Profiting from the lethargy of the rational world, it moves on to promote the coming-in-being of other "holy" states whose riotous emergence from the womb of religion defines its nature in advance by an abrogation of all humane conduct toward non-adherents—individuals and communities.

This retrogressive motion is not hidden; on the contrary it flaunts itself, arrogantly, blindly, territorially insatiable, exulting in its rejection of dissent and contemptuous of rational restraints. In the course of its global rampage it does indeed effect genuine cases of personal conversion. When this captive is a political leader or Head of State, political power becomes conflated with a sense of divine mission; an internal trail of disaster grows into a blood-stained highway as the convert becomes increasingly obsessed by a mystic mandate to recreate all citizens within his borders in his spiritual image. Such has been the costly experience of Sudan under Numeiry. Yet even in this instance, political opportunism was not a negligible factor. A need to attract the political support of the extremist Islamic Brotherhood led to Numeiry's decision to further desecularise a nation already split in two on the altar of religion. Public floggings, resumption of execution by stoning for "impieties," amputations etc etc. . . . Eventually a venerated Islamic leader, who, however, dissented from certain tenets of Numeiry's new-found fundamentalism, paid with his life, publicly hanged. Three of his disciples were to follow, but even as he set the supreme example of steadfastness by stepping onto the gallows, he ordered his followers to recant. In our contemporary experience, this must be the highest act of symbolic offering, harrowingly clear-sighted in the strategy of resistance.

And the consequences of Numeiry's aberration continue til today in the intensified struggle of the predominantly animist South, the nearly three decades old strife which is still known to many as the Anyanya rebellion. How insanely provocative then can we account the action of Numeiry's neighbour who, with this exorbitant, ongoing haemorrhage as warning, nevertheless attempts to foment further religious strife on the continent with his fanatic's exhortations in the state of Burundi? Yet hardly one African leader was moved to comment or protest; the outside world gave it no more than a passing glance. All pretend not to see the conflagration that is threatened, until of course it consumes us in our rational complacency.

Now what is fanaticism? Fanaticism is much easier to define in the observance than in its essence. And the history of fanaticism is not recent. Hardly ever in human history, however, has this recurrent epidemic of irrationality claimed a sacrosanct status in its international relations. Any claims to selectionist theory of ideology or faith is in itself a form of fanaticism, but such selectionist faith, the belief in self, clan, community or race as the "chosen" can be harmless as long as it is contained within the bosom of the faithful. It becomes an explosive mixture, how-ever, when it allies itself with the divine mission of self-extension, and with global ambitions. The enslavement of an entire continent, first by Islamic, then Christian invaders, was an indirect result of this imperialist compulsion in the name of divine will. The economic factor was of course preeminent, no one glosses over that materialist drive. What we need to remind ourselves of, in my chosen context, is that the crossover line between being considered a free man and a slave was often contiguous with a readiness for conversion. Of course when the slave trade got thoroughly underway, this nice distinction became somewhat irrelevant. But willingness to be converted frequently affected the captive's treatment even in the enslaved condition. . . .

Wole Soyinka, Nigerian playwright, won the Nobel Prize for Literature in 1986

It was perhaps this immersion in the triumph of fanaticism in the African past that nerved that African leader—Ghadafi, who else?—to storm the heartland of the African continent and, in a formal address, incite the black African polity to rise against their governments, not on the grounds of economic privation or political oppression, but to ensure that only the "faithful" are permitted the mantle of leadership. Islam, he declared, was the only authentic African religion. The gratuitous insult offered by his pronouncement to millions of African peoples still faithful to their own authentic religions was clearly lost on him. He was of course acting not much differently from yet another alienated African—a historian and intellectual Ali Mazrui, who filmed and narrated a television series titled *The Africans* for the Public Television Service of the USA. The explicit thesis of his series was the contest for the African soul by the two religious superpowers—Christianity and Islam. In the process, a subtle act of denigration of African authentic spirituality becomes apparent. Even though as a scholar, Mazrui is compelled to pay lip-service to African deities which existed before the advent of Islam and Christianity, such religions to him obviously lacked substance, depth or relevance to contemporary society. A spiritual vacuum, in effect, existed into which Islam and Christianity stepped, as the dynamic of nature dictated. Of these two of course, his private superstitious bent, the Islamic, emerged the clear winner. Ignored was the historic transfer of African religions to the Americas, their thriving integration with the religious symbols, rituals, festivals and forms of worship in South America and in the Caribbean. A series which was dedicated to redressing the appalling ignorance and misrepresentation of a vast continent ended up being just another expensive propaganda for the racial-religious superiority of seductive superstitions imported into, or forced down the throat of the African continent.

When we recall history therefore, or speak of the dangers of a lack of egalitarian acceptance of other cultures, we are not instituting courts for the determination of guilt or altruistic errors; we

speak of an ongoing perpetuation of myths of superiority, the denigration of other people's past in whom the present is very much rooted. Fanaticism is not merely the overt, physical degradation of the physical "other" but the consolidation of myths, documentation, which reduce the peoples to secondary, even tertiary levels of validity in the emergence of human civilisation. That today's iteration of the low points of human conduct still fails to address—to name this one example—the commencement of the suicide of European humanism in the most quantitatively monstrous decimation of a people in the African slave trade—sanctified by the contesting idioms of Islam and Christianity—has its roots in this convenient excision of history. No one underplays the guilt of the Africans themselves in the sordid commerce of those bleak centuries; it is, however, necessary to remind the world, whenever it seeks explication of later, self-inflicted wounds on its humanism, that it was the world of Shakespeare, Goethe, Hegel, Voltaire, Molière, Mozart etc, that profited from and sustained this inhuman event. It is the same world that found yet an "other" in a later age: one result Auschwitz. To date the history of the decay of European humanism to the latter event is to continue to admit that, even till this moment, the African has not entered the consciousness of the European as yet another segment of the human family. And the tragic evidence today is the fanatical self-righteousness of the religion of Apartheid.

The menace is real, and extensive. We are confronted today by societies whose leadership blithely counters accusations of inhumane conduct with the response: "The standards of the rest of the world do not apply to us." This was the incredible response of the Iranian leadership to Amnesty International which listed 65 forms of torture routinely employed by that nation in the name of Islam. It is of course a very familiar defence or, more accurately, escape from defence. We have variants of this retreat from the human community from other dens of repression on the African continent where denunciations of torture and illegal imprisonment are neatly shelved under "inapplicable" Western perspectives—when they are not simply dismissed as Western propaganda.

I have asked myself often: what is the unique perspective of any race or nation on the reality of human pain and suffering? What, for instance, is the Asian cry of anguish, involuntarily wrung in protest against the abuse of Asiatic flesh? Is pain experienced in cultural terms? Have hunger and starvation always been purely religious phenomena? Must every race now present its human credentials to its own kins, to its current overlords and givers of life and death—from the barely recognisable form wallowing in his own vomit in a Kenyan prison to the aboriginal Indian whose drama of extermination in parts of the South American continent is still largely shrouded from the glare of world concerns? Perhaps we should translate into every spoken language in the world, emphasising their sheer ordinariness, the words of the much-abused Merchant of Venice:

> Hath not a Jew eyes? Hath not a Jew hands, organs, dimensions, senses, affections, passions? If you prick us, do we not bleed? If you poison us, do we not die?

How, I wonder, does it translate in Afrikaans? Would it read alien in Kwazulu? Lud? Or, most pertinently, in view of the recent horrors in the occupied Gaza strip—in Hebrew? For it would appear that the object of Shakespeare's ambiguous humanism has forgotten the right of other beings to inclusion in such quite mundane, observable definitions. And to move back closer home, I picture a little scene: Daniel Arap Moi and Píeter Botha seated together, listening to a simultaneous translation of these prosaic lines in their own native languages, delivered by a representative victim from either state. Would we be greeted by a simultaneous guffaw from both, a conspiratorial wink and chuckle from our august listeners?

It is necessary to reduce the arrogance implicit in the denial of freedom of thought, sensibility, intuition and action to its banal dimensions. And when such a denial is anchored in superstitious structures called religion, no terms should be considered excessive for the categorisation of such conceits. What can we say, for instance, of any faith in whose name its adherents empty a bus of its passengers, line them up on a desolate highway, and riddle their bodies with bullets—then douse them with gasoline and burn them for good measure? And this for no other reason than that these victims do not belong to a specific sect of a specific faith. We can catalogue *ad infinitum* such manifested aberrations of the human mind, its capacity for limitless cruelty in many areas of the world—the Sikhs in India or the Hindus and Tamils in Sri Lanka for instance—where the quest for political separatism has been lavishly fuelled by the religious imperative. But the horror which we experience at the numerous instances of maverick insanity, in which one contending group does actually "claim credit" for discreditable acts, can be absorbed by the knowledge that the perpetrators of such acts are not "legitimate" entities. They make no claims on the respect of the world, nor on its recognition. Diplomats do not entertain them—except furtively when their political interests coincide—nor have they a voice in the gathering of nations. Their acts are, we may argue, reflexes of desperate conditioning, their reasoning pure unreason.

What response, however, can we offer, when even more horrifying events are sanctioned and promoted by a corporate existence which we call a state, when mass executions are routine, for no other cause than the courage of the victims which nerve them to resist state demands that they renounce their faith? A state where women are publicly lashed and even stoned to death for their refusal to submit to the jealously guarded dictatorship of male priesthood in matters of dressing or appearance? Where criminals, dissidents, adherents of dissenting faiths and economic saboteurs are lumped together under convenient titles as "agents of Satan on earth," "enemies of the Living Faith" and other versions of religious rhetoric which then become their own authority for their consequent imprisonment, torture and dehumanisation. The time has come, I believe, to address this twentieth-century anomaly in a blunt manner, to question whether such states, wherever they exist, actually qualify to be counted among a community of nations. And this call upon the attention of the world is not rhetorical. Even as far away as my own corner of the world, Nigeria, we have experienced, in very recent times, variants of this extremist virus, and it is an unsettling fact that some of the instigators of these destabilising events were creations of the export trade of this aggressive machinery for the imprisonment of the human mind through far-flung agencies of the "holy state."

Of course, such concerns must seem remote to a large part of the world, where secularism, even side by side with the existence of state religions, has long been recognised as the same route to internal stability within the state. Yet even such fortunate nations cannot pretend that their political decisions are not often governed by the vagaries, the unpredictability of these theocracies whose political pathology can be described, at best, as unstable. We must not of course underestimate the historical and political content of such instabilities, nor indeed the aspect of unequal economic relations which drive smaller nations to reflexive hostility, manifested in acts which appear inexplicable and contradictory. These injustices exist, and we would be foolish to deny them. It is impossible for instance to deny the long history of the subject or inferior relation imposed by European nations on Third World countries which have resulted, in many cases, in a reflex of hostile suspicion, unfortunately directed inward at their own kind in those familiar exercises of national self-recovery or psychological reconstitution. But we cannot continue eternally with such special pleading, and certainly not when we can point to other Third World nations, with identical historical conditioning, who have nevertheless transcended the morbid temptations of the past by understanding that its citizens are equal partners in the fashioning of a new, authentic national character. Such exemplars do exist, though the count is sadly modest. And where the political strategy for such emergence is complicated by

the religious factor, the result, as we have seen, is the retrogressive enthronement of the enslavement experience.

The twenty-first century man or woman cannot be a creature of medieval fantasies and dogmatic superstition. What follows now is, I know, a highly unlikely proposition, but who knows? After all, hardly any dominant religion—Christianity, Islam, Hinduism, etc. has not had its contemporary share of disaster through contending sects within its own adherents—the murderous consequences of Iranian extremists in Saudi Arabia is one very fresh example which must never be permitted to fade from world consciousness. So, perhaps the following notion would find adherents in quite unlikely places. And so to the proposition—if the United Nations, or more probably UNESCO, has not yet found a theme for the closing decade of this century, what about declaring it a *Decade for Secular Options?* Let me hasten to add that I do not advocate an attempted (and quite impossible) demolition of religious thought, practices or any reduction in the cultural status of their physical structures—mosques, churches, temples, shrines etc. As a mythopoet, I have drawn from far too deep and rich resources in religious essence to trivialise or despise the pervasiveness of religion in human actions. But it is time, surely, to come to terms also with the anomaly of the theocratic state at the close of the twentieth century, especially when, as inhumanely chronicled by the upsurge of hitherto unthinkable atavism of the past few decades, this idealistic striving of the human imagination has been ordained as principles for the reversion of gains in the liberating of that same human mind.

These, then, are the realities, not any abstract or idealistic notion of human rights. We know of the wrongs of economic privation, of the explosive inequity of inegalitarian societies, of the lack of organisational will or sheer leadership irresponsibility which routinely condemn entire peoples to slow starvation, forced migrations, a pathetic canvas that is painted and repainted over with the same monotonous strokes, year after year. But a conspiracy of diplomatic silences appears to overtake the civilised world where the ravages of religious extremism plead with us for urgent redress. It is time, surely, for an aggressive recognition of the aggressive face of religion. "Toward a Secular Understanding?"

"Action for Secular Politics?" "Decade for Religious Tolerance?" "Decade for Secular Options?" Whatever title it goes by, this reordering of the human mind must reach beyond mere rhetoric into the twenty-first century.

ANONYMOUS
TESTIMONY OF AN EX-CENSOR

In 1987, the periodical *Index on Censorship* published an account of how censorship works in Syria, written by a journalist who was once a censor in the Ministry of Information. The journalist, who insisted on anonymity, describes here the process by which the state controlled all cultural and political expression.

Censorship as we know it now in Syria began with the first *coup d'état* in 1947 which was led by Housni al-Zaim, and which was followed by a series of coups. With each new coup, censorship increased and was further tightened. By the time of the last coup, led by Hafiz al-Assad in 1970, the whole state structure was transformed into one large intelligence and censorship apparatus.

As early as elementary school, files are kept on each student and transferred to secondary schools and so on. This system, started in 1979, ensures that the authorities have records of all your activities, friends, and other important details. Teachers and headmasters are responsible for the compilation of those files. Some teachers chose to quit their jobs rather than act as intelligence officers in schools. In the universities, half of the academic staff are, in fact, working for the intelligence service. Nowadays in Syria, a person is not innocent until proven guilty. It is the accused's responsibility to prove themselves innocent of any charges raised by the intelligence.

Your question about Syrian journalists is not a valid one since there are no journalists in Syria anymore. Real Syrian journalists are either dead, or living in exile, working for other Arab periodicals published in the West or the Middle East. Meanwhile, a whole new generation of "journalists" has been raised by the state. In 1975, for

example, the state introduced a university degree for journalists with both faculty and curriculum chosen and carefully monitored by the state. That is understandable, as reporters and writers later became government employees. Editors have to be members of the ruling Ba'ath Party.

In 1963 I became editor of a weekly magazine, *al-Mawqef al-Arabi*, then the editor of a children's magazine as well as of another cultural weekly. Those publications are all owned by the government, and every time I got out of line I was removed from my job and given a desk job at the Ministry of Information, either doing nothing or working in the office of the censor or just staying at home and cashing my salary.

The crunch came in 1977 as a result of a current affairs column I wrote alternately with a colleague on one of the dailies. After I wrote a critical piece about the Shah of Iran, a decree was issued to ban me from further writing. I was fired from my position as editor of the cultural magazine *al-Marifa*, because I published a selection of the works of a nineteenth-century writer that called on people to refuse living as meek subjects under the rule of an oppressor. Even though the famous nineteenth-century verse was available in any Syrian or Arab library, I was called by the intelligence office to be questioned about that as well as about a column I wrote for an Arab publication in London, *al-Dastour*. I was told at the end of the interrogation that writers like me have no place in Syria. So I left my country for good. . . .

There used to be a number of privately owned newspapers and magazines, but now all periodicals are owned by the government and its various departments. The major papers are *al-Ba'ath*, the organ of the ruling party, published in Damascus; *Tishreen*, which represents the presidential palace, also published in the capital; and *al-Thawra*, published by the Ministry of Information in Damascus. There are local papers in the cities of Homs, Aleppo, Hama and Lazikia, all published by the state.

The Ministry of Information and the "official" Writers Union each publish four magazines and the Army publishes five. There are no underground publications in Syria.

As for Arabic language and foreign periodicals published outside Syria, the general rule is that they are all banned from entering the country. However, a foreign publication may apply for distribution in Syria by submitting an application to the Ministry of Information together with copies of the publication. The censor's office in the Ministry of Information may or may not respond, but unless the publication receives permission, it may not be distributed. But even permission to distribute does not mean the publication has an automatic right to do so, since each issue has to obtain the censor's prior approval. If there is an offending article, the issue is seized. Some papers, like *al-Safir* of Lebanon, often print stories which the Syrian government considers important alongside items that may be offensive to the Syrian authorities. Usually such an issue is permitted after the offending item has been deleted.

The law restricting the import of periodicals, passed in 1974, was later extended to include books. Before a book can be distributed, it has to be submitted to the censor's office, which stamps its approval or disapproval. Any publication sent to an individual in the mail is censored by a special office established by the Ministry at the post office. Tapes, records, and video cassettes are all handled by the censor's office in the Ministry of Culture.

There are private publishing houses in Syria, but this means nothing since all manuscripts have to be presented to the Ministry of Information, which will stamp each page it approves. After publication, the book, along with the manuscript, must again be presented to the censor to check that nothing has been changed or added. This applies to everything published in Syria. There are also government publishing houses which print the books of several semigovernmental organisations such as the Writers Union or those of the Ministry of Culture. If there is any question regarding the publication of a book, it is sent to the Cultural Office of the Ba'ath Party to see whether it is fit for publication.

A list of censored books is regularly sent to the political security department of the Ministry of the Interior. This department, in turn, makes spot checks on all bookshops to ensure that no banned book is on sale or even in stock. Members of this department wear civilian clothes.

Books and periodicals brought in from abroad are usually confiscated. These publications are then listed and the list must be taken to the Ministry of Information to be stamped. On leaving the country one must hand the list to the authorities and only then are the books handed back. No books or periodicals can be taken out of the country without prior permission of the Ministry of Information, which takes down the title, author, and the name of the person who wishes to take the book abroad.

All key positions in radio and television are manned by members of the Ba'ath Party. However, everything from songs to scientific programmes and news has to first pass the different censorship committees. So to keep in touch with the world, Syrians listen to foreign stations for news, like the BBC World Service, Radio Monte Carlo, Voice of America, or Egyptian Radio.

The film censorship committee checks the script of each film before permission to shoot is granted. It then reviews the film after it has been produced to see that the screenplay has not been changed. Some movies are produced by the state, through "the General Organisation for the Cinema," and are subject to censorship within this organisation. Like books and periodicals, there is a law that makes the import of films a state monopoly. Nothing in Syria evades the censor—even Friday sermons in the mosques have to be written down and presented to the Ministry of Religious Affairs for approval before being preached.

A major difficulty is that there are no guidelines whatsoever for what cannot be included in artistic works. It is all according to someone's whim: the censor, a prominent party member, the president, the president's brother, and so on. In some instances, when the authorities like to be regarded as "revolutionary," they permit some songs, like those of Sheikh Imam of Egypt, or the poetry of the Iraqi, Mudhafar al-Nawab, not permitted anywhere else in the region, as long as they are not about the Syrian Ba'ath Party.

They even permit the famous Syrian actor, Ghawar al-Toushi, to stage plays critical of Arab governments as a whole and the lack of democracy in the Middle East. This does not directly attack them and gives Syrian art an air of reality which at present is absent from all other aspects of Syrian life.

NABIL JANABI
MEMOIR OF TERROR

Nabil Janabi, an Iraqi poet, was arrested in 1976 and sentenced to five years in jail for criticizing the Iraqi government's repression of the Kurdish independence movement. When Janabi was released from prison in 1981 he was harassed for refusing to support the Iraqi war against Iran. He eventually was forced into exile in Britain, where he writes for Arab newspapers and magazines. An account of his ordeal follows.

It was very cold at the end of that winter, in March, after the execution of the young poet Abdul Jabbar Issa, from Basra, southern Iraq, who was accused of publishing some poems against the Iraqi dictatorial regime. After his execution, on 11 March, I went to Mogul, 400 hundred miles north of Baghdad, to celebrate with the Kurds the anniversary of the independence of Kurdistan from Iraq.

I had written a poem asking for freedom and democracy for my Iraqi people. I read that poem to an assembly of Kurds at Sinjar, Western Mogul. At 6 P.M. on that day I was arrested by the security forces and taken by Land Rover, escorted by six gunmen, to their headquarters in Mogul.

My friend Mattow, who had been my escort, was arrested with me.

We arrived in Mogul at 3 A.M. They pushed us

into a dank, wet room, the floor of which was covered with dirty water. There were four tins full of human dirt in a row by the wall, put there as a bed for anybody who wanted to sleep. There was no proper bed and nowhere dry on the floor.

My friend rang the bell to ask for another room to spend the rest of that night. A gunman came.

"What do you want?" he asked.

"We want to sleep," replied my friend.

"There's the bed." He pointed with his machine gun to the tins of dirt by the wall.

"Could *you* sleep on them?" I asked.

"I am not a traitor." he replied. "This is the bed of traitors."

"You're right," I said. "Everybody who asks for freedom and democracy is a traitor," I added.

"You will be able to test your nice democracy and freedom in the morning." He was blackmailing me.

Realising what we were to face in the morning, I asked my friend Mattow to be quiet.

We spent the next four hours talking, each perched on tins like a couple of cats trying to escape from a flood. At 7:30 A.M. the heavy door was opened and we were handcuffed together.

We were interviewed by two security officers who certainly knew nothing about freedom or democracy. One of them wrote down my name and asked me, "What is your occupation?"

"A director at the Ministry of Industry," I replied.

"What are you doing here in Mogul?" he asked.

"I came to celebrate with the Kurds at Sinjar."

"Are you Kurdish?"

"No."

"Why then do you celebrate if you're not Kurdish?"

"What is wrong with that?" I asked.

"It means you're a traitor," he explained.

"No I am not," I told him.

Then he left me and started, along with other officers, to torture my friend Mattow, who was a Kurd. They tortured him by hitting him with electric rods, shaving his beard upside-down, hitting his head against the wall.

When they found that he had nothing to say, they released him and said they would take me to Baghdad to face my own "Hell."

They handcuffed me and put me into a Volkswagen car. I was escorted in the car by two officers, and four others followed in another car. They were all armed with machine guns. After four hours, at 4 P.M., we arrived in Baghdad.

I was taken to the headquarters of the Baghdad security forces. They ordered me to sit on the cold floor in Reception as they waited to find a place for me in their overcrowded cells. I did as they ordered but it was very difficult for me, a proud poet, to sit on the floor before stupid young officers who knew nothing about poets or poetry, who had never been educated, only brainwashed.

After three hours of sitting on the floor, I was taken by two very big gunmen into a single, cold, dark cell with no bedding. I found only a tin for my waste, but I felt better because at least this cell wasn't flooded.

I took my jacket and shoes off to make a pillow, a very hard pillow. I slept that night in terror. The door of the cell was opened at 3 A.M. They took me out, blindfolded to an unknown place. After walking for 10 minutes round the building I was led, still blindfolded to the first floor.

They asked me to explain the poem which I had read to the assembly in Mogul. After I had done this they started torturing me by attaching one end of an electric wire to my left big toe and the other end to my penis. They put the power on and I lost consciousness for about an hour, then they repeated this with the electric wire attached to my right foot. Again I passed out. While I lay half dead on the floor they tried to revive me by torturing me with cigarettes and steel rods.

When I regained consciousness again, they tied my head and both legs together and put me into a tire. They started to spin it; two men on either side kept spinning me round and round. In addition to all this, I was completely naked, they'd even taken off my pants.

Then they started to beat me. Two men were

beating me with electric rods, hitting my testicles. Afterwards, my testicles were so enlarged they came down to my knees.

I stopped eating food, couldn't walk, couldn't talk and my whole body was inflamed.

Next day they hit and kicked me on the inflamed parts of my body to hurt me even more.

My head was injured, my nose was bleeding, my urine was full of blood.

Eventually, a military doctor was called. He told them to stop torturing me otherwise I would die. But they didn't. They made me sign a piece of paper without telling me what was on it. After about six months of torture they sent me for trial to a military—so-called "revolutionary"—court, without a solicitor or any legal defence.

After a trial which lasted two minutes the court decided to jail me for five years for publishing a poem "calculated to incite people to act against the government."

Then the court decided to destroy the poem, and banned it from being read or copied out or recorded on cassette or sold or bought, forever.

The poem was:

Those words I said through my poetic travels
Were my entrance to my real novels.
I was—I imagine—the gate I had to pass
To reach the bottom of my poetic palace.
It was musical freedom, but it could not sing:
The singer himself was banned from singing.
I do not know why I could not get in
To that poetic room to sleep,
Between those virgin poems to weep.
Before knocking there we must be sure
That poems are allowed to meet the core
That people are ready for poetry
Like a child on his first day at school
Or the earth in her first meeting with the seed
Or the artist preparing to meet the
Theatre lights.

Through those poetic travels, I brushed

All the Arab world, I discovered that the
        word is
Absolute power, a queen who can't give up
Her throne.
I discovered that the word is a woman who
        can
Move mountains from their places,
Water from the seas,
Governments from their seats
And repeat the writing of history round the
        world.

Some rulers find the word their enemy.
Some cut her hair,
Cut off her tongue
Force her to put on
Her veil to cover the truth.
Some of them want the word as
Slave and prostitute.
Want her to love them, not to share
Their rule but live with them
As slave and prostitute.
And if she does, they will be
Generous to her with gold, silver
And jewels.

Some rulers jail the word
In prisons for women.
They chain her feet, they shut her mouth,
Give her no cigarettes to smoke,
No paper to read,
No book, not even a piece of paper
To write her will on
And no pencil to write with.
But despite all the rulers, despite their power,
All the radar and missiles that cover the
Poem's sky,
The word will continue to fly
All over the world.
No power can ban it or stop it
From landing at any airport
For the word is a bird
That needs no entry visa
For freedom
For democracy.

SHERKO BEKAS

THE ROOTS and SEPARATION

The Kurds are an ethnic and linguistic group who live in contiguous areas of Iran, Iraq, and Turkey. After the dissolution of the Ottoman Empire, the Kurds were left without a homeland. The Turkish government tried to assimilate them forcibly, as did Iran and Iraq. However, attempts to suppress Kurdish culture and religious life have seemed only to enflame Kurdish nationalism.

In Iraq, where Kurds are nearly twenty percent of the population, the government permitted them limited self-rule in 1974. However, Kurdish nationalists continued their agitation for independence. In 1988, the Iraqi government put down the Kurdish rebellion with poison gas, killing thousands of Kurdish people. In 1991, following the Persian Gulf War, an estimated 1,000,000 Kurds fled Iraq and sought refuge in Turkey and Iran, trying to escape the brutal regime of Saddam Hussein.

Sherko Bekas (1940–   ) was born in southern Kurdistan in Iraq; his father was a famous Kurdish poet. He was educated in Sulaymaniya and Baghdad, and his first collection of poems was published in 1968. Bekas was deeply involved in the Kurdish National Liberation Movement, which sought independence from Iraq. He joined the movement in 1965 and worked for its radio station. Since 1987 Bekas has lived in Sweden, where he continues to write poetry. In 1987 he won the Swedish Pen Club's Tucholsky prize, presented to him by the Swedish prime minister. Two of his poems are reproduced here.

The Roots

Those birds who are killed in skies
though stars, clouds, wind
        and the sun do not testify
against the murderers
And the horizon does not want
        to listen
Mountains and waters forget
        them.
Yet some tree must
        have witnessed the crime
And will write the names of the
        murderers on its roots.

Separation

If within my poems
You take out the flower
From the four seasons
One of my seasons will die
If you exclude love
Two of my seasons will die
If you exclude bread
Three of my seasons will die
And if you take away freedom
All four seasons and I will die.

LUIS AGUILAR
IN DEFENSE OF FREE SPEECH

In May 1960 *Diario de la Marina*, the oldest and most conservative newspaper in Cuba, was taken over by its workers, ending the paper's criticism of the Castro regime. On May 13, 1960 the following protest by Luis Aguilar (1926–   ) appeared in *Prensa Libre*. Two days later, *Prensa Libre* suffered the same fate as *Diario de la Marina*. Aguilar's article was the last defense of free speech permitted in Fidel Castro's Cuba.

The Cuban-born Aguilar attended college and received a law degree at Havana University, where Fidel Castro was also a student. Aguilar studied philosophy in Madrid and contemporary problems in France. On his return to Cuba, he practiced law, was a professor at the University of Oriente, and wrote articles critical of the Batista regime. After the Cuban revolution he was named a member of the Revolutionary Institute of Culture.

After the trial of Hubert Matos, one of the heroes of the Cuban Revolution, Aguilar resigned from the Revolutionary Institute of Culture. Shortly after the following article was published Aguilar received a visit from the Minister of Justice, an old friend, who suggested that it was time for him to leave Cuba. He emigrated to the United States in 1960, where he became a professor of Latin American studies, most recently at Georgetown University.

I thoroughly disagree with what you say, but I shall defend to the death your right to say it.
—Voltaire

I want a hundred ideas to germinate in my country, and a hundred buds to sprout.
—Mao Tse-Tung

Freedom of speech, if it is to be real, must be extended to all and not be the prerogative or special gift of anyone. That is the crux of the problem. It is not a question of defending the ideas maintained by the newspaper *Diario de la Marina*. It is a question of defending the *Diario de la Marina*'s right to express its ideas, and the right of thousands of Cuban citizens to read what they think is worth reading. Hard battles have been fought in Cuba on behalf of that freedom of expression and freedom of choice. And it has been said that if one began by persecuting a newspaper for maintaining an idea, he would end up persecuting all ideas. And it has been said that there was a desire for a regime in which there would be room for the newspaper *Hoy*, of the Communists, and the *Diario de la Marina*, of

conservative leanings. Despite that, the *Diario de la Marina* has disappeared as a vehicle of thought. And the newspaper *Hoy* remains freer and more firmly established than ever. Evidently the regime has lost its determination to maintain balance.

For those of us who long for full freedom of expression to be crystallized in Cuba once and for all, for those of us who are convinced that in this country of ours union and tolerance among all Cubans are essential for carrying forward the purest and most fertile ideals, the ideological death of another newspaper produces a sad and somber echo. For, however it may be presented, the silencing of a public organ of thought or its unconditional enlistment in the government line implies nothing less than the subjugation, by one means or another, of a tenacious critical posture. All the massive propaganda of the government was not enough. There was the voice and there was the argument. And since they did not want or were not able to debate the argument, it was indispensable to choke off the voice. The method is an old one, the results are well known.

Now the time of unanimity is arriving in Cuba, a solid and impenetrable totalitarian unanimity. The same slogan will be repeated by all the organs of news. There will be no disagreeing voices, no possibility of criticism, no public refutations. Control of all the media of expression will facilitate the work of persuasion, collective fear will take charge of the rest. And underneath the sound of the vociferous propaganda, there will remain . . . the silence. The silence of those who cannot speak. The implicated silence of those who, being able to speak, did not venture to do so.

But, it is shouted, the fatherland is in danger. Well then, if it is, let us defend it by making it unattackable both in theory and in practice. Let us wield arms, but also our rights. Let us start by showing the world that here there is a free people, a truly free people, and that here all ideas and attitudes can coexist. Or is it that in order to save our national liberty we must begin by suffocating civil liberties? Or is it that in order to defend our sovereignty we must limit the sovereign rights of the individual? Or is it that in order to demonstrate the justice of our cause we must make common cause with the injustice of totalitarian methods? Would it not be much more beautiful and much more worthy to offer all America the example of a people that makes ready to defend its freedom without impairing the freedom of anyone, without offering even the shade of a pretext to those who suggest that we here are falling into a government of force?

Unfortunately, that does not seem to be the path that has been chosen. Instead of the sane multiplicity of opinions, the formula of a single guide, a single watchword, and common obedience is preferred. This way leads to compulsory unanimity. And then not even those who have remained silent will find shelter in their silence. For unanimity is worse than censorship. Censorship obliges us to hold our own truth silent; unanimity forces us to repeat the truth of others, even though we do not believe it. That is to say, it dissolves our own personalities into a general, monotonous chorus. And there is nothing worse than that for those who do not have the herd instinct.

HEBERTO PADILLA

POEMS OF THE CUBAN REVOLUTION

After Fidel Castro led the revolution in Cuba that overthrew dictator Fulgencio Batista, he organized a Marxist-Leninist state and prohibited any opposition to the Communist party. In its zeal to impose ideological conformity, the Castro regime closely regulated artistic expression, speech, and the press; such democratic freedoms were scorned as "bourgeois freedoms."

In 1971 the Cuban poet Heberto Padilla was arrested because of criticism expressed in some of his poems. Padilla had won an international prize in 1968 for his book *Fuera del Juego (Out of the Game)*. Two weeks after Padilla's arrest, he confessed his "sins" and was released soon afterwards. In May 1971 an international group of writers who had previously supported the Cuban revolution—including Jean Paul Sartre, Simone de Beauvoir, Alberto Moravia, and Susan Sontag—denounced Padilla's confession. It was "a pitiful text," they said, that "could have only been obtained by methods which are the negation of legality and revolutionary justice."

In disgrace, Padilla worked mainly as a translator. In 1980, he was allowed to leave Cuba. He emigrated to the United States and settled in Princeton, New Jersey. The following poems were among those that caused his arrest.

Don't Tell Me

Don't tell me there are crimes more or less beautiful
because there are no beautiful crimes.
There are no degrees in crime.
Don't attempt to convince me that every hope
has to be for a time in the hands of
    executioners.

I want a value to judge my era by, even though
    you may shout
that a tribe of sad old men
already invented it for me! You were also
    invented
by the same old men: you and I are children
    of sadness.

To Write on the Scrapbook of a Tyrant

Protect yourself from those who vacillate,
because one day they will know what they
    don't want.
Protect yourself from those who mumble,
Juàn-the-stutterer, Pedro-the-mute,

because one day they shall find their strong
    voice.
Protect yourself from the timid and the
    frightened,
because one day they will not rise when you
    enter.

Instructions to Enter a New Society

First, optimistic
Secondly, neat, measured, and obedient.
(To have passed all the physical fitness tests.)
And finally to walk like every member:

one step forward
and two or three backward,
but always applauding.

MAURICIO REDOLES
PRESS CONFERENCE

Born in Santiago, Chile, Mauricio Redoles studied law in Valparaiso. After the 1973 coup, which brought a brutal military government to power, Redoles was imprisoned for nearly two years. He was expelled from Chile in 1975 and went to England, where he studied sociology. His poems, one of which, "Press Conference," is reproduced here, have been published in anthologies and magazines in Latin America, North America, and Europe.

Even Chile could not resist the democratic tide in Latin America in the 1980s. The military dictator Augusto Pinochet held a plebiscite in October 1988, which he lost

Pinochet then stepped aside to permit free elections in December 1989. The election was won by Christian Democrat Patricio Alywin, who represented the united opposition and who promised to restore democracy to Chile.

"In Chile there are no political prisoners
The ones there are are
politicians who are prisoners
are
Prisoners who are not political
just
prisoners"
Since when do we have to
explain so many things?
  (the general perspires)

"Here we've put an end to Marxism

There are no more social classes
They were abolished the
proletariat was dissolved through proclamation
Number twenty whatever"
  (the general smiles)

"No, no, no
Our economic policies
Benefit no one
Here we all have to tighten our belts we
are all equal
Yes

Protesters in Chile in 1988 hold photographs of family members and friends, all part of "the disappeared"—citizens who had vanished during the reign of the military junta. Chileans experienced human rights abuses until free elections were held in December 1989.

There is unemployment, hunger, but . . ."

"No, no, no, no," I said, "it rankles
  unemployment, it rankles"
you get that?
"Yes
Put that down yes
put it down and send it to the embassy"
  (the general sighs)

"The disappeared?
There have always been disappeared people in
    Chile
For example Lieutenant Bello in the illustrious
    history . . .

In the history of our . . .
In the air force . . .
Lieutenant Bello, for example
You understand?"
    (the general looks at his adviser slyly)

"Freedom of the press yes
Yes there is freedom of the press any
Person who does not contravene our norms
Has the right to publish whatever
He wishes but
He'd better respect our arms . . .
I mean norms"
    (the general has lost his color)

OCTAVIO PAZ

LATIN AMERICA AND DEMOCRACY

A major figure in world literature, Octavio Paz (1914–   ) was awarded the Nobel Prize for Literature in 1990. Born in Mexico City, Paz is a poet, critic, essayist, social philosopher, editor, and diplomat. Educated at the National University of Mexico, he served for many years in the diplomatic corps, including several years as Mexican ambassador to India. Paz has taught at the University of Texas, Cambridge University, and Harvard University. Although his earliest political sympathies were leftist, Paz was one of the first Latin American intellectuals to condemn the brutality of the Castro regime in Cuba at a time when it was revered by intellectuals in Latin America and Europe. The following is an excerpt from an essay included in his book, *One Earth, Four or Five Worlds: Reflections on Contemporary History.*

. . . For almost two centuries now, misapprehensions about the historical reality of Latin America have been accumulating. Even the names used to designate it are inexact: Latin America, Hispanic America, Iberoamerica, Indioamerica. Each of these names leaves out a part of reality. Nor are the economic, social, and political labels that are pinned on it any more apt. The notion of underdevelopment, for example, can be applied to economics and technology, but not to art, literature, ethics, or politics. The expression "Third World" is even vaguer, a term that is not only imprecise but actually misleading: what relation is there between Argentina

and Angola, between Thailand and Costa Rica, between Tunisia and Brazil? . . .

Architecture is the mirror of societies, but a mirror that shows us enigmatic images that we must decipher. The opulence and refinement of Mexico City or Puebla in the middle of the eighteenth century stand in sharp contrast to the austere simplicity, bordering on poverty, of Boston or Philadelphia. A deceptive splendor: what was a dawn in the United States was a twilight in Hispanic America. Americans were born with the Reformation and the Enlightenment—that is, with the modern world; we were born with the Counter-Reformation and

Neo-Scholasticism—that is, against the modern world. We had neither an intellectual revolution nor a democratic revolution of the bourgeoisie. The philosophical foundation of the absolute Catholic monarchy was the body of thought of Francisco Suárez and his disciples of the Society of Jesus. These theologians renovated, with genius, traditional Thomism and converted it into a philosophical fortress. The historian Richard Morse has shown, with penetrating insight, that the function of Neo-Thomism was twofold: on the one hand, at times explicitly and at others implicitly, it was the ideological cornerstone of the imposing political, juridical, and economic edifice that we call the Spanish Empire; on the other, it was the school of our intellectual class and modeled their habits and their attitudes. In this sense—not as a philosophy but as a mental attitude—its influence still lingers on among Latin American intellectuals.

In the beginning, Neo-Thomism was a system of thought aimed at defending orthodox beliefs against Lutheran and Calvinist heresies, which were the first expressions of modernity. Unlike the other philosophical tendencies of that era, it was not a method for exploring the unknown but a system for defending the known and the established. The Modern Age began with a criticism of first principles; Neo-Scholasticism set out to defend those principles and demonstrate their necessary, eternal, and inviolable nature. Although this philosophy vanished from the intellectual horizon of Latin America in the eighteenth century, the attitudes and habits that were consubstantial with it have persisted up to our own day. Our intellectuals have successively embraced liberalism, positivism, and now Marxism-Leninism; nonetheless, in almost all of them, whatever their philosophy, it is not difficult to discern—buried deep but still alive—the moral and psychological attitudes of the old champions of Neo-Scholasticism. Thus they display a paradoxical modernity: the ideas are today's; the attitudes yesterday's. Their grandfathers swore by Saint Thomas and they swear by Marx, yet both have seen in reason a weapon in the service of a Truth with a capital T, which it is the

mission of intellectuals to defend. They have a polemical and militant idea of culture and of thought: they are crusaders. Thus there has been perpetuated in our lands an intellectual tradition that has little respect for the opinion of others, that prefers ideas to reality and intellectual systems to the critique of systems. . . .

. . . [I]t may be said that the nineteenth century began with three great revolutions: those waged by the American colonies, by the French, and by the nations of Latin America. All three won a victory on the battlefield, but the political and social results were quite different in each case. In the United States the revolution brought the birth of the very first society that was wholly modern, despite the taint it bore of black slavery and the extermination of the Indians. Although the French nation suffered substantial and radical changes, the new society that emerged from its revolution, as Tocqueville demonstrated, was in many respects a continuation of the centralist France of Richelieu and Louis XIV. In Latin America, the various peoples achieved independence and began to govern themselves; the revolutionaries, however, did not succeed in establishing, except on paper, regimes and institutions that were truly free and democratic. The American Revolution founded a nation; the French Revolution changed and renewed a society; the Latin American revolutions failed to achieve one of their fundamental objectives: political, social, and economic modernization.

The French and American revolutions were the consequence of the historical evolution of the two nations; the Latin American movements were limited to the adoption of the doctrines and programs of others. I underscore the word: "adoption," not "adaptation." In Latin America the intellectual tradition that, since the Reformation and the Enlightenment, had shaped the minds and consciences of the French and American elite, did not exist; nor did there exist the social classes that corresponded, historically, to the new liberal and democratic ideology. A middle class barely existed, and our bourgeoisie had scarcely gone beyond the mercantilist stage. There had been an organic relationship between the revolutionary groups in France and their ideas, and the same thing can be said of the American Revolution; in our case, ideas did not correspond to social classes. Ideas served the function of masks; they were thus converted into an ideology, in the negative sense of that word—that is, into veils that interfere with and distort the perception of reality. Ideology converts ideas into masks: they hide the person who wears them, and at the same time they keep him from seeing reality. They deceive both others and ourselves. . . .

. . . On the collapse of the Spanish Empire and its administration, power fell into the hands of two groups: economic power fell to the native oligarchs, political power to the military. The oligarchies did not have sufficient power to govern in their own name. Under the Spanish regime, civil society, far from prospering and developing as it had elsewhere in the West, had lived in the shadow of the State. The focal reality in our countries, as in Spain, was the patrimonialist system. Under this system, the head of government—prince or viceroy, *caudillo* or president—directs the State and the nation as an extension of his own patrimony—that is, as though it were his own household. The oligarchies, made up of owners of large estates and traders, had lived in subordination to authority and lacked both political experience and influence on the populace. On the other hand, the ascendancy of the clergy was enormous, as was, though to a lesser degree, that of lawyers, doctors, and other members of the liberal professions. These groups—the seed of the modern intellectual class—embraced, immediately and fervently, the ideologies of the era, some liberal and others conservative. The other force, the decisive one, was the military. In countries without democratic experience, with rich oligarchies and poor governments, the struggle between political factions inevitably led to violence. The liberals were no less violent than the conservatives—or, rather, they were as fanatical as their adversaries. The endemic civil war produced militarism, and militarism produced dictatorship.

For more than a century, Latin America has lived amid disorder and tyranny, anarchical violence and despotism. Attempts have been made to attribute the persistence of these evils to the absence of the social classes and the economic structures that made democracy possible in Europe and in the United States. That is quite true: we have lacked really modern bourgeoisies; the middle class has been weak and numerically small; the proletariat is recent. But democracy is not simply the result of the social and economic conditions inherent in capitalism and the industrial revolution. Castoriadis has shown that democracy is a genuine political *creation*—that is to say, a totality of ideas, institutions, and practices that constitute a collective *invention.* Democracy has been invented twice, once in Greece and again in the West. In both cases it was born of the conjunction of the theories and ideas of several generations and the actions of different groups and classes, such as the bourgeoisie, the proletariat, and other sectors of society. Democracy is not a superstructure, but a popular creation. Moreover, it is the condition, the basis, of modern civilization. . . .

. . . [I]t is significant that the frequency of military coups d'état has never obscured the principle of democratic legitimacy in the awareness of our peoples. Its moral authority has never been challenged. Hence, invariably, on taking over power, all dictators solemnly declare that their rule is provisional and that they are prepared to restore democratic institutions the moment circumstances permit. They very seldom keep their promise, it is true; but this does not matter. What strikes me as revealing and worth stressing is that they feel obliged to make the promise. This is a phenomenon of major importance, the meaning of which very few have pondered: until the second half of the twentieth century, no one dared challenge the proposition that democracy represents historical and constitutional legitimacy in Latin America. Our nations were democratic by birth, and, despite crimes and tyrannies, democracy was a sort of historic act of baptism for our peoples. The situation has changed in the last twenty-five years, and this change calls for comment.

Fidel Castro's movement stirred the imagination of many Latin Americans, particularly students and intellectuals. He appeared as the heir to the great traditions of our peoples: the independence and unity of Latin America, anti-imperialism, a program of radical and necessary social reforms, the restoration of democracy. One by one these illusions have vanished. The story of the degeneration of the Cuban Revolution has been recounted a number of times, among others by such direct participants in the revolution as Carlos Franqui, so I shall not repeat the details yet again. I shall merely note that the unfortunate involution of the Castro regime has been the result of a concatenation of circumstances: the very personality of the revolutionary leader, who is a typical Latin American *caudillo* in the Hispano-Arabic tradition; the totalitarian structure of the Cuban Communist Party, which was the political instrument for the imposition of the Soviet model of bureaucratic domination; the insensitivity and obtuse arrogance of Washington, especially during the first phase of the Cuban Revolution, before it was taken over by the communist bureaucracy; and finally, as in the other countries of Latin America, the weakness of our democratic traditions. This last circumstance explains why, even though its despotic nature becomes more palpable and the failures of its economic and social policy more widely known with each passing day, the regime still preserves part of its initial ascendancy among young university students and certain intellectuals. . . .

I have already pointed out that Latin American dictatorships consider themselves to be exceptional, provisional regimes. None of our dictators, not even the most brazen of them, has ever denied the historical legitimacy of democracy. The first regime to have dared to proclaim a different sort of legitimacy was Castro's. The foundation of his power is not the will of the majority as expressed by free and secret vote, but a conception that, despite its scientific pretensions, bears a certain resemblance to the Mandate of Heaven of ancient China. This conception, fabricated out of bits and pieces of

Marxism (both the true variety and the apocryphal ones), is the official credo of the Soviet Union and of the other bureaucratic dictatorships. I shall repeat the hackneyed formula: the general, ascendant movement of history is embodied in a class, the proletariat, which hands it over to a party, which delegates it to a committee, which entrusts it to a leader. Castro governs in the name of history. Like divine will, history is a superior authority, immune to the erratic and contradictory opinions of the masses. . . .

. . . [T]he absolute monarch exercised power in the name of a superior and supernatural authority, God; in totalitarianism, the leader exercises power in the name of his identification with the party, the proletariat, and the laws that govern historical development. The leader is universal history in person. The transcendent God of the theologians of the sixteenth and seventeenth centuries descends to earth and becomes "the historical process"; "the historical process" in turn becomes incarnate in this or that leader: Stalin, Mao, Fidel. Totalitarianism usurps religious forms, empties them of their content, and cloaks itself with them. Modern democracy had completed the separation between religion and politics; totalitarianism unites them once more, but they are now inverted: the content of the politics of the absolute monarch was religious; today politics is the content of totalitarian pseudo-religion. . . .

The antidemocratic nature of this conception is as disturbing as its pseudo-scientific pretensions. Not only are the acts and the politics of the Castro regime a negation of democracy; so, likewise, are the very principles on which it is founded. In this sense the Cuban bureaucratic dictatorship is a real historical novelty on our continent: with it began not socialism but a "revolutionary legitimacy" aimed at taking the place of the historical legitimacy of democracy. Thus the tradition on which Latin America was founded has been broken. . . .

The problems of Latin America, it is said, are those of an underdeveloped continent, yet the term "underdeveloped" is misleading: it is not a description but a judgment. That statement says something without explaining. Underdevelopment of what, why, and in relation to what model or paradigm? It is a technocratic concept that disdains the true values of a civilization, the physiognomy and soul of each society, an ethnocentric concept. This does not mean that we should ignore the problems of our countries: economic, political, and intellectual dependence on the outside, iniquitous social inequalities, extreme poverty side by side with wealth and extravagance, lack of civil freedoms, repression, militarism, unstable institutions, disorder, demagogy, mythomania, empty eloquence, falsehood and its masks, corruption, archaic moral attitudes, machismo, backward technology and scientific lag, intolerance in the realm of opinion, belief, and mores.

The problems are real; are the remedies equally real? The most radical of them, after twenty-five years of application, has produced the following results: the Cubans today are as poor as or poorer than they were before, and far less free; inequality has not disappeared: the hierarchies are different, and yet they are not less rigid but more rigid and draconian; repression is like the island's heat: continuous, intense, and inescapable; it continues to be economically dependent on sugar, and politically dependent on the Soviet Union. The Cuban Revolution has petrified: it is a millstone about the people's neck. At the other extreme, military dictatorships have perpetuated the disastrous and unjust *status quo*, abolished civil rights, practiced the cruelest repression, succeeded in resolving none of the economic problems, and in many cases exacerbated the social ones. And, gravest of all, they have been and are incapable of resolving the central political problem of our societies: that of the succession—that is, of the legitimacy—of governments. Thus, far from doing away with instability, they foster it.

Latin American democracy was a late arrival on the scene, and it has been disfigured and betrayed time and time again. It has been weak, hesitant, rebellious, its own worst enemy, all too eager to worship the demagogue, corrupted by money, riddled with favoritism and nepotism. And yet almost everything good that has been achieved in Latin America in the last century and a half has been accomplished under democratic rule, or, as in Mexico, a rule *heading toward* democracy. A great deal still remains to be done. Our countries need changes and reforms, at once radical and in accord with the tradition and the genius of each people. In countries where attempts have been made to change the economic and social structures while at the same time dismantling democratic institutions, injustice, oppression, and inequality have become stronger forces than ever. The cause of the workers requires, above all else, freedom of association and the right to strike, yet this is the very first thing that their liberators strip them of. Without democracy, changes are counterproductive; or, rather, they are not changes at all.

To repeat again, for on this point we must be unyielding: changes are inseparable from democracy. To defend democracy is to defend the possibility of change; in turn, changes alone can strengthen democracy and enable it to be embodied in social life. This is a tremendous, twofold task. Not only for Latin Americans: for all of us. The battle is a worldwide one. What is more, the outcome is uncertain, dubious. No matter: the battle must be waged.

MARIO VARGAS LLOSA

LATIN AMERICA: THE DEMOCRATIC OPTION

Born in Peru, Mario Vargas Llosa (1936–   ) is one of the most highly regarded novelists in the world today. He attended the University of San Marcos and the University of Madrid, where he earned a doctorate. He worked as a journalist during the 1960s and has taught in many universities. His first novel *(The Time of the Hero)* was published in 1966. At one time an admirer of the Communist revolution in Cuba, Vargas Llosa became an opponent of tyrannies of left and right in the early 1970s. In his widely praised novel, *The War of the End of the World*, Vargas Llosa depicts the vast social tragedies that grow out of fanaticism, violence, and corruption. In an unusual departure for a novelist, Vargas Llosa ran for president of Peru in 1990 (and lost).

Vargas Llosa explains the democratic tide—and what is needed to sustain it—in the following excerpt from a speech to the Trilateral Commission in San Francisco, California in March 1990.

Latin America today justifies our cautious optimism. Never before in the history of our nations—that is, since we became independent from Spain and Portugal—has our part of the world had as many governments created by (more or less) free elections. Put another way, never before have there been so few authoritarian regimes. Bloody tyrannies in Argentina and Uruguay have yielded to civilian governments—the same has happened in Brazil—as has the shameful anachronism until recently embodied by Baby Doc, ex-"perpetual president" of Haiti. Countries in which no elected president could finish out his term in office—Venezuela and the Dominican Republic, for example—are today models of pluralism and co-existence, where antagonistic political parties are voted in and out of power and where the extreme right and the extreme left receive fewer and fewer votes in each succeeding election. Even in Central America, the region that has traditionally suffered most from political oppression, we have begun to see military regimes resign themselves—not always willingly, of course—to holding elections and yielding power to civilians.

But it would be misleading to celebrate this process of democratization merely in statistical terms. Of much greater importance, I think, is the way in which this process is taking place. If we compare it with the period following World War II, when a democratic wave ran through the continent, we see that the current situation is not the result of external pressures or the work of local elites.

For the first time, democracy—or, in some cases, incipient democratic forms of government—is being established with clear popular support. Today, the antidemocratic alternatives of Marxist revolution or military dictatorship are the monopoly of economic or intellectual elites. The bulk of the populace has expressed overwhelming support for moderate regimes: center-left, center, or center-right—whichever seems to offer the best chance of achieving democracy. My own country, Peru, is a good example: in the 1985 elections, which extremists tried to sabotage by unleashing a terror campaign to keep people away from the polls, only 7 percent of the registered voters stayed home, a real achievement when you consider the level of voter apathy in the more advanced democracies.

Such huge numbers of people have been spurred to turn to democracy by the terrible violence of which they have been the victims. This violence, the result of intolerance, fanaticism, and dogma, has been practiced by both revolutionary terrorists and political or military counterterrorists, and has littered our continent with the dead, the tortured, the kidnapped, the disappeared—and the vast majority of the victims have been the poor. These people, on whom political extremists have inflicted their violence—as if economic exploitation and social discrimination were not misfortune enough—have decided to support that system which they think, intuitively and instinctively, will best be able to defend human rights and social stability, and will attempt to extirpate the pistol, the bomb, and the electric prod from political life.

This unheralded fact of Latin American life—a democratizing process that originates with the people themselves—has presented us with a unique opportunity: we Latin Americans now have the chance to consolidate our legal, free regimes and to eliminate forever the vicious circle of revolutions and military coups. We have the chance to link our destiny to something of which we have always in fact been a part: the liberal, democratic West.

Naturally, this will not be easy. The democratization of Latin America, even though it has today an unprecedented popular base, is very fragile. To maintain and extend this popular base, governments will have to prove to their citizens that democracy means not only the end of political brutality but progress—concrete benefits in areas such as labor, health, and education, where so much remains to be done. But, given Latin America's current economic crisis, when the prices of its exports are hitting record lows and the weight of its foreign debt is crushing, those governments have virtually no alternative but to demand that their citizens—especially the poor—make even greater sacrifices than they've already made.

I am not one of those who believe that the problem of foreign debt should be met with demagogic gestures or with a declaration of war against the international financial system. If such a war were to break out, Western banks might be affected; but our countries would fare even worse, because one of the first casualties of the hostilities would be the democratic system. It's hard to imagine how it would survive the chaos and paralysis that would result from an economic boycott by the developed world.

Still, the industrialized nations—their governments and their banks—must understand that if our democratic governments are forced to pay the service on their debts by implementing policies that will have extremely high social costs, the result, purely and simply, will be the collapse of those governments and the return of military dictatorships. We have already seen, in the Dominican Republic, Mexico, and Brazil, the explosions of rage and despair that can take place when the fabric of society is stretched too thin.

Military dictatorships are not only the best

breeding ground for Marxist revolutionaries. They are also models of ineptitude in the field of economics, as all recent Latin American military regimes have demonstrated. And who will reap the benefit should such regimes return? Certainly not Western banks and Western governments.

A realistic and ethically sound approach that our creditors could take would be to demand that each debtor nation pay what it can without placing its stability in jeopardy. At the same time, our creditors should provide both the stimulus and the aid necessary to reactivate the economies of the debtor nations; the more their economies grow, the more able these countries will be to pay back their debts. President Paz Estenssoro of Bolivia, a veteran revolutionary who is today a genuine believer in democracy, has devised a policy which deserves serious consideration: the service on our debt should be tied to the prices of our exports on the international market, and should "float" with them. If the banks and the industrialized nations are interested not merely in being paid what they are owed but in seeing that our nations emerge from underdevelopment in solidarity with the West, they should entertain such an approach.

I am not trying to suggest that the future of our democracies depends on you. We and we alone are responsible. Moreover, I am convinced—although I'm not sure whether to be happy or sad about it—that when a Latin American nation chooses democracy, it chooses not only freedom and the rule of law but the most extreme form of independence as well. This is because no form of government receives less support from the West—or seems to have less "sex appeal" as far as the West's communications media and intellectual elites are concerned—than those regimes in the Third World that try to live according to the ideals of freedom and pluralism, which are the West's greatest contribution to the world. While I have no figures to prove it, I doubt that any democratic nation in the underdeveloped world has received the credits and subsidies Cuba has received from the Soviet Union. And it is certainly true that no Latin American nation struggling to live in peace and freedom within the law has ever aroused the militant sympathy that Sandinista Nicaragua has inspired in the liberal and progressive circles of the West. To the contrary, when it doesn't simply inspire indifference, the struggle for democracy in the underdeveloped countries usually inspires skepticism and disdain from those who should be its most enthusiastic supporters. But perhaps this isn't such a bad thing after all. Because if we Latin Americans do win the battle for freedom, we can say we won it ourselves—against our enemies and despite our friends.

If we want democracy to take hold in our countries, our most urgent task is to broaden it, give it substance and truth. Democracy is fragile in so many countries because it is superficial, a mere framework within which institutions and political parties go about their business in their traditionally arbitrary, bullying way. Of course, the degree of democracy varies so much from country to country that it is impossible to generalize. An abyss separates Costa Rica's exemplary democracy from Mexico's dubious one-party democracy, with its institutionalized corruption, or Panama's democracy, where the civilian authorities govern but the National Guard rules. In Venezuela and the Dominican Republic, democratic tendencies have permeated the armed forces as well as the extreme right and left, and have drawn these elements into the political process. In Guatemala, Uruguay, and Ecuador, on the other hand, the military still exercises a kind of guardianship, an aloof autonomy that limits the actions of the civilian government.

In many countries, the separation of powers is a myth, as is equality of opportunity. And the fact that huge sectors of the economy are nationalized—and almost always deficit producing—continues to be a source of inflation, corruption, and inequality. Democratic governments are no more or less to blame than dictatorships for promoting demagogic nationalism, which has been the major obstacle to regional cooperation and the primary reason so much money is wasted on weapons. Freedom of

the press frequently degenerates into defamation; the right to criticize into libel and insult. And the politicians with the most democratic programs often act in private like the henchmen of all-powerful *caudillos.*

I could go on and on with this catalogue of the deficiencies of our democracies, but why bother? What really matters is that our democracies not only survive but learn to criticize themselves and better themselves. If they don't, they will perish. No democracy is born perfect, and none ever gets to be perfect. Yet democracy is superior to authoritarian and totalitarian regimes because, unlike them, democracy is perfectible. Perhaps the hardest struggle we Latin Americans will have will be against ourselves. Centuries of intolerance, of absolute truths, of despotic governments, weigh us down—and it won't be easy to shake that burden off. The tradition of absolute power that began with our pre-Columbian empires, and the tradition that might makes right that the Spanish and Portuguese explorers practiced, were perpetuated in the nineteenth century, after our independence, by our *caudillos* and our oligarchies, often with the blessing or direct-intervention of foreign powers.

Indeed, the belief that violence is the answer is not new, much less revolutionary, in Latin America—contrary to what our messianic ideologues think. In fact, violence represents the worst kind of conformism. It means continuing—albeit using different rhetoric and different rituals—in the same old tradition of barbarism and *machismo* that is in large measure to blame for our backwardness and the social inequities that plague our countries.

What is truly original, truly revolutionary for Latin America is the other option. The one that teaches a long-overdue lesson to Latin America's privileged classes, for whom military dictatorships represent a guarantee of order, and to its intellectual elites, for whom the myth of Marxist revolution, of returning to a *tabula rasa*, is still alive despite the fact that history has shown it to be a lie. The other option is the one that the poor and the innumerable victims of repression have spontaneously chosen and are now defending. Will the result be a new era in Latin American history, one that is more humane, more respectful of human dignity? This is neither the time nor the place for prophecy. But I do have a suggestion: Let us all make an effort, each one of us, within the limits of our own spheres of action, using the means at our disposal, to contribute whatever we can to see that democracy works.

THE CHARTER OF PARIS FOR A NEW EUROPE

On November 21, 1990 the leaders of 34 nations in Europe and North America endorsed the Charter of Paris for a New Europe, which proclaimed the dawn of an era of democracy, human rights, and the rule of law. The Charter spelled out a new Bill of Rights for the nearly one billion people who live in the signing countries. It described a common vision for the future that embraced democracy as "the only system of government of our nations" and detailed the basic human rights and economic freedoms to which all people are entitled.

Most remarkable about this ceremony was that the signers included not only the leaders of well-established democracies like France, Britain, Germany, Canada, and the United States, but of the new democracies in Czechoslovakia, Poland, and Hungary. No less significant was the inclusion of the Soviet Union, whose president, Mikhail Gorbachev, was lauded for permitting the nations of Eastern Europe to abandon Communism.

The Charter of Paris signalled the end of the Cold War, the result of the collapse of Communism in Europe. The euphoria that followed the political transformation of Europe was tempered, however, by the dangerous revival of ethnic, nationalistic, and religious tensions in the post-Communist nations, as well as by their dire economic and environmental problems. Having finally escaped the tyranny of the omnipotent state, these nations turned to democracy as the best means with which to address their formidable political, economic, social, and cultural problems.

We, the heads of state or government of the states participating in the Conference on Security and Cooperation in Europe, have assembled in Paris at a time of profound change and historic expectations. The era of confrontation and division of Europe has ended. We declare that henceforth our relations will be founded on respect and cooperation.

Europe is liberating itself from the legacy of the past. The courage of men and women, the strength of the will of the peoples and the power of the ideas of the Helsinki Final Act have opened a new era of democracy, peace and unity in Europe.

Ours is a time for fulfilling the hopes and expectations our peoples have cherished for decades: steadfast commitment to democracy based on human rights and fundamental freedoms; prosperity through economic liberty and social justice; and equal security for all our countries. . . .

We undertake to build, consolidate and strengthen democracy as the only system of government of our nations. . . .

Human rights and fundamental freedoms are the birthright of all human beings, are inalienable and are guaranteed by law. . . .

Democratic government is based on the will

of the people, expressed regularly through free and fair elections. . . .

Democracy, with its representative and pluralist character, entails accountability to the electorate, the obligation of public authorities to comply with the law and justice administered impartially. No one will be above the law.

We affirm that, without discrimination, every individual has the right to:

- Freedom of thought, conscience and religion or belief,
- Freedom of expression,
- Freedom of association and peaceful assembly,
- Freedom of movement.

No one will be:

- Subject to arbitrary arrest or detention,
- Subject to torture or other cruel, inhuman or degrading treatment or punishment.

Everyone also has the right:

- To know and act upon his rights,
- To participate in free and fair elections,
- To fair and public trial if charged with an offense,
- To own property . . . and to exercise individual enterprise,

- To enjoy his economic, social and cultural rights.

We affirm that the ethnic, cultural, linguistic and religious identity of national minorities will be protected. . . .

Full respect for these precepts is the bedrock on which we will seek to construct the new Europe.

Economic liberty, social justice and environmental responsibility are indispensable for prosperity.

The free will of the individual, exercised in democracy and protected by the rule of law, forms the necessary basis for successful economic and social development. We will promote economic activity which respects and upholds human dignity. . . .

Aware of the dire needs of a great part of the world, we commit ourselves to solidarity with all other countries. Therefore, we issue a call from Paris today to all the nations of the world. We stand ready to join with any and all states in common efforts to protect and advance the community of fundamental human values.

MOSCOW NEWS BOARD OF DIRECTORS
BLOODY SUNDAY IN VILNIUS

The euphoria of 1989 gave way in the following months and years to the hard, often frustrating work of institution-building and economic recovery. The signing of the Charter of Paris on November 21, 1990 raised hopes for a new democratic order in Europe. That dream was smashed less than two months later, on January 12 and 13, 1991 when the Soviet military attacked government offices in Vilnius, Lithuania. The Soviet government sought to impose control through force at a time when the world's attention was focused on events in the Persian Gulf, on the eve of a war there to force Iraq to end its occupation of Kuwait.

The attack on the elected government of Lithuania by Soviet troops left more than a dozen unarmed civilians dead. Advocates of democracy in the Soviet Union were stunned. Bloody Sunday, as they called the events in Vilnius, threatened not only the fragile Lithuanian independence movement, but the democratic reforms recently launched in the Soviet Union.

In response to the bloodshed in Vilnius, the Board of Directors of the independent weekly *Moscow News* printed a front-page editorial protest, bordered in black. The audaciousness of the editorial, reprinted here, was a testament to the press freedom that had been unleashed under the policy of *glasnost*. The 30 signers of the editorial included some of the leading democrats in the Soviet Union, including Gavriil Popov, the mayor of Moscow, and Stanislav Shatalin, an economist who had been one of Gorbachev's closest advisers. Less than eight months later, the hard-line Communists who planned the attack on Vilnius led an abortive coup against Mikhail Gorbachev. The failure of the coup discredited the Communist Party of the Soviet Union, opening an era of unimagined democratic possibilities.

The attack on democracy in Lithuania was a reminder to the world that democracy is fragile; that its victory is not inevitable; that it is ever a threat to those who rule without the consent of the people; and that it must be fought for and defended.

Today's issue of Moscow News is printed with black borders. We are mourning the Baltic victims, but not only them. On the bloody Sunday of January 13, guns were fired at democracy. For the first time in the Soviet Union, a blow was dealt to a government freely elected by the people.

A regime in its death throes has a last-ditch stand: economic reform has been blocked, censorship of the media reinstated, brazen demagogy revived, and an open war on the Republics declared.

The attempted coup in Lithuania has been masterminded by the leadership of the Lithuanian Communist Party which is part and parcel of the CPSU. The latter stood up to defend its property in the Baltic Republics with the help of the state's institutions of force: the Army and the Interior Ministry.

The right to self-determination of all Soviet nations has been violated. The events in Lithuania can be unambiguously classified as *criminal.* It is a crime against one's own people to push them towards civil war. There is no need to turn the Union of fraternal nations into a fraternal cemetery to keep them together.

The situation in Vilnius is partly due to the fact that the Republic's leadership had withdrawn from the Soviet Union's democratic forces. Lithuanian people's deputies have been absent for almost a year from the U.S.S.R. Supreme Soviet, a fact that could not but have negative consequences.

Today the desire for independence is growing in other Union Republics. Never before has it been clearer than now that none of them will be able to hold out on their own. Anonymous committees of national salvation like the one set up in Lithuania may any day spring up in other Baltic Republics, in Moscow, Leningrad, or Yerevan. It is crystal clear whose power these salvation committees seek to salvage.

Last Monday, speaking at the U.S.S.R. Supreme Soviet, the U.S.S.R. President and General Secretary of the CPSU Central Committee tried to justify their actions in Lithuania. If it hadn't been for his address, we might have demanded the resignation of Interior Minister Pugo, of Gosteleradio Chairman Kravchenko (for misinforming the nation), or of Defence Minister Marshal Yazov (for confusing the Garrison and Guard Duty Regulations with the U.S.S.R. Constitution). We would have had every right to insist on an impartial investigation of the crime and on the institution of criminal proceedings against the secret members of Lithuania's national salvation committee, on charges of anticonstitutional activities.

But who will answer for what happened?

After the bloody Sunday in Vilnius, what is left of our President's favourite topics of "humane socialism," "new thinking" and the "European home"? Virtually nothing. Lithuania is more than a tragic page in the history of the U.S.S.R.'s internal affairs. The events in Lithuania have undermined the hopes the entire world community cherished with respect to the Soviet Union, and

In August 1991, most of the leadership of the Soviet Union joined in an unsuccessful coup attempt by placing Soviet premier Mikhail Gorbachev under house arrest. When the coup collapsed after three days, there was mass revulsion against the dictatorship of the Communist Party. Not only were Communist party headquarters closed down in many republics, but statues of Marx, Lenin, Stalin and other Communist heroes were pulled down from their pedestals all over the Soviet Union. This photograph was taken in Riga, Latvia, where the coup brought down the monuments and hastened the drive by the Baltic nations for restoration of their independence.

violated the international accords signed on behalf of the Soviet people.

The Lithuanian tragedy, however, must not fill our hearts with despair. While opposing the onslaught of dictatorship and totalitarianism, we are pinning our hopes on the leadership of other Union Republics.

We appeal to reporters and journalists: if you lack courage or opportunity to tell the truth, at least abstain from telling lies! Lies will fool no one anymore. They are evident today.

We are counting on mass protests against the antidemocratic wave inundating the Baltic Region and threatening the entire country. If sympathy and mercy are still alive in our hearts, let us declare a nationwide mourning for the victims of the Vilnius tragedy on January 20.

AUTHOR'S INDEX

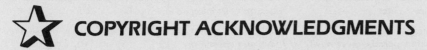# COPYRIGHT ACKNOWLEDGMENTS

PHOTO CREDITS

Page ii: Reuters/Bettmann.

Page xiv: Alinari/Art Resource. 3: Culver Pictures, Inc. 6: Culver Pictures, Inc. 13: Culver Pictures, Inc. 15: Alinari/Art Resource. 19: Culver Pictures, Inc. 30: Culver Pictures, Inc. 33: Culver Pictures, Inc. 42: Library of Congress. 49: Culver Pictures, Inc. 53: Culver Pictures, Inc. 58: Culver Pictures, Inc. 61: National Portrait Gallery, London, Painting by J. Partridge. 64: Culver Pictures, Inc. 67: *Radio Times*, Hulton Picture Library. 75: Culver Pictures, Inc. 79: Library of Congress. 81: *Radio Times*, Hulton Picture Library. 87: UPI/Bettmann Newsphotos.

Page 96: Chrysler Museum, Norfolk, Virginia, gift of Edgar William and Bernice Chrysler Garbisch. 104 both: Culver Pictures, Inc. 110: Philadelphia Museum of Art. 126: Culver Pictures, Inc. 132: Culver Pictures, Inc. 135: Culver Pictures, Inc. 138: The New-York Historical Society. 143: Culver Pictures, Inc. 146: Smithsonian Institution. 151: Culver Pictures, Inc. 157: Culver Pictures, Inc. 160: Culver Pictures, Inc.

162: Georgia Historical Society. 165: Library of Congress. 168: Culver Pictures, Inc. 171: Culver Pictures, Inc. 177: Culver Pictures, Inc. 183: Franklin Delano Roosevelt Library, Hyde Park. 195: UPI/Bettmann Newsphotos.

Page 198: Abbas/Magnum Photos, Inc. 203: Culver Pictures, Inc. 206: UPI/Bettmann Newsphotos. 209: W. Spitter/Magnum Photos, Inc. 213: Susan Meiselas/Magnum Photos, Inc. 225 both: Courtesy of *Index on Censorship*, London. 232: Jean Gaumy/Magnum Photos, Inc. 241: Joseph Koudelka/Magnum Photos, Inc. 246: Milon Novotny/Magnum Photos, Inc. 249: Abbas/Magnum Photos, Inc. 252: Leonard Freed/Magnum Photos, Inc. 257: Reuters/Bettmann. 262: Reuters/Bettmann. 273: Abbas/Magnum Photos, Inc. 275: Stuart Franklin/Magnum Photos, Inc. 283: Cartoon by Benson. 286: Ian Berry/Magnum Photos, Inc. 295: Gideon Mendel/Magnum Photos, Inc. 301: Reuters/Bettmann. 307: Cartoon by Plantu. 314: Susan Meiselas/Magnum Photos, Inc. 326: Reuters/Bettmann.